ROUTLEDGE LIBRARY
PHILOSOPHY OF

Volume 8

CLARITY IS NOT ENOUGH

CLARITY IS NOT ENOUGH
Essays in Criticism of Linguistic Philosophy

Edited by
H. D. LEWIS

Routledge
Taylor & Francis Group

LONDON AND NEW YORK

First published in 1963 by George Allen & Unwin Ltd

This edition first published in 2017
by Routledge
2 Park Square, Milton Park, Abingdon, Oxon OX14 4RN

and by Routledge
711 Third Avenue, New York, NY 10017

Routledge is an imprint of the Taylor & Francis Group, an informa business

British Library Cataloguing in Publication Data
A catalogue record for this book is available from the British Library

ISBN: 978-1-138-68428-7 (Set)
ISBN: 978-1-315-52145-9 (Set) (ebk)
ISBN: 978-1-138-69152-0 (Volume 8) (hbk)
ISBN: 978-1-138-69156-8 (Volume 8) (pbk)
ISBN: 978-1-315-53473-2 (Volume 8) (ebk)

Publisher's Note
The publisher has gone to great lengths to ensure the quality of this reprint but points out that some imperfections in the original copies may be apparent.

Disclaimer
The publisher has made every effort to trace copyright holders and would welcome correspondence from those they have been unable to trace.

CLARITY IS
NOT ENOUGH

Essays in Criticism of
Linguistic Philosophy

EDITED BY
H. D. LEWIS

LONDON: GEORGE ALLEN & UNWIN LTD

PRINTED IN GREAT BRITAIN
in 11 on 12 point Imprint type
BY UNWIN BROTHERS LIMITED
WOKING AND LONDON

PREFACE

The title of this book has been taken from the title of the contribution by Professor Price with which it begins. I have to thank Professor Price for allowing me to take over the title in this way, and I hope that it will be understood in the sense, and in the spirit, in which he uses it. Professor Price devotes much of his space to defending the clarifiers, as he calls them, and to showing in how many different ways clarity is essential in philosophy. His own work has always been a model of clarity. No contributor to this volume is likely to feel that we can have too much clarity. On the other hand we need many other things, not least the wisdom praised by Professor Price at the close of his address.

The dominant trend of philosophy in English speaking countries during the last thirty years has been some form of linguistic analysis. There have been many varieties of this, some much more rigid than others, and little would be gained by attempting to specify them here. It is not so well known how much work of the highest order has been done during this period by philosophers who have not shared the prevailing preoccupation with language. In this there are included some sustained and discerning critical discussions of linguistic philosophy. These are by writers who differ much in other ways from one another, and some of them have substantially affected the course of linguistic philosophy itself. This book provides samples of such criticisms.

A rough chronological order is preserved, but the main plan of the book is as follows. We begin with the reactions of three fairly traditional philosophers and then proceed to discussions of certain basic questions which, without being strictly linguistic, form much of the background of linguistic philosophy today. The central theme is taken up again with Professor Max Black's discussion of language and reality, and this is followed by a number of papers dealing expressly with attempts to solve philosophical questions in linguistic ways. These papers converge, towards the latter half of this book, on the problem of mind and body which I take to be in many ways a crux in modern philosophy, and this prepares the way, in the closing stages, for studies which might well be described as second thoughts about linguistic philosophy by certain thinkers, Hampshire, Ayer and Findlay who, without having been strictly linguistic philosophers at any time, have known this movement in philosophy closely from within and been much influenced by it. Their critical comments should carry particular weight.

In order to limit the scope of the book I have kept it to fairly general themes, mainly in logic and epistemology, and I have had to omit many papers which at first I had hoped to include. There are no papers on ethics or religion or kindred matters, but it may be possible to provide these in a further volume.

It is hoped that this book will be useful to students of philosophy and their teachers in the universities and elsewhere. I have also had in mind the needs of the layman, although he must be warned that he may find some of the papers, including those which discuss the background of linguistic philosophy, more technical and harder to follow than others. It will be gratifying if the book helps to create a somewhat less one-sided impression of the course of recent philosophy than prevails in many quarters at present. By correcting the perspective in which we view our own achievements we may also help those who come to study them at a later day. We may likewise be enabled to see better what our new tasks should be. There has been much talk of late of a return to metaphysics. This I, for one, very much welcome. But we have also to be exceptionally careful to ensure that it is the right sort of return. No one wants to revive the absurdities, the vagueness and allusiveness and the irresponsible play with metaphors which brought much metaphysics in the past into ill repute and provoked very sharp reactions in our time. The lessons of recent empiricism and the philosophy of analysis must be well heeded, and we have to attempt some more patient and strenuous reflection on the situations in which we find ourselves and a more disciplined, if also adventurous, use of philosophical imagination than may be found in loose generalizations culled from the arts or literary criticism—the 'metaphysics without tears' which we sometimes encounter today. On the other hand, the real, as distinct from a verbal, recognition of the possibility and propriety of metaphysical inquiry can hardly come easily to philosophers long habituated to regarding 'metaphysics' as a term of abuse. It would be unreasonable to expect for some time yet much metaphysical writing that is not hampered by the persistence of assumptions which have their warrant only in an earlier anti-metaphysical view of philosophy. For this situation the present work may provide some remedy.

The original place of publication is indicated, in the case of each paper, in a footnote to the title of it. I am much indebted to the editors and publishers concerned for permission to reproduce the papers here.

I am also very grateful to my friend Mr L. E. Thomas of University College, Bangor, for reading the whole of this book in proof and for making the index.

H. D. LEWIS

CONTENTS

CHAPTER I

CLARITY IS NOT ENOUGH[1]

H. H. Price

Professor Emeritus, University of Oxford

I think it is fitting that at this meeting, the first we have had
after six years of war, we should consider the present position and
future prospects of philosophy in this country. It is psychologic-
ally impossible that we should just begin again where we left off
six years ago. And even if we could, I do not think we should wish
to. For it is felt by quite a number of people, rightly or wrongly,
that during the twenty years between the two wars philosophy had
somehow taken the wrong turning. It is even said sometimes that
the wrong turning which it took was one of the main causes of the
disasters which have befallen civilization. I should not myself
attach so great an importance to the things philosophers say and
do. And such importance as I would attach to them is in any case
a long-term one; it seems to me that the social and political
effects of even the greatest philosopher's work only show themselves a generation or two after his death. I do think, however,
that the prevalent outlook of civilized mankind during the inter-
war period was an important cause-factor in bringing about these
disasters, quite as important as the political and economic cause-
factors. And I also think that the preoccupations of philosophers
during that period were one characteristic manifestation of that
outlook. It would not therefore be surprising if there were something wrong with them. The complaints and appeals of those who
say that there was indeed something seriously wrong have accordingly a claim on our attention. Now is the time to consider them,
and to ask whether, or how far, they are justified. And if they are
in any degree justified, now is the time for good resolutions, so
that we may set about amending our ways.

These complaints, roughly summed up in the dictum 'Clarity

[1] Presidential address to the Mind Association delivered at the Joint
Session of the Mind Association and Aristotelian Society in July 1945 and
published in the *Proceedings of the Aristotelian Society* Supplementary
Vol. XIX.

is not enough' which I have taken for my text, are addressed to us not merely as philosophers, but also (perhaps even more) as teachers of philosophy. As pure philosophers, we may think about what we like, and nobody has the right to stop us, or to tell us that we ought to think about something else instead. But as teachers of philosophy, we have a duty to the community; and it is alleged, rightly or wrongly, that we have not been doing it. Not that any authority, academic or political or ecclesiastical, has the right to dictate to us in detail what we should teach or how we should teach it. God forbid! Nevertheless, it is argued, there is a certain job which the philosophical teacher is paid to do, a certain sort of intellectual good which he is paid to provide for those who need it. If you want a name for it, I do not think there is a better one than 'wisdom'. And it is alleged that in the inter-war period he did not in fact provide it; it is even alleged sometimes that he made no serious effort to do so.

Let us now consider whether there is any justification for these complaints. The task is not an easy one. And I should like to say at once that it will not do to put the complainants off with a merely 'clever' rejoinder, which admits of no answer but produces no conviction. If the critics have not stated their own case properly (and I think that in some respects they have not) it is our business to state it better. If it appears to us that the demands which they make upon us are nonsensical as they stand, we must try to reformulate them in a way which does make sense. Then, but not before, we may express our disagreement with them. This laborious procedure is necessary because the majority of the critics are not themselves professional philosophers, though it is true that a few of them are. The majority of them are onlookers, not participants, in philosophical discussions; readers of philosophical books, but not writers of them; persons interested in the future of higher education, or even in the future of civilization as a whole; persons who look at philosophy from the point of view of the consumer, if I may put it so, rather than the point of view of the producer.

I think that there is one historical fact upon which we can all agree. In the period between the two wars it came to be very widely accepted, among professional philosophers at any rate, that clarification is the fundamental aim of philosophy. Philosophy, it was often said, gives us no new knowledge; it only makes clear to us what we know already. The philosopher's task is to *analyse* the statements of science, of history and of common sense, including of course ethical statements, and I suppose religious statements too, though in practice not much attention was paid to these. The word 'analysis', it is true, was sometimes associated with a particular school of philosophers, the so-called Cambridge school. But many philosophers who did not subscribe to all the tenets and methods of that school would have agreed with this conception of philosophy. For the purposes of this discussion, then, I propose to use the words 'clarification' and 'analysis' (both of which are metaphors after all) as if they were synonyms; and I do not think that this will lead to any serious injustice or confusion.

But the statement that philosophy 'makes clear to us what we already know' is itself in need of interpretation. For in one sense of the word 'know', what the philosopher had to clarify was not necessarily something known. It need not even be something true; it might just as well be something false. We start, for instance, by asking ourselves what exactly we are knowing when we know that there is a chair in the bedroom which is not at the moment observed by anyone. But it soon occurs to us that it makes no difference whether we do know this or not, or whether there is or is not as a matter of fact an unobserved chair there. What matters is merely what is *meant* by the statement 'there is an unobserved chair in the bedroom'. It does not matter whether this statement is true or false; whether it is known to be true, or only believed, or merely considered without either belief or disbelief. And a sentence of similar meaning which we are quite sure is false, e.g. 'there is an unobserved crocodile on the roof', would do just as well. Thus the knowledge which has to be clarified is not, or not mainly, a knowledge of facts, but a knowledge of the meanings of statements. Similarly, it would be said that the moral philosopher's task is to ask what I *mean* by saying 'I ought to keep the promise I have made to Jones'; even though in fact I have made no promise to Jones and know that I have not, or even though, knowing that I have made one, I know also that I ought not to keep it, owing to the demands of some more urgent duty.

Such is the programme of analytic or clarificatory philosophy. A very simple-minded person might feel some surprise at it. Is there any point in asking what such statements mean, since admittedly we already know their meaning to begin with? I remember a story about a celebrated authoress who addressed a meeting in Oxford, and made some very peculiar statements about the nature of literature. At the end an undergraduate got up and asked her what she had meant by one of them. She replied, 'You know English, don't you?' He had to admit that he did, and was silenced. But of course he ought not to have been silenced. (I do not think he can have been a student of philosophy.) He ought to have said, 'Oh yes, in one sense I know perfectly well what you meant: but in another sense I do not, because I do not know it clearly'. The original statement was puzzling or muddling in some way; and what he wanted was an equivalent statement, or set of statements, which would not be puzzling or muddling. The new understanding with which the Analytic Philosopher provides us is not like that which we get when we learn a new technical terminology, e.g. that of navigation or of chemistry, though incidentally we may find ourselves acquiring one. It is like the new understanding which we get when a puzzle is solved. The darkness, out of which we are to advance into light, is the darkness of perplexity, not of ignorance.

Hence the analytic conception of philosophy developed very naturally into a 'therapeutic' conception of it. The philosopher's job, it was said, is to cure us of muddles or headaches, generated by language; either by everyday language, or by the technical language of some science. But it would appear that nobody could suffer from headaches of that particular sort unless he were already a philosopher. The word 'I' for example has caused many headaches, but the plain man does not suffer from any of them. And so we witness the curious spectacle of the professional philosopher deliberately and methodically causing the headaches which he is subsequently going to cure. The student spends the first year of his philosophy course laboriously catching the disease, and then he spends the second year being cured of it. A strange sort of therapy! But unless things were done that way, the therapist would have no patients.

To this it would be replied that *some* of the headaches are sure to arise spontaneously, sooner or later, in almost everybody. To that extent everybody is by nature a philosopher. The disease, in a mild form, is endemic. But you can only be cured of it, if you catch it 'good and proper'. To say the same thing in a more old-fashioned way: philosophical problems arise spontaneously in everyone's mind sooner or later, when he begins to reflect upon himself and upon the world. But other people must teach us to state these problems in their most general form, to grasp the full implications of each problem and the connexion between one problem and another; that is why we study the history of philosophy. When we have learned these things, but not before, we can profitably consider what solutions are possible.

But however the analytic conception of philosophy should be formulated—whether in a 'therapeutic' way or in some other—it is clear that a good many people have become dissatisfied with it. Perhaps, as I have hinted already, this is one result of the general change in the climate of opinion which the Second World War has brought about. Our main task is to consider this dissatisfaction and to ask ourselves whether there are any good grounds for it. Perhaps those who feel it might state their case as follows. Philosophy, they might say, is admittedly a very difficult subject. To master it—if it can be mastered at all—takes a lifetime. To attain even a reasonable Honours standard in it takes two or three years. Now the individual and the community as a whole have only a limited amount of time and energy to spare. Is it really wise to spend so much of it on something so trivial as the analysis of sentences? It is a question of 'priorities', of the optimum allocation of scarce resources. This spring-cleaning, this clearing up of the muddles which some of these sentences engender, is no doubt quite a good thing. But is it really a very important occupation? Should it not be left to a few, a very few, specialists who happen to have a talent for it? Is it a thing which every educated man should know something about, and quite a large number should know quite a lot? If philosophy is only clarification, does it deserve the place it has traditionally had in a liberal education? It acquired that place on the strength of a claim to be something much more than this. If that claim has now been abandoned, would it not be well for the claimant to stand down? Was it originally made at a time when philosophy included much of what would be called science today, and not only natural science, but also 'human' sciences such as psychology, sociology, economics?

To say the same thing less politely, we are being told that there is a danger that we shall lose both our readers and our pupils if

things go on as they have been going; that by our own confession
we ought to lose most of them; and that with the gradual spread
of enlightened views of what philosophy is, philosophy will
extinguish itself. Or at least, it will have to retire into a small
and remote corner of the intellectual world, or an even smaller
corner of the educational world, and there be left to cultivate its
little garden, by the curious method of first planting weeds and
then pulling them up again. And if the analysis of sentences is
its sole job, can we honestly maintain that it deserves a more
important place than this?

What answer shall we make to these candid friends? Up to a
point, I think they can be answered. They have blackened the
picture too much. Let us see what can be said on the other side.

In the first place, the complaint which is often made that
'philosophers nowadays talk about nothing but words' is not
altogether just. For one thing, the clarificatory conception of
philosophy need not be stated in a linguistic form at all. The
analytical philosopher is not bound to maintain that the aim of
philosophy is just to analyse the meaning of sentences. He can
equally well say that its aim is to analyse our experience, or again
to analyse certain types or forms of fact: not of course certain
individual facts, for example the fact that there is a table in the
next room, but certain *types* of fact, of which this one is an
instance. The antithesis between non-philosophical knowledge
which is concerned 'with the world', and philosophical knowledge
which is concerned 'only with the sentences in which we talk
about the world', is liable to mislead us; as if philosophy were just
grammar or lexicography, which no analytic philosopher really
believes that it is. Words only matter because words are what we
think with. So you could equally well say, as some clarificatory
philosophers do say, that philosophy is the analysis of certain
very general and very fundamental concepts—such as Thing,
Self, Cause, Duty—or that it is an analysis of categories. And
then, in your definition of philosophy, you need not mention words
or sentences at all.

If, however, you do think fit to mention them, there is nothing
to be ashamed of in that. In all ages, philosophers have in fact
been greatly concerned about words, whatever their official
definition of philosophy might be. I need only mention Socrates.
If anyone was ever a 'linguistic analyst', surely Socrates was.

No one was more concerned with the unravelling of linguistically generated muddles, the curing of 'headaches' arising from linguistic usages. Nor were his therapeutic methods very different from those which are practised today. We even observe that, like our modern practitioners, he usually began by exacerbating the headaches which he then proceeded to cure. To be sure, he got little thanks for it from his contemporaries. We may suppose that a lot of them said 'This verbal stuff is not philosophy at all; it is not at all the sort of thing we used to get in the good old Ionian days'. And persons who were concerned about the future of higher education accused him of corrupting the youth. Nevertheless, his successors have thought him not unworthy of admiration.

This brings me to another point which I have not hitherto mentioned. The clarificatory philosophers of the inter-war period were often accused of writing and speaking as if philosophy had begun in the year 1900. It was said that they neglected the history of philosophy; that they altogether ignored the 'great problems' which our predecessors have handed down to us, and the solutions of them which our predecessors have offered; and that instead they concentrated on trivial and new-fangled puzzles of their own devising. Now perhaps some of them did neglect the history of philosophy, though I do not think they all did (I seem to remember hearing a good deal of discussion of the views of Locke, Berkeley, Hume and Kant, for instance). But there was nothing in their principles which obliged them to neglect it. For clarification or analysis, even in the most strictly 'verbalistic' interpretation of it, is as old, or almost as old, as philosophy itself. In all periods from Socrates' time to our own, with the possible exception of the darkest part of the Dark Ages, clarification has been regarded as an essential part of the philosopher's job, though not generally as the whole of it. The practice of clarification has a long and very honourable history. And that history is relevant to our modern clarificatory techniques in two ways. It is worth studying for its own sake, as one of the monuments of human genius, and we shall study it more effectively if we have been taught to do some clarification for ourselves. The student of the Socratic dialogues will benefit from a reading of the works of Lord Russell or Professor Moore. Conversely, the modern clarifier who really wants to know the answers to the philosophical problems or muddles which puzzle him—some people speak as if there were something unscholarly and almost indecent in this desire for an answer, but for my part I disagree— the modern clarifier is surely very foolish if he neglects what has been said on the subject by the clarifiers of previous ages. Nor will he necessarily suppose that the analysts of the nineteenth or early twentieth century have more to teach him than the analysts of the fourth or fifth century BC. He will gladly accept any illumination he can get from any writer, however old or however new. Thus if the traditional 'great problems' of philosophy be problems of clarification—as many of them undoubtedly are— our modern clarifiers have every reason for studying them, and every reason also for studying what the great philosophers of the past have had to say about them. It is fair to add that if some modern clarifiers have looked with some suspicion on the history of philosophy, their mistake has not been without excuse. For too often the history of philosophy has been confounded with mere *Quellenforschung*. The clarifying philosopher is not interested in the question whether A borrowed such and such a theory from B or from C or from D. Why should he be? It is no concern of his. He only wants to know what the theory in question is, and whether it is illuminating, no matter who invented it or when.

I turn now to another charge which is brought against the analytical or clarificatory philosophers of the inter-war period. They are accused of neglecting moral philosophy. But again there is nothing in their principles which should oblige them to neglect it; quite the contrary. Ethical statements are no less puzzling than perceptual or scientific or mathematical statements, and are equally in need of clarification. But in any case the charge is not true, as the published works of the clarifying philosophers bear witness, beginning with Professor Moore's *Principia Ethica*. And the moralists of my own university, though they might not accept all the tenets of the 'Cambridge Analysts', would agree that the aim of moral philosophy is clarification, and have pursued that aim with no little energy.

But sometimes a different, and indeed logically incompatible, charge is brought against the clarificatory philosophers. They are accused not of neglecting moral philosophy, but of perverting it. (We may notice that so far they are in good company, since the charges brought against Socrates were not very different.) It has been argued that the source of this perversion was the

'Realistic' theory of knowledge, the theory that knowledge makes no difference to what is known. From this theory it is supposed to follow that an understanding of what morally good action is will not make us act any better than before. And from this again it is supposed to follow that no moral philosopher of the 'Realistic' school will even attempt to make his pupils better men. Whereas the moral philosophers of the school of T. H. Green, who did not hold a 'Realistic' theory of knowledge, were able to reject this unreal distinction between theory and practice; they held that a man who understands ethical principles will act more virtuously in consequence. They therefore conceived that it was part of their task as moral philosophers to make their pupils better men; and what is more, they succeeded. In fact, they took moral philosophy seriously, whereas the 'Realistic' clarifiers regard it merely as an intellectual game.

Now, with all respect, I cannot see much force in this argument. In the first place, the dictum that knowledge makes no difference to what is known seems to me not so much a truth as a truism. Even the most subjectivistic moralist accepts it, though he would give a somewhat peculiar account of what it is that is being known; he would say that our ethical knowledge is a knowledge of the emotional or volitional attitudes of other human beings, or of their social conventions. But still he would admit, indeed he would insist, that they do in fact have these attitudes and these conventions, whether we know it or not, and even though we falsely believe that they have quite different ones, or none at all.

Secondly, and even more important, although knowledge makes no difference to what is known, it may still make a very great difference to the knower. Likewise when one acquires a clear knowledge of something which one has previously known in a vague or confused manner, this it is true makes no difference to the thing known. The principles of right action are what they are, whether we are muddled about them or clear about them. But if the 'clarifying' moral philosopher enables us to get a clear knowledge of these principles, that may make a very great difference to us, though it makes no difference whatever to them. And the difference which it makes to us can hardly fail to affect our conduct. Certainly it will affect our judgements about other people's actions. We shall judge them more fairly and more charitably if we have learned to discriminate clearly between motive and intention, between rightness and conscientiousness if we have learned to ask ourselves whether a man's duty depends on the facts as they are, or only on the facts as he believes them to be. And if we judge other people more fairly, our emotions towards them will be more appropriate, and our behaviour towards them more just. Similar results will follow if we sit down in a cool hour to judge our own actions, past or proposed (and everyone has cool hours sometimes). If we have a clear grasp of the distinctions I have mentioned, and a well-constructed terminology for formulating them, our emotions of self-approval and self-disapproval will be more appropriate to their object. These emotions cannot fail to affect our future conduct, and that conduct will in consequence be more likely to be right.

It is true, I think, that such an increase of clarity will not make us more conscientious. It will only make us more likely to do the things which are objectively right, and then only if we already have a desire to do what is right. If we have no conscience to begin with, and no desire to do what is right, the clarifying philosopher cannot give us these things. If 'better' means 'more likely to judge fairly and to act rightly', he can make us better men, provided always that we have some modicum of goodness to start with. But if 'better' means 'more conscientious', then he cannot make us better; and still less can he provide us with a conscience if we have none.

But can any philosopher, however anti-analytical, make us more conscientious? One would suppose that this is the function not of philosophers but of preachers, though certainly every preacher would be the better for a training in moral philosophy. Perhaps, however, the real point of the attacks on the clarificatory moral philosophers lies here. Perhaps it is thought that every moral philosopher ought also to be a preacher; that he ought to make right conduct more attractive to us, or less unattractive, as well as showing us clearly what right conduct is. And I suppose that this *is* part of the meaning of the word 'moralist' in ordinary language. Certainly many of the moral philosophers of antiquity were also, in a wide sense, preachers. Even Aristotle, analyst as he is, says somewhere that there would be no point in studying moral philosophy if it did not improve our characters. Is it felt, perhaps, that the moral philosophy of our contemporary analysts is too disinterested? (When it is said to be 'too academic', this is a less polite way of saying the same thing.) Are they supposed to give the impression that goodness itself does not matter, and that the only thing which does matter is to make clear what goodness is? If my aim is merely clarity, shall I not be as much interested in vice as in virtue; and would it be surprising if I induced a like impartiality in my pupils?

In this connexion, complaints are also made about the particular moral problems which the analytical moralists discuss. It is said that the examples they select for analysis are almost always trifling or trivial ones. I have promised to return a detective story which I have borrowed. I pack it up carefully and post it myself, but it does not arrive. Have I done right or wrong? Certainly such problems are trifling in a sense. When the lender fails to get his book back on the appointed day, the wrong I have done him (if indeed I have done him any) is not a very great one. It is nothing to get excited about. It really does not matter very much whether he gets his detective story back or not.

But what is it that the anti-analytical philosopher is demanding? Is he demanding that all our examples in moral philosophy should be about murder or high treason or declarations of war? Well, perhaps some of them should be. I think we must admit that the choice of examples does have quite an important psychological effect. It is not altogether a good thing if our pupils come to think of moral philosophy as the branch of philosophy which discusses unimportant promises, minor 'white lies', trifling conflicts of duties where it does not matter very much which way you decide. I do not mean that any of them will explicitly say, except as a joke, that this is the sort of thing that moral philosophy is about. I am thinking rather of what I can only call 'the impression which is made on them' by the way the subject is treated, and of the permanent attitude which results. Such impressions and attitudes are below the level of explicit thinking; they are subconscious or unconscious. Nevertheless they are important, indeed for that very reason. For they condition our explicit thoughts and estimations of the subject without our being aware of it; they may prevent us from recalling the clarificatory teachings of the moralist on just those important occasions when the recalling of them would make all the difference to our judgements or our actions.

But of course, there is also a sense in which these 'trivial' examples are not really trivial at all. The principles they illustrate are not trivial, and it is for the sake of these principles that the analytic moralist makes such a fuss about them. Moreover, those who object to such examples are not entitled to complain (as they also do) that the analytic sort of moral philosophy is 'out of touch with real life'. For most men at most times life is made up of trivialities. Indeed, this is an analytic proposition; that is what the word 'trivial' means. Perhaps the analytic moralist has not always made clear in what sense his examples are trivial and in what sense they are not, thereby falling short of his own clarificatory ideals. And so perhaps he does sometimes leave in the minds of his less intelligent pupils the unconscious 'impression' I spoke of—the impression that moral philosophy is concerned with subjects which are in themselves unimportant, or only important because of the intellectual puzzles they raise, like the cryptic statements in a cross-word clue. 'Our discussion is not about an unimportant matter,' says Socrates in the *Republic*, 'but about the way one ought to live.' Socrates, as I have said, was an analytic moralist if ever there was one; but it must be admitted that his modern successors do not often speak in that tone of voice. And I would suggest that in so far as there is any force in the criticisms which are made of them, it is their tone or their style which the critic ought to object to, rather than the substance of what they have to say. Perhaps he might fairly add that of the three departments into which John Grote divided moral philosophy—'eudaemonics', 'aretaics' and 'deontics'—they have concentrated too much on the second and third and have somewhat neglected the first. And 'eudaemonics', the investigation and evaluation of the different types of happiness or well-being, is an important subject, and one about which the moralists of previous ages had a good deal to say. You may object that it is in part an empirical one; and that it is the business of psychologists, not philosophers, to discuss it. Yes, you may leave it to the psychologists if you like. But you know perfectly well that they will not in fact say anything about it; and in practice the result will be that nobody will talk about it at all. Moreover, it seems to me that Bishop Butler was not far wrong when he said we can owe no man anything except happiness. Thus our treatment of 'deontics' itself will not be altogether satisfactory if 'eudaemonics' is neglected.

I do not think, however, that moral philosophers can really be blamed for not being preachers; unless the word 'preacher' is a misleading name for an expert in eudaemonics, as possibly it is sometimes. By all means let them preach if they feel a call to do so; but we cannot fairly impose it upon them as part of their job. Their job is to tell us what goodness is, not to make us good. I admit, however, that 'preaching' in a wide sense of that term is a very important social function. If our existing preachers are not listened to, owing to the widespread decay of religious belief among educated people, perhaps there is need of a special order of purely ethical preachers, like some of the Stoics of the Roman Imperial period, or the Confucian teachers of China. And I agree that such persons should have a philosophical training, though they should not necessarily be professional philosophers.

On the whole, then, I do not think there is much justice in the attacks which have been made on the clarificatory moral philosophers. The complaint that clarity is not enough should be addressed to another quarter. The function of moral philosophy *is* to make clear to us what we already know; except possibly for some parts of 'Eudaemonics' where certain empirical generalizations about human nature, not necessarily known to everyone, must be taken into account. And it is *not* its function to improve our conduct (though incidentally it may have that effect, as I have argued); still less to increase our conscientiousness; and least of all to provide us with a conscience when we have none to begin with.

Let us turn then to the other main departments into which philosophy has traditionally been divided: logic, theory of knowledge, and metaphysics. We need not say much about logic. In formal logic (of whatever brand) it is obvious at once that clarity *is* enough, though we are not to infer that clarity is easily attained. As for what is sometimes called philosophical logic, this seems to be a branch of the theory of knowledge: the branch of it which studies thinking, as opposed to other forms of cognitive consciousness. So let us consider the theory of knowledge.

Now of course it has always been acknowledged that clarification is an essential part of the epistemologist's function. It is true that the epistemologists of previous ages would not have laid the same stress on language as our modern clarifiers do (though it is worth remembering that a whole book of Locke's *Essay* is called 'Of Words'). They would generally have said that *what* they were clarifying—the *datum clarificandum* so to speak—was 'ideas' or 'thoughts' or 'conceptions' rather than words or sentences. But this is not much more than a difference of idiom. For it is not words considered as noises or black marks which the modern clarifier is interested in, but words in their use, as instruments of private thought and public communication. Moreover, in practice, as I have pointed out already, the philosophers of former times were greatly occupied with words and sentences, and with verbally-generated 'headaches'. So far, the analysis or clarification in which modern philosophers engage does not differ at all from what is generally called the theory of knowledge, a highly respectable and very ancient branch of philosophy.

Nevertheless there is one important difference, in appearance at any rate. The old epistemologists would not generally have said that their inquiries gave us no new knowledge but only made clear what was known already. For they generally supposed that it was their job, not merely to clarify, but also to criticize or evaluate the ideas or thoughts or conceptions of the plain man, the scientist, the theologian, or whoever it might be. They regarded it as an open question whether the knowledge claimed by non-philosophical people really did deserve the name of knowledge. It might be only a body of opinions or beliefs; and even though these opinions might be found on examination to be true in the main, yet to turn them into knowledge one would have to provide reasons or justifications for them. For example, the unphilosophical person's beliefs in the existence of matter or of other minds had to be justified, as well as clarified. And it might turn out that they were justifiable only in part, not wholly. Thus he might be quite wrong about secondary qualities, though substantially right about the primary ones; and it was possible in principle that he might be wrong altogether, and that there was no material world at all. Likewise with the beliefs of the scientist. It was thought that the experimental method entailed certain presuppositions of which the scientist was unconscious, and which he himself made no attempt to justify. It was the philosopher's business to state those presuppositions clearly. But that was only the first part of his job. The second, and even more important, part was to consider whether or how they could be justified. Nor was he entitled to assume beforehand that they were justifiable at all. He must consider and find out. He might be obliged to conclude that they were entirely unjustifiable.

This attitude might be summed up by saying that the task of the theory of knowledge was conceived to be a *critical* as well as clarificatory task; and further that the beliefs which were to be criticized were not so much the conscious and explicitly formulated beliefs of the plain man, scientist, theologian, etc., but rather the unconscious or half-conscious assumptions lying behind them. Hence it was often said that the epistemologist's function was to 'criticize the presuppositions' of science or common sense or theology; or again to criticize the methods by which plain men, scientists, or other non-philosophical persons acquired what they called their knowledge.

Now, in appearance at any rate, the modern clarifier does differ from the old epistemologists at this point. He would agree that unphilosophical persons make assumptions which they do not formulate, and that it is his job to formulate them. But he would not agree that it is his job to justify them, nor that they need any justification; and he would not agree that it is in principle possible that these assumptions might be false, either wholly or partly. He sticks to it that what he is to clarify is something which we already know; not merely claim to know, but really do know. For example, he will tell us that it is not his business to prove that there is a material world, or that there are laws of nature, or that there were events before this present moment. He says we know these things already; his task is merely to make clear what it is that we are knowing, and how—by the use of what methods—we have come to know it. Thus he will tell us clearly what methods we use to distinguish a real object from a mirror-image or an hallucination, or what methods we use to distinguish between a real causal relation and a run of coincidences. But he has not to justify these methods. He has merely to discover what they are, and to formulate them in their full generality and as unambiguously as possible.

Thus it looks as if the modern analytical philosopher had abandoned the 'critical' or 'justificatory' part of the old epistemological programme and retained only the 'clarificatory' part. But I think this difference is more apparent than real. For one thing, when he is on his guard he only maintains that we know that there is 'in some sense' a material world, that 'in some sense' memory certainly gives us knowledge of past events, and so on. And as to what sense it is, we are allowed full liberty of conjecture. The material world which we know to exist, may turn out to exist only in a highly Pickwickian sense of the word 'material' and even of the word 'exist'. At any rate this possibility cannot be ruled out *a priori*. Nor can we lay down any limit *a priori* to the degree of Pickwickianity which would be permissible. It may easily turn out that these entities which we know to exist— material objects, other minds, past events—are logical constructions of a quite unsuspected and indeed staggering complexity. Thus what I called the critical (as opposed to clarificatory) part of the old epistemological programme has not really been abandoned. It has only been moderated a little. We have merely to take care to save the face of our client, the plain man or the scientist, by saying to him 'of course the statements you make are in *some* sense true, and in *some* sense you really do know the things you claim to know'. After this diplomatic preface, we may go on very much as before.

Nor is this all. Although the modern analyst maintains that it is not his job to justify the statements of common sense or science, we nevertheless find him refuting other philosophers who attempt to cast doubt on them. He says it is not his job to justify these statements themselves, but he admits that it *is* his job to justify the statement that they need no justification. He accordingly argues that they cannot 'really' or 'seriously' be questioned. He tries to show that the doubts which old-fashioned philosophers have expressed concerning them are 'pseudo-doubts'; and how these pseudo-doubts arise from the illegitimate generalization of genuine doubts about particular cases, e.g. the genuine doubt whether this particular perceptual experience is veridical or illusory, or whether this particular object now before me is a waxwork or an animate human organism with a mind like my own. He also urges that the 'laments' which old-fashioned philosophers have uttered from time to time, when the problem of justifying common-sense statements appeared to them insoluble, are only 'pseudo-laments': as for example when they say 'Oh dear, oh dear, we can never know the causes of our sensations'.[1] No doubt this amounts to maintaining that the problem of 'justification',

[1] Cf. Mr Wisdom's very instructive essay on 'Philosophical Perplexity', *Aristotelian Society Proceedings*, 1937.

with which previous epistemologists were preoccupied, was a pseudo-problem. But we must not take the prefix *pseudo-* too seriously. For it is not an ordinary pseudo-problem, like 'how shall I go from here to the middle of next week?' A 'pseudo-problem' in this context means a *philosophical* problem, and you only call it 'pseudo' because you think you have solved it. If you like, it is a muddle rather than a problem. It requires to be untangled rather than answered, and when someone asks us the way out of it, we have to reply 'you ought not to have started from here'. But anyway it is a philosophical muddle, one which it is proper for a philosopher to be worried by. It is philosophical thinking, not any other sort of thinking, which will untangle it. And by offering to untangle it, the analytical philosopher admits that it does exist and deserves his professional attention, though he refuses to call it a problem and prefers to call it 'a worry' or 'a muddle' or 'a headache' instead.

I conclude then that the modern analytic or clarificatory philosophers are studying nothing more nor less than the theory of knowledge. Their programme does not differ in essence from the traditional programme of that ancient and highly respectable department of philosophy. It is not they, but their critics who say that a philosopher has no business to waste his time on such subjects, who are the dangerous and new-fangled persons, repudiating the whole European philosophical tradition. It is true that our modern clarifiers have more to say about words and sentences than their predecessors had, and even profess sometimes to be concerned with nothing else. But they are only interested in words and sentences because words and sentences are what we think with; and in practice the epistemologists of the past were almost as interested in words and sentences as they are. No doubt the sentences which are nowadays selected for clarification are in themselves trivial, and even sometimes rather ridiculous. As Dr. Joad points out,[1] it does seem peculiar to worry oneself overmuch about the sentence 'this is a rocking-horse covered with pink spots'. Perhaps examples of this sort may have an unfortunate psychological effect upon the philosopher's pupils or readers, as I have already admitted that trivial examples in ethics may. All the same, I should like to quote against Dr. Joad what the poet says of the flower in the crannied wall. If we could

[1] 'Appeal to Philosophers', *Aristotelian Society Proceedings*, 1940, p. 33.

really be clear about the meaning of this sentence concerning the rocking-horse, which bristles with philosophical puzzles, I do not say that 'we should know what God and man is', but I think we should be in a much better position for finding out.

In my opinion, the most that we can fairly say against our modern clarifiers on this head, is that they have sometimes paid too little attention to pre-verbal or non-verbal thinking. For we do also think in images as well as in words, and there is even a sense (I believe) in which we may be said to think 'in' actions and motor attitudes, without even using images. And such pre-verbal thinking seems to me important, both in the theory of knowledge and in the theory of conduct. Of course you may refuse to call it thinking if you like, but it does seem to be a very important kind of symbolic cognition. Perhaps it has also been forgotten sometimes that when we do think in words, the language we use is by no means always the 'full dress' language which would satisfy a grammarian or a governess; for example, syntactical words like 'and', 'if', 'some' are not always present. I do not think that these considerations are merely psychological (whatever exactly is meant by that abusive epithet) since they may well throw valuable light on what thinking is. Even if they were, it seems to me that they are not likely to be much studied in psychological laboratories, and if philosophers think it beneath them to discuss such subjects, they will not be discussed by anyone at all.

Are we to conclude then that clarity *is* enough, and that the dissatisfaction widely aroused by the 'clarificatory' conception of philosophy is wholly, or almost wholly, unjustified? I do not think so. I think that clarification is a part of the philosopher's task; an indispensable part moreover, and one which he must be allowed to fulfil by whatever methods—verbalistic or other—may seem good to him. But I do not think that it is the whole of his task. And certainly clarification is not all that the educated public demands of him. Then what else does it demand, if clarification is the primary function alike of moral philosophy, logic, and theory of knowledge? The simplest answer is 'metaphysics'. Let us consider whether it is the right one.[1]

[1] Miss D. M. Emmet's recent book *The Nature of Metaphysical Thinking* (especially ch. 9, on Metaphysical Analogies) contains a number of points which are highly relevant to this section of my paper, which was unfortunately written before her book came into my hands.

As we all know, metaphysics was sadly blown upon in the second half of the inter-war period. Metaphysical statements were declared to be meaningless, not even false; indeed the adjective 'metaphysical' became almost a term of abuse. To be sure, a number of the subjects previously included under metaphysics might still be studied under other names, even by the most advanced thinkers. It was quite proper to study the notions of substance and cause, for example, provided one said one was studying the analysis of thing-propositions and causal propositions. You might still discuss the nature of the self or of personal identity, provided you called it 'the analysis of "I" sentences'. You might even have been allowed to discuss the relation of mind and body, if you were prepared to change the label and say you wanted to talk about the relation between psychological statements and physiological statements. Thus although many of our modern analysts would profess to have abolished metaphysics, this revolution—like others—is not quite such a clean sweep as it appears. And I think the revolutionaries themselves would admit this.

Nevertheless, they would insist that something has been abolished; and certainly there is something which has been rendered very unpopular among professional philosophers. It is *speculative* metaphysics, the construction of metaphysical systems: what has been called 'philosophy in the grand manner'. And perhaps those who tell us that clarity is not enough are really saying that the attempt to abolish speculative metaphysics was a fundamental mistake, indeed a kind of intellectual suicide.

Is this because they are not convinced by the reasoning which purports to show that the sentences written by the speculative metaphysicians are meaningless? Partly, no doubt. It is indeed very difficult to decide just how much this reasoning establishes. I am inclined to think that in the last resort it only establishes this much: that it is illegitimate to argue to a conclusion concerning matters of fact if there are no matters of fact among your premises. But so far as I can see, the only important metaphysical argument which would be put out of court by this is the ontological argument for the existence of God. And although many constructors of metaphysical systems have used this argument, in one form or another, it is not true that they all have; and even when a speculative metaphysician does use the ontological argument, it is not necessarily true that his whole metaphysical

B

system depends on it, so that a part of his system might still be sense even though another part might be nonsensical.

I think, however, that the main reason, or motive, behind these protests against the abolition of speculative metaphysics is a different one. When the critics say that a philosopher ought to concern himself with the construction of metaphysical systems, or at least with the exposition of other people's metaphysical systems if he can construct none of his own, I think they mainly have in mind what I have called the interests of the consumer; that is, the needs of the educated public which reads philosophical books or is influenced by those who do, and sends its sons and daughters to philosophical lectures at universities. Now of course it is conceivable that even though the educated public does have these needs, it is impossible in principle that they should be satisfied; and the speculative metaphysicians who have professed to satisfy them in the past may have been confusing both themselves and their readers. But when we consider the long line of speculative metaphysicians from Plato to Whitehead, when we reflect that many of them were admittedly men of the very highest genius, can we really feel very comfortable about this conclusion? Or if we do feel comfortable about it, may we not be the victims of a kind of temporal parochialism? *Securus judicat orbis terrarum.* Is it not more likely that such men were talking sense (in *some* good sense of the word 'sense') than that the arguments which purport to prove that they were talking nonsense are correct?

Moreover, this is not the first time that speculative metaphysics has been abolished. The sceptics of the later Classical period abolished it. It revived in the form of Neoplatonism and of Christian metaphysical theology. In the eighteenth century Hume abolished it, and Kant imposed the most drastic restrictions on it. But not for long. It arose again, more vigorous than ever, in the great speculative systems of the Romantic period. The Positivists and Agnostics of the later nineteenth century abolished it once more; and once more it revived in the speculative systems of Bergson, Alexander and Whitehead. If what I called the needs of the consumer are in principle incapable of being satisfied (as the modern anti-speculators assert), we may nevertheless be pretty confident that fresh attempts will in fact be made to satisfy them in the future, whether we like it or not. It looks as if there were a kind of rhythm in the history of human thought on metaphysical subjects. A long period of speculative thinking is followed by a shorter period of criticism and agnosticism, and then speculative thinking begins again in a different form. At the moment we happen to be living in one of the critical and agnostic periods; and perhaps the widespread complaint that 'clarity is not enough' is itself one of the symptoms that the period is approaching its end. Certainly in other departments of human thought and culture the 'de-bunking' which went on in the inter-war period has begun to look a little old-fashioned; as the saying is, it begins to 'date'. I suspect that if the complainants are asking for a revival of speculative metaphysics, they will in fact get what they want in the end, though they may not get it from the present generation of professional philosophers; and perhaps they will not get it from professional philosophers at all, but from other and less well-qualified persons.

But what exactly are these 'needs of the consumer' which—if I am right—are what the critics of the purely clarificatory conception of philosophy are mainly concerned about? And how would these needs be satisfied by a system of speculative metaphysics? What the consumer mainly needs, I think, is a *Weltanschauung*, a unified outlook on the world. This is what he is asking for when he asks the philosopher for wisdom or guidance, or a clue to 'the meaning of the Universe'; and this is what the analytic philosophers are failing to give him. I am afraid he is not particularly interested in the arguments by which this or that world-outlook is recommended; at any rate not in the detail of them. But he is not wholly disinterested in them either. For the outlook which he demands has to be a *reasoned* outlook. If it is supported merely by the *ipse dixit* of some authority, or by the dictates of the heart, it will not satisfy him, or not for long. But the reasoning which supports it need not be the sort of reasoning which the anti-metaphysical philosophers disapprove of. It need not be that 'pure thought' which tries to establish existential conclusions by means of wholly *a priori* premises. In every one of his arguments, the speculator might use one empirical premiss at least. Nor is it at all necessary that any of his arguments should be completely demonstrative. His conclusions must be recommended by reasoning; but they need not be strictly proved, in a way which would satisfy a professor of formal logic.

Does this amount to saying that what is demanded of the speculative metaphysician is a kind of explanatory hypothesis, capable of accounting for all the main types of facts which are empirically known to us? That is one way of putting it, but perhaps the word 'hypothesis' may mislead us. For one thing, his hypothesis—if you call it that—must be more comprehensive than any scientific or historical hypothesis. It must cover all the main departments of human experience, including experiences which it is not fashionable nowadays for philosophers to talk about: religious and mystical experience, for instance, and the queer or 'supernormal' experiences which psychical researchers investigate, such as telepathy and precognition. Moreover, his theory will not, I think, be capable of conclusive refutation by future empirical data. New empirical facts may turn up which are (as we say) 'difficult to reconcile with it'; but by sufficiently ingenious interpretation it will always be possible to explain them away. Indeed, even the word 'theory' is not altogether a suitable one, for it has come to be used mainly in a scientific sense ('the Evolution Theory', 'the Quantum Theory'). For the same reason words like 'explain' and 'account for' may be misleading. 'Explanation' has come to mean primarily causal explanation, or at any rate explanation in terms of inductively established regularities of sequence, whether deterministic or statistical. And this is not the speculative metaphysician's business. It would be better to say that what we demand of him is just a unifying conception, or to use some still vaguer expression like 'point of view' or 'outlook': thus we speak of the theocentric point of view of the Mediaeval Schoolmen, or the biocentric outlook of Bergson.

This has some bearing on a very puzzling question: in what sense can a system of speculative metaphysics be called true or false? I do not think that the words 'true' and 'false' are rightly applicable to the sentences in which the metaphysician formulates his speculative theses, though they do of course apply to the statements which he makes in support of them. In saying this, I am not agreeing with those who maintain that a system of speculative metaphysics is just an expression of emotion, akin to a work of art. There is some force in this analogy, no doubt. But I think a much better one would be a map or chart. This is a kind of picture, if you like, and it may well have aesthetic merits. But it is also something more. It is a systematic representation of a certain set of geographical facts. And the question whether this or that stretch of green paint or blue ink shall be put in or left out, or what shape it shall have, is not settled by the emotions of the map-maker. It is settled by two considerations in conjunction: by the geographical facts on the one hand (is it empirically true that there is a wood here, and a brook there?) and on the other by the principle of representation which he has adopted.

Now two maps of the same tract of territory may be very different indeed. If your map of the world is a schoolroom globe, it will differ in many ways from a flat map constructed according to Mercator's projection; on a one-inch map a main road may be broader than the river Thames, whereas on a six-inch map it will be the other way round. But we do not say on that account that the Mercator map is 'wrong' and the schoolroom globe 'right', nor that the six-inch map is 'right' and the one-inch map is 'wrong'.

It seems to me that systems of speculative metaphysics differ from each other in somewhat the same way. We may regard them as alternative modes of conceptual arrangement by which the body of empirical data is systematically ordered: for example, the speculative system of Alexander is a mode of conceiving the universe as a hierarchical arrangement, ordered by means of the three notions of space-time, quality and emergence. What the metaphysician has to show is that his method or arrangement— his principle of systematic representation—is a possible one, that the facts can be ordered in accordance with it, but not that it is the only one possible; no more than Mercator has to show that his method of projection is the one and only 'right' one and all the others 'wrong'. We may of course find that a particular metaphysical system leaves out some of the facts altogether; not because the metaphysician was unaware of them (if that is all, the defect can be remedied by his successors) but because in the system of representation which he has adopted they cannot be put in, just as in some types of maps there is no way of representing telegraph lines or level-crossings. Religious experience has been omitted by some metaphysicians in this way, moral experience by others; while 'supernormal' experiences, such as telepathy, have been omitted by almost all. Or we may find that his system of representation is so obscure that we cannot see how to apply it to new facts which he himself did not know;

or still worse, we cannot see how he applied it himself to the old ones he did know. But though we may discover defects of these sorts in a particular metaphysical system, we ought not to say on that account that it is wrong, or false, or that it has been refuted (as the Phlogiston Theory has been refuted). We ought rather to say, and indeed we often do say, that it is inadequate or unsatisfactory in this or that respect, though perhaps satisfactory in others; which is much like what we say of Mercator's map of Greenland. And we shall then look about for another metaphysical system which is more illuminating. But in the meantime we shall not just throw the old one into the waste-paper basket, on the ground that it has been 'refuted', for the notion of refutation does not apply in this case. On the contrary, we shall continue to study it carefully in order to get all the illumination out of it we can; only we shall hope to invent another (or rediscover an ancient one) which will illuminate more comprehensively. Thus the choice between different systems of speculative metaphysics is not a choice between the true and the false, at least in the ordinary sense of those words. It is rather a choice between the less good and the better, or even between several things which are good, but good in different ways. And even a little illumination is much better than none at all.

Let us now return to the needs of the consumer. What he is alleged to need is a unified conceptual scheme of the sort I have been trying to describe. And I think it is true that he does need it. When the ordinary educated man speaks of 'a philosophy', it is a conceptual scheme of this kind which he has in mind. Such a scheme, he thinks, will provide him with the wisdom which philosophers are traditionally supposed to supply. He needs, as it were, a map of the universe so far as our empirical information has disclosed it; and not a map of the physical world only, but one which makes room for all the known aspects of the universe, physical, spiritual, and whatever others there may be. He needs it nowadays more than ever, since for good reasons or bad the Christian metaphysical scheme has lost its hold over him; and science does not give him what he wants either, since he feels (in my opinion rightly) that there are a number of very important questions on which science has nothing to say. And he complains that just when his need is greatest, the philosophers are refusing to satisfy it. The prevalence of the purely clarificatory conception of philosophy prevents them from even making the attempt. They will not even discuss and expound for his benefit the speculative systems of the past, so that he may avail himself of such illumination and guidance as these old-fashioned 'maps of the universe' have to offer. It is true that they are not by any means uninterested in the history of philosophy, as I have argued already. But they *are* uninterested in the history of speculative metaphysics.

It would seem then that the complaint 'clarity is not enough' is in one important respect justified, in so far as the contemporary clarifying philosophers have neglected speculative Metaphysics, which is one of the things which philosophers are traditionally paid to know about. They have neglected it, not of course through mere laziness or inadvertence, but on principle, because they have thought that the speculative metaphysician is trying to do something which is from the nature of the case impossible: namely, to establish conclusions about matters of fact by means of purely *a priori* premisses. But if I am right, that is not what he is trying to do, except in occasional moments of aberration. He is trying to do something much less extravagant and much more important: to produce a unified conceptual scheme under which all the known types of empirical fact may be systematically arranged. And there is nothing in this enterprise which even the most sensitive philosophical conscience need object to.

Yet if this be so, it might be said, the statement that clarity is not enough is hardly the best way of formulating the legitimate complaints of the consumer. For, it may be suggested, there are more sorts of clarity than one. The function of the map-maker, to whom I have compared the speculative metaphysician, is surely in a sense to make things clear which were not clear before. And the speculative metaphysician, at least as I have conceived him, could even accept the dictum that 'philosophy gives us no new knowledge, but only makes clear to us what we already know'. For certainly it is not his function to give us new information about matters of fact, but rather to devise a conceptual scheme which brings out certain systematic relationships between the matters of fact we know already—including those queer and puzzling ones about which we know only a little. His job is to make things comprehensible, not to establish what things are. In short, is there not such a thing as *synoptic* clarity, as well as analytical clarity? And if we are careful to remember that the word 'clarity' covers both of them, could we not conclude that clarity *is* enough after all?

Perhaps we could. But I should like to add a final word of caution, and it is probably the most shocking of all the shocking things I have said this evening. It has been maintained that whatever can be said at all, can be said clearly; from which it follows that if a thing cannot be said clearly, then it cannot be said at all. We should all like to believe this. It presents itself as a kind of charter of liberation, lifting a vast load of twaddle and muddle from our shoulders. But I think we ought not to accept this freedom which is offered to us, until we have considered carefully what the word 'can' means in this context. I am afraid that it only means 'can in principle', not 'can in practice'. A man may be saying something, even something of fundamental importance, and yet it may be quite impossible for *him* to say it clearly, and impossible equally for any of his contemporaries; and this not through lack of cleverness on his part or theirs, but simply because the existing terminology is not adequate for the task. We must not, however, allow ourselves to conclude—as this dictum might tempt us to, unless carefully interpreted—that he would have done better not to speak at all. There may very well be some things which in the terminology available at the time can only be said obscurely; either in a metaphor, or (still more disturbing) in an oxymoron or a paradox, that is, in a sentence which breaks the existing terminological rules and is in its literal meaning absurd. The man who says them may of course be just confused. But it is possible that he is saying something important; or he may be confused in some degree, and yet he may at the same time be saying something important. Nevertheless, his successors may be able to divine what he is trying to convey. The terminological rules may eventually be changed. And the wild metaphor or outrageous paradox of today may become the platitude of the day after tomorrow. The old saying that a philosopher's reach should exceed his grasp has no doubt been grossly abused in the past, and has enabled many solemn muddles to masquerade as profound truths. But it is not a wholly silly statement all the same. And the denial or neglect of it may be even more deleterious than the abuse of it. I think we are in danger of neglecting it. If we do, we shall only succeed in being clear at the expense of being superficial; and in our zeal to 'disinfect' our language from muddles, we shall only succeed in sterilizing it. To use another analogy, we shall have made its rules so rigid that it becomes a strait-jacket, and prevents us even from asking questions which ought to be asked and from understanding the non-professional outsider who (in a confused way, very likely) is trying to ask them. Has it not happened sometimes that an important question was first asked by poets and religious teachers and other unphilosophical persons, who were blissfully ignorant of the terminological rules which the philosophers of their day had laid down? 'Nonsense! Nonsense!' says the professional philosopher, when he is told of the question these people have asked. But his successors a generation or two later may call it unconscious wisdom or untutored insight; and having altered the terminological rules so as to make the question a permissible one, they may spend their lives in looking for the answer. In that case the philosopher who said 'Nonsense!' will appear a little ridiculous. Let us take care that this does not happen to ourselves, and let us not allow our zeal for 'tightening up language' to run away with us. Even though we allow for the distinction between analytic clarity and synoptic clarity, it may still be true that clarity is not enough.

CHAPTER II

TWO LECTURES ON THE NATURE OF PHILOSOPHY[1]

C. D. Broad

Professor Emeritus, University of Cambridge

LECTURE I

Anyone who is a professional teacher of philosophy must be well aware that many of his colleagues regard his subject as at best extremely queer and at worst completely bogus. He knows too that this impression is not confined to stupid or ignorant or unfriendly persons, whose opinions on the matter he can lightheartedly set aside. We may usefully begin by asking ourselves what are the causes of this unfavourable estimate, and how far, if at all, they are valid reasons.

We may remind ourselves at the outset that doubts about the validity and the fruitfulness of philosophy, as hitherto pursued, have not been confined to outsiders. At least three of the most eminent European professionals, Descartes, Locke, and Kant, were moved to initiate the philosophic developments for which they are famous by their profound dissatisfaction with all that had gone under the name of 'philosophy' before their time. It is true that each of them claimed to have found a remedy and to have set philosophy at long last on the right course. But their successors can derive little comfort from this. For, whilst we cannot but admit that each of these great men was largely justified in his criticisms on philosophy as practised up to his time, we must also own that the remedy proposed by each of them has to all appearances failed to cure the disease. The philosophies of Descartes, of Locke, and of Kant seem to be open to very much the same kind of objections as those writers launched against the philosophy in which they were brought up.

These objections may be summarized as follows. (1) Philosophy claims to be a branch of knowledge or of well-founded

[1] Two lectures delivered in the University of Oslo in March 1955 and published in the Norwegian journal *Inquiry*, Vol. I, No. 2, 1958.

belief. It is not content to be regarded as mythology or poetry or the expression of a personal emotive reaction. Now, if this claim were valid, we should expect philosophy to be a co-operative work, in which generally agreed results are reached by common and accepted methods. There would, no doubt, be plenty of legitimate disagreement. There would also be a certain amount of heated and needless controversy, due to common human defects and to the personal failings of particular individuals. All this we find in other branches of human inquiry, such as mathematics, natural science, and history. But we should expect the controversies to have led to a very large amount of agreement at any moment among experts, and we should expect such agreed results to form a firm basis for further developments. Now, it will be said, we do not find this or anything like it in philosophy. At any moment we find philosophers divided into sects and schools, whose problems, methods, and very language are so alien to each other that mutual understanding is difficult and fruitful discussion and co-operation impossible. One has only to note, e.g. the co-existence at the present time of a school of logical positivists and a school of existentialists, in order to illustrate this contention. At most we may find one fashion prevailing for some years and over a considerable area, and ousting temporarily another fashion which sooner or later returns. In illustration of this it is amusing to compare and contrast the titles of articles in the famous philosophical journal *Mind* today and fifty years ago. At the beginning of this century many pages in each number were devoted to the discussion of intimate details in the life of the Absolute. Nowadays it is rare indeed for the very phrase 'the Absolute' to occur in a number of *Mind*, except perhaps in a book-review. Now no one in his senses would allege that, e.g. Bradley and Bosanquet and McTaggart and Royce were any less able or learned or devoted to their subject than the leaders of English and American philosophy today. The inference which suggests itself is that there is something radically wrong with the subject.

It is worth while to remark that Descartes and Bacon quite fairly brought a similar objection against the *natural science* which had prevailed up to their time. They thought that the defect could be remedied by the introduction of certain new methods, and the subsequent history of natural science has abundantly confirmed their anticipations. Descartes, who had himself invented a method which revolutionized the treatment of geometrical problems, had similar high hopes for philosophy. It must be admitted that these hopes have been completely disappointed. Yet we can hardly be surprised that the wonderful transformation wrought in geometry and in physics by the introduction into each of an appropriate new method should have encouraged in other philosophers too, such as Locke and Kant, the belief that their own subject might in a similar way be 'set in the sure path of science'. The repeated frustration of such hopes strongly suggests that the analogies which seemed to justify them were illusory. Either philosophy is not a branch of knowledge at all, or, if it is, it is radically unlike both pure mathematics and natural science.

(2) I think that the considerations which I have outlined constitute the main cause of widespread dissatisfaction with philosophy. Critics who are familiar with the history of scientific thought in Europe may be inclined to reinforce these objections with the following reflexions. They will say that the various branches of human knowledge which are now recognized sciences, e.g. astronomy, mechanics, and formal logic, began by being parts of philosophy. So long as they remained in that state they exhibited all the characteristic defects which have been noted above. But sooner or later the appropriate concepts, methods, and principles were discovered in each case, and thereafter the subject began to progress and at the same time ceased to be a part of philosophy. It might be alleged with some plausibility that we can see this process taking place in our own day with psychology. Does not this strongly suggest that philosophy is not a genuine branch of human knowledge at all, but is simply the ever-diminishing field within which baseless speculation and profitless controversy still have free play because the appropriate conditions for scientific treatment have not yet been elicited?

(3) If one considers the way in which philosophy is taught to students, and contrasts it with the methods of teaching in subjects which are admittedly genuine branches of human knowledge, one may well be confirmed in these suspicions. A considerable part of the training of a student of philosophy consists in studying the writings of eminent philosophers of the past, such as Plato, Aristotle, Descartes, and Kant. But it is no part of the training of a mathematician or physicist to read and criticize the works of Archimedes, of Newton, of Faraday, and of Maxwell.

The methods and results of these great men, so far as they have proved to be valid and useful, have been embodied in the science and now appear in simplified and improved form in contemporary textbooks. If the original writings are now studied at all, this is only because of their historical interest as milestones on the road of mathematical or physical progress. Does not this peculiarity in the method of training students of philosophy reinforce the suspicion that the subject is not a branch of human knowledge, but only a collection of *obiter dicta* dressed up in argumentative form?

Many professional philosophers nowadays would be ready to admit that there is a great deal of truth in these contentions, and would be content to make very modest claims for their subject. An influential contemporary school, with many very able adherents in England and the United States, would reduce philosophy to the modest task of attempting to cure the occupational diseases of philosophers. In their writings the word 'philosopher' is commonly used to denote the holder of some opinion, or more accurately the utterer of some sentence in the indicative mood, which the writer regards as characteristically fatuous. If this is what one thinks about one's own occupation, it is certainly *honest* to announce the fact. It is not for me to judge whether it is altogether *prudent* for professional philosophers thus publicly to proclaim that their business is to take in and wash each other's dirty linen. Nor will I speculate on how long an impoverished community, such as contemporary England, will continue to pay salaries to individuals whose only function, on their own showing, is to cure a disease which they catch from each other and impart to their pupils.

What in older idioms were called 'philosophical problems' are often referred to by such philosophers as 'worries', with the implication that they are comparable to the pimples and emotional upsets of adolescence. The 'treatment' proposed for these 'worries' ranges from the agonized soul-searchings of the late Professor Wittgenstein and his pupils in Cambridge to the avuncular man-of-the-world good sense of Professor Ryle in Oxford. We might perhaps respectfully summarize the latter prescription in the phrase: 'I've been through it myself in my time, my boy, and I know that it hurts like Hell; but I came through, and so will you if you'll only look at it sensibly.'

On the other hand, philosophers nowadays find themselves repeatedly admonished, not only by well-meaning non-professionals, but also by some of their professional colleagues, to be up and doing and to deliver a message which shall restore to humanity its lost spiritual values and save civilization. How gladly would I deliver such a message, if I had one which I believed to be well-founded, and if I saw any reason to think that it would not be either ignored or misunderstood or deliberately suppressed or distorted where it was most needed!

Those who make this demand may be invited to consider the following facts. In the first place, even if it be part of the business of philosophy to produce a *Weltanschauung*, it is no part of the business of any philosopher to produce one on demand in order to stop a leak in the ship of civilization. Secondly, there is no guarantee whatever that an honest attempt to philosophize will lead to a view of the world and of human nature and society which liberal-minded contemporary Western Europeans and Americans would find to their liking. Plato, Spinoza, Hobbes and Hegel were all great philosophers who had thought very deeply on these matters, and their philosophies constitute fairly impressive instances to the contrary. Lastly, we may remind ourselves that the cruelty and violence and loss of liberty, which now prevail in a great part of the world, are the products of a fanatically held philosophical *Weltanschauung*. If we want to find an historical parallel to them, we have only to go back to the seventeenth century in Europe. Now at that time all those philosophical doctrines, to the decline of which our present troubles are often confidently ascribed, were in full bloom. Almost everyone that mattered believed quite seriously in the existence and providence of God, in the immortality of the human soul, in an objective system of moral law, and in rewards and punishments in a future life. The prevalence of these elevating and consolatory views of man and the universe did not prevent the sack of Magdeburg or the reduction of parts of Central Europe to starvation mitigated by cannibalism. Indeed, if these doctrines had never been heard of, the combatants in the Thirty Years War would have needed to seek, and would doubtless have found, other pretexts for fighting and persecuting.

I think that we may at once concede the following points to the critics of philosophy. The facts adduced by them are largely genuine. These facts do make it certain that philosophy, as hitherto pursued, is not a science or a collection of several sciences, either in the sense in which pure mathematics is so or in the sense in which physics, chemistry, biology, etc., are so. Some of these facts, moreover, make it almost certain that philosophy never can become a science in either of these senses, and that hopes that it may do so or regrets that it has not done so are based on a complete misunderstanding of its nature.

Whilst accepting all this, I would like before going further to make the following three remarks: (1) We must distinguish between being *non*-scientific and being *un*-scientific. What I have admitted is that philosophy is a subject which is almost certainly of its very nature *non*-scientific. We must not jump from this purely negative statement to the conclusion that it has the positive defect of being unscientific. The latter term can be properly used only when a subject, which is capable of scientific treatment, is treated in a way which ignores or conflicts with the principles of scientific method.

(2) One of the adverse comments which we noted above was that philosophy makes no progress and that opposite views on the same question simply alternate with each other again and again. I think that, at any rate in some important instances, this is a superficial appearance which is greatly modified by closer inspection and more intimate knowledge of the facts.

We must first distinguish here two different cases, viz. certain very general and far-reaching alternative types of philosophic theory, and alternative views on certain fairly specific problems. As an example of the former we might take what I call 'Substantival Monism' and 'Substantival Pluralism', with the philosophy of Spinoza and that of Leibniz as typical and extreme instances of each. As an example of the latter we might take the cluster of interconnected problems about the nature of sense-perception and its objects.

As regards alternative theories of the first kind, I think we must expect them to co-exist with each other at every period in the history of philosophy. Unity and plurality, in intimate correlation, are obvious features in the world as it presents itself to any reflective person. The aspect of unity appeals intellectually and emotionally to thinkers of one temperament, and that of plurality appeals equally strongly to those of another. Each type of theory is likely to be held, though in various specific forms, by equally intelligent philosophers at every period of history. Neither party is in the least likely to convert the other to its own view by argument. At best argument may be used to show that a particular theory of one or other of these alternative types fails to do justice to a certain important aspect of unity or of plurality, as the case may be. Apart from this it is a waste of time to argue. One has to make one's choice of one or another of these *types* of theory on grounds which cannot be presented in the form of arguments appealing equally to all intelligent and instructed persons. Having done this, one may try to develop the chosen type of theory into as coherent and comprehensive a specific form as possible. In that undertaking there is plenty of room for argument, and there is no reason why there should not be progress.

As an example of the second case we might take the controversies about sense-perception and its objects which have so much occupied English philosophers from the time of Locke to the present day. It might well seem to an unsympathetic external observer that idealistic and realistic answers have merely alternated with each other and that no progress has been made. Now that is certainly a mistake. The course of philosophical thought here, amongst really able and expert thinkers at any rate, has taken the form of a spiral and not of a mere circle. Any competent philosopher who puts forward either a realistic or an idealistic answer to these questions nowadays must state it in a far more subtle and qualified form than his remote predecessors would have done, just because of the distinctions which have been drawn and the criticisms which have been made by intermediate philosophers in the course of their controversies with each other. In consequence of this his theory, of whichever type it may be, should at least be immune to many of the objections which have been legitimately brought against earlier forms of the same type of theory.

Another excellent illustration of the same fact is provided by the controversies in regard to phenomenalism and the so-called 'verification-principle' which have taken up so much of the energies of philosophers in England and the United States during the last twenty-five years. I think it might fairly be said that phenomenalism began as a new gospel, that its adherents strove with immense ingenuity and evangelical fervour to apply the verification-principle to cases which seemed *prima facie* to be most recalcitrant, and that in the end it has had to be admitted that a satisfactory phenomenalist analysis of, e.g., material-object propositions or memory-propositions, cannot be given. To an unsympathetic observer it might well seem that we were simply back at where we started, and that a number of very able men, who might surely have been better occupied, had wasted a quarter of a century in desperately defending positions which any sensible person could have seen at the outset to be untenable.

I am quite sure that such a judgement is superficial and mistaken, though I must confess that I have sometimes myself felt inclined to say such things in my haste. The fact is that, in the course of the defence and the attack, ambiguities in the at first vaguely formulated verification-principle have been noted and cleared up, and much light has been thrown on the conditions which must be fulfilled by any satisfactory analysis of material-object propositions or of memory-propositions.

I think that the fate of the verification-principle provides an instance in favour of a rather depressing generalization which the history of philosophy suggests. It is this. Time and again some new general principle is brought forward with a flourish of trumpets. As originally formulated it is vague and ambiguous, but this is not at first apparent. In the course of controversy the ambiguities are cleared up, and then it is found to cover two or more alternatives. On one interpretation it is certainly true, but is little more than a tautology and has no interesting consequences. On the other interpretation it is synthetic and would have exciting consequences, but there is no reason to think it true. The time for evangelical fervour is when the ambiguity is still undetected and the principle seems to be at once evidently true and fruitful in consequences. This depressing generalization extends beyond the field of philosophy. It is admirably illustrated, e.g. by the so-called 'economic interpretation of history'. Such illusions are not to be despised. They may be compared with those which cause men to marry and beget children. They are carrots which nature dangles before the noses of philosophers, luring them on to do much valuable thinking which would otherwise never have been undertaken.

(3) The last remark which I will make here is the following. There certainly are changes of fashion in philosophy. When a

new kind is in vogue many things in the philosophy of an earlier day, which are of permanent value and perhaps highly relevant to contemporary problems, tend to be altogether forgotten or carelessly and ignorantly dismissed, simply because they occur in an out-of-date setting and are clad in an unfashionable dress. It is now quite certain that much of permanent value in Scholastic philosophy was ignored or contemned from this cause by Locke, Berkeley, Hume and their followers. I have little doubt that the same is true *mutatis mutandis* of the attitude of many present-day philosophers towards the systems of monistic idealism which were fashionable at the beginning of this century. It is consoling to a philosopher's vanity not to pry too closely into the history of his subject, for otherwise he is liable to find that his discoveries have been anticipated and his fallacies refuted in advance by predecessors whom he has ignored or despised.

I want now to consider in some detail a view of the nature of philosophy which has been accepted in recent years by a number of very able thinkers in England and the United States. It may be formulated roughly as follows. The sole or the main business of philosophy is to analyse the various kinds of proposition which constitute the common-sense view of the world. For many philosophers this line of thought originates in the paper 'A Defence of Common Sense', which was Professor G. E. Moore's contribution to the collection of essays published in 1925 under the title *Contemporary British Philosophy*. It will be worth while to devote some careful attention to this famous and very influential essay of Moore's.

Moore does not attempt to define the word 'common sense' or the phrase 'a common-sense proposition'. Instead he begins by enumerating a long list of propositions, each of which would, I think, readily be admitted to be a common-sense proposition. In order to classify them briefly and intelligibly I will begin by introducing a few simple technical terms. Let us call a proposition 'epistemic' if and only if it asserts that a certain individual, or someone or other, or everyone *knows* a certain proposition or *knows* a proposition of a certain class. Thus the following propositions would be epistemic: Jones knows that the angles at the base of an isosceles triangle are equal; Everyone knows that twice two is four; Some people know all the propositions in the First Book of Euclid. On the other hand, the proposition $2 \times 2 = 4$

would be non-epistemic. An epistemic proposition may be of the first or the second or of a still higher *order*. The examples which I have given are all of the *first* order. But the proposition: I know that Jones knows that 2 × 2 = 4 is an epistemic proposition of the second order.

The first point to be noted is that Moore's propositions fall into two primary groups. The first consists of a large number of *non-epistemic* propositions. The second consists of a single *epistemic* proposition of the *first order* concerning the members of the first group.

The non-epistemic propositions which constitute the first primary group may themselves be subdivided first into *physical* and *psychological* propositions. The physical propositions may then be subdivided into *autobiographical, heterobiographical* and *non-biographical*. The autobiographical physical propositions are assertions *by Moore himself* of the existence, and certain spatial and other relationships, of Moore's own body during a certain period. The heterobiographical ones are similar assertions made by Moore about other living human bodies and the same or earlier periods. The non-biographical ones are similar assertions made by Moore about certain ostensibly non-living bodies, e.g. the earth and the sun, and the same or earlier periods. Finally, the psychological non-epistemic propositions may be subdivided into a number of *autobiographical* ones and a single *heterobiographical* one. The autobiographical ones are assertions by Moore that he himself has from time to time had experiences of each of certain specific kinds. The single heterobiographical one is an assertion by Moore, with regard to the human bodies other than his own whose existence he asserted in the heterobiographical physical propositions. It is that many of these have been the bodies of *persons* who have had during the lifetime of their bodies experiences of the various kinds which Moore himself has had during the lifetime of his present body.

So much for the first primary group, i.e. the *non*-epistemic propositions. We come now to the second primary group which, as I have said, consists of a single *epistemic* proposition of the *first order*. This may be put as follows. It is true of many of the persons other than Moore himself, whose existence is implied by the heterobiographical psychological proposition just stated, that they have often during the lifetime of their present bodies *known* propositions corresponding *mutatis mutandis* to each of those enunciated in the first primary group. The *mutanda* here are of course such terms as the person denoted by the proper name 'Moore', the date at which Moore was born, the date at which he wrote the essay, and so on, in the autobiographical propositions.

Now Moore claims to *know* many propositions in each subdivision of the first group. Since this is an assertion of knowledge, it is an *epistemic* proposition. Since all the propositions in the first group are *non*-epistemic, it is an epistemic proposition of the *first order*. But Moore also claims to *know* the one proposition in the second group. Since this is itself an *epistemic* proposition of the *first order*, the assertion that Moore knows it is an epistemic proposition of the *second order*.

We may sum up this complicated business as follows: (1) Moore claims to *know* that he has a *body* of a certain kind, viz. a living human body, and that he has had *experiences* of certain kinds. He claims to know that there are *other living human bodies* beside his, and that there are *bodies of other kinds*, e.g. trees, chairs, etc. He claims to *know*, with regard to each living human body, that it is the body of a *person* who has had experiences of the same kinds as he himself has had. [All this is an epistemic proposition of the *first order*.] (2) Moore claims to *know*, with regard to each such person, that *that person knows* facts corresponding *mutatis mutandis* to each of the kinds of fact enumerated above which Moore himself claims to know. [This is an epistemic proposition of the *second order*.]

The next point to be noted is this. The word 'know' is used in English in such a way that it would be nonsensical to say of a proposition that it is known by someone but may yet be false. Therefore anyone who admits Moore's claims must admit that there are true propositions in all the subdivisions of Group I. He must also admit that the proposition which is the only member of Group II is true. There are two ways in which he might seek to whittle down this admission. One is to say that in each of the final subdivisions enumerated above there are propositions which are at any rate partly true, though every one of them is also partly false. The other is to say that for the propositions in each of the final subdivisions it is possible to find an *interpretation* in which some of them are wholly true, though in their ordinary sense they are all false. We must note that Moore explicitly rejects both these expedients. He is committed to holding that in each of the final subdivisions there are propositions which, when taken *in their ordinary sense,* are *wholly* true.

This last point deserves further consideration. Moore asserts that each of the common-sense propositions which he has taken as examples, and which he claims to know, has *one and only one* meaning, and that everyone who knows English understands that meaning. Take, e.g., the proposition: There is a penny on the table before me now. Moore would say that this has one and the same *meaning* (allowing for the systematic ambiguity of the words 'I' and 'now') for everyone who understands English. But he says that there might be, and in fact are, great differences of opinion as to the *right analysis* of this and similar propositions, and he does not claim to know the right analysis of them. Unfortunately he does not further discuss these two vitally important notions of the *meaning* and the *correct analysis* of a proposition, nor does he explain in any detail how he supposes the two to be connected. All that he says on that point is this. It is impossible to raise the question: What is the correct analysis of such and such a proposition? unless one understands the meaning of the proposition.

On this I would make the following comments. (1) Surely it is not propositions, but *sentences,* which can significantly be said to have a meaning. A proposition is what a sentence means, or more accurately it is the common meaning of a whole multitude of equivalent sentences, spoken or written in English and in German, and so on. If that be so, we must substitute for Moore's original assertion some such statement as follows. Any person who knows English will think of one and the same proposition whenever he sees or hears or utters or images an instance of the type-sentence 'there is a penny on the table before me now'. Now this seems to me to be an empirical assertion about the behaviour of members of a certain class of men when placed in situations of a certain kind. I do not see how Moore or anyone else can be justified in affirming it with complete confidence. On general grounds it seems to me highly doubtful. The utmost that I could admit is that we could describe fairly accurately the kind of circumstances which would be *necessary,* though not sufficient, conditions for a sane waking adult Englishman to utter or to write (as distinct from babbling or scribbling) an instance of this type-sentence. We could also describe fairly accurately the sort of circumstances which would be held to be relevant for testing the truth or falsity of such an utterance.

(2) Since a *proposition* cannot significantly be said to have a meaning, we cannot significantly contrast the meaning of a proposition with its analysis. We must substitute for this the contrast between a proposition *itself* and that set of interconnected propositions which together constitute the correct analysis of it. For Moore's assertion about meaning and correct analysis we could then substitute the following statement. Although everyone who understands English thinks of one and the same proposition whenever he sees or hears or utters or images an instance of the type-sentence 'There is a penny on the table before me now', yet there is no agreement as to the set of interconnected propositions which together constitute the correct analysis of that proposition. I have already commented adversely on the first part of this assertion. Let us, however, waive these objections and consider the second part of it.

(3) I suppose it would be admitted that in order for a con-junction of propositions p_1 & p_2 & . . . p_n to count as the correct analysis of a proposition p the following conditions are *necessary*: (i) That if p is true, then p_1 & p_2 & . . . p_n is true, and conversely. (ii) that this equivalence is not merely contingent, like the equivalence between being a ruminant and having cloven hoofs, but is in some sense *necessary*. (iii) That the equivalence, though necessary, is *not merely linguistic*. By this I mean that it really is a case of two different propositions, viz. p, on the one hand and p_1 & p_2 & . . . p_n, on the other, and not merely a case of two different *sentences*, e.g. 'This is a negro' and 'This is a black man', which in a certain language stand for *one and the same* proposition.

Now, although these conditions are severally necessary for a set of propositions to count as the correct analysis of a given proposition, I think it is certain that they are not jointly sufficient. Some further condition seems to be needed, and I do not know what it is. I think that this can be made plain by the following example.

Take the sentence 'n is a prime number'. Here I think it is probably true that practically everyone who understands English and has learned elementary mathematics does attach one and the same meaning to it, viz. that n is an integer which is not exactly divisible by any other integer. Now consider the following sentence: 'The immediate successor of the product of all the integers less than n is divisible by n.' I think it is plain that this really does mean a different proposition from that which is meant by the sentence 'n is a prime number'. So our third condition is fulfilled. Now it can be proved that the proposition which is meant by this sentence entails and is entailed by the proposition which is meant by the sentence 'n is a prime number'. (This mutual entailment is known as Wilson's Theorem.) So the first and second of our conditions are also fulfilled. But, although all three conditions are thus fulfilled, would anyone be prepared to say that this complicated proposition is the 'correct analysis' of the proposition that n is a prime number? I do not think that anyone would.

If anyone did, he might be invited to consider the following questions. There are plenty of other complicated propositions which can be shown to entail and be entailed by the proposition that n is a prime number. Are *all* of them to be counted as correct analyses of the proposition that n is a prime number? If so, the phrase '*the* correct analysis' has no application. If, on the other hand, one of them is to be singled out as *the* correct analysis, whilst the rest are to count only as logical equivalents and not as analyses, on what principle is the distinction to be drawn?

The only suggestion that I can make here is the following. It might be said that the proposition that n is a prime number does not *by itself* entail the proposition that the immediate successor of the product of all the integers less than n is divisible by n. The latter proposition is entailed only by the *conjunction* of the former with the axioms of arithmetic. Similarly the former proposition is entailed, not by the latter *alone*, but only by the *conjunction* of the latter with the axioms of arithmetic. We are inclined to overlook this because these axioms are themselves necessary propositions which are the common premisses of all deductions within pure arithmetic. Perhaps, then, we ought to add the following as a fourth condition which is necessary if a conjunction of propositions p_1 & p_2 & ... p_n is to count as an *analysis* of a given proposition p. The proposition p must *suffice by itself* to entail the conjunctive proposition p_1 & p_2 & ... p_n, and similarly the latter must suffice by itself to entail the former. Whether these four conditions are jointly sufficient as well as severally necessary to mark out an analysis, I do not know. Nor do I feel any confidence that the fourth of them is compatible with the third, viz. the condition that analyzandum and analysis shall be two *propositions* and not just two different *sentences* which in a certain language mean the same proposition.

(4) I think that I can sometimes say with confidence that a certain set of propositions is *not* an analysis at all (and therefore not the correct analysis) of what I understand by a certain sentence. But I cannot state any satisfactory criterion by which I decide this. Still less can I state any criterion by which I could recognize that a certain set of propositions *is* the correct analysis of what I understand by a certain sentence when that is in fact the case. In view of all this, I do not think that it is particularly illuminating to say that what is *meant* by such a sentence as 'There is a penny on the table before me now', when understood in its ordinary sense, is and is known to be wholly true, and that the business of philosophy is to seek for the *correct analysis* of such propositions and not to question their truth.

It should be noted that Moore himself never alleged that this was the *only* business of philosophy. Still less did he claim that the philosophical analyses of common-sense propositions must themselves be expressed in the language of common sense. Some philosophers in recent years seem to me to have written as if they held the latter view. If anyone really does hold it, I can only say that it seems to me completely unjustifiable. The philosophical analysis of common-sense propositions, whatever it may really consist in, is obviously a reflective activity carried out by certain specialists upon materials provided by common sense. It is no part of the business of common sense itself. There is therefore not the least reason to expect that the language of common sense would contain a suitable terminology for expressing the results of philosophical reflexion even on nothing but common-sense propositions. So it is no *prima facie* objection to a proposed philosophical analysis that it is expressed in technical terms, e.g. 'sense-datum', 'appearance', 'pure ego', etc., which either do not occur at all in common-sense language or occur there in a different and non-technical sense. One might as well object to a theoretical physicist because he uses the word 'entropy', to which no word in everyday speech corresponds, or because he uses the word 'energy' in a specialized technical sense which is very different from that which it has in daily life.

Certainly it is most desirable to bring high-sounding technical terminology to the test of concrete situations, as Professor Moore has so often done with such devastating effect. It is also true and important to note that a technical term may and often does presuppose a certain theory, and that those who habitually use it are therefore in danger of unwittingly assuming that theory without question when it is in fact open to doubts and objections. But, provided that a philosopher always bears these facts in mind, he need not reproach himself if he sometimes expresses the results of his reflexions in terms which would be unintelligible to his bedmaker or unfamiliar to his bookmaker. It is as well to remember that the word 'jargon', which is sometimes bandied about in this connexion, is a question-begging epithet. In practice it generally denotes simply the technical terminology favoured by one's opponents.

I will conclude today's lecture by summarizing my own reaction to the view that philosophy is or should be the analysis of common-sense propositions.

I think that *one* very important part of philosophy *is* something which it is convenient to call the 'analysis' of various important types of proposition, though I must confess that I cannot give a satisfactory definition of 'philosophical analysis' or a criterion for deciding whether a certain set of propositions is or is not the correct analysis of what is meant by a certain sentence. I also think that *one* very important class of propositions to be subjected to philosophical analysis are those which plain men and philosophers alike express by the sentences which they utter, and understand by the sentences which they hear, in the most ordinary business of their everyday life.

I would point out, however, that, in my opinion, the importance of these latter propositions, and therefore the importance of a correct analysis of them, would be very little diminished if I rejected, as I am inclined to do, Moore's claims to knowledge here. Suppose I were content to say that in my unreflective moments I *unhesitatingly believe* such non-epistemic propositions as Moore claims that he and I *know*, including propositions that there are other living human bodies and that many of them are the bodies of persons who have experiences of similar kinds to those which I *unhesitatingly believe* myself to have had. Suppose, further, I were content to say that in my unreflective moments I *unhesitatingly believe* that these other persons, whom I unhesitatingly believe to exist and to have experiences like mine, *unhesitatingly believe* in *their* unreflecting moments propositions similar *mutatis mutandis* to those which *I* unhesitatingly believe in *my* unreflective moments. Then the importance to *me* of these propositions, and therefore of a correct analysis of them, would still be very great. And presumably the importance of similar propositions *mutatis mutandis* to another person would be no less great if, as I unhesitatingly believe in my unreflective moments, there are other persons like myself.

However that may be, I do *not* think that the analysis of propositions of various important kinds is the *whole* business of philosophy. Nor do I think that the propositions of common sense, as exemplified by Moore in his list, are the *only* suitable materials for philosophical analysis. It seems to me that another important part of the business of philosophy is to consider the *consistency* of common-sense propositions of various kinds with each other and with propositions of other important kinds, e.g. those of mathematics, of natural science, of morality, of psychical research and of religion. It is also part of its business to consider the internal consistency of each of these systems of propositions.

Both for this reason, and for its own sake, it is part of the business of philosophy to try to analyse, e.g. scientific propositions and moral propositions, as well as common-sense propositions. Here we shall have to extend the phrase 'analysis of propositions' to cover the attempt to show that certain kinds of sentences in the indicative, e.g. moral ones such as 'Lying is wrong' and 'People ought to pay their debts', do not in fact express or convey propositions at all. This extension can easily be made by substituting for the phrase 'analysis of propositions' the phrase 'analysis of what is expressed by sentences in the indicative'.

In this lecture I have confined myself in the main to negative and critical statements about philosophy itself and about certain views as to its nature and functions. In the next lecture I shall try to develop and to illustrate the ideas which I have thrown out in the course of my criticism of the view that the sole function of philosophy is to analyse common-sense propositions.

LECTURE II

In the present lecture I shall be covering in part the same ground as in the address, entitled 'Some Methods of Speculative Philosophy',[1] which I gave at the joint session of the Mind Association and the Aristotelian Society at Cambridge in July 1947. As I have not substantially altered my views since then, it is inevitable that I should to some extent repeat my own words. For this I must apologize to those who happen to have read and to remember that address.

We may begin with the platitude that philosophy is what philosophers do. If, then, we want to decide what philosophy is, we shall naturally begin by considering what kind of activities have been pursued by men whom everyone would regard as great philosophers when engaged in what everyone would regard as their characteristically professional work. There would be no great difficulty in giving instances which would satisfy most people. Spinoza and Leibniz were great philosophers; Shakespeare and Gibbon, though men of the highest intellectual calibre, were not philosophers at all. Spinoza was engaged in philosophical work when he wrote his *Ethics* and not when he wrote his *Hebrew Grammar*, and Leibniz was so engaged when he wrote his *Monadology* and not when he wrote his history of the House of Brunswick. But there are undoubtedly plenty of marginal cases. One and the same man may be eminent both as a philosopher and as a scientist or a mathematician. Descartes, Leibniz and Whitehead are obvious examples. Then, again, it may be impossible to draw a sharp line between philosophical and non-philosophical activities in many cases. Einstein, e.g., was obviously a great mathematical physicist and not primarily a philosopher, but it might well be held that the reflexions which led him to formulate first the special and then the general theory of relativity were predominantly philosophical. Leibniz's writings on dynamics and on the differential calculus seem to be an intimate blend of what everyone would call 'science' and what most people would call 'philosophy'.

We may notice next that what would generally be admitted to be philosophical activities seem to cover at least two very different kinds of intellectual undertaking. Hume's attempt to analyse causal propositions and Spinoza's attempt to establish by deductive

[1] *Proceedings of the Aristotelian Society, Supplementary Vol. XXI.*

argument the fundamental nature of God or the Universe are extreme instances of the two. In the philosophical work of most great philosophers these two kinds of activity are blended in various proportions. But it is not at all obvious that there is any necessary connexion between them. It might be held that the former is a practicable and useful activity, which should continue to be pursued; whilst the latter is an impracticable but seductive activity, which should be dropped, and against which the unwary should be warned. (Those who take this view might claim to find analogies in the original amalgam of astronomy with astrology and of chemistry with alchemy.)

Now I am inclined to think that there is one feature which is characteristic of all work that would generally be regarded as philosophical. This I will call 'Synopsis'. I am inclined to think that there are certain other features, of which the following things may be said. One or more of them must be present, in addition to synopsis, in any work which would be called 'philo-sophic'. But they need not all be present. In some work which everyone would call 'philosophic' one or more of these features may be absent or evanescent. I distinguish four such features, and I will give to them the following names, 'Analysis of Propositions and Concepts', 'Detection and Formulation of Presuppositions', 'Critical Appraisal of Presuppositions', and 'Synthesis'. The first three of these are very closely bound up with each other, and together they are characteristic of what I call 'critical philosophy'. The fourth, viz. synthesis, is specially characteristic of what I call 'speculative philosophy'. The rest of this lecture will be devoted to explaining and illustrating the above statements and pointing out interconnexions between these various features. I will begin with *synopsis*, which I regard as fundamental.

There are different departments of fact, or different regions or levels within a single department, which are very seldom viewed together or seen in their mutual relationships by the plain man or even by the professional scientist or scholar. Yet they do co-exist and are relevant to each other and must presumably be interconnected into some kind of coherent whole. All men at most times, and many men at all times, conduct various parts of their living and thinking in relatively watertight compartments. They turn blind eyes to awkward, abnormal, or marginal facts, and they skate over the surface of phenomena. A strong and persistent desire to see how the various aspects of experience hang together is perhaps the one characteristic common and peculiar to philosophers. I understand by the word 'synopsis' here the deliberate attempt to view together aspects of human experience which are generally viewed apart, and the endeavour to see how they are interconnected. To illustrate what I have in mind I will take two of the examples which I used in my address of 1947.

As our first example we will take the problem of sense-perception. We commonly think of a material thing as something which has all the following characteristics. It is something which has at every moment a certain shape, size and position in a common three-dimensional space; which has at every moment various qualities, such as colour and temperature, in certain determinate forms; which has various causal properties, such as inertia, impenetrability, elasticity, etc.; and which persists, moves or rests, retains or alters its determinate shape, size, qualities, and causal properties, and interacts with other material things through impact, gravitation, radiation, etc. We commonly think that our senses reveal to us the presence and certain of the qualities, mutual relations, changes, and causal properties of certain bodies. We assume that these bodies would have existed; would have had precisely the same qualities, mutual relations, and causal properties; and would have undergone precisely the same changes; even if they had never been perceived by anyone, human or non-human. We take for granted that at the time when a person sees a certain object, e.g. a star, that object exists and is in the state and at the place in which it then visually appears to him to be. We think that the same person can perceive the same part of the same body at the same time by different senses, e.g. sight and touch; and that different persons can perceive the same part of the same body at the same time by the same sense, e.g. sight.

Now there is a problem about sense-perception for the following reasons. (1) If we attend carefully, we note such facts as these. (i) Of two persons, who would be said to be seeing the same part of the same thing at the same time, one may see it, e.g. as round and the other as elliptical. (ii) One and the same person, who would be said to be seeing and feeling the same part of the same thing at the same time, may, e.g., see it as elliptical and feel it as round. (iii) One and the same person, who would be said to have been seeing the same *unchanged* part of the same thing at different times from different positions, may, e.g., see it on one occasion as round and on the other as elliptical. Common sense is more or less aware of such minor systematic variations in normal sensible appearances, and it has certain modes of expression for describing them, but in the main it ignores them. Certain sciences and arts, e.g. geometrical optics and perspective drawing, deal explicitly with some of them.

(2) There are visual perceptual experiences which are abnormal in various ways and degrees, but are similar to and continuous with normal visual perceptions. They range, e.g. from mirror-images and sticks which feel straight but look bent when half immersed in water, through 'seeing double' when one eyeball is pressed aside or the percipient is drunk, to dreams and full-blown waking hallucinations. Now those which come at the latter end of this scale cannot plausibly be interpreted in the naïvely realistic way which ordinary language inevitably suggests for normal sense-perceptions, and yet qualitatively the series is continuous from one end to the other.

(3) There are certain highly relevant facts which are still quite unknown except to a minority of grown-up and educated persons. These must have been completely hidden from everyone at the time when the language in which we express our perceptual experiences was first formed and for thousands of years afterwards. One of these is the *physical* fact that light takes time to travel, and that a visual experience referring to an event in a remote object does not begin until light which left that object simultaneously with that event reaches the percipient's eye. A consequence is that an experience which would naturally be described as 'seeing a certain remote object at a certain moment' does not guarantee the existence of any such object at *that* moment, nor does it reveal the *contemporary* shape, size, position, colour, etc., of such an object if it does still exist. At the best such an experience guarantees only the existence of such an object in the more or less remote *past*, and reveals only the shape, size, position, colour, etc., which it *then* had. To this physical fact we must add the *physiological* fact that visual appearances vary with certain differences in the percipient's eye, optic nerve, and brain, even when the retinal stimulus is the same. We must also add the *psychological* fact that visual perceptions are determined to some extent by the

percipient's past experiences and present mental attitude and expectations.

Now there is a philosophical problem of sense-perception for those and only for those who try to envisage all these facts together and to give an account of sense-perception and its objects which fits them all into a coherent pattern. The language in which we express our sense-perceptions and talk about material things was formed unwittingly in prehistoric times to deal in a practical way with a kind of normalized extract from our total perceptual experience. It was formed in utter ignorance of a whole department of highly relevant physical, physiological and psychological facts. It would surely be nothing short of a miracle if it were theoretically adequate and if it were not positively misleading in some of its implications. If a synoptic view is to be taken, it must be taken by persons with philosophic interests and training, who are adequately informed of these and other relevant facts beside the beliefs and linguistic usages of common sense.

As my second example I will take what may roughly be called the 'mind-body' problem. Here the main facts to be viewed synoptically are the following.

(1) Everyone knows that many of his sensations and feelings follow closely upon, and vary concomitantly with, certain events in his eyes, ears, skin, joints, etc. On the other hand, many experiences, e.g. those of day-dreaming, reasoning, deliberating, etc., do not seem *prima facie* to be co-variant with events in one's body. Then, again, everyone knows that certain of his overt bodily movements follow closely upon, and vary concomitantly with, certain of his experiences, e.g. his intentions to express certain thoughts or to make certain changes in his own or foreign bodies. There is no doubt at all that the common-sense notions of cause and effect, and the associated ideas of agent, instrument and patient, and so on, are mainly derived from such facts as these.

(2) The sciences of anatomy and physiology make it almost certain that the *immediate* bodily antecedents and correlates of our sensations are *not* events in our eyes, ears, skin, etc., but are slightly *later* chemical or electrical changes in our brains. These can be made perceptible to the senses only indirectly through elaborate technical devices, such as the electro-encephalograph. These sciences also make it almost certain that the *immediate* bodily consequents and correlates of setting oneself to fulfil an

intention are *not* the overt bodily movements which one is setting oneself to make, but are slightly *earlier* chemical or electrical changes in one's brain. Of these one is completely ignorant. It is further alleged, on the authority of these sciences, that there are immediate cerebral antecedents and correlates, of the same general nature, even for those mental processes, such as day-dreaming, reasoning, deliberating, etc., which do not seem *prima facie* to be co-variant with events in the body.

(3) The physical sciences have developed a concept of causation in terms of regular sequence and concomitant variation. In this the notions of agent and patient, activity and passivity, etc., play little if any explicit part. So far as the notion of acting and being acted upon survives in physics it comes to this. The physicist thinks of one system as acting on another when energy is transferred from the former to the latter, or when the former, without doing work on the latter, modifies the direction of motion of some of its parts by fixed constraints. Now there is fairly good empirical evidence that a living organism never gains or loses energy except by transference from or to some other part of the *material* world. And it is difficult to imagine a volition exercising guidance without work on moving atoms or electrons in the brain, as a material constraint, such as the rod of a pendulum, does on a moving macroscopic body, such as a pendulum-bob.

Now these various mutually relevant facts and concepts and principles are hardly ever viewed synoptically except by philosophers. Common sense is quite ignorant of many of them, and common language has grown up and crystallized before they were known or suspected. On the other hand, scientists, though familiar with all of them, tend to concentrate on one at a time and temporarily to ignore the rest. When they confine their attention to the chemical, physical and physiological facts they are inclined to take the view that men are 'conscious automata', i.e. that all our mental states, including processes of deliberating, imagining, reasoning, etc., are mere by-products of states of the brain, which are themselves completely determined by physical and physiological antecedents. But their daily lives and all their professional activities in designing, carrying out, and interpreting experiments presuppose a view which is shared by plain men and which seems *prima facie* to be incompatible with the 'conscious-automaton' theory.

A scientist always assumes in practice that, when he designs an experiment and carries it out, he is initiating certain changes in the material world which would not have taken place then and there unless he had thought them out beforehand, willed them, and deliberately prepared the conditions for them. He assumes that his assent to or dissent from the various alternative explanations which might be put on the results of an experiment is determined by processes of *reasoning*, demonstrative or probable, in which assent is given or withheld in accordance with *evidence*, which may be favourable or unfavourable, weak or strong or coercive. Now all this *certainly* involves concepts, and seems *prima facie* to involve modes of causation, completely different from those in terms of which the 'conscious-automaton' theory is formulated.

To sum this up briefly. A scientist who investigates and theorizes about man and his powers and activities is himself a man exercising certain characteristically human powers and activities. But the account which he is led to give of man, when he treats him as an object of scientific investigation, seems difficult to reconcile with the occurrence and with the validity of his own most characteristic activities as investigator, experimenter and reasoner. It seems no less difficult to reconcile with what non-scientists, and the scientist himself in his daily life, unhesitatingly take for granted about themselves and their fellow-men in ordinary social intercourse. There is obviously need for synopsis by someone who is aware of all the main facts and can hold them steadily together in one view. It is for that reason that there is a philosophical problem of body-and-mind, even if the solution of it should consist in showing that it has been wrongly stated.

I think that these two examples should suffice to show what I understand by 'synopsis' and why I think that it is a mental operation which is peculiarly characteristic of philosophy. Synopsis is, however, no more than an essential first stage. From it philosophical thinking may develop in various ways. I will now try to describe and illustrate these.

Suppose that the results of taking a synoptic view of a number of different mutually relevant departments of knowledge or belief were to show that they all obviously fit together without difficulty into a single coherent whole. Then there would be little or no occasion there for philosophy. But actually, as illustrated by my

c

examples, this is often not the case. It often happens that each of the several mutually relevant regions, which we habitually contemplate and react to separately, gives rise to its own system of concepts and principles; that each such set seems fairly satisfactory and coherent in isolation; but that, when we contemplate the various departments together, we find that the several sets of concepts and principles seem *prima facie* to conflict with each other. It is synopsis, revealing *prima facie* incoherence, which is the main motive to philosophical activity.

When we are faced with apparent conflict between different sets of propositions which, taken separately, seem to be satisfactory and evidently true, the most obvious first step is to try to analyse the terms in them and to formulate the propositions themselves more carefully. Such a process is an indispensable step towards deciding whether the inconsistency is real or only apparent, and towards formulating it precisely if it is real. And this is a precondition of any reasonable attempt to deal with the difficulty.

Now the general principles, in accordance with which people do in fact think and behave in their everyday life, in their professional activities as scientists, in their religious life, and so on, are seldom if ever explicitly before their minds. They have never explicitly formulated these presuppositions for themselves, and they might not recognize them if another person were to do so for them. It is an important part of philosophic activity to try to elicit and formulate the presuppositions of each of the various important departments of knowledge and belief which are to be brought into one synoptic view. This is obviously a difficult and delicate task. It is particularly so in connexion with the presuppositions of common sense. For here the philosopher is trying to do for the plain man what the latter could not attempt to do for himself without ceasing, by definition, to be plain. It is evident that there is a serious risk of putting into the mouths of babes and of sucklings what could have occurred only to the wise and prudent. Nevertheless this danger must, I think, be faced if we are to get anywhere.

I will now give some examples of attempts to elicit and formulate presuppositions. I have already outlined one instance in the account of the common-sense view of material things and our perception of them with which I introduced my first example of synopsis. Another admirable example is Sidgwick's attempt in his

Methods of Ethics to formulate the main principles of the morality of common sense. He tries there to elicit and to state clearly the presuppositions at the back of everyday moral judgements about truth-telling, promise-keeping, justice, etc., and their opposites lying, promise-breaking, injustice, etc. This seems to me a typically philosophical undertaking, performed with exemplary acuteness, fairness and thoroughness.

It is often far from easy to discover what is presupposed by a certain system of beliefs or behaviour. What one tries to do may be described very roughly as follows. One tries to formulate a minimal set of fairly general propositions which would make it logically necessary or logically reasonable for a person who accepted them, and who thought and acted consistently, to believe and to act in particular relevant situations in the ways in question. Here it is important to remember that we cannot safely assume that people do think and act consistently. We know that each of us is occasionally inconsistent in detail, and it would not be surprising if all of us were always more or less inconsistent in principle in important departments of our belief and behaviour. It may therefore be impossible, from the nature of the case, to formulate a mutually consistent set of presuppositions even for a particular department of human thought and action, e.g. for common-sense morality or for the common-sense beliefs about sense-perception and material things. Sidgwick, at any rate, found it impossible to do so for common-sense morality. If the presuppositions of any important department of belief or action seem to be mutually inconsistent, or if those of one department seem to be inconsistent with those of another which is obviously closely connected with the former, then the need for a careful analysis of the propositions concerned becomes pressing.

We can illustrate this also from the problem of sense-perception. In order to deal with *prima facie* conflicts and difficulties here we need to analyse carefully such notions as the following: the notion of perceiving the same part of the same thing by two different senses, e.g. sight and touch; the notion of two persons simultaneously seeing the same part of the same thing; the notion of a thing remaining objectively unchanged during a period in which one and the same part of it presents varying visual appearances to an observer; the notion of a perceived thing having parts, e.g. a back and an inside, which are not at the moment being seen or felt; and the notion of a perceptible thing existing and having a history during periods when no one is perceiving it.

Another good example is provided by the problem of free-will and determinism. The situation here may be described roughly as follows. (1) There is a sense of 'could' in which each of us in his daily life is quite convinced that on many occasions he and others *could* have acted otherwise than they in fact did. (2) Unless this conviction is significant and true, *all* judgements of the form: You *ought* to have done *X* (which you did *not* do), or: You *ought not* to have done *Y* (which you *did* do), are in *principle* false. Moreover, if that be so, such morally directed emotions as remorse, moral indignation, etc., are and have always been altogether without appropriate objects. (3) On the other hand, it seems evident to many people on reflexion that, given the circumstances in which any event happened and the laws of nature, including those of psychology, it is *inevitable* that precisely such an event should have happened then and there. In science and a large part of our daily life we do seem to pre-suppose this.

Now, in view of this *prima facie* conflict of presuppositions, the first business of the philosopher is one of analysis. He must try to analyse the sense of 'could' in which each of us is convinced that he and others *could* on many occasions have done otherwise than they did. He must try to analyse the sense of 'could' in which the conviction that persons could have acted otherwise than they did seems to be presupposed by a whole class of ordinary moral judgements and morally directed emotions. He must ask whether these are the same or different. Then he must try to analyse the sense of 'could' in which it seems evident to many that, given the circumstances in which an event happened and the laws of nature, nothing else *could* have happened. He may find that the senses are different, and that 'could' in the former sense or senses does not conflict with 'could not' in the latter. If so, the problem vanishes. If not, we have at least taken the essential first steps towards any possible solution of it.

I have now explained and illustrated what I mean by 'synopsis', 'detection and formulation of presuppositions', and 'analysis of concepts and propositions'. We can next consider what I have called 'critical appraisal of presuppositions'.

It is one problem, and often a very difficult one, to elicit and formulate the *de facto* presuppositions of a certain department of human belief or conduct. It is another problem to analyse these presuppositions and the notions involved in them, though these two processes generally go on together and interact with each other. But, when all this is done to the best of our ability, the question remains: Is there any good reason for us as critical philosophers to accept these analysed and formulated presuppositions, even if as plain men or as scientists or as religious men we cannot help continuing to believe and to act in accordance with them? This is the question of critical appraisal.

Suppose that the presuppositions of a certain department conflict with each other, as Sidgwick thought that those of common-sense morality do. Or suppose that those of one sphere of thought and action conflict with those of another intersecting sphere, as, e.g., it might well be held that the presuppositions of common-sense morality and everyday social intercourse do with those of biology, physiology and experimental psychology. Then it is plain that a rational reflective person cannot continue in theory to accept either of the conflicting propositions without reservation. But, even when there is no apparent conflict after careful analysis has been made, a situation may arise which I will illustrate by comparing and contrasting the cases of deductive and inductive logic.

Consider the rules of the syllogism as formulated by Aristotle and his successors. There is a considerable class of deductive arguments which can without great violence be reduced to syllogistic form. Those of them which would universally be admitted to be cogent break none of the traditional rules of the syllogism, whilst those which would universally be admitted to be invalid break one or more of those rules. We may say therefore that Aristotle and his successors formulated the presuppositions of valid reasoning for an important class of deductive arguments.

Now these rules do not appear to conflict with each other or with the presuppositions of any other department of human activity. So far, so good. But it must be admitted that few if any of them have any trace of self-evidence. Is it in the least obvious, e.g., that a syllogism with two negative premisses cannot be valid; or that, if the conclusion of a valid syllogism is negative, then one of the premisses must be negative? Surely not. But in this case we can get behind the traditional rules to more ultimate principles which entail them and which are self-evident. This can be done in various ways which we need not consider in detail. So here the situation may be regarded as satisfactory.

Now contrast this with the case of inductive reasoning and the endeavours which have been made by Bacon, Mill, Venn, Jevons, Johnson, Keynes and others to formulate and justify its principles. We need not concern ourselves here with the *eliminative* methods elaborated by Bacon, Mill and Johnson. For, although these raise many interesting and subtle questions of detail, as Professor von Wright has well shown, they are essentially *deductive* arguments of a perfectly familiar kind. They state the conditions under which we can *reject* as false certain proposed generalizations. They give us no direct information as to the conditions under which we may *accept* a proposed generalization. Nor do they justify us even indirectly in accepting any generalization unless the following conditions are fulfilled. We must already know somehow that one or another of a certain set of alternative generalizations is true, and we must have empirical evidence which enables us to reject all but one of them in accordance with these principles of elimination.

It is plain, then, that the essential problem is that of inductive generalization. In its simplest form the question may be stated as follows. Suppose that a number of instances of a class α, e.g. swans, which is in principle unlimited in extent, have been observed, and that they have all been found to have a certain property P, e.g. whiteness. What justification is there for concluding, either with certainty or with high probability, that every past instance of α had P, that every present instance of it has P, and that every future instance of it will have P? We all assume that many such arguments are valid, and the whole of natural science is built on that assumption. What is at the back of this conviction?

Now one thing is evident on a moment's reflexion. The subject of the instantial premiss is *some*, but *not* all, members of α, viz. those which have been observed up to date. But the subject of the inductive generalization is all members of α. The predicate is the same in both cases, viz. the property P which all the observed instances were found to have. It is therefore clear that any attempt to regard the argument as *demonstrative* and leading to a conclusion which is certain must be mistaken. It does not matter what one supposes the suppressed premiss to be. *No* premiss, however strong, added to a particular premiss, will enable one validly to deduce a universal conclusion with the same subject and predicate. If such arguments can be defended at all, then, the line taken must be that the instantial premiss, either by itself or in conjunction with some other concealed premiss, makes the inductive conclusion *highly probable*.

It follows at once that, if inductive generalization can be justified at all, some at least of its presuppositions must be certain formal principles of the logic of probability. These may perhaps be regarded as self-evident, like the ultimate principles on which the traditional rules of the syllogism rest. We must remember, however, that the correct analysis of probability-propositions is a matter of acute controversy. It might well be held that the only senses of 'probability' in which these formal principles of probability are self-evident are quite different from the sense in which the conclusion of a well-established inductive generalization is highly probable.

Let us, however, waive this difficulty. Even so, it is generally admitted by experts that the utmost that could be proved is the following. In accordance with the formal principles of probability all that favourable evidence can do is to multiply the *initial probability* of a generalization. If and only if this initial probability exceeds a pre-assigned fraction, which may itself be as small as you please, then an indefinitely long repetition of exclusively favourable instances will raise the final probability as near as you please to unity.

Now, if this analysis be accepted, an essential presupposition of inductive generalization must be a proposition to the following effect. For any conceivable inductive generalization there is some fraction ϵ, such that the probability of this generalization, *prior to* the observation of any relevant instances, favourable or unfavourable, is greater than ϵ. Now, *if* this is an intelligible statement, I do not think that it conflicts with anything that we positively know or with the presuppositions of any other department of thought or action. But one might well ask whether it is even intelligible. What exactly are we to understand, e.g. by the probability, prior to any observations on the colour of swans, of the generalization that all swans are white?

But, even if the sentence be intelligible, is there the faintest reason to accept the proposition which it states? Obviously it has no trace of *self*-evidence, and equally obviously it would be circular to offer *inductive* grounds for it. In its lack of self-evidence it is indeed no worse off than some of the traditional rules of the syllogism. But in the present case no one has been able to suggest any proposition or set of propositions which fulfil the two essential conditions of being self-evident and entailing this proposition. All suggestions that I know of, e.g. the *Uniformity of Nature* of J. S. Mill or the *Principle of Limited Variety* of Lord Keynes, break down on both tests. They are not in the least self-evident, and they are far too abstract to entail anything so determinate as the proposition in question.

The fate of this attempt to elicit, formulate and critically appraise the presuppositions of a very important department of human thought is typical of what may happen. When one tries to appraise critically the presuppositions which one has elicited and formulated one may find that, although they do not conflict with each other or with those of any other department of thought or action, yet there appears to be no reason, direct or indirect, for accepting them. They are not self-evident, and one cannot discover any set of self-evident propositions from which they follow.

The last topic which I shall treat is the activity which I have called 'synthesis' and which I said was specially characteristic of speculative philosophy.

The purpose of synthesis is to supply a set of concepts and principles which shall cover satisfactorily all the various regions which are being viewed synoptically. The concepts and principles characteristic of each separate region, in so far as they are valid, must be shown to follow from, or at least to cohere closely with, this more general set under the special conditions and limitations peculiar to that region. The apparent conflict between the concepts and principles characteristic of different but overlapping spheres of thought or action must be shown to arise from the valid application of these common concepts and principles in different contexts and under different special limitations. Even when there is no conflict to be solved it is likely that the synoptic contemplation of several regions, which are usually contemplated and reacted to separately, will reveal certain analogies between their contents or their structure and certain interrelations between them as collective wholes.

As an example of philosophic synthesis I will return to Sidgwick's *Methods of Ethics*. I have already given his account of the presuppositions of common-sense morality as a good example of the processes of eliciting, formulating and critically appraising the presuppositions of an important department of human thought and action. I will now take his Utilitarianism as an example of an attempt at synthesis.

It appeared to Sidgwick that the presuppositions of common-sense morality are neither severally self-evident nor collectively consistent. On the other hand the following propositions did seem self-evident to him. (1) When several mutually exclusive alternative courses of action are open to a person in a given situation he will do *rightly* if and only if he enacts one of them which will have *at least as good consequences* as any of the others would have if he were to enact it. (2) The only things that can be *intrinsically good or bad* are *actual experiences*, and the only feature of an experience which makes it intrinsically good or bad is its *pleasantness* or *unpleasantness*, respectively. (3) Two alternative states of affairs, in which the same net balance of pleasant over unpleasant experience is distributed among wholly or partly different individuals or is differently distributed among the same individuals have precisely the same *intrinsic* value. These three principles may be called respectively the *Utilitarian Principle*, *Ethical Hedonism* and the *Indifference Principle*.

Now none of these principles seems in the least evident to most people at first sight. So Sidgwick tries to point out and remove a number of confusions and irrelevancies which tend to make people think that they are contemplating *these* propositions when they are in fact contemplating, and quite rightly doubting or rejecting, certain others which they confuse with these. His hope is that, when they really contemplate the propositions which he has in mind, they will find them as self-evident as he does. This is evidently the only possible method of procedure in such cases.

Suppose now that we take into account the actual psychological and sociological facts about men living in communities. One important fact of this kind is the limitation of men's natural sympathies, of their knowledge of others, and of their power of affecting others for good or ill. Another such fact is the importance for human welfare of having general rules of conduct in certain

c*

frequently recurring situations, which men can be relied upon to follow, without pausing to reflect on the utilitarian reasons for doing so, even when following them goes much against the grain. Sidgwick then tries to show in detail the following two things. He tries to show that, from his three self-evident principles and these psychological and sociological facts about human nature, the rules of common-sense morality follow as generally reliable *recipes* for maximizing happiness and minimizing unhappiness in a number of important types of situation in which men are frequently placed. He also tries to show that his three principles, together with these facts about human nature, provide a reasonable basis for deciding what a person ought to do in those marginal cases where the rules of common-sense morality conflict with each other. He thinks that common sense is itself inclined on the whole to appeal to the utilitarian principle when faced with such situations. I am not called upon here to express any opinion on the success or failure of this attempt of Sidgwick's. What I do say is that it provides a most excellent example of an attempt at philosophic synthesis, based upon synopsis and subsequent formulation, analysis and critical appraisal of presuppositions.

This example relates, however, to synthesis *within* a single region, and not to synthesis of a number of overlapping and mutually relevant regions, such as I had in view when I gave as examples of synopsis the mind-body problem and the problem of freewill and determinism. It is attempts to make a synthesis which shall cover a number of such regions, or which shall even be all embracing, that are characteristic of the great speculative philosophers, such as Plotinus, Leibniz, Spinoza, Hegel, Whitehead, McTaggart and Alexander. I have left the mention of such forms of philosophizing to the extreme end of my lecture because I have recently said all that I have to say about them in the address on *Some Methods of Speculative Philosophy* which I referred to at the beginning.

All that I will say here in conclusion is this. To many people these are the most typical and the most exciting products of philosophical activity. But they are also the ones for which it is most difficult at the present day to put up a convincing defence, if they are to be regarded, as their authors would wish them to be, not as poetry or mythology addressed to our emotions, but as speculations about the nature of things, to be accepted or rejected after critical examination by our intellects. For this reason I have preferred to dwell upon those philosophical activities which, as I have tried to show by examples, probably can be pursued with some hope of genuine, if neither continuous nor spectacular, progress. I suspect that synopsis, analysis, the formulation and appraisal of presuppositions, and limited attempts at synthesis, will suffice to keep philosophers innocently, and perhaps even usefully, occupied for as long as the social conditions are likely to last which make philosophizing economically and politically possible.

CHAPTER III

THE PHILOSOPHY OF ANALYSIS[1]

Brand Blanshard
Professor of Philosophy, Yale University

I

To a visitor from abroad, by far the most interesting fact about
British philosophy in the past half-century is the long swing of
its pendulum from the philosophy of idealism to the philosophy
of analysis. It has been my privilege, greatly prized, to visit
England at intervals of roughly a decade over a period of nearly
forty years, and to note, at each return, the new mark that the
pendulum had reached. When I came first as an Oxford undergraduate in 1913, idealism was so much in the ascendant and
blazing so brightly at the zenith as to obscure everything else
in the sky. To be sure, there were other signs if one cared to
look for them. There was Dr Case's physicalism, which still led
a fugitive life in quadrangle corners; there was an intermittent
shower of sparks from Corpus where Dr Schiller kept his supply
of pragmatic fireworks; to the eastward there was a cloud, no
bigger than a man's hand, but, as some thought, of ill foreboding,
which marked the spot where G. E. Moore sat brooding over
sense data. But on the whole, it was a time of philosophic peace
corresponding to the outward peace of those remote and unsus-
pecting days. The philosophic capital of Britain was undoubtedly
Oxford, and in Oxford the great figure of Bradley, rarely seen by
anyone, and magnified now to legendary proportions, hovered
everywhere over the scene. No doubt the turn of fortune that
sent me to his college of Merton, and his own kindness which,
though he never taught, permitted me some small access to him,
gave me a veneration for him not held by all; but it is I think
safe to say that his way of thinking held the field. Two of the
three professors, J. A. Smith and J. A. Stewart, were metaphysical

[1] Annual Philosophical Lecture delivered to the British Academy in
March 1952 and published in the *Proceedings of the British Academy*,
Vol. XXXVIII.

idealists, and perhaps, too, the third, Cook Wilson, though Wilson had ventured some sharp criticism of Bradley's theory of knowledge; and scarcely less influential than the professors were a distinguished group of like-minded dons—Joachim, Rashdall, Joseph, Webb, Lindsay, Moberly, Collingwood, for example— who, though their differences then seemed important, appear far less widely separated as one looks back from a time—*quantum mutatus ab illo*—when all their doctrines equally are out of fashion. Even at Cambridge both the professors, Ward and Sorley, were idealists, as was that other figure, destined probably to a larger place than either, McTaggart. Nor was the story different if one went outside the older universities. Dean Inge, Lord Haldane, Bishop Temple, Bernard Bosanquet, all preached the idealist creed from their pulpits or studies, and in the provincial universities Muirhead and Hetherington, A. E. Taylor and J. B. Baillie, Kemp Smith and Mackenzie, de Burgh, Hoernlé, Henry Jones, and many others, were teaching similar doctrine.

You will recall what that doctrine was. Put briefly, it was this: start anywhere in experience, develop what is implied in what is before you, and you will find yourself committed, on the principle of the flower in the crannied wall, or of the widening circles in the pool, to an all-comprehensive system in which everything is bound by necessity to everything else. To judge that this is a flower is to use a universal. But the universal, when you attend to it, burgeons. It is necessarily connected through genus and species with a hierarchy above it. Its appearance at this spot and moment is connected spatially, temporally, and causally with every other event in the universe. And these relations, if we saw clearly enough, would turn out to be necessary also. We cannot now prove this in detail, but as philosophers we must make it our working assumption till nature flouts us, and there is no reason to expect that she will. The business of philosophy is to understand; to understand is to explain; and to explain is to place things in a context that reveals them as necessary. Such explanation is genuine discovery; the necessities thought discerns in things are not made by us, and neither are such values as beauty, or the goodness of justice or happiness. What from our point of view is increasing understanding of the world is thus from another point of view an increasing self-revelation of the Absolute in finite minds.

This will remind you of the sort of outlook that prevailed among British philosophers forty years ago. And now it has all but vanished. There has been perhaps no period of equal length in the history of British thought that has seen a transformation so complete. What has taken the place of the older view? It is the philosophy of analysis, an elusive and protean philosophy that is in course of such rapid development that what one says about it may be out of date in a month. I have neither the time nor the knowledge to give a complete account of the new way of thinking. All I can do in this lecture is to review the chief points at which it has challenged and, in the opinion of many, vanquished the older philosophy, though it is fair to add that its theses at these points are, in my judgement, its principal theses. Of these, there seem to me to be five.

(1) As against the rationalist view that the building bricks of the universe are concepts or universals, it has offered a doctrine of meaning which would in effect abolish such things. This doctrine is that the meaning of any statement of fact lies in what would verify it in sense perception. The theory came from Vienna, where its most effective proponent was Moritz Schlick, but it has been defended in Britain with much persuasiveness by Professor Ayer. (2) As against the conviction held unanimously by rationalists from Plato to McTaggart that reason can supply us with knowledge of the world, and also extend it by inference, analysts have commonly held that no necessary insights give knowledge of the world at all; they only explicate meanings already in mind. The chief support for this view in Britain came from Wittgenstein, who seems to have persuaded his teacher, Lord Russell, of its truth. (3) As against the view that both concepts and things are so linked together that each depends for its very nature on its relations to others, stands the theory of 'logical atomism', namely, that none of the ultimate bricks of which the universe is built is necessarily related to any other. This is a view which, contrariwise, Wittgenstein learned from Russell. (4) As against the view that values such as good and evil, beauty and ugliness, were in some sense out there in the frame of things, that nature itself, for example, 'means intensely and means good', arose the conviction that judgements of value were not really judgements at all, but exclamations expressing or reporting nothing but our own feelings. This conviction, widely held

among British analysts, has received its fullest statement from an American, Charles Stevenson. (5) As against the view of the absolute idealists that philosophy, through criticizing the assumptions and systematizing the conclusions of science, was an important means to truth, comes the contention that the philosopher's office is the far humbler one of clarifying the meaning of statements whose truth or falsity is otherwise known. One particularly interesting form of this contention is that the business of philosophy is to clear up the vagueness and ambiguity of ordinary language, a doctrine taught by Professor Moore and adopted as a point of departure by the new analytic school at Oxford. The purpose of this lecture is to offer brief comment on each of these teachings.

Let us note at the outset, however, that these doctrines do not form a system, like those of idealism; they are largely independent of each other, and hence philosophers who would call themselves analysts may hold some of them without holding all. Thus logical positivism, which has been the most conspicuous form of the philosophy of analysis, consists essentially of positions (1), (2), and (4), but positivists would not all accept (3), and they would place their own restrictions on (5). The Oxford analysts, who would accept (5), often differ sharply with the positivists about one or all of their three main contentions. Again, though Moore is often accounted a founder of the analytic movement, he sits extraordinarily loose to it in his actual conclusions, for, if I am not mistaken, he would reject (1), (2), and (3), question (4) very strongly, and not uniformly give his assent even to (5). Wittgenstein, on the other hand, accepted and urged all five positions; and for this reason, though not only for this, he has undoubtedly been the central and decisive force of the movement in this country.

It may be thought arbitrary to group into a single school philosophers who differ so widely, and the criticism is undoubtedly just. They are not so much members of a school as co-workers in a movement. What unites them is less a body of common conclusions than a common opposition to the metaphysics of the past, a dislike of anything pompous or high-flown in language, example, speculation, or moral claim, the demand for a sharp and sceptical dissection of notions that long formed the currency of philosophical discussion, a stress on the importance of sense experience, and a preoccupation with language. Widely as the conclusions of Professors Wisdom, Ayer, Ryle and Findlay, for example, would differ, no reader could fail to remark an underlying affinity in method, aim, and temper, which sets them at the other horizon from such writers of the last generation as Bradley, Taylor, and Royce.

II

First among the widely held new conclusions stands a fresh doctrine of meaning. This doctrine is offered as a test of whether a statement is meaningful or not and a way of determining what, if so, its meaning is. Among lay readers there has been some impatience that philosophers should gravely occupy themselves with such a problem. 'We can see the importance', they would say, 'of finding out whether what I mean to say is true or false, but why make a difficulty about *what* I mean? Surely, I can know that by simply looking into my own mind.' But the matter is not so easy, as philosophers have long known. Indeed, just as philosophers knew before Freud that one's real motives were hard to catch, so they have known since Socrates that meanings one would swear one was clear about are as hard to catch as fire-flies. For the most part we have no trouble in recognizing actions as just, but what precisely do we mean by 'just'? Socrates struggled to find an answer through ten books of the *Republic*, and some college students have thought him none too luminous at the end. Many of the problems of philosophy would seem to be problems of just this kind. What do you mean by saying that a flash of lightning *caused* a peal of thunder? What do you mean by a *thing*? What by the word 'I', or by the word 'God', or the word 'good'? We can say about such words what Augustine said of time, that we know perfectly well what we mean by them till we are asked. When the layman objects to such questions, he is showing himself naïve. They are not only very difficult; they are questions of great philosophical importance.

It was to clear up such obscurities as this in our thought about the nature of things that the *Wiener Kreis* offered its now famous principle of meaning as mode of verification. We must say a word about this Vienna Circle. It was a group of younger men bound together by a common interest in philosophy, but all coming to the subject from one or other of the sciences, generally mathematics or physics. At first very loosely formed, the group was more firmly organized when Schlick came to Vienna in 1922, and in 1928 it took the name of the *Verein Ernst Mach*. The name was significant. Ernst Mach, the distinguished professor of physics at Vienna at the turn of the century, was the leading advocate of the view that metaphysics should live up to its name and stay outside the boundaries of physics. He thought that when physicists began talking of atoms, light waves, ether, and other such entities which were, and always would be, imperceptible, they were forfeiting their claim to be empirical scientists; they could form no clear notion of such entities; they could not even prove that they existed. The proper field for an empirical science was experience, actual or possible. The science of physics, for example, could be restated entirely in such terms without losing anything worth keeping. What Boyle's law stated was that if a given volume of gas was pressed into half the space, its pressure as recorded by instruments was twice as great. So long as the statement was confined to that, it dealt with changes in volume and pressure that had a perfectly definite meaning, verifiable by sense. But if you go on to talk, as Clifford did, about millions of sub-microscopic bullets flying about within the volume and hitting the inside of the container twice as often when the volume is halved, you have entered the realm of conjecture and are talking about something that no one has perceived or perhaps ever will perceive. If such terms are to be used at all, it should be as mathematicians use $\sqrt{2}$, that is, as something that fills in gaps in equations but is not assumed to stand for any existing quantity.

Though Planck and other notable scientists repudiated this doctrine, it seemed to the Circle sound. They delighted in the way in which it squeezed the speculative water out of physics. But what excited them even more was the reflexion that if it was sound in physics, it must be sound in principle, that if sound in principle, it must be sound also in philosophy, and that if it was sound in philosophy, they had a potent weapon by which to explode the pretensions of the academic German philosophy of the day. This philosophy still moved in the idealist tradition of Kant and Hegel; it had immense prestige; it spoke a language that was certainly obscure and was assumed to be profound; it looked down on science as possessing a less exalted kind of know-ledge; and yet no two of the German philosophers seemed to agree as to what it was that speculative insight should disclose. The Circle strongly suspected that what lay beneath this *hauteur* and these irreconcilable differences was the fact that the philo-sophers did not descend to earth often enough to be found out. When they occasionally did, as in Hegel's famous deduction that there must be just seven planets, disproved a week later by the discovery of an eighth, the results were not reassuring. Indeed the Circle came to think that the whole claim to such speculative insight was unconscious hocus-pocus.

The weapon with which they sought to dispatch the philo-sophers was the principle of verification. As formulated by Schlick, this read: 'the meaning of a statement can be given only by indicating the way in which the truth of the statement is *tested*.'[1] And it soon appeared that what was conceived to test any statement of fact was sense perception; 'there is no way', Schlick wrote, 'of understanding any meaning without ultimately referring to ostensive definitions . . .'.[2] If a term is to mean anything, that is, it must refer to the sort of thing that you could point at. This doctrine went through a series of interpretations. I shall refer to three of the most important of them.

The first was the 'methodological solipsism' accepted in the early days by Wittgenstein and Carnap. If I am speaking meaning-fully only when I am referring to something I could point at, it seems clear that I can refer to nothing outside my own experience; if I did, I should be speaking of the unverifiable; 'the world', said Wittgenstein, 'is my world'.[3] But in using the term 'my world', one seems to be referring to oneself, and on the theory, what is that? Realizing that there were no sense impressions one could point to and say 'that is myself', Wittgenstein went on to say that if the criterion were applied to the word 'I', it, too, would be found meaningless; hence his position was described as 'solipsism without a subject'. The only meaningful statements were those that could be resolved into what Carnap called *Protocollsätze*, that is, propositions about what was given here and now, without reference to any self to which it was given. These were the ultimate statements, by which the meaning and

[1] *Gesammelte Aufsätze*, p. 179.   [2] *Ibid.*, p. 341.
[3] *Tractatus*, 5.62.

truth of all others were to be tested. But this went too far for most of the positivists. Reichenbach protested that on this view ' "I see a sparkling spot on a black line and some numbers on a brass instrument" is all that astronomy aims to say; and it cannot wish to say more because that would be impossible'.[1] This was odd, to say the least of it. Neurath pointed out a consequence that was more disquieting still. Even *Protocollsätze*, as reports of the given, must come later, even if very little later, than what they report. Since what they report is then gone, and the only way of checking statements about it is to point at it, the statements never can be checked, even assuming what on the theory must be questionable, that they have any meaning at all. Hence they may all be mistaken. But since they are the foundation of knowledge generally, to call them dubious is in effect to deny that anything properly called knowledge is open to us.

I do not think this position was held for long, even by those who formulated it. Most positivists inclined to a second and more liberal interpretation of their criterion. Might they not say that though reference must be to what is given in my own sense experience, still this reference need not be to what is given at the moment, but to anything in that experience, past, present or future? Though I might then refer to the absent, I still meant something with which I had had, or might have, direct contact in sense. This seemed more reasonable. But what about verifiability? Positivists insisted that this must figure in the test; I must refer not only to something that was or might be given, but to that particular given by which I should verify my statement. But that gave rise to the gravest difficulties. Suppose I remarked that Cleopatra had a long nose. Such a statement seems to make sense, and yet, pleasant as it might be to verify it by inspection, that is not at this date a very practicable course. The best I can do is to run down statements in the British Museum library which might support my conjecture. On the theory, these statements, in the sense of black marks on a white surface, would be what my words referred to, since they would be the sense perceptions by which I should verify what I said, and my statement would be a declaration that I should find them if I looked. When Professor Ayer published his *Language, Truth and Logic* in 1936, he seemed to have accepted this view; he held that statements about the

---

[1] *Journal of Philosophy*, xxxiii, p. 149.

past were 'rules for the prediction of those "historical" experiences which are commonly said to verify them'.[1] Now it is clear that any criterion of meaning that leads to such a conclusion is assuming a large burden of proof, since we are far more certain that we are referring to the Cleopatra of the past than that any theory is reliable which tells us we are not. Besides, if our original statement referred not to Cleopatra, but to future verificatory statements about her, then when, in the light of these, we say our original statement was true, we are not talking about *it*, but about something again in the future. So that not only can we never say anything about Cleopatra, we cannot even discuss the question whether our supposed judgement about her was meaningful, or whether, if so, it was true or false. It is a credit to Professor Ayer's candour and good sense that he abandoned this view in his second edition.

Another embarrassing consequence of the theory was its implication regarding our knowledge of other minds. If, when I talk about your headache, for example, I am talking about those observations of my own which would serve to verify it, my reference to your headache must really be to such words, grimaces, or gestures of yours as I can see or hear. Professor Ayer wrote that 'each of us must define the experiences of others in terms of what he can at least in principle observe', from which it followed that 'I must define other people in terms of their empirical manifestations—that is, in terms of the behaviour of their bodies, and ultimately in terms of sense contents',[2] that is, my own sense contents. It was significant to talk of one's own headache, since that was something one could verify, but it was meaningless to attribute a headache in the same sense to anyone else, since, telepathy apart, this could not be directly verified. Now there are many doubts that one may legitimately entertain about our knowledge of other minds, as a distinguished lecturer in this series, Professor Webb, reminded us; one may even doubt, though it would seem a rather silly doubt, whether they think and feel at all. But to say that the very suggestion that they think and feel as we do is meaningless is not to discredit the suggestion, but rather to discredit the absurd criterion of meaning that would require us to abandon it. Most positivists have now, I think,

[1] *Language, Truth and Logic*, p. 147.
[2] *Ibid.*, pp. 202, 203.

discarded the 'physicalism' and behaviourism that they formerly held, though not all seem to have realized that in admitting the reference to other people's pleasures and pains they have really abandoned the principle of verifiability itself. But it seems clear that they have.

Towards the end of his life, which was tragically cut short in 1936, Professor Schlick adopted a third and greatly liberalized version of the principle. Instead of the strong verification which we should have been discussing, and which required that what was meant should itself be presentable in sense, he introduced the notion of weak verifiability, which would grant meaning to a statement if any relevant *evidence* for it could be presented in sense. And by 'could be so presented', he meant 'could *logically* be so presented'. Thus if a statement was such that anyone could conceivably offer empirical evidence that was relevant to it, then and then only was it meaningful. This was an immense step beyond the earlier formulations. But whereas they proved too narrow to suit the positivists' purpose, this last one was far too broad. For now all the metaphysical and theological propositions for whose exclusion the criterion was formulated came trooping back *en masse*, each wearing the official badge of approval. God, freedom, and immortality, for example—all notions which had been driven out because they referred to nothing sensible—were now welcomed home again, since it was clearly possible to find sense observations which had *some* bearing for or against them. Self, cause, the Absolute, the soul, the world as unobserved, all came back into the fold. Thus by a process of internal development, a criterion of meaning designed to exclude speculative philosophy had found itself compelled to readmit it.

Looking back on this development, I think we can see that in the criterion of verifiability there were two fundamental blunders. One was the confusion of what is meant by a proposition with what will serve to verify it. Between what a proposition asserts and the evidence which we use to establish it there may be a very great gap. Most physicists, when they talk about electrons, do not mean only the paths in a cloud-chamber which they would offer as evidence for them. If we speak of this desk as existing when no one is in the room we do not mean merely what people see and feel when they *are* in the room, and, of course, what they might see *if* they were there is not evidence.

Secondly, it is begging a major question to assume that experience is confined to sense experience. Here logical empiricism has not been empirical enough. If it had been, it would surely have recognized that we do in fact think of many relations such as 'a century earlier', of many mental acts such as recollection or assertion, of many numbers possessed by existing groups in common, whose nature makes it impossible to sense them. It is idle to tell us, on the strength of a preconceived theory, that statements which everyone has been making for centuries and everyone recognizes as significant are really meaningless. Whoever offers such a criterion must admit that there are cases in which we know already, and without regard to it, what we mean—otherwise the statement of the criterion itself would have no meaning—and that the criterion must fit this independent evidence, not legislate what evidence will be received. And unless this evidence is ruled out *a priori*, it vetoes the criterion.

III

The second point that the philosophers of analysis have attacked in the older philosophy is its belief that by the use of pure reason we can know the nature of things. Rationalists from Plato down have been attracted by mathematics as providing a model of understanding: Descartes and Spinoza believed that one could start from self-evident propositions, and spin from them, if clever enough, a complete knowledge of the world, and, if I remember rightly, there were only two points in McTaggart's system where he found it necessary to introduce empirical propositions at all. Positivists are convinced that the rationalist claim to such knowledge is a mere blunder in analysis. Rightly understood, they say, these self-evident propositions and deductions upon which the rationalist lays such stress do not state fact at all; they have a totally different aim. What is this aim? Strictly speaking, to report how the speaker is using words, to explain what he means when he uses certain symbols. $3 + 3 = 6$; we know, to be sure, that wherever we go in the universe, we shall find that true; and this has been supposed to be an important insight into the structure of things. But not at all, say the positivists. It is true enough that you will never find an exception, but that is because, by the terms of your statement, you announce that you will not allow one to occur. If someone added three lambs to three lions and got a sum of three lions, or three drops of quicksilver to three others and got one, would you consider that an exception? Not in the least, for you were not talking about animals or quicksilver, but about number, and no such instances could show that the number you meant by '3 + 3' was different from that meant by '6'. But why are you so sure they could not? Simply because you see that what you mean by '3 + 3' and by '6' is the same; no parade of facts could affect this in the least. A definition of meaning is a statement of different order from a statement of fact. And all necessary statements *are* such statements of meaning. 'A straight line is the shortest line'; yes, of course, because in Euclidean geometry, being the shortest is what being straight means. 'Whatever is red is coloured'; naturally; being coloured is obviously part of the meaning of 'red'. Rationalists have bowed their heads and swung their censers before such statements as expressions of profound insight into reality. They were wasting their incense. These statements, one and all, are reports of arbitrary verbal usage.

I think you will agree with me that this view has high plausibility; it has, in fact, convinced most of the philosophers of analysis. But there is one circumstance that may make us hesitate about it; if it is true, nearly all philosophers of first rank from Plato down have suffered from an odd myopia which led them to confuse systematically what was trivial and arbitrary with what was objectively true, certain, and important. All philosophers nod at times, but could the specialists in critical thinking be as chronicially muddled as this? That would certainly be surprising. Still it must be admitted to be possible. At any rate philosophers felt that the new doctrine must have a fair hearing. This it seems now to have received. But the hearing has brought to light that the new doctrine has several slightly different senses. I shall have time to comment on two only, though these, I think, are the most important.

According to the first of these senses, necessary statements are reports of linguistic conventions. Unfortunately this, too, is ambiguous. Does it mean that when we make our statement about red or a straight line, we are reporting the way in which the words are actually used by ourselves or others? This has sometimes been said by positivists, but there are obvious difficulties.

For one thing, necessary or *a priori* statements were supposed to say nothing about fact, but if they are now admitted to be reports of how people actually use language, they are empirical statements after all, and the main point of the new doctrine is abandoned. Secondly, what is being interpreted is *necessary* statements, but no statement about actual usage is necessary; we use the sound 'eagle' to refer to a bird, but we could perfectly well use it, as the Germans do, to mean a hedgehog. Thirdly, the positivists make a great point of saying that all necessary statements are analytic, that they merely explicate our meaning, whereas all statements of actual usage are synthetic. The view, then, that necessary statements are reports about actual usage involved the positivists in at least three self-contradictions.

This view was soon abandoned, if indeed it was ever more than verbally held. 'I think', Professor Ayer wrote in 1936, 'that our view must be that what are called *a priori* propositions do not describe how words are actually used, but merely prescribe how words are to be used. They make no statement whose truth can be accepted or denied. They merely lay down a rule which can be followed or disobeyed.'[1] Carnap took a similar view; necessary statements are not descriptions but prescriptions, and arbitrary ones, about the use of words. This interpretation has been widely accepted by positivists.

But it, too, has broken down. In the first place, it has been seen that a statement can hardly be called in the same breath 'necessary' and also a mere rule of language about which, in Carnap's words, 'we have in every respect complete liberty'. Secondly, it has had to be admitted that such propositions as '3 + 3 = 6' are true, and 'red is an odour' false. But if they were merely rules in the sense of prescriptions, they could no more be true or false than a request to open the window. Thirdly, and most significantly, if these statements were really conventions, the only force that could prevent our changing them would be our own wills, whereas, when we reflect on their meaning, we see that there is another force constraining us which is wholly independent of our wills and has nothing whatever to do with our manipulations of language. We can, of course, use the word red to mean anything we like, and in that sense its use is arbitrary. But the quality red that we mean by it—are we really at liberty

---

[1] *Analysis*, iv, p. 20.

to conceive *that* as entailing, or not entailing, colour? That is the only point of any interest or importance to us, and it is clear that there is no choice about it. Red and colour are plainly different, for what has colour need not be red. But if a thing is red, it is and must be coloured, not through any choice of ours, for we could not make it otherwise if we tried, but because 'nature has said it'.

The same will be found true all along the line. It is true, for example, of those most important of necessary propositions, the laws of logic. If these were conventions merely, we could dismiss them and get new ones. But we cannot. Of course there has been much discussion of alternative logics, but these all seem to turn upon an Ur-logic to which itself there is no alternative. So far as I know, they all depend upon either (*a*) interpreting a familiar law in a quite new way before questioning it, as Brouwer did with excluded middle, (*b*) finding new senses within the meanings of the older logic, as Dr Waismann does when he suggests as a substitute for 'true and false', 'true', 'nearly true', 'not quite false', and 'entirely false', or (*c*) defining implication in various ways. But these are not really new logics in the sense that the validity of the basic laws of traditional logic are impugned by them. In all these systems, when a logician says that something 'follows', he seems to mean the same thing by it; and when positivists argue that logic is conventional, they give no signs of supposing that the logic they use in establishing this is itself merely conventional. Indeed, such sturdy antiques as the law of contradiction have a way of playing disagreeable tricks upon those who try to take them as conventional merely. The very statement that this law is conventional comes flying back at you, for to say this is to say that there is an alternative to the law; to say this is to say that it makes sense to deny it; to deny it is to say that it is false; but since, if it is false, both sides of a contradiction may be true, it may still be true after all.

The doctrine that necessary propositions are statements of our own meaning has more than one interpretation, as I have pointed out. With one kind of emphasis it means that all such statements are linguistic conventions; with another it becomes the somewhat different doctrine that they are all tautologies. If this latter doctrine is true, it is plainly of great importance. Rationalist metaphysics consists very largely of deductions, and, according to this doctrine, every valid deduction merely makes explicit what the premisses have said already. Similarly, in a necessary statement there is no advance to anything new, for the predicate sets out all or part of what is already meant by the subject. To put it in a way that positivists commonly prefer, the contradictory of such a statement is self-contradictory; to deny that a Euclidean straight line is the shortest, or that what is coloured is extended, denies of the subject what, in naming it, you are indicating that it contains.

Now this doctrine also has failed to maintain itself. Discussion has brought to light many statements, admittedly necessary, in which the predicate is clearly not contained in the subject in any plausible sense. Take as a simple instance Professor Langford's example about a cube. Are there not persons, even in an assembly like this, who, if suddenly asked how many edges a cube has, would be momentarily nonplussed? Of course they know what a cube is, and they could identify a lump of sugar as an example without the least hesitation, but if asked how many edges such a figure has, they would ignominiously pick up the lump and count twelve. But if having twelve edges were part of what they meant by a cube, they would not know the lump was a cube till after the counting was done, which is contrary to fact. It is quite possible to know some of the attributes of a cube without knowing all of them, for example, the property of being a solid whose faces are squares, and to see that new properties wholly distinct from any we know are entailed by these. Similarly, there are many necessary propositions about the relation of sense qualities that have resisted all attempts to exhibit them as analytic. Most critics would admit that if anything is coloured, it must be spatially extended, but it is surely clear that however necessary spatial extension may be to that which is coloured, we do not *mean* the same, in whole or in part, when we refer to its colour and to its extension. Nor do we mean by calling anything purple that it falls between blue and red, though we can see on reflexion that it does and must fall there. Indeed I think Mr Joseph was right in saying that never in actual thought do we use tautologies; there would be no point in doing so. In such thought, propositions are either synthetic or not worth making.

What lies behind this not very convincing doctrine that all necessary statements are tautologies? Partly, no doubt, the revived

influence of Hume, who held that none of the qualities of an
object entailed any other, that even geometry contained no
necessities, and that if these appeared anywhere, it was only in
defining meanings. But what is at work is partly also the puzzle
how, if we do have necessary knowledge, we could ever have
acquired it. We plainly could not have drawn it from experience,
if that means sense experience, since no run of sensed cognitions
of blue and extension will give us a *must* between them, and even
if the must were there, it could not be sensed. The problem was
solved by Plato, Hegel, and Bradley by the forthright procedure
of saying that non-sensible universals and the links between them
were directly laid hold of by a special cognitive faculty, νόησις,
Vernunft, or intellect. Analysts look on this faculty as a patent
improvisation to grasp entities themselves improvised. They have
long been moving toward the view that there is nothing in the
world but particulars. If we are to see why, we must turn to the
third line that analysts have taken against the older philosophy.

IV

We saw that according to the positivists, the capital of philosophy
consisted chiefly of watered stock and that with the aid of the
verification theory of meaning they could squeeze the water out.
Wittgenstein attempted a sketch of the world one would live in
if one took this theory seriously. It was a world of atomic exis-
tents no one of which was necessarily connected with any other.
How natural such a conclusion is it is not difficult to see. Take
any ordinary judgement and strip the fat off it, everything, that
is, except the assertion of verifiable fact; take, for example, 'This
gentian is blue'. The first thing to realize is that you are making
not one statement but two, since what you are saying could be
denied either by 'That is not a gentian', or by 'That is not blue'.
You must be saying, then, both 'This is a gentian' *and* 'This is
blue'. Next, when you say 'This is a gentian', what do you refer
to by 'this'? Are you referring to an *it* which *has* the various
qualities of a gentian as opposed to those qualities themselves?
If you think you are, it must be pointed out that no such thing
is verifiable in sense; substances of this kind have been banished
from the analyst's world; all that is verifiable seems to be a cluster
of qualities presenting themselves together. And when you look

more closely at what you are entitled to say, you find it is not 'This flower as a whole is blue', but 'These five triangular petals are blue'. But you obviously cannot stop at that, for it can be broken up into at least sixteen different statements, such as 'this is triangular', 'this is a petal', 'these are five'; and some of these statements can again be broken up into still simpler statements. How far can this process go on? It can go on till all the component statements are themselves atomic statements. Each would then report an atomic fact, a fact, that is, which resists analysis into simpler facts. Perhaps the nearest approach to an atomic statement would be the report about a minute spot, 'This is blue'. But though an atomic fact has no further facts within it and cannot be expressed by anything simpler than the clause 'that x is y', still it does have components within it, a sort of logical proton and electron, designated by subject and predicate, for example, *this* and *blue*. These components are called 'objects', and ideally each of them is so simple as to resist further breaking down. In this analysis there is a clear and important implication. It is that if we break up the world as we know it into its ultimate components, it will be found to consist of an enormous aggregate of sensory simples.

The question now is how these simples are connected. The answer given by Wittgenstein at least was an uncompromising one: no object within a fact is necessarily connected to any other object in it, and no fact is necessarily connected with any other fact. Take the statement 'This is blue'. Is there anything in being this spot that would require it to be blue rather than red, or anything about red that would require it to be here rather than elsewhere? Nothing. The same mutual indifference that obtains among objects obtains also among facts. If I report 'blue now', there is nothing in this fact to require that anything should have been blue a moment ago or should be blue a moment hence. This is Hume once more, with his doctrine that every distinct perception is a distinct existence, which could either be or not be while everything else remained the same. When we come down to the actual givens of which our world is composed, we find nothing but brute facts; once and again there may be rhyme in them, but never reason; the world is a kaleidoscope in which qualities are variously but always unintelligibly put together. That an apple is round does not entail that it should be red or juicy.

We say of Mr Churchill that he is bald, an orator, of so many stone and inches, a painter of pictures and layer of bricks, a statesman, a connoisseur of cigars, admired by Americans, a stylist, cherubic of countenance. But when analysts and psychoanalysts have done their best, does not Mr Churchill remain what a lion was for Empedocles, a happy conflation of atoms? No one of these facts about him requires or explains any of the others; any of them could be denied without making us withhold any other.

At this point some possessor of what was once called the philosophic mind may enter a demurrer. 'After all,' he may say, 'the characters of a mind are not just thrown together like marbles in a box. Indeed we can see as much in the present case; that a man who is a statesman should also be an orator is not an accident merely, nor is it mere chance that an orator should be a stylist. Deny if you will that between these characters in my present loose way of conceiving them there is the sort of necessity one finds in a syllogism, still if you say that this togetherness is simply and wholly unintelligible, you are surely overshooting the mark.' Philosophy—and philosophic history, psychology, and politics— used to be full of generalizations of this kind which are supposed to express essential insights—insights, that is, into the connexion of essences or 'as suches', universal characters whose nature and affiliations could be considered in the abstract. According to the philosophy now widely received, all such insights are illusions unless they report merely that such and such characters are more or less frequently conjoined. Why has this view come to seem so plausible? It is in part, at least, because the present-day logical fashion compels us to formulate such insights as if nothing beyond conjunction were involved in them.

I will not take in illustration such an insight as that the love of oratory entails an interest in style, or that humour involves intelligence, because the mere analysis of the terms would embroil us in a discussion of 'dispositional' and behaviouristic interpretations that would carry us far afield. So let us take an old case whose simplicity may atone for its dullness, 'blueness entails extension'. This is a universal statement. Will you not agree with me that what we mean to say by it, whether this is true or not, is that the character of being blue is *such that* whatever has it must also be extended? We surely suppose ourselves to see some sort of intrinsic connexion between being blue and being extended.

This is a connexion between what has traditionally been called the intensions of the terms. But the logic now in vogue and accepted by the analysts is wholly extensional. This means two things. It means first that the logic is designed to deal exclusively with particulars. If we try to state the above proposition as this logic would state it, we must do so in accordance with its own formula for the universal proposition which is $(x). (\phi x \supset \psi x)$, and that gives us, 'for all values or cases of x, "x is blue" implies "x is extended" '. Now, of course, if being blue entails being extended, then in all cases where anything is blue, it will also be extended, and we may be asked whether the two ways of putting the matter do not amount to the same. The answer is that so far from being the same they imply two different views of the universe. According to the second, all you are entitled to affirm is that being extended accompanies being blue; according to the first, you are reporting not only that extension accompanies blue, but that there is a reason for it, a reason that you have seen. The extensional logic, by confining itself to the conjunction or disjunction of instances to the exclusion of all connexion between intension, has in effect begged the question in which the rationalist is most interested. It silences him by first insisting that if he is to speak with accuracy he must use a certain idiom, and then so arranging the idiom that he cannot say what he means in it. It is no wonder that this sort of logician, with a competence in mathematics which his opponent can seldom claim and with a display of symbols not always governed by Occam's razor, leaves the rationalist intimidated and speechless.

Someone may object that though necessary linkage is ignored in one part of the formula for universal assertions, it is supplied in another. In the statement, 'for all cases of x, "x is blue" implies "x is extended" ', 'all cases' is extensional merely, but what about 'implies'? Does not that restore the lost necessity? Far from it. Indeed the fact that it does not is one of the most familiar facts about the newer logic. $P \supset q$ means merely $\sim (p . \sim q)$ or $\sim p \vee q$; or, putting the relation in words, p implies q in every case except where p is true and q false, or more fully still, p implies q wherever both propositions are true, both false, or p false and q true. This is the second sense in which the newer logic is extensional; a statement of implication is not a statement of necessary connexion, but a statement about the conjoint 'truth-values' of the two propositions in question. On this view, all true propositions will imply each other, as will likewise all false propositions, and every one that is false will imply every one that is true; the assertion that Caesar died in infancy will imply that *The Times* now sells for fourpence. And when the insight that what is red must also be extended is cast into logical form, it is cut off by logical convention from the privilege of expressing anything more definite than this. But, of course, that is no refutation of necessary connexions; it is merely a method of gagging their proponents.

Both the logic and the empirical analysis of the present-day analysts thus converge towards an atomic world which stands at the opposite pole from the close-knit monistic world in which philosophers lived at the turn of the century. For Bosanquet every true judgement of fact was so connected with every other that its falsity would carry down with it the truth of all the rest; for Wittgenstein no such judgement was so connected with any other. Where exactly the truth lies as between these opposite extremes it is not my present business to conjecture, but I do not think that philosophy can live and breathe in a world where all is thus turned to dust. Indeed the analyst cannot do so. He finds that, against his will, the particles are coagulating, even as he describes them as isolated. To take a few examples: (*a*) Our nearest approach to atomic fact is sometimes exemplified by such statements as 'here blue' or 'now pain'. But already in these the isolation has broken down. 'Here' and 'now' have no meaning except in relation to there and then, and if one is to specify that meaning, one must go indefinitely beyond these to others, and beyond these others again. Space, time, number, and degree are orders in which things and qualities actually exist, and they involve necessary connexions; if *a* is earlier than *b*, for example, and *b* than *c*, *a must* be earlier than *c*. Kant was surely right in saying that in all judgements of fact we are committed to using such orders. (*b*) Analysts seem at times to be trying to avoid them. The nearest approach to the truly atomic is taken as 'this is blue', and the givenness of blue at a point is supposed to be an ultimate inexplicable surd. But then this, as it stands, expresses no judgement at all. In actual thinking, 'this' never points to a mere denotation, as Mill thought proper names did: a 'that' without a 'what' cannot be a component in a fact; 'this' refers to some presented character, if nothing more than a spot. And to see this is to see further that the presentation of the blue is after all not a *mere* brute fact; between being a spot and being blue the relation is not wholly external; the spatial character of the spot is a necessary condition of its being blue. The idealists used to insist that the spirit of necessity is beginning to awake even in the simplest demonstrative judgement. In this I suspect they were right. (*c*) The old logic was ready to say that in asserting 'man is mortal', one is asserting *mortality* of man. The new logic protests, and with reason, that one ought not to use a noun to name something whose nature is adjectival, so it uses for mortal a propositional function, '*x* is mortal', indicating that 'mortal' stands for that which is incomplete, which depends in its very nature on something else. This insight is a genuine one. But to say that something is thus dependent, and also quite independent, lacks consistency. (*d*) Even when such judgements as 'humour entails intelligence' are interpreted extensionally, it is not easy to exclude universals; 'all cases of humour' suggests an identity present in all the cases. And so long as there are universals, the world is obviously something more than an aggregate of particulars. Analysts have tried hard to analyse universals away. Even numbers are not conceded to be universals; 'three' means the class of classes or groups similar to a class that I point at. But when one asks, In what *respect* are the other classes similar to the one I point at? the universal seems to creep back again, as it does also when one asks whether the term 'similar', on the various occasions of its use, has the same or only similar meanings. These questions cannot be pursued here. Suffice it to say that though they have been canvassed with great acuteness, I am not myself satisfied that universals can be dispensed with. (*e*) Indeed I am inclined to think that the falsity of atomism follows merely from what is involved in the relation of difference. An object or fact, *A*, is related by this relation of difference to everything else in the universe. Is this an internal or an external relation? If an internal relation means one that could not be absent while leaving its terms the same, it is clearly internal. But a universe in which everything is internally related to everything else, even in this very general way, is not a world of independent atoms.[1]

[1] I have been much helped in my thinking on these matters by Mr Joseph's unpublished lectures on 'Internal and External Relations'.

V

I come now to the fourth thesis maintained against the older philosophy, and happily one that may be put very briefly. So far we have been discussing analyses of judgements of fact and judgements of necessity. But what about judgements of value? The absolute idealists regarded values, like necessary connexions, as part of the fabric of the real world; Professor Kemp Smith says that the distinctive thing about idealism is the view that 'spiritual values have a determining voice in the ordering of the Universe'. The view generally held among positivists, and shared by many other analysts, is the extreme antithesis of this. It is the view that an assertion of value—such a statement as 'that gargoyle is ugly', or 'Himmler was a wicked man', or 'happiness is intrinsically good'—is not a judgement at all, but an expression of the speaker's own attitude of feeling, will, or desire. This view is often described as subjectivism, and this indeed it is, in an extreme form. But we may note that it is not the same as the subjectivism of Westermarck, for whom the statement 'that act is wrong' meant 'I feel disapproval for it', nor yet the subjectivism of Hume, for whom the statement roughly meant 'men generally disapprove of it'. In both these forms of subjectivism, a judgement of value *is* a judgement, that is, an assertion that may be true or false. On the view of Lord Russell and many other analysts, it is neither true nor false, since it is not a judgement or assertion at all. It is essentially an interjection or expression of feeling like 'Bah!' or 'Hurrah!'

We have already intimated that this fourth thesis of the analysts forms the third main thesis of the positivist school. Its connexion with their other two theses is easy to see. Suppose you say that every factual statement refers to what might be given in sense; is a judgement of value a factual statement? Clearly not. For when you say 'that act is wrong', 'wrong' does not refer to any quality of the act, like green or hard, that you could see or touch or point at. Is the statement then a necessary one, in the sense that wrongness is part of what you mean when you name the act? No, that too seems clearly untrue. But if an assertion asserts neither fact nor necessity, what is left for it to assert? Nothing, positivists say. These two kinds of assertion are the only ones recognized in their theory of knowledge. In that

D

theory there is therefore no place for judgements of value. Hence out they go.

Though the emotive theory of value fits in admirably with the other contentions of the positivists, it has caused some heart-burning among those analysts who hold that the office of philosophy is to analyse common-sense beliefs, since this particular analysis throws common sense to the winds. Common sense certainly believes, for example, that we can contradict each other about the rightness or wrongness of conduct; according to the view before us, this is impossible, since your feeling when you say an act is right does not contradict my feeling when I say it is wrong; our feelings are merely different. According to common sense, we can argue for moral convictions and offer evidence for them; according to this view no evidence could establish them, or, strictly speaking, be relevant to them. According to common sense, one's duty may notoriously conflict with one's feeling; according to this view, all one expresses in calling it duty is the way one feels about it. According to common sense, when two persons or nations quarrel, there is a standard of right or wrong independent of their passions, in the light of which one or other, or both, can be pronounced wrong; on the theory before us, there is no such standard.

For those analysts who take philosophy, including ethics, as the analysis of common sense, this catalogue of conflicts with common sense, which could be greatly extended, is enough to refute the theory. For those who admit common sense to be an unsafe guide, the refutation would have to go farther and show that in such conflicts common sense is right. Has this been shown? I think it has. Take one case only, the case of past pain. An aviator crashes and burns in the mountains, and in his last moments suffers intensely. Someone comes across the wreckage and remarks what a bad thing it was that the unfortunate man should have suffered so. According to the emotive theory, he is saying nothing about the suffering at all, but only expressing his own present feeling. It would be meaningless to say that the suffering *was* bad; the only badness that the words could express came into being when the suffering was over and the observer made his remark. I find this most unconvincing. If intense pain is ever evil—and it is surely evil if anything is—it is evil when it occurs and by reason of what it is, not by reason of what someone else feels about it. Nor is there any escape from the paradox by saying that the suffering really was evil when it occurred because of the sufferer's own repugnance to it. On the emotive theory, that is a judgement we cannot make. We can, of course, say that he felt repugnance, but that is a purely descriptive judgement from which the expression of value has evaporated. If we try to say that anything *bad* entered in by way of his repugnance, what we are again expressing is not anything belonging to the past, but something happening in us now. Indeed there has been nothing evil in the universe till we learn about it and take up some attitude toward it. There is something deeply amiss in such a theory.

VI

We turn now to the last of our analytic theses, that which would demote philosophy to the position of a critique of language. You will recall that, according to the older view, philosophy was an independent means to knowledge, to be placed on the level of science, or rather above it. With the prodigious advance of science in the present century, this view has become harder and harder to maintain. If the philosopher was asked by the scientist *what* knowledge his discipline offered, he could only answer stammeringly, for there was virtually nothing at all on which philosophers agreed. It was inevitable that someone should draw the natural conclusion from this; and it was drawn at about the same time by the Vienna Circle on the Continent and by Russell in Britain: what is knowledge is science, and what is not science is not knowledge. Did this exclude philosophy altogether? Not quite. Schlick said at the Oxford Congress of 1930 that the business of philosophy was to clarify the basic statements of science. Moore, in a famous essay of 1925, proposed that the function of philosophy should be to analyse the beliefs of common sense. Since the roots of the newest school of analysis run to Cambridge rather than to Vienna, let us dwell for a moment on Moore's proposal.

Moore's essay, which he entitled 'A Defence of Common Sense', and which was written, as his manner is, in the simplest and clearest terms, cheered the hearts of many who had come to find in philosophy more obscurity than profundity. He gave a long list of propositions, often challenged by philosophers, of which he claimed to be absolutely certain, such propositions as that the earth existed long before he was born and that material things now exist. If the philosopher questioned this belief about material things, the proper way to deal with him was merely to hold up one's hand and say, 'Here *is* a material thing, so you must be wrong'. No argument philosophers offered against such propositions seemed to Moore to have anything like the certainty of the propositions themselves; so he proposed that instead of philosophy's setting up as the critic of common sense, common sense should serve as the touchstone of philosophy, and that if a philosopher offered conclusions at odds with such common-sense beliefs, we should say to him, 'We know already that your conclusions are wrong, so your arguments for them must be invalid'. Of course not all philosophers took this in good part. If common sense was enough in itself to give certainty about an ancient bone of philosophic contention, what exactly was left for them to do? Moore's answer was that instead of trying to correct beliefs that were more certain than anything they could put in their place, they turn to analysing these beliefs. For the strange fact was, he said, that we could understand a belief, and know that it was true, without knowing what it meant, in the sense of knowing the right analysis of it.

Now there is something very odd in saying that you can be sure a proposition is true before you know what it means. Moore explained that the statements he had in mind bore familiar and standard meanings, and that it was these that were clear and certain; he went on to make sport of philosophers who, when asked whether they believed the earth had existed for many years, wagged their heads and said it all depended on what was meant by 'the earth', and 'existed', and 'years'. Now this is an attractive position. But common sense is not always so helpful. As Professor Barnes has pointed out, if Moore were asked whether he knew the meaning of 'this is an inkstand', he would reply, 'That all depends on what you mean by knowing its meaning; if you mean understanding the meaning, Yes; if you mean being able to analyse the meaning, No'. But this implies that the statement 'I know the meaning' has no standard meaning that can give us secure guidance. And sometimes, instead of two or more normal meanings, such meaning presents a blur, resoluble only by the process of analysis that was supposed to follow understanding rather than precede it. For example, Moore professes to know that this is an inkstand, but when he tries to analyse this knowledge, he concludes that the inkstand 'is certainly *only* known to me as the thing which stands in a certain relation to this sense-datum'.[1] But in saying this he has already gone beyond the common-sense meaning, in which sense data do not figure. And he goes much farther. He asks what precisely this relation of thing to sense datum may be. He can think of only three plausible suggestions, and having explored these, he admits that there are the gravest objections to all of them; 'I am completely puzzled', he writes, 'as to what the true answer can be.'[2] Now it is surely strange to say that one knows a proposition with absolute certainty when the only definite meanings one can attach to it are all admitted to be extremely uncertain.

The attempt to take common-sense propositions as certain, then, and to make philosophy the analysis of them, seemed to have run into a culvert. But at this point Moore's followers—with how much of his own approval I do not know—gave to his doctrine an interpretation that they believed would make it tenable. When one says that it is absurd to question the certainty of common-sense propositions, what one means, or ought to mean, is that to call them uncertain *conflicts with ordinary usage*. One can sensibly say one is uncertain whether it will rain tomorrow, but only fools or philosophers would stand in a downpour and express doubt whether it was raining or not; and there was more than a hint that these classes overlapped. When people did express doubt on such points, they were not really doubting what the rest of us accepted, for that was not possible for a sane mind; what they were really doing was using the *words* 'rain' or 'inkstand' or 'certain' in a new way. That, indeed, was what philosophers generally were doing. The paradoxes they pressed upon us to the effect that material things did not exist, that time and space were unreal, and so on, were not peculiarly profound insights, but simply a set of proposals that ordinary usage be abandoned and a new one substituted. Was there any point in this? None whatever. It would only substitute a new rule for an old one that was just as good. And if there is an established rule, it is idle to call usage that is in accordance with it incorrect, for accordance with it is precisely what correctness means; 'it is not possible', writes an advocate of this view, 'for an ordinary form of speech to be

[1] *Philosophical Studies*, p. 233.   [2] *Ibid.*, p. 231.

improper'. 'The philosophizing of most of the more important philosophers has consisted in their more or less subtly repudiating ordinary language.' 'Moore's great historical role consists in the fact that he has been perhaps the first philosopher to sense that any philosophical statement which violates ordinary language is false. . . .'[1]

Here we come in full sight of that preoccupation with language which is one of the most curious aspects of the current philosophy of analysis. A philosophy which in the early twenties was ready, however reluctantly, to abandon common-sense belief if the analysis of fact required it, had become by 1942 a philosophy for which conformity with ordinary usage was a criterion of truth itself. It is easier to feel sure that this view is mistaken than to give one's reasons for feeling so. My own reasons, for what they are worth, are these: first, it imposes upon philosophy a needless fundamentalism, which would make advance very difficult. If we are to take the conventional meaning of 'this is an inkstand' as inviolable and accept nothing at odds with it, what is the point of Moore's own illuminating discussions of the relation of sense-data to physical things and of Russell's ingenious perspective theory? Many of the meanings suggested in such explorations are clearly at odds with ordinary belief, but are they, for that reason, worthless? We should here enter a plea for Moore against the Mooreans. Secondly, it is surely untrue that 'any philosophical statement which violates ordinary language is false'. When the plain man says 'grass is green', he means, I suppose, that it is green whether anyone sees it or not. But is Berkeley really answered by pointing out this fact? That is far too short and easy a way to escape him. For he was not proposing a new usage; indeed he was quite ready to speak with the vulgar if he could think with the learned; he was maintaining that the plain man, in supposing grass to be green when no one saw it, was universally mistaken in the plain sense of 'mistaken', and about one of his plainer meanings. I think that in this he was probably right. Thirdly, as already suggested, words may have a variety even of standard meanings, so that if, to settle a question, *the* meaning is required, no settlement is possible. I use the term 'know' with equal propriety in 'I know that two and one are three', 'I know

[1] Professor N. Malcolm, in *The Philosophy of G. E. Moore*, pp. 362, 365, 368.

that cruelty is wrong', and 'I know that the sun will rise tomorrow', but what is the value of ordinary usage to the student of knowledge if it throws a common verbal blanket over meanings as diverse as these? Fourthly, common usage is often so blurred at the edges as to give no clear answer to one's questions, one way or the other. Someone has asked whether the word 'brother' covers half-brothers? I doubt if Sir James Murray himself could have answered that. Fifthly, there are many philosophic questions which are beyond the ken of common thought or discussion, and hence no common usage about them has ever developed. Language is a very dim and flickering taper with which to explore infinity, or freedom, or causality, or substance, or universals. In such questions common-sense meanings can, at the best, provide a point of departure, and one from which the critical mind makes its departure rapidly and into distant places.

The newest type of analysis, now practised chiefly at Oxford, differs widely from this. The influence of Moore is still apparent in it, but it is an influence that has been filtered through the thick texture of Wittgenstein. In his curious *Tractatus*, Wittgenstein stated his theory of philosophy as a critique of language so obscurely and incoherently, and later revised it so extensively, that comment on him is most safely left to that inner circle whom he allowed to sit at his feet. But it is clear that he gave much thought to the nature of an ideal language, and concluded that it would be one in which every sentence reflected in its own structure the structure of the fact it reported. Such reflexion was already achieved in very simple statements like 'this is blue', where there is a word for each component of the fact, and where the linkage of the words mirrors the linkage in nature. But in dealing with complex cases our language utterly breaks down. Now without committing themselves to Wittgenstein's 'picture' theory, which is pretty clearly untenable, the present-day Oxford analysts have taken from him their central idea that the structure of ordinary language is misleading regarding the structure of facts, and that the business of philosophy is to search out the ways in which it misleads and guard against them.

We say 'the Great Pyramid is square', and such a statement of such an object could mislead nobody. We then say 'the Great Pyramid exists', and our words, though they do not mislead the plain man do befuddle 'the man who has begun to generalize about sorts or types of states of affairs and assumes that every statement gives in its syntax a clue to the logical form of the fact that it records'.[1] The philosopher has only too often been this sort of man. He has assumed that because 'square' names an attribute of the Great Pyramid, 'exists' names an attribute too. And then various forms of disaster, including the ontological argument, quickly follow. Or he says that unpunctuality is a vice, and because 'unpunctuality' is a subject, just as 'the Great Pyramid' is, he assumes that, like the latter, it is some sort of *thing*, and then there is born that doctrine of universals which has bedevilled philosophy from Plato on. Or he refers to 'the top of a tree', and because that sounds very much like 'the top twig of a tree', he assumes that he is referring to something similar in the nature of things, whereas ' "the top of the tree" does not refer to anything, but signifies an attribute, namely the having of a relative position. . . .'[2] Professor Ryle is inclined to think that philosophy is made up of these pseudo-problems, generated by the too ready assumption that forms of language reflect the forms of fact, and suggests that 'the sole and whole function of philosophy' is to identify and correct these misleading forms of language.

I am sure that many besides myself will have been surprised and impressed by the brilliant way in which this theory has been applied by the Oxford analysts. They have, to my mind, proved in a very instructive and illuminating way how easy it is to go off on thoroughly wrong philosophical scents because of assumptions drawn from one's form of expression. There is no idolatry here of common usage; on the contrary, it is precisely the forms of common usage that, adequate for their own uncritical purposes, are branded as the chief source of philosophical delusion.

Grateful as one must be to this new school, however, one may be allowed a murmur or two. The place given language seems to me not only false but itself misleading as to what the school is really doing. Apparently in order to be an analyst in these days, it is *de rigueur* to talk much about language; and the new interest is reflected in the titles of many recent books: *The Logical Syntax of Language, Language, Truth and Logic, Ethics and Language,*

---

[1] Professor G. Ryle in *Logic and Language* (First Series), ed. by A. G. N. Flew, p. 17.

[2] *Ibid.*, p. 28.

Language and Intelligence, Logic and Language. In some cases such titles have been a useful signal to the philosopher that his problems were not being discussed and that he could go on his way. But this would be quite untrue of such analysts as Professor Ryle. His case against the forms of common speech rests upon a prior analysis of the forms of being, an analysis that is pure metaphysics. It is precisely because he has seen so clearly that the kinds of being we refer to by 'idea', 'thing', 'top', 'red', 'exists', are so various that he is able to draw up his indictment against language for confusing them, and the real interest of his work lies in such contentions as that there are no such things as universals, and no such activity as thinking as distinct from bodily behaviour. Of course one can discuss these questions as if they were problems of the right use of words, as one can any other question, but they are not primarily problems of this kind and could be discussed with perfect clearness without referring to usage at all. These analysts, who have something philosophically important to say, have hid their light perversely under their linguistic bushel, and when they preach avoidance of misleading expressions might well be urged to begin at home.

No doubt they would reply that they have shown philosophic confusions to be really linguistic. If that means they have shown that mistaken analogies in the use of words have actually led many philosophers to confusion about the nature of things, it is undoubtedly true, and more generally true than we realized before they insisted on it. But to say that *all* philosophic problems have arisen out of verbal confusions seems to me almost certainly false; I do not think that the problems of evil or immortality first pressed themselves on men's minds because of linguistic confusions, nor do I think that when we now wonder whether chairs and tables continue to be when unobserved our puzzlement has anything to do with language or has a linguistic cure. But even if every philosophical problem without exception arose out of linguistic confusions, it would still not follow that philosophy *is* essentially the detection and correction of such confusions. When one takes a gun and goes hunting in a populous jungle, one's failures will probably arise from the misuse of one's instrument, but the aim of hunting is not simply to avoid such misuses. The aim of hunting is to bag game, to which the avoidance of misuses is merely a means. When one begins to philosophize, one's puzzles

D*

may first be occasioned by confusions in usage, but to avoid those confusions is not therefore the aim of philosophy. The aim of philosophy is to know the nature of things in its more fundamental features. And if the philosopher is interested in avoiding misuses, it is solely because by avoiding them he can see things more clearly as they are.

VII

We have been examining some special theses of the analytic movement; let us close with a brief impression of the movement as a whole. On the negative side:

(*a*) If its main contentions are those we have examined, not one of them seems to have been made out. These theses are the chief points at which the new schools have challenged the philosophic tradition. If they are invalid, the road is still open for constructive speculation.

(*b*) Nevertheless, such speculation has been retarded by the preoccupation of the newer philosophy with its instruments. Philosophers who are convinced that their prime concern is with language will not attempt such constructions as those of Bradley or Alexander, McTaggart or Whitehead. Why should they? the analysts may ask. And it must be admitted that these constructions are largely mistaken at the best, since they disagree widely with each other. But simply to brush them aside, either as false or as unilluminating, would be absurd; with all their defects, they are cultural achievements of a high order, and they won for Britain the philosophic primacy in the years that followed the First World War. It has been claimed that the new analysis is a return from such wanderings into the true British tradition of empiricism. I should have supposed, on the contrary, that the acceptance of the five theses we have discussed would eviscerate every British system except Hume's—even Locke's and Berkeley's. And though this, too, is debatable, I doubt whether the mere whetting of knives to whatever keenness of edge is enough to hold the primacy. Are there others to whom it might pass? Not Russia certainly, where philosophy is in fetters. Possibly to Germany again, if her old spirit can rise from the ruins. Possibly to America, where the enormous quantity of philosophic activity—she has about a thousand teachers of philosophy—is producing, here and there, work of distinguished quality.

(c) The rise of analytic philosophy has had another consequence which some would describe as the assumption by philosophy of a place appropriate to her new and modest status, and others more roundly as a loss of influence and prestige. The new philosophy is more intimately connected than the old with mathematics and natural science, and less intimately with literature, art, and religion; it sets comparatively little store by the history of philosophy, which, consisting largely of metaphysics, is chiefly a chronicle of confusion; and since it regards the search for a *summum bonum* as also confusion, ethics has turned its attention from the ends of life either to reviewing the forms of behaviour or to analysing the language of our emotions about them. Among the qualities required of the philosopher those that used to be summed up under culture play a smaller role, while logical subtlety and acuteness play a larger role. This means in turn that philosophy is losing some part of that connotation of *wisdom*[1] that it once carried. If the present trend continues, philosophy, I suppose, must retreat from a central place in education to a more peripheral place, where it will be pursued by those with special talent for logical and linguistic inquiry. Not all will regard this as an entry for the debit column. I do.

Fortunately as against these debits there are genuine gains:

(a) There has been a general tightening up of philosophical thinking. The elaborate study of the conditions words must fulfil if they are to avoid being vague and meaningless has put the fear of the rod into a whole generation. It has made discussion in philosophy harder; it has made writing harder; it has also in a sense made reading harder, since if, with the new criticism working in one's blood, one tries to read some eminent philosophers of a generation ago, one finds them intolerably loose. The analysts have tried to introduce into philosophy as much as they can of the precision of the mathematician and the empirical definiteness of the scientist, with the result that they have probably attained a higher level in these respects than any other philosophical school, past or present.

(b) Perhaps in consequence of this stress on clear and precise

---

[1] Cf. Professor Price's paper, p. 38 above. [Ed.]

thinking, there is a stress among the leading analysts on simple and lucid writing. Whether their other practices are in the English tradition or not, this clearly is. Moore, Russell, Ayer, Ryle (and here one feels moved to include two other writers, second to none, who stand a little outside the movement, Broad and Price) are worthy successors to Berkeley, Hume, and Mill. An American or a German can only look with envy on a galaxy of writers who are able to combine, as these do, subtle and technical thinking with unfailingly clear and straightforward writing. Perhaps it should be added in fairness that all these men are products of the older Oxford and Cambridge, and that in reading some of the younger analysts one wonders, after all, how much of the credit should go to analysis.

(c) More important is the achievement of the analysts in bringing philosophy and science together. Every member of the influential Vienna group came into philosophy from science. The home of British analysis for many years was Cambridge, and it is hardly possible for Cambridge philosophers to remain unaware of science. By the researches of Frege, Russell, and Whitehead, the chief instrument of the philosophers, logic, has been shown to be continuous with the chief instrument of the natural scientists, mathematics. When positivists talk about scientific method, they commonly do so with a larger acquaintance with the sciences than their non-positivist colleagues. It is to be doubted whether any philosopher of equal competence in the future can attempt so ambitious a construction as Bradley did at Oxford or McTaggart even at Cambridge with so slender an equipment on the scientific side. To many workers in philosophy the new affiliation with science is, of course, an embarrassment. In the end, it should prove a great gain.

That, indeed, would be my judgement of the analytic movement as a whole. It has not, I think, made out its case as it hoped to do. It has not succeeded in showing that speculative philosophy is meaningless. It has not crushed—far from it—the speculative interest or impulse in philosophically minded Britons. In the splendidly impractical bosom of the allegedly practical Englishman that impulse, like the poetic, has been a strong and fruitful one. The new movement has stung him, bewildered him, flouted him, angered him, made him thrash out at it in desperate, frustrated indignation. It has also chastened him. He will find, I hope and expect, that all this whetting of knives has been in his service. It has at least given him a weapon of very sharp edge which, if he knows how to use it, will win him even more honourable trophies than those that are now on his walls.

CHAPTER IV

TWO DOGMAS OF EMPIRICISM[1]

W. V. O. Quine
Edgar Pierce Professor of Philosophy, Harvard University

Modern empiricism has been conditioned in large part by two dogmas. One is a belief in some fundamental cleavage between truths which are *analytic*, or grounded in meanings independently of matters of fact, and truths which are *synthetic*, or grounded in fact. The other dogma is *reductionism*: the belief that each meaningful statement is equivalent to some logical construct upon terms which refer to immediate experience. Both dogmas, I shall argue, are ill-founded. One effect of abandoning them is, as we shall see, a blurring of the supposed boundary between speculative metaphysics and natural science. Another effect is a shift towards pragmatism.

1. *Background for Analyticity*

Kant's cleavage between analytic and synthetic truths was foreshadowed in Hume's distinction between relations of ideas and matters of fact, and in Leibniz's distinction between truths of reason and truths of fact. Leibniz spoke of the truths of reason as true in all possible worlds. Picturesqueness aside, this is to say that the truths of reason are those which could not possibly be false. In the same vein we hear analytic statements defined as statements whose denials are self-contradictory. But this definition has small explanatory value; for the notion of self-contradictoriness, in the quite broad sense needed for this definition of analyticity, stands in exactly the same need of clarification as does the notion of analyticity itself. The two notions are the two sides of a single dubious coin.

Kant conceived of an analytic statement as one that attributes to its subject no more than is already conceptually contained in the subject. This formulation has two shortcomings; it limits itself to statements of subject-predicate form, and it appeals to

[1] First published in the *Philosophical Review* and subsequently included in *From a Logical Point of View*, Harvard Press.

a notion of containment which is left at a metaphorical level. But Kant's intent, evident more from the use he makes of the notion of analyticity than from his definition of it, can be restated thus: a statement is analytic when it is true by virtue of meanings and independently of fact. Pursuing this line, let us examine the concept of *meaning* which is presupposed.

Meaning, let us remember, is not to be identified with naming. Frege's example of 'Evening Star' and 'Morning Star', and Russell's of 'Scott' and 'the author of *Waverley*', illustrate that terms can name the same thing but differ in meaning. The distinction between meaning and naming is no less important at the level of abstract terms. The terms '9' and 'the number of the planets' name one and the same abstract entity but presumably must be regarded as unlike in meaning; for astronomical observation was needed, and not mere reflexion on meanings, to determine the sameness of the entity in question.

The above examples consist of singular terms, concrete and abstract. With general terms, or predicates, the situation is somewhat different but parallel. Whereas a singular term purports to name an entity, abstract or concrete, a general term does not; but a general term is *true of* an entity, or of each of many, or of none. The class of all entities of which a general term is true is called the *extension* of the term. Now paralleling the contrast between the meaning of a singular term and the entity named, we must distinguish equally between the meaning of a general term and its extension. The general terms 'creature with a heart' and 'creature with kidneys', for example, are perhaps alike in extension but unlike in meaning.

Confusion of meaning with extension, in the case of general terms, is less common than confusion of meaning with naming in the case of singular terms. It is indeed a commonplace in philosophy to oppose intension (or meaning) to extension, or, in a variant vocabulary, connotation to denotation.

The Aristotelian notion of essence was the forerunner, no doubt, of the modern notion of intension or meaning. For Aristotle it was essential in men to be rational, accidental to be two-legged. But there is an important difference between this attitude and the doctrine of meaning. From the latter point of view it may indeed be conceded (if only for the sake of argument) that rationality is involved in the meaning of the word 'man' while two-leggedness is not; but two-leggedness may at the same time be viewed as involved in the meaning of 'biped' while rationality is not. Thus from the point of view of the doctrine of meaning it makes no sense to say of the actual individual, who is at once a man and a biped, that his rationality is essential and his two-leggedness accidental or vice versa. Things had essences, for Aristotle, but only linguistic forms have meanings. Meaning is what essence becomes when it is divorced from the object of reference and wedded to the word.

For the theory of meaning a conspicuous question is the nature of its objects; what sort of things are meanings? A felt need for meant entities may derive from an earlier failure to appreciate that meaning and reference are distinct. Once the theory of meaning is sharply separated from the theory of reference, it is a short step to recognizing as the primary business of the theory of meaning simply the synonymy of linguistic forms and the analyticity of statements; meanings themselves, as obscure intermediary entities, may well be abandoned.

The problem of analyticity then confronts us anew. Statements which are analytic by general philosophical acclaim are not indeed far to seek. They fall into two classes. Those of the first class, which may be called *logically true*, are typified by:

(1) No unmarried man is married.

The relevant feature of this example is that it not merely is true as it stands, but remains true under any and all reinterpretations of 'man' and 'married'. If we suppose a prior inventory of *logical* particles, comprising 'no', 'un-', 'not', 'if', 'then', 'and', etc., then in general a logical truth is a statement which is true and remains true under all reinterpretations of its components other than the logical particles.

But there is also a second class of analytic statements, typified by:

(2) No bachelor is married.

The characteristic of such a statement is that it can be turned into a logical truth by putting synonyms for synonyms; thus (2) can be turned into (1) by putting 'unmarried man' for its synonym 'bachelor'. We still lack a proper characterization of this second class of analytic statements, and therewith of analyticity generally, inasmuch as we have had in the above description to lean on a notion of 'synonymy' which is no less in need of clarification than analyticity itself.

In recent years Carnap has tended to explain analyticity by appeal to what he calls state-descriptions. A state-description is any exhaustive assignment of truth values to the atomic, or noncompound, statements of the language. All other statements of the language are, Carnap assumes, built up of their component clauses by means of the familiar logical devices, in such a way that the truth value of any complex statement is fixed for each state-description by specifiable logical laws. A statement is then explained as analytic when it comes out true under every state-description. This account is an adaptation of Leibniz's 'true in all possible worlds'. But note that this version of analyticity serves its purpose only if the atomic statements of the language are, unlike 'John is a bachelor' and 'John is married', mutually independent. Otherwise there would be a state-description which assigned truth to 'John is a bachelor' and to 'John is married', and consequently 'No bachelors are married' would turn out synthetic rather than analytic under the proposed criterion. Thus the criterion of analyticity in terms of state-descriptions serves only for languages devoid of extralogical synonym-pairs, such as 'bachelor' and 'unmarried man'—synonym-pairs of the type which give rise to the 'second class' of analytic statements. The criterion in terms of state-descriptions is a reconstruction at best of logical truth, not of analyticity.

I do not mean to suggest that Carnap is under any illusions on this point. His simplified model language with its state-descriptions is aimed primarily not at the general problem of analyticity but at another purpose, the clarification of probability and induction. Our problem, however, is analyticity; and here the major difficulty lies not in the first class of analytic statements, the logical truths, but rather in the second class, which depends on the notion of synonymy.

2. Definition

There are those who find it soothing to say that the analytic statements of the second class reduce to those of the first class, the logical truths, by *definition*; 'bachelor', for example, is *defined* as 'unmarried man'. But how do we find that 'bachelor' is defined as 'unmarried man'? Who defined it thus, and when? Are we to appeal to the nearest dictionary, and accept the lexicographer's formulation as law? Clearly this would be to put the cart before the horse. The lexicographer is an empirical scientist, whose business is the recording of antecedent facts; and if he glosses 'bachelor' as 'unmarried man' it is because of his belief that there is a relation of synonymy between those forms, implicit in general or preferred usage prior to his own work. The notion of synonymy presupposed here has still to be clarified, presumably in terms relating to linguistic behaviour. Certainly the 'definition' which is the lexicographer's report of an observed synonymy cannot be taken as the ground of the synonymy.

Definition is not, indeed, an activity exclusively of philologists. Philosophers and scientists frequently have occasion to 'define' a recondite term by paraphrasing it into terms of a more familiar vocabulary. But ordinarily such a definition, like the philologist's, is pure lexicography, affirming a relation of synonymy antecedent to the exposition in hand.

Just what it means to affirm synonymy, just what the interconnexions may be which are necessary and sufficient in order that two linguistic forms be properly describable as synonymous, is far from clear; but, whatever these interconnexions may be, ordinarily they are grounded in usage. Definitions reporting selected instances of synonymy come then as reports upon usage.

There is also, however, a variant type of definitional activity which does not limit itself to the reporting of pre-existing synonymies. I have in mind what Carnap calls *explication*—an activity to which philosophers are given, and scientists also in their more philosophical moments. In explication the purpose is not merely to paraphrase the definiendum into an outright synonym, but actually to improve upon the definiendum by refining or supplementing its meaning. But even explication, though not merely reporting a pre-existing synonymy between definiendum and definiens, does rest nevertheless on *other* pre-existing synonymies. The matter may be viewed as follows. Any word worth explicating has some contexts which, as wholes, are clear and precise enough to be useful; and the purpose of explication is to preserve the usage of these favoured contexts while sharpening the usage of other contexts. In order that a given definition be suitable for purposes of explication, therefore, what is required is not that the definiendum in its antecedent usage be synonymous with the definiens, but just that each of these favoured contexts of the definiendum, taken as a whole in its antecedent usage, be synonymous with the corresponding context of the definiens.

Two alternative definientia may be equally appropriate for the purposes of a given task of explication and yet not be synonymous with each other; for they may serve interchangeably within the favoured contexts but diverge elsewhere. By cleaving to one of these definientia rather than the other, a definition of explicative kind generates, by fiat, a relation of synonymy between definiendum and definiens which did not hold before. But such a definition still owes its explicative function, as seen, to pre-existing synonymies.

There does, however, remain still an extreme sort of definition which does not hark back to prior synonymies at all: namely, the explicitly conventional introduction of novel notations for purposes of sheer abbreviation. Here the definiendum becomes synonymous with the definiens simply because it has been created expressly for the purpose of being synonymous with the definiens. Here we have a really transparent case of synonymy created by definition; would that all species of synonymy were as intelligible. For the rest, definition rests on synonymy rather than explaining it.

The word 'definition' has come to have a dangerously reassuring sound, owing no doubt to its frequent occurrence in logical and mathematical writings. We shall do well to digress now into a brief appraisal of the role of definition in formal work.

In logical and mathematical systems either of two mutually antagonistic types of economy may be striven for, and each has its peculiar practical utility. On the one hand we may seek economy of practical expression—ease and brevity in the statement of multifarious relations. This sort of economy calls usually for distinctive concise notations for a wealth of concepts. Second, however, and oppositely, we may seek economy in grammar and vocabulary; we may try to find a minimum of basic concepts such that, once a distinctive notation has been appropriated to each of them, it becomes possible to express any desired further concept by mere combination and iteration of our basic notations. This second sort of economy is impractical in one way, since a poverty in basic idioms tends to a necessary lengthening of discourse. But it is practical in another way: it greatly simplifies theoretical discourse *about* the language, through minimizing the terms and the forms of construction wherein the language consists.

Both sorts of economy, though prima facie incompatible, are valuable in their separate ways. The custom has consequently arisen of combining both sorts of economy by forging in effect two languages, the one a part of the other. The inclusive language, though redundant in grammar and vocabulary, is economical in message lengths, while the part called primitive notation, is economical in grammar and vocabulary. Whole and part are correlated by rules of translation whereby each idiom not in primitive notation is equated to some complex built up of primitive notation. These rules of translation are the so-called *definitions* which appear in formalized systems. They are best viewed not as adjuncts to one language but as correlations between two languages, the one a part of the other.

But these correlations are not arbitrary. They are supposed to show how the primitive notations can accomplish all purposes, save brevity and convenience, of the redundant language. Hence the definiendum and its definiens may be expected, in each case, to be related in one or another of the three ways lately noted. The definiens may be a faithful paraphrase of the definiendum into the narrower notation, preserving a direct synonymy as of antecedent usage; or the definiens may, in the spirit of explication, improve upon the antecedent usage of the definiendum; or finally, the definiendum may be a newly created notation, newly endowed with meaning here and now.

In formal and informal work alike, thus, we find that definition —except in the extreme case of the explicitly conventional introduction of new notations—hinges on prior relations of synonymy. Recognizing then that the notion of definition does not hold the key to synonymy and analyticity, let us look further into synonymy and say no more of definition.

3. *Interchangeability*

A natural suggestion, deserving close examination, is that the synonymy of two linguistic forms consists simply in their interchangeability in all contexts without change of truth value— interchangeability, in Leibniz's phrase, *salva veritate*. Note that synonyms so conceived need not even be free from vagueness, as long as the vaguenesses match.

But it is not quite true that the synonyms 'bachelor' and 'unmarried man' are everywhere interchangeable *salva veritate*. Truths which become false under substitution of 'unmarried man' for 'bachelor' are easily constructed with the help of 'bachelor of arts' or 'bachelor's buttons'; also with the help of quotation, thus:

'Bachelor' has less than ten letters.

Such counter-instances can, however, perhaps be set aside by treating the phrases 'bachelor of arts' and 'bachelor's buttons' and the quotation 'bachelor' each as a single indivisible word and then stipulating that the interchangeability *salva veritate* which is to be the touchstone of synonymy is not supposed to apply to fragmentary occurrences inside of a word. This account of synonymy, supposing it acceptable on other counts, has indeed the drawback of appealing to a prior conception of 'word' which can be counted on to present difficulties of formulation in its turn. Nevertheless some progress might be claimed in having reduced the problem of synonymy to a problem of wordhood. Let us pursue this line a bit, taking 'word' for granted.

The question remains whether interchangeability *salva veritate* (apart from occurrences within words) is a strong enough condition for synonymy, or whether, on the contrary, some heteronymous expressions might be thus interchangeable. Now let us be clear that we are not concerned here with synonymy in the sense of complete identity in psychological associations or poetic quality; indeed no two expressions are synonymous in such a sense. We are concerned only with what may be called *cognitive* synonymy. Just what this is cannot be said without successfully finishing the present study; but we know something about it from the need which arose for it in connexion with analyticity in § 1. The sort of synonymy needed there was merely such that any analytic statement could be turned into a logical truth by putting synonyms for synonyms. Turning the tables and assuming analyticity, indeed, we could explain cognitive synonyms of terms as follows (keeping to the familiar example): to say that 'bachelor' and 'unmarried man' are cognitively synonymous is to say no more nor less than that the statement:

(3) All and only bachelors are unmarried men

is analytic.

What we need is an account of cognitive synonymy not presupposing analyticity—if we are to explain analyticity conversely with help of cognitive synonymy as undertaken in § 1. And indeed such an independent account of cognitive synonymy is at present up for consideration, namely, interchangeability *salva veritate* everywhere except within words. The question before us, to resume the thread at last, is whether such interchangeability is a sufficient condition for cognitive synonymy. We can quickly assure ourselves that it is, by examples of the following sort. The statement:

(4) Necessarily all and only bachelors are bachelors

is evidently true, even supposing 'necessarily' so narrowly construed as to be truly applicable only to analytic statements. Then, if 'bachelor' and 'unmarried man' are interchangeable *salva veritate*, the result:

(5) Necessarily all and only bachelors are unmarried men

of putting 'unmarried man' for an occurrence of 'bachelor' in (4) must, like (4), be true. But to say that (5) is true is to say that (3) is analytic, and hence that 'bachelor' and 'unmarried man' are cognitively synonymous.

Let us see what there is about the above argument that gives it its air of hocus-pocus. The condition of interchangeability *salva veritate* varies in its force with variations in the richness of the language at hand. The above argument supposes we are working with a language rich enough to contain the adverb 'necessarily', this adverb being so construed as to yield truth when and only when applied to an analytic statement. But can we condone a language which contains such an adverb? Does the adverb really make sense? To suppose that it does is to suppose that we have already made satisfactory sense of 'analytic'. Then what are we so hard at work on right now?

Our argument is not flatly circular, but something like it. It has the form, figuratively speaking, of a closed curve in space.

Interchangeability *salva veritate* is meaningless until relativized to a language whose extent is specified in relevant respects.

Suppose now we consider a language containing just the following materials. There is an indefinitely large stock of one-place predicates (for example '*F*' where '*Fx*' means that *x* is a man) and many-place predicates (for example, '*G*' where '*Gxy*' means that *x* loves *y*), mostly having to do with extralogical subject-matter. The rest of the language is logical. The atomic sentences consist each of a predicate followed by one or more variables '*x*', '*y*', etc.; and the complex sentences are built up of the atomic ones by truth functions ('not', 'and', 'or', etc.) and qualification. In effect such a language enjoys the benefits also of descriptions and indeed singular terms generally, these being contextually definable in known ways. Even abstract singular terms naming classes, classes of classes, etc., are contextually definable in case the assumed stock of predicates includes the two-place predicate of class membership. Such a language can be adequate to classical mathematics and indeed to scientific discourse generally, except in so far as the latter involves debatable devices such as contrary-to-fact conditionals or modal adverbs like 'necessarily'. Now a language of this type is extensional, in this sense: any two predicates which agree extensionally (that is, are true of the same objects) are interchangeable *salva veritate*.

In an extensional language, therefore, interchangeability *salva veritate* is no assurance of cognitive synonymy of the desired type. That 'bachelor' and 'unmarried man' are interchangeable *salva veritate* in an extensional language assures us of no more than that (3) is true. There is no assurance here that the extensional agreement of 'bachelor' and 'unmarried man' rests on meaning rather than merely on accidental matters of fact, as does the extensional agreement of 'creature with a heart' and 'creature with kidneys'.

For most purposes extensional agreement is the nearest approximation to synonymy we need care about. But the fact remains that extensional agreement falls far short of cognitive synonymy of the type required for explaining analyticity in the manner of § 1. The type of cognitive synonymy required there is such as to equate the synonymy of 'bachelor' and 'unmarried man' with the analyticity of (3), not merely with the truth of (3).

So we must recognize that interchangeability *salva veritate*, if construed in relation to an extensional language, is not a sufficient condition of cognitive synonymy in the sense needed for deriving analyticity in the manner of § 1. If a language contains an intensional adverb 'necessarily' in the sense lately noted, or other particles to the same effect, then interchangeability *salva veritate* in such a language does afford a sufficient condition of cognitive synonymy; but such a language is intelligible only in so far as the notion of analyticity is already understood in advance.

The effort to explain cognitive synonymy first, for the sake of deriving analyticity from it afterward as in § 1, is perhaps the wrong approach. Instead we might try explaining analyticity somehow without appeal to cognitive synonymy. Afterward we could doubtless derive cognitive synonymy from analyticity satisfactorily enough if desired. We have seen that cognitive synonymy of 'bachelor' and 'unmarried man' can be explained as analyticity of (3). The same explanation works for any pair of one-place predicates, of course, and it can be extended in obvious fashion to many-place predicates. Other syntactical categories can also be accommodated in fairly parallel fashion. Singular terms may be said to be cognitively synonymous when the statement of identity formed by putting '=' between them is analytic. Statements may be said simply to be cognitively synonymous when their biconditional (the result of joining them by 'if and only if') is analytic. If we care to lump all categories into a single formulation, at the expense of assuming again the notion of 'word' which was appealed to early in this section, we can describe any two linguistic forms as cognitively synonymous when the two forms are interchangeable (apart from occurrences within 'words') *salva* (no longer *veritate* but) *analyticitate*. Certain technical questions arise, indeed, over cases of ambiguity or homonymy; let us not pause for them, however, for we are already digressing. Let us rather turn our backs on the problem of synonymy and address ourselves anew to that of analyticity.

4. *Semantical Rules*

Analyticity at first seemed most naturally definable by appeal to a realm of meanings. On refinement, the appeal to meanings gave way to an appeal to synonymy or definition. But definition turned out to be a will-o'-the-wisp, and synonymy turned out to be best understood only by dint of a prior appeal to analyticity itself. So we are back at the problem of analyticity.

I do not know whether the statement 'Everything green is extended' is analytic. Now does my indecision over this example really betray an incomplete understanding, an incomplete grasp of the 'meanings', of 'green' and 'extended'? I think not. The trouble is not with 'green' or 'extended', but with 'analytic'.

It is often hinted that the difficulty in separating analytic statements from synthetic ones in ordinary language is due to the vagueness of ordinary language and that the distinction is clear when we have a precise artificial language with explicit 'semantical rules'. This, however, as I shall now attempt to show, is a confusion.

The notion of analyticity about which we are worrying is a purported relation between statements and languages: a statement S is said to be *analytic* for a language L, and the problem is to make sense of this relation generally, that is, for variable 'S' and 'L'. The gravity of this problem is not perceptibly less for artificial languages than for natural ones. The problem of making sense of the idiom 'S is analytic for L', with variable 'S' and 'L', retains its stubbornness even if we limit the range of the variable 'L' to artificial languages. Let me now try to make this point evident.

For artificial languages and semantical rules we look naturally to the writings of Carnap. His semantical rules take various forms, and to make my point I shall have to distinguish certain of the forms. Let us suppose, to begin with, an artificial language L_t whose semantical rules have the form explicitly of a specification, by recursion or otherwise, of all the analytic statements of L_0. The rules tell us that such and such statements, and only those, are the analytic statements of L_0. Now here the difficulty is simply that the rules contain the world 'analytic', which we do not understand! We understand what expressions the rules attribute analyticity to, but we do not understand what the rules attribute to those expressions. In short, before we can understand a rule which begins 'A statement S is analytic for language L_0 if and only if . . .', we must understand the general relative term 'analytic for'; we must understand 'S is analytic for L' where 'S' and 'L' are variables.

Alternatively we may, indeed, view the so-called rule as a conventional definition of a new simple symbol 'analytic-for-L_0', which might better be written untendentiously as 'K' so as not to seem to throw light on the interesting word 'analytic'. Obviously any number of classes K, M, N, etc., of statements of L_0 can be specified for various purposes or for no purpose; what does it mean to say that K, as against M, N, etc., is the class of the 'analytic' statements of L_0?

By saying what statements are analytic for L_0 we explain 'analytic-for-L_0' but not 'analytic', not 'analytic for'. We do not begin to explain the idiom 'S is analytic for L' with variable 'S' and 'L', even if we are content to limit the range of 'L' to the realm of artificial languages.

Actually we do know enough about the intended significance of 'analytic' to know that analytic statements are supposed to be true. Let us then turn to a second form of semantical rule, which says not that such and such statements are analytic but simply that such and such statements are included among the truths. Such a rule is not subject to the criticism of containing the un-understood word 'analytic'; and we may grant for the sake of argument that there is no difficulty over the broader term 'true'. A semantical rule of this second type, a rule of truth, is not supposed to specify all the truths of the language; it merely stipulates, recursively or otherwise, a certain multitude of statements which, along with others unspecified, are to count as true. Such a rule may be conceded to be quite clear. Derivatively, afterward, analyticity can be demarcated thus: a statement is analytic if it is (not merely true but) true according to the semantical rule.

Still there is really no progress. Instead of appealing to an unexplained word 'analytic', we are now appealing to an unexplained phrase 'semantical rule'. Not every true statement which says that the statements of some class are true can count as a semantical rule—otherwise *all* truths would be 'analytic' in the sense of being true according to semantical rules. Semantical rules are distinguishable, apparently, only by the fact of appearing on a page under the heading 'Semantical Rules'; and this heading is itself then meaningless.

We can say indeed that a statement is *analytic-for-L_0* if and only if it is true according to such and such specifically appended 'semantical rules', but then we find ourselves back at essentially the same case which was originally discussed: 'S is analytic-for-L_0 if and only if. . . .' Once we seek to explain 'S is analytic for L' generally for variable 'L' (even allowing limitation of 'L' to artificial languages), the explanation 'true according to the semantical rules of L' is unavailing; for the relative term 'semantical rule of' is as much in need of clarification, at least, as 'analytic for'.

It may be instructive to compare the notion of semantical rule with that of postulate. Relative to a given set of postulates, it is easy to say what a postulate is: it is a member of the set. Relative to a given set of semantical rules, it is equally easy to say what a semantical rule is. But given simply a notation, mathematical or otherwise, and indeed as thoroughly understood a notation as you please in point of the translations or truth conditions of its statements, who can say which of its true statements rank as postulates? Obviously the question is meaningless—as meaningless as asking which points in Ohio are starting-points. Any finite (or effectively specifiable infinite) selection of statements (preferably true ones, perhaps) is as much *a* set of postulates as any other. The word 'postulate' is significant only relative to an act of inquiry; we apply the word to a set of statements just in so far as we happen, for the year or the moment, to be thinking of those statements in relation to the statements which can be reached from them by some set of transformations to which we have seen fit to direct our attention. Now the notion of semantical rule is as sensible and meaningful as that of postulate, if conceived in a similarly relative spirit— relative, this time, to one or another particular enterprise of schooling unconversant persons in sufficient conditions for truth of statements of some natural or artificial language L. But from this point of view no one signalization of a subclass of the truths of L is intrinsically more a semantical rule than another; and, if 'analytic' means 'true by semantical rules', no one truth of L is analytic to the exclusion of another.

It might conceivably be protested that an artificial language L (unlike a natural one) is a language in the ordinary sense *plus* a set of explicit semantical rules—the whole constituting, let us say, an ordered pair; and that the semantical rules of L then are specifiable simply as the second component of the pair L. But, by the same token and more simply, we might construe an artificial language L outright as an ordered pair whose second component is the class of its analytic statements; and then the analytic statements of L become specifiable simply as the statements in the second component of L. Or better still, we might just stop tugging at our bootstraps altogether.

Not all the explanations of analyticity known to Carnap and his readers have been covered explicitly in the above considerations, but the extension to other forms is not hard to see. Just one additional factor should be mentioned which sometimes enters: sometimes the semantical rules are in effect rules of translation into ordinary language, in which case the analytic statements of the artificial language are in effect recognized as such from the analyticity of their specified translations in ordinary language. Here certainly there can be no thought of an illumination of the problem of analyticity from the side of the artificial language.

From the point of view of the problem of analyticity the notion of an artificial language with semantical rules is a *feu follet par excellence*. Semantical rules determining the analytic statements of an artificial language are of interest only in so far as we already understand the notion of analyticity; they are of no help in gaining this understanding.

Appeal to hypothetical languages of an artificially simple kind could conceivably be useful in clarifying analyticity, if the mental or behavioural or cultural factors relevant to analyticity—whatever they may be—were somehow sketched into the simplified model. But a model which takes analyticity merely as an irreducible character is unlikely to throw light on the problem of explicating analyticity.

It is obvious that truth in general depends on both language and extralinguistic fact. The statement 'Brutus killed Ceasar' would be false if the world had been different in certain ways, but it would also be false if the word 'killed' happened rather to have the sense of 'begat'. Thus one is tempted to suppose in general that the truth of a statement is somehow analysable into a linguistic component and a factual component. Given this supposition, it next seems reasonable that in some statements the factual component should be null; and these are the analytic statements. But, for all its *a priori* reasonableness, a boundary between analytic and synthetic statements simply has not been drawn. That there is such a distinction to be drawn at all is an unempirical dogma of empiricists, a metaphysical article of faith.

5. *The Verification Theory and Reductionism*

In the course of these sombre reflections we have taken a dim view first of the notion of meaning, then of the notion of cognitive synonymy, and finally of the notion of analyticity. But what, it may be asked, of the verification theory of meaning? This phrase has established itself so firmly as a catchword of empiricism that we should be very unscientific indeed not to look beneath it for a possible key to the problem of meaning and the associated problems.

The verification theory of meaning, which has been conspicuous in the literature from Peirce onward, is that the meaning of a statement is the method of empirically confirming or infirming it. An analytic statement is that limiting case which is confirmed no matter what.

As urged in § 1, we can as well pass over the question of meanings as entities and move straight to sameness of meaning, or synonymy. Then what the verification theory says is that statements are synonymous if and only if they are alike in point of method of empirical confirmation or infirmation.

This is an account of cognitive synonymy not of linguistic forms generally, but of statements. However, from the concept of synonymy of statements we could derive the concept of synonymy for other linguistic forms, by considerations somewhat similar to those at the end of § 3. Assuming the notion of 'word', indeed, we could explain any two forms as synonymous when the putting of the one form for an occurrence of the other in any statement (apart from occurrences within 'words') yields a synonymous statement. Finally, given the concept of synonymy thus for linguistic forms generally, we could define analyticity in terms of synonymy and logical truth as in § 1. For that matter, we could define analyticity more simply in terms of just synonymy of statements together with logical truth; it is not necessary to appeal to synonymy of linguistic forms other than statements. For a statement may be described as analytic simply when it is synonymous with a logically true statement.

So, if the verification theory can be accepted as an adequate account of statement synonymy, the notion of analyticity is saved after all. However, let us reflect. Statement synonymy is said to be likeness of method of empirical confirmation or infirmation. Just what are these methods which are to be compared for likeness? What, in other words, is the nature of the relation between a statement and the experiences which contribute to or detract from its confirmation?

The most naïve view of the relation is that it is one of direct report. This is *radical reductionism*. Every meaningful statement is held to be translatable into a statement (true or false) about immediate experience. Radical reductionism, in one form or another, well antedates the verification theory of meaning explicitly so called. Thus Locke and Hume held that every idea must either originate directly in sense experience or else be compounded of ideas thus originating; and taking a hint from Tooke we might rephrase this doctrine in semantical jargon by saying that a term, to be significant at all, must be either a name of a sense datum or a compound of such names or an abbreviation of such a compound. So stated, the doctrine remains ambiguous as between sense data as sensory events and sense data as sensory qualities; and it remains vague as to the admissible ways of compounding. Moreover, the doctrine is unnecessarily and intolerably restrictive in the term-by-term critique which it imposes. More reasonably, and without yet exceeding the limits of what I have called radical reductionism, we may take full statements as our significant units —thus demanding that our statements as wholes be translatable into sense-datum language, but not that they be translatable term by term.

This emendation would unquestionably have been welcome to Locke and Hume and Tooke, but historically it had to await an important reorientation in semantics—the reorientation whereby the primary vehicle of meaning came to be seen no longer in the term but in the statement. This reorientation, explicit in Frege ([1] § 60), underlies Russell's concept of incomplete symbols defined in use; also it is implicit in the verification theory of meaning, since the objects of verification are statements.

Radical reductionism, conceived now with statements as units, set itself the task of specifying a sense-datum language and showing how to translate the rest of significant discourse, statement by statement, into it. Carnap embarked on this project in the *Aufbau*.

The language which Carnap adopted as his starting-point was not a sense-datum language in the narrowest conceivable sense, for it included also the notations of logic, up through higher set theory. In effect it included the whole language of pure mathematics. The ontology implicit in it (that is, the range of values of its variables) embraced not only sensory events but classes, classes of classes, and so on. Empiricists there are who would boggle at such prodigality. Carnap's starting-point is very parsimonious, however, in its extralogical or sensory part. In a series of constructions in which he exploits the resources of modern logic with much ingenuity, Carnap succeeds in defining a wide array of important additional sensory concepts which, but for his constructions, one would not have dreamed were definable on so slender a basis. He was the first empiricist who, not content with asserting the reducibility of science to terms of immediate experience, took serious steps toward carrying out the reduction.

If Carnap's starting-point is satisfactory, still his constructions were, as he himself stressed, only a fragment of the full programme. The construction of even the simplest statements about the physical world was left in a sketchy state. Carnap's suggestions on this subject were, despite their sketchiness, very suggestive. He explained spatio-temporal point-instants as quadruples of real numbers and envisaged assignment of sense qualities to point-instants according to certain canons. Roughly summarized, the plan was that qualities should be assigned to point-instants in such a way as to achieve the laziest world compatible with our experience. The principle of least action was to be our guide in constructing a world from experience.

Carnap did not seem to recognize, however, that his treatment of physical objects fell short of reduction not merely through sketchiness, but in principle. Statements of the form 'Quality q is at point-instant x; y; z; t' were, according to his canons, to be apportioned truth values in such a way as to maximize and minimize certain over-all features, and with growth of experience the truth values were to be progressively revised in the same spirit. I think this is a good schematization (deliberately over-simplified, to be sure) of what science really does; but it provides no indication, not even the sketchiest, of how a statement of the form 'Quality q is at x; y; z; t' could ever be translated into Carnap's initial language of sense data and logic. The connective 'is at' remains an added undefined connective; the canons counsel us in its use but not in its elimination.

Carnap seems to have appreciated this point afterward; for in his later writings he abandoned all notion of the translatability of statements about the physical world into statements about immediate experience. Reductionism in its radical form has long since ceased to figure in Carnap's philosophy.

But the dogma of reductionism has, in a subtler and more tenuous form, continued to influence the thought of empiricists. The notion lingers that to each statement, or each synthetic statement, there is associated a unique range of possible sensory events such that the occurrence of any of them would add to the likelihood of truth of the statement, and that there is associated also another unique range of possible sensory events whose occurrence would detract from that likelihood. This notion is of course implicit in the verification theory of meaning.

The dogma of reductionism survives in the supposition that each statement, taken in isolation from its fellows, can admit of confirmation or infirmation at all. My counter-suggestion, issuing esentially from Carnap's doctrine of the physical world in the *Aufbau*, is that our statements about the external world face the tribunal of sense experience not individually but only as a corporate body.

The dogma of reductionism, even in its attenuated form, is intimately connected with the other dogma—that there is a cleavage between the analytic and the synthetic. We have found ourselves led, indeed, from the latter problem to the former through the verification theory of meaning. More directly, the one dogma clearly supports the other in this way: as long as it is taken to be significant in general to speak of the confirmation and infirmation of a statement, it seems significant to speak also of a limiting kind of statement which is vacuously confirmed, *ipso facto*, come what may; and such a statement is analytic.

The two dogmas are, indeed, at root identical. We lately reflected that in general the truth of statements does obviously depend both upon language and upon extralinguistic fact; and we noted that this obvious circumstance carries in its train, not logically but all too naturally, a feeling that the truth of a statement is somehow analysable into a linguistic component and a factual component. The factual component must, if we are empiricists, boil down to a range of confirmatory experiences. In the extreme case where the lingusitic component is all that matters, a true statement is analytic. But I hope we are now impressed with how stubbornly the distinction between analytic and synthetic has resisted any straightforward drawing. I am impressed also, apart from prefabricated examples of black and white balls in an urn, with how baffling the problem has always been of arriving at any explicit theory of the empirical confirmation of a synthetic statement. My present suggestion is that it is nonsense, and the root of much nonsense, to speak of a linguistic component and factual component in the truth of any individual statement. Taken collectively, science has its double dependence upon language and experience; but this duality is not significantly traceable into the statements of science taken one by one.

The idea of defining a symbol in use was, as remarked, an advance over the impossible term-by-term empiricism of Locke and Hume. The statement, rather than the term, came with Frege to be recognized as the unit accountable to an empiricist critique. But what I am now urging is that even in taking the statement as unit we have drawn our grid too finely. The unit of empirical significance is the whole of science.

6. *Empiricism without the Dogmas*

The totality of our so-called knowledge or beliefs, from the most casual matters of geography and history to the profoundest laws of atomic physics or even of pure mathematics and logic, is a man-made fabric which impinges on experience only along the edges. Or, to change the figure, total science is like a field of force whose boundary conditions are experience. A conflict with experience at the periphery occasions readjustments in the interior of the field. Truth values have to be redistributed over some of our statements. Re-evaluation of some statements entails re-evaluation of others, because of their logical interconnexions—the logical laws being in turn simply certain further statements of the system, certain further elements of the field. Having re-evaluated one statement we must re-evaluate some others, which may be statements logically connected with the first or may be the statements of logical connexions themselves. But the total field is so underdetermined by its boundary conditions, experience, that there is much latitude of choice as to what statements to re-evaluate in the light of any single contrary experience. No particular experiences are linked with any particular statements in the interior of the field, except indirectly through considerations of equilibrium affecting the field as a whole.

If this view is right, it is misleading to speak of the empirical content of an individual statement—especially if it is a statement at all remote from the experiential periphery of the field. Furthermore, it becomes folly to seek a boundary between synthetic statements, which hold contingently on experience, and analytic statements, which hold come what may. Any statement can be

E

held true come what may, if we make drastic enough adjustments elsewhere in the system. Even a statement very close to the periphery can be held true in the face of recalcitrant experience by pleading hallucination or by amending certain statements of the kind called logical laws. Conversely, by the same token, no statement is immune to revision. Revision even of the logical law of the excluded middle has been proposed as a means of simplifying quantum mechanics; and what difference is there in principle between such a shift and the shift whereby Kepler superseded Ptolemy, or Einstein Newton, or Darwin Aristotle?

For vividness I have been speaking in terms of varying distances from a sensory periphery. Let me try now to clarify this notion without metaphor. Certain statements, though *about* physical objects and not sense experience, seem peculiarly germane to sense experience—and in a selective way: some statements to some experience, others to others. Such statements, especially germane to particular experiences, I picture as near the periphery. But in this relation of 'germaneness' I envisage nothing more than a loose association reflecting the relative likelihood, in practice, of our choosing one statement rather than another for revision in the event of recalcitrant experience. For example, we can imagine recalcitrant experiences to which we would surely be inclined to accommodate our system by re-evaluating just the statement that there are brick houses on Elm Street, together with related statements on the same topic. We can imagine other recalcitrant experiences to which we would be inclined to accommodate our system by re-evaluating just the statement that there are no centaurs, along with kindred statements. A recalcitrant experience can, I have urged, be accommodated by any of various alternative re-evaluations in various alternative quarters of the total system; but, in the cases which we are now imagining, our natural tendency to disturb the total system as little as possible would lead us to focus our revisions upon these specific statements concerning brick houses or centaurs. These statements are felt, therefore, to have a sharper empirical reference than highly theoretical statements of physics or logic or ontology. The latter statements may be thought of as relatively centrally located within the total network, meaning merely that little preferential connexion with any particular sense data obtrudes itself.

As an empiricist I continue to think of the conceptual scheme of science as a tool, ultimately, for predicting future experience in the light of past experience. Physical objects are conceptually imported into the situation as convenient intermediaries—not by definition in terms of experience, but simply as irreducible posits comparable, epistemologically, to the gods of Homer. For my part I do, *qua* lay physicist, believe in physical objects and not in Homer's gods; and I consider it a scientific error to believe otherwise. But in point of epistemological footing the physical objects and the gods differ only in degree and not in kind. Both sorts of entities enter our conception only as cultural posits. The myth of physical objects is epistemologically superior to most in that it has proved more efficacious than other myths as a device for working a manageable structure into the flux of experience.

Positing does not stop with macroscopic physical objects. Objects at the atomic level are posited to make the laws of macroscopic objects, and ultimately the laws of experience, simpler and more manageable; and we need not expect or demand full definition of atomic and subatomic entities in terms of macroscopic ones, any more than definition of macroscopic things in terms of sense data. Science is a continuation of common sense, and it continues the common-sense expedient of swelling ontology to simplify theory.

Physical objects, small and large, are not the only posits. Forces are another example; and indeed we are told nowadays that the boundary between energy and matter is obsolete. Moreover, the abstract entities which are the substance of mathematics— ultimately classes and classes of classes and so on up—are another posit in the same spirit. Epistemologically these are myths on the same footing with physical objects and gods, neither better nor worse except for differences in the degree to which they expedite our dealings with sense experiences.

The over-all algebra of rational and irrational numbers is under-determined by the algebra of rational numbers, but is smoother and more convenient; and it includes the algebra of rational numbers as a jagged or gerrymandered part. Total science, mathematical and natural and human, is similarly but more extremely under-determined by experience. The edge of the system must be kept square with experience; the rest, with all its elaborate myths or fictions, has as its objective the simplicity of laws.

Ontological questions, under this view, are on a par with questions of natural science. Consider the question whether to countenance classes as entities. This, as I have argued elsewhere, is the question whether to quantify with respect to variables which take classes as values. Now Carnap [6] has maintained that this is a question not of matters of fact but of choosing a convenient language form, a convenient conceptual scheme or framework for science. With this I agree, but only on the proviso that the same be conceded regarding scientific hypotheses generally. Carnap ([6], p. 32 n.) has recognized that he is able to preserve a double standard for ontological questions and scientific hypotheses only by assuming an absolute distinction between the analytic and the synthetic; and I need not say again that this is a distinction which I reject.

The issue over there being classes seems more a question of convenient conceptual scheme; the issue over there being centaurs, or brick houses on Elm Street, seems more a question of fact. But I have been urging that this difference is only one of degree, and that it turns upon our vaguely pragmatic inclination to adjust one strand of the fabric of science rather than another in accommodating some particular recalcitrant experience. Conservatism figures in such choices, and so does the quest for simplicity.

Carnap, Lewis, and others take a pragmatic stand on the question of choosing between language forms, scientific frameworks; but their pragmatism leaves off at the imagined boundary between the analytic and the synthetic. In repudiating such a boundary I espouse a more thorough pragmatism. Each man is given a scientific heritage plus a continuing barrage of sensory stimulation; and the considerations which guide him in warping his scientific heritage to fit his continuing sensory promptings are, where rational, pragmatic.

CHAPTER V

ARE NECESSARY TRUTHS TRUE BY CONVENTION?[1]

William Kneale

White's Professor of Moral Philosophy, University of Oxford

I once heard an American philosopher say of a colleague: 'He was an interesting man in discussion until he went to Cambridge for a sabbatical year. After that he got so he couldn't understand.' Whether the change described by this remark was a loss or gain for philosophy I cannot say, but it was evidently annoying to my informant; and this is not surprising, for philosophers are always at their most irritating when they say they cannot understand. It is therefore with some misgiving that I announce I have gotten so I cannot understand the question we have been set to discuss.

If words are to be taken in their ordinary senses, it seems obvious that necessary truths cannot be true by convention. In common speech the word 'necessary' means much the same as 'indispensable', 'inevitable', 'without any possible alternative'. Consider, for example, its use in the opening statement of the Athanasian creed: 'Whosoever will be saved: before all things it is necessary that he hold the Catholick Faith. Which Faith except every one do keep whole and undefiled: without doubt he shall perish everlastingly.' Admittedly the phrase 'necessary truth' belongs to philosophers' jargon rather than to common speech, but its origin is clear enough. Philosophers say that a proposition is a necessary truth if it is impossible that it should not be true, i.e. if there is no possible alternative. But in common usage the phrase 'by convention' always implies the possibility of an alternative. If someone tells me that it is only convention which makes black the colour of mourning in Europe, I understand him to mean that the connexion established in our civilization is not

---

[1] This paper was originally published as the third contribution to a symposium in the *Proceedings of the Aristotelian Society*, Supplementary Volume XXI (1947). For the present reprinting the author has corrected some errors in the examples.

inevitable; and I think it very good evidence for his assertion, when he goes on to tell of some people on the other side of the world who use scarlet where we should use black. It seems clear, therefore, that anyone who speaks of necessary truths as true by convention is guilty of self-contradiction, unless one or more of the terms he uses has a special sense in this context. Taken according to ordinary usage, his statement means that truths without alternatives nevertheless have alternatives.

It is rather surprising that neither Mr Britton nor Mr Urmson has anything to say about the appearance of paradox in the question we have been set to discuss. Mr Britton does not speak of alternatives at all until the end of his paper, but when he does, he boldly heads his section: 'Alternatives to the Necessary Truths'. Mr Urmson, after insisting, quite rightly, that the thesis of this section is essential to the doctrine that necessary truths are true by convention, goes on to state that, for some necessary truths at least, there obviously are alternatives. I assume nevertheless that neither of them is guilty of the absurdity to which I have just referred, and so I must look for some special interpretation which makes the question debatable.

In the introduction to his paper Mr Britton makes it clear that when he talks of necessary propositions as true by convention he is using words in a special way, although not in a way private to himself. Necessary propositions, he tells us, are not propositions in the ordinary sense, and they cannot be said to have truth in the ordinary sense. In other words, we have here a kind of metaphor which may be seriously misleading to persons who do not understand the complexity of their own language. What is commonly called the assertion of a necessary proposition is really one way of formulating (and teaching) a rule, a way which involves the construction of an illustrative sentence. For in practice the acceptance of a proposition as necessary is shown by 'the adoption of certain procedures of inference or transition from one statement to another'. Although (as Mr Urmson says) the views expressed here by Mr Britton do not involve the conclusion that all necessary truths are true by convention, they do at least allow him to put the conventionalist thesis in a new way. He can now say that, when he uses the paradoxical expression 'alternatives to the necessary truths', he is referring only to the possibility of adopting procedures or rules other than those we have adopted. And he does in fact follow this line of argument in the last section of his paper. Having insisted that our adoption of a certain set of rules is an empirical fact, he there draws the conclusion that we might have different rules.

When Mr Britton speaks of a necessary truth, he means apparently a truism such as 'If a person is a grandparent, then he is the parent of a parent'. And when he speaks of a transformation rule or of a procedure for passing from one statement to another, he means apparently a rule of usage such as might be expressed in a sentence of the command form, e.g. 'For "parent of a parent" write "grandparent" '. I think that the truistic character of truisms is to be explained by the rules of usage of the symbols which they involve, and that truisms are often uttered, as Mr Britton says, for the purpose of drawing attention to rules of usage. But I do not think that the rules of usage of symbols are what Mr Britton supposes them to be, nor yet that his account of the relation between truisms and rules of usage is enough to show why truisms are said to be necessarily true. Before examining the conventionalist thesis in the form which he has given to it, I must say something about these two points.

In the first place, rules of usage cannot properly be treated as positive commands to say this or that in certain circumstances. I hope that I use the word 'grandparent' correctly, but I certainly do not observe a rule of writing (or saying) 'grandparent' whenever I see (or hear) the words 'parent of a parent'. Why should I? What would be the value of conforming to such a rule? The rules which I do observe are rather such as might be expressed by sentences like 'Do not say "grandparent" where you are not allowed to say "parent of a parent" '. In short, all rules of usage which determine meaning are prohibitions. This is true not only of dictionary definitions like that just considered, but also of ostensive definitions. A child does not yet know how to use the word 'red' unless he has learnt that he is not to apply it to green things. And there is nothing mysterious in this restrictive character of linguistic rules. Nature provides us with a disposition to chatter freely: we make languages for ourselves by adopting rules which canalize that activity. Once this point has been realized, my second point, i.e. that about truisms, can be made quite simply. A statement is truistic in a given language if, and only if, (*a*) it consists of symbols for which restrictive rules exist in that language, and (*b*) all statements inconsistent with it are forbidden by the rules of that language. It is not surprising that such a statement should be said to be *necessarily* true, for there is indeed no alternative to its truth. Knowledge of the rules enables us to certify this, apart from all reference to experience.

If this account of the matter (or something like this) is correct, what are we to say of the suggestion that there might be different rules of usage for our symbols? Taken in the most natural and obvious way, this remark is a platitude. Everyone now admits that linguistic rules are conventional—at least in a wide sense of that word which does not commit us to saying that they were adopted by a deliberate act, like the rules of cricket and bridge. We can suppose, for example, that the sound 'green' might have been subjected by Englishmen to the same restrictive rules as now apply in English to the sound 'scarlet', and we can say that if this had happened, the set of sounds 'All green things are red' would have been a necessarily true statement. But is this *all* that the conventionalists wish to maintain? When they tell us that necessary truths are true by convention, they speak with an air of conscious audacity, as though they were waiting for an explosion of shocked disapproval. Surely their doctrine is something more than a tame consequence of the universally accepted view that linguistic rules are conventional. But what exactly is the novelty they wish to add?

I suspect that some philosophers who profess conventionalism may be under the impression that we can vary the rules of usage of our symbols at will *without altering the meaning* of those symbols. According to this interpretation conventionalism would at least be something startling; but a little reflexion shows that it would also be quite untenable. For sounds and shapes acquire meaning only by being made subject to restrictive rules of usage, and an alteration of the rules must alter the meaning. If I decide to allow inference from 'This is green' to 'This is red' (i.e. if I lay it down that 'This is red' must not be denied when 'This is green' is asserted), I adopt a new code in which one or other of the sounds 'green' and 'red' no longer has the same meaning as in English. If, on the other hand, I decide to use these sounds with the meanings that they have in English, I am not at liberty to change the rules which govern their usage. I cannot, for example, abandon the rule which forbids their use in conjunction.

What is more, if there exist in any other language two words which fulfil the same roles as 'green' and 'red' fulfil in English, those words must be subject to corresponding restrictions.

Since these points seem very obvious, when once they have been stated, it may perhaps be doubted whether anyone has ever maintained the absurdity mentioned above. My reason for attributing it to some conventionalists is the fact that they talk of necessary *propositions* as true by linguistic convention. The proposition that $2 + 2 = 4$ is not itself a set of symbols, although we must use symbols from some language in order to refer to it. If, then, anyone supposes that the truth value of this proposition could be altered by an alteration of the rules for the use of symbols '2', '+', '=' and '4', he must be assuming in a muddled way that a change of rules of usage which sufficed to alter the truth value of the *formula* '$2 + 2 = 4$' might nevertheless leave it still expressing the proposition that $2 + 2 = 4$.

I derive no help, therefore, from Mr Britton's references to rules. If conventionalism is the doctrine that we might have adopted other rules for the use of the sounds and marks we now use as symbols, it is platitudinous. If it is the doctrine that we could vary all the rules of usage of our symbols while leaving their meanings unchanged, it is absurd. I hesitate to identify Mr Britton's thesis with either doctrine, but I cannot find any third interpretation.

Mr Urmson insists, quite rightly, that the possibility of having alternatives is implied by the doctrine that necessary truths are true by convention. His own view seems to be that some necessary truths have alternatives whereas others have not. Indeed, he thinks that, if the conventionalists confined themselves to saying that *some* necessary truths have alternatives, their contention would be obviously correct, because they could settle the matter by producing indisputable examples. He writes: 'We have several alternative geometries, and commutative and non-commutative algebra, that is to say, there is an algebra in which "$a \times b = b \times a$" is a necessary truth, and an algebra in which it is not.' Now in a discussion like ours an agreed example is very valuable, and I agree with Mr Urmson at least in thinking that his references to geometry and algebra are fair examples of the detailed assertions that conventionalists may be expected to make. It appears to me that a great deal of modern talk about the depen-

E*

dence of necessary truths on convention has been inspired by reflexion on the developments of mathematics which he mentions. It is important, therefore, to consider these examples carefully. Here, if anywhere, it seems we may expect to discover the correct interpretation of the conventionalist thesis.

When Mr Urmson speaks of alternative geometries, I do not think he is referring to the distinctions between topology, projective geometry and metrical geometry. For these studies are alternatives only in the sense in which physics and chemistry are alternatives, i.e. a person may study one without studying the other; and perhaps even this analogy is not quite appropriate, since the topological properties of figures *are* presupposed by their projective properties, and these in turn by their metrical properties. We certainly do not have to *choose* between topology and metrical geometry, holding to the one and rejecting the other, any more than we have to choose between the calculus of unanalysed propositions and the calculus of propositional functions in mathematical logic. I assume, therefore, that the several alternative geometries mentioned by Mr Urmson are the geometries which have been distinguished in the course of discussions about Euclid's parallels axiom. This is obviously the most hopeful interpretation of his example.

For simplicity let us confine attention to Lobachevsky's geometry, and for convenience of reference let us introduce short names for certain propositions according to the following scheme:

'$\mathscr{E}$' for Euclid's axiom of parallels, or rather for Playfair's substitute, i.e. for the proposition that through a given point there can be drawn one and only one line parallel to a given straight line;

'$\mathscr{R}$' for the conjunction of the other axioms of Euclidean geometry;

'$\mathscr{L}$' for Lobachevsky's axiom that more than one line can be drawn through a given point parallel to a given straight line.

At one time it was thought that $\mathscr{E}$ and $\mathscr{R}$ were both necessary truths. Non-Euclidean geometry started with the attempts of Saccheri and others to improve Euclid's exposition by showing that $\mathscr{E}$ followed from $\mathscr{R}$ and so need not be taken as an axiom. Some mathematicians thought that this could be established by an *ad absurdum* proof in which the conjunction of $\mathscr{R}$ with the negation of $\mathscr{E}$ would be found to entail a self-contradiction.

But the effort to construct such a proof failed; for no self-contradiction was derived from the conjunction of 𝓡 with the negation of 𝓔. On the contrary it was presently realized that 𝓛 could be conjoined with 𝓡 to produce a self-consistent system. The admission of 𝓛 as a real alternative to 𝓔 implies, however, abandonment of the view that 𝓔 is a necessary truth of mathematics; and so the word 'axiom' is now to be understood in all geometry, whether Euclidean or non-Euclidean, as equivalent to 'postulate'. Where, then, are the alternatives to necessary truths which Mr Urmson suggests we may find in non-Euclidean geometry? Surely not in such a statement as 'If 𝓡 and 𝓛 are both true, the interior angles of a triangle are together less than two right angles'. For this is in no way inconsistent with the corresponding statement of Euclidean geometry, 'If 𝓡 and 𝓔 are both true, the interior angles of a triangle are together equal to two right angles.' We do not have to choose between these two hypothetical statements. On the contrary, we can and do assert both. In short, where there are real alternatives, i.e. in the composition of axiom sets, there is no necessity, and where there is real necessity, i.e. in the entailment of theorems by axioms, there are no alternatives. The moral to be drawn by philosophers from the development of non-Euclidean geometry is nothing like conventionalism, but simply the cautionary remark that propositions which are not self-evidently necessary may sometimes appear so because we have not tried hard enough to conceive alternatives.

Let us now consider the alternatives which are said to be found in the development of algebras. Mr Urmson states that in one algebra '$a \times b = b \times a$' is a necessary truth, in another not. Clearly he cannot be thinking here of abstract algebras, i.e. uninterpreted calculi. For the expression '$a \times b = b \times a$', considered as part of an abstract algebra, is not a necessary truth, or indeed a truth of any kind, but merely an uninterpreted formula. He must therefore have in mind the various ways in which the symbol '$\times$' is used in connexion with numbers of different types. In order to understand this we must make clear to ourselves what we have done with this symbol in the course of the development of mathematics.

Historically, we all begin by using the sign '$\times$' for an operation performed on natural numbers. Then we go on to use it with signed integers, rational numbers, real numbers and complex numbers as its operands. For a rigorous development of mathematics all algebraic laws like the commutative law of multiplication should be proved afresh at each stage. The expression '$a \times b = b \times a$' takes on a new sense when its variables have a new range of values; and we have no right to assume without more ado that, because it holds at some lower stage, it will hold also at the next higher stage. There are, indeed, a number of different universal propositions expressed together with systematic ambiguity by this formula as it is used in a non-rigorous development of mathematics. Multiplication of complex numbers is *not the same operation* as the multiplication of numbers of any lower type, although the propositions which hold true of it can be expressed by sentences of the same pattern as are used for expressing truths about multiplication at lower levels. The history of mathematics shows other examples of the interest of mathematicians in retaining old patterns of expression when dealing with new entities.

If we take all this for granted without a proper appreciation of our own procedure, we may be surprised when presently we find ourselves led on to talk of hyper-complex numbers for which the commutative law of multiplication does not hold. But we have no good reason for amazement. At this level multiplication has to be defined afresh, and there is no inconsistency whatsoever between our old statement '$a \times b = b \times a$', where 'a' and 'b' mark gaps for the symbols of numbers of any type up to and including complex numbers, and our new statement '$a \times b \neq b \times a$', where '$a$' and '$b$' mark gaps for the symbols of hyper-complex numbers (e.g. quaternions). Since the mark '$\times$' does not mean the same in the two different contexts, there is no sense in talking as though we had discovered necessary truths which were alternatives to each other. What we have found are only alternative uses of the same mark. If we used a different mark to symbolize the operation which can be performed on hyper-complex numbers and ceased to call these entities numbers at all—as well we might, the whole mystery would disappear. Such puzzle as there is we have made for ourselves by using old symbols in a new situation with no more justification than a partial analogy.

I can find nothing then in these mathematical examples which helps me to understand the conventionalist thesis in philosophy. What exactly is the moral Mr Urmson wishes to draw from them?

Both Mr Britton and Mr Urmson cite in support of their view a recent paper by Dr Waismann on the question 'Are there Alternative Logics?'[1] I have read this paper several times with the pleasure which I get from reading anything written by Dr Waismann, but I confess I do not understand why he should link his views with conventionalism, as he does in his first paragraph. He has indeed shown that there are alternative logics, but only in a very wide sense of the word 'alternative' which makes it equivalent to 'distinguishable' and I doubt whether this is enough to satisfy those who call themselves conventionalists. In order to make my point as clearly as I could wish, it would be necessary to consider each of his examples in turn, but this would take much too long, and I shall therefore notice only two which seem to me especially interesting.

The first example I wish to consider is the system of intuitionist logic first sketched by Brouwer[2] and then later formalized by Heyting.[3] This is undoubtedly different from the system of classical logic, i.e. the system expounded with varying degrees of generality by Aristotle, Boole, Frege, Russell and Lewis, and yet it can properly be described as logic, since it provides patterns of valid inference. But what exactly is its difference from classical logic? All the exponents, following Brouwer, say that its peculiarity is the dropping of the law of excluded middle. This seems to me a very curious way of putting the matter. It is true that the new logic can be obtained from classical logic by an omission, but it is surely a mistake to suggest that the new logic contains a sign with the ordinary meaning of 'not' and yet differs from classical logic in failing to prescribe for this sign one of the rules which give 'not' its ordinary meaning. It is more correct, I think, to say that intuitionist logic contains no symbol equivalent to 'not' and therefore cannot contain the law of excluded middle or any other logical principle concerned with ordinary negation. This interpretation is suggested by the phraseology of Brouwer in some of the papers where he gave the first informal exposition

---

[1] *Proceedings of the Aristotelian Society*, Vol. XLVI (1945–6), p. 77.

[2] E.g. 'Intuitionistische Mengenlehre', *Jahresbericht des Deutschen Mathematiker-Vereins*, 28 (1920), and 'Über die Bedeutung des Satzes vom ausgeschlossenen Dritten', *Journal für Mathematik*, 154 (1924).

[3] 'Die formalen Regeln der intuitionistischen Logik', *Sitzungsberichte der Preussischen Akademie*, 1930.

of the system. Instead of talking of negation, as one might expect
if the question at issue were about the traditional law of excluded
middle, he speaks of absurdity. He says, for example, that we can
always argue from the truth of a proposition to the absurdity of
its absurdity but not *vice versa*.[1] We have here a clue which enables
us to understand how the new system is related to the classical.

Let us suppose that we have a version of the modal system
called by Lewis S4, with '$\sim$', '&', and '$\square$' as primitive symbols
signifying respectively negation, conjunction, and necessity. It
is well known that with these all the concepts of the ordinary
modal logic of propositions can be defined. Let us, then, suppose
further that the symbols '$\daleth$', '$\wedge$', '$\vee$', and '$\supset$' have been introduced according to the following rules of abbreviation

$$\text{'}\daleth P\text{'} \quad \text{for '}\square\sim\square P\text{'}$$
$$\text{'}P \wedge Q\text{'} \text{ for '}\square P \mathbin{\&} \square Q\text{'}$$
$$\text{'}P \vee Q\text{'} \text{ for '}\sim(\sim\square P \mathbin{\&} \sim\square Q)\text{'}$$
$$\text{'}P \supset Q\text{'} \text{ for '}\sim(\square P \mathbin{\&} \sim\square Q)\text{'}$$

and that all the principles of S4 which can be formulated by use
of these abbreviating signs are so formulated. If we now strike
out from the system all formulae which can be formulated only
by means of the three original symbols (as distinct from the new
abbreviating signs), what remain are the formulae of Heyting's
system, though these must naturally be rearranged for presentation in the order of his calculus.[2] In this latter system the four
signs which we introduced for purposes of abbreviation are now
independent, i.e. none of them can be defined in terms of the
others, but all their mutual relations remain unaltered, and so
they may be said to retain the same sense as in the fuller system.
There are indeed some logical theses concerning these four logical
notions which cannot be asserted in the lesser system, but this
means only that a symbol which is required for their formulation
cannot be provided from within the resources of the system.

Since the lesser system does not contain an ordinary negation
sign, it does not allow for the statement of the classical law of

[1] 'Intuitionistische   Zerlegung   mathematischer   Grundbegriffe',
Jahresbericht des Deutschen Mathematiker-Vereins, 33 (1925).

[2] K. Gödel, 'Eine Interpretation des intuitionistischen Aussagen-
kalküls', *Ergebnisse eines mathematischen Kolloquiums*, iv (1933).

excluded middle, or indeed of any other thesis concerning simple negation. Exponents of the system usually speak of '$p \vee \neg p$' as a formulation of the principle of excluded middle, and say it is characteristic of their system that it does not contain this formula either as an axiom or as a theorem. They are correct, of course, in saying that the formula is alien, but I wish to maintain that they are mistaken in supposing that it is a formulation of the law of excluded middle, as that is ordinarily understood. According to the interpretation which is suggested by Brouwer's terminology and confirmed by the derivation I have just outlined, the formula '$p \vee \neg p$' means the same as '$\sim (\sim \Box p \mathbin{\&} \sim \Box \Box \sim \Box p)$', which can be reduced in Lewis's S4 to '$\sim (\sim \Box p \mathbin{\&} \sim \Box \sim \Box p)$' and signifies in ordinary English 'Either it is necessary that p or it is necessary that it is not necessary that p'. In fact it is a version of the strong reduction principle which gives its peculiar character to the system of modal logic called by Lewis S5.

It seems then that intuitionist logic is a fragment of a well-known system of modal logic rather than an alternative to classical logic in the strict sense of something incompatible with the latter. But why, it may be asked, should the intuitionist construct this narrow calculus for himself? Is it because he wishes to reject all arguments that cannot be presented within this calculus? I think not. Brouwer has stated repeatedly that he has no objection to the law of excluded middle when its application is restricted to propositions about finite sets. This is as much as to say that he does not entirely reject that part of classical logic which is excluded from the intuitionist calculus. His thesis is concerned only with propositions about infinite sets, where it seems difficult, and perhaps even impossible, to distinguish between truth and necessity; and what he says is that we should not try to establish any such proposition by assuming that it is either necessary or necessarily not necessary. Now although the assumption which he rejects has not always been regarded as a truth of logic, it is commonly thought to hold for propositions of the kind in which he is interested, namely those of pure mathematics. For anyone who claims that every mathematical problem is soluble in principle asserts in effect that any proposition concerned solely with notions of logic and pure mathematics is either necessary or necessarily not necessary. And so Brouwer's thesis comes to this: when trying to solve a mathematical problem we are not entitled to use any argument which rests on the assumption that every problem is soluble.[1] Whether or not he is right in seeking to impose this restriction on mathematical proofs seems to me at least a sensible question, and I do not see how it helps to say that we can settle the matter as we choose by arbitrary convention.

The second of Dr Waismann's examples which I wish to consider is that of many-valued logic. In recent years a number of logicians have tried to work out a many-valued system of logic, but none has won general acceptance for his system, because so far none has been able to interpret his calculus in a way which justifies him in calling it a new logic. Dr Waismann suggests, however, that a many-valued system which deserves the name of logic can be constructed with the notion of graduated negation. It may perhaps be objected that the illustrations by which he tries to show the need for such a system are all of a rather limited kind and so do not entitle us to talk of the proposed calculus as logic. For there are only a few special fields, such as the estimation of measurements, in which we can talk reasonably of infinitely many degrees of falsity, and logic is not concerned with what is peculiar to special kinds of subject-matter. I shall not try to express an opinion on this question, but content myself with pointing out that, if a many-valued logic can be developed on the basis of Dr Waismann's interesting suggestion, it will be related to classical logic much as S4 is related to intuitionist logic, that is to say, it will contain classical logic as a proper part and provide for the definition of a concept which is taken as fundamental in classical logic.

For simplicity let us consider first a three-valued system in which '~', the symbol of ordinary negation, does not occur but there are instead two primitive symbols, say '*' and '!', which divide the work of negation between them. In ordinary English these two symbols may perhaps be translated by the phrases 'not quite' and 'not at all', but such translation is misleading if it suggests that the symbols have sense only through a definition which contains the word 'not' or some equivalent; within the system they are to be taken as undefined. If, however, there exists within the system a symbol of disjunction (i.e. a symbol with rules *analogous* to those of disjunction within the ordinary

[1] Cf. his 'Intuitionistische Betrachtung über den Formalismus', *Sitzungsberichte der Preussischen Akademie*, 1928.

two-valued system), ordinary negation can be re-introduced by definition as a disjunction of the two operations which have been said to divide its work. We then have '$\sim P$' in our system as an abbreviation for '$* P \lor ! P$'. In a system with more than three truth values the definition of simple negation would naturally be more complicated, but the mere number of distinguishable truth values would not introduce any new difficulty of principle. On the contrary it should make clearer what is happening. In this connexion Dr Waismann himself writes: 'One might here apprehend ordinary negation as an equivalent of a sum of operations in a logic with infinitely many truth values. In other words, ordinary negation can be split up into an infinite disjunction of precise operations; I say precise because each of these operations leaves the communication value of the original statement unaltered. By extending the disjunction over an increasing number of terms we "dilute" the original statement more and more; *the limit of this process of diluting is ordinary negation.* Thus certain features of ordinary logic are fully understood only in the light of many-valued logic.'[1] But this is surely as much as to say that, when we interpret a many-valued calculus in a way which justifies us in calling it logic, the calculus turns out to be an amplification and refinement of classical logic rather than an alternative in any strict sense. And if this is so, I do not see why we should suppose that talk of conventions will help to illuminate the situation.

Although I cannot understand the thesis of the conventionalists in detail, I think I can guess the reason why they try to explain necessary truth as a product of convention. They believe that in this way, and in this way only, they can escape from the dangers of talking about intellectual intuition. Now it must be admitted that philosophers who appeal to intuition often report different answers from their oracle. Some indeed report nonsense. It may therefore seem hard-headed to say that all necessity is *imposed* by our own legislation. But if this is the conventionalist's motive for developing his theory, he is doomed to disappointment. Whenever he hopes to get clarity and determinateness by setting out his rules and considering their implications, he will find that he is forced to rely once more on intellectual intuition, although this time it may be only insight into logical connexions. The effort to dispense with intellectual intuition is, indeed, an attempt

[1] In the article cited, pp. 90–1.

to dispense with all thinking; for anyone who notices that something is of a certain kind, e.g. red, must be intuitively aware of the mutual exclusion of some kinds, e.g. red and green. But the absurdity of the enterprise is especially clear in the limiting case just mentioned, where it is supposed that the conventionalist has only to apply rules of his own making.

Perhaps Mr Britton has this objection in mind when he insists that agreement is the sole test of correctness in the application of rules. His emphasis on this statement suggests that he is trying to be as thoroughly conventionalist as he can at a point where he anticipates attack. Now everyone will allow that if two attempts to apply a rule, whether made by different men or by one man at different times, yield different results, one at least must be faulty, whereas if two attempts yield the same result, there is some presumption that they are both correct. And it may even be said that agreement with other attempts is the sole *external* test of the correctness of any attempt to apply a rule. But it is surely conceivable that all the attempts to apply a given rule which are made within some finite period are incorrect together; and so the correctness of attempts to apply a rule cannot be *defined* as agreement between the results of the attempts. Yet nothing less would enable Mr Britton to evade the admission of a necessity which is not imposed by convention. For so long as we distinguish rules from descriptive generalizations about human behaviour and talk in the ordinary way of the correctness or incorrectness of attempts to apply them, we assume in effect that there are principles of logic independent of our conventions.

CHAPTER VI

THE LINGUISTIC THEORY OF *A PRIORI* PROPOSITIONS[1]

A. C. Ewing
Reader in Philosophy, University of Cambridge

The question I shall ask tonight is whether *a priori* propositions are 'true' and deductive reasoning 'valid' simply because to deny the *a priori* proposition or to refuse to accept the reasoning would be to contradict the rules of language or combine words in a way which according to the rules of language conveys no meaning. It is plain that, if such a view is adopted, it must mean the end of metaphysics in the old sense. That it would mean something more still, which would strike most of the members of the audience as a good deal worse, I hope to show in the course of this paper. I must warn my audience, however, that I shall not provide a rival *explanation* of *a priori* knowledge. I have no explanation of *a priori* knowledge to offer, nor do I think that it requires one, any more than empirical knowledge. I merely accept it as a fact that we can sometimes know that one proposition entails or one characteristic necessarily involves another. Why should we not have the power of seeing this, as we seem to have? Or do we know *a priori* the synthetic proposition that we cannot know *a priori* any synthetic propositions? All I wish to do in this paper is to refute attempts to reduce *a priori* reasoning and knowledge to something which they are not, and to supplement misleading analogies, which unless supplemented and thus counteracted obscure rather than help our understanding of the subject.

My friends at Cambridge are, however, very difficult people to argue with because, if challenged, they are apt to beat a strategic retreat and say that the principle under criticism is not put forward as a dogma or a truth to be believed, but as a method or a slogan which is not to be taken too literally but is useful as an epigrammatic way of emphasizing likeness or difference in the usage of words. Thus used, such principles as the verification

---

[1] *Proceedings of the Aristotelian Society*, New Series, 1939–40, Vol. XL. The author has shortened the original version of this paper. [Ed.]

principle and the principle I have mentioned concerning deductive reasoning and *a priori* propositions are claimed to be very valuable 'medicines for the cure of philosophical diseases'. (I am afraid I myself regard the remedy as much worse than the disease.) These philosophers may even say that they are not *asserting* anything when they talk as they do talk, but are merely pointing out and emphasizing a certain likeness between *a priori* principles and the rules of language or the rules of a game. If so, well and good. There is a certain analogy between the two things compared, and to emphasize it may be a useful medicine for certain philosophical diseases. But to emphasize the likeness without emphasizing the difference seems to me most misleading, and I think that the medicine, however useful for certain purposes, requires an antidote which I shall proceed to administer with the utmost of what poor medical skill I have at my command. So in considering what follows, the verificationist or logical positivist may, if he likes, look upon it not as a contradiction but as a supplementation of what he has to say. To be frank, however, I cannot myself help believing that even those exponents of the principle I am discussing who would, if challenged, say that it was merely methodological are apt to treat it in their own thoughts as if it were not merely a method but a dogma, and that the whole manner of their treatment of such problems is so different from that which I favour as to constitute an opposition as fundamental and as far-reaching in its effects as almost any that separates different philosophical schools, but, be that as it may, I claim that I can at any rate show that, whatever truths the metaphors of games and rules of language as applied to *a priori* propositions and deductive reasoning may suggest, there are also very important respects in which such metaphors give a totally misleading impression. My view is that it is, at the very least, far nearer the truth to say that *a priori* propositions and deductive reasoning give us new information about the real and that their necessity is quite independent of human convention than to say that they are based on language conventions and that they give no new information except perhaps about the use of words. Of course, if the philosophers who talk in this way are really not expressing any views or making any assertions, as they sometimes say, they cannot be refuted, but at least what they say suggests certain ideas and what I am doing is to supplement these ideas by suggesting others, though I am afraid I am not as modest as they are, and in suggesting these ideas do propose to make some assertions.

Now under what circumstances could an *a priori* proposition be true or a deductive inference valid if these depended merely on rules of language, and how could they be known to be true? They certainly cannot be learnt from books of grammar or dictionaries, but no doubt it can be retorted that people may learn the ordinary rules of grammar too without being taught them formally as such or finding them given in a book. But the fact that our knowledge of ordinary grammatical rules does not have the least tendency to make us think they express necessary logical truths should surely make us suspicious of the explanation given of *a priori* propositions. This appearance of necessity which differentiates *a priori* propositions from rules of language or games must be explained if the linguistic account of *a priori* propositions is to be at all plausible, and as far as I know nothing has really been done in this direction. My opponents cannot reply that the appearance of necessity in the propositions arises because it is an invariable empirical fact that everything we observe as being $5 + 7$ we find also to be 12 or that the same thing is never both red and green all over, because if, as they hold, the sentences '$5 + 7$ is sometimes not equal to 12' or 'something is both red and green all over' are meaningless combinations of words, there can be no sense in saying that it is an empirical fact that no red thing is ever green or that $5 + 7 = 12$.

How do we come to learn that the statement that a red thing is also green all over is always inadmissible? Not by learning it by heart in a book. Not by finding that it contains single words which have no meaning or that the words are arranged in a way which defies ordinary grammatical rules. Not by merely failing to understand the words—I cannot understand many statements in higher mathematics, but it would be the height of impertinence for me therefore to condemn them as logically absurd, and as regards the sentence 'the same thing is both red and green all over', I do understand the words perfectly well but use them to assert something false. Not by merely noting the fact that people do not use words in this way, for there are many sentences which in all probability have never been used by anybody and yet have a perfectly good meaning and are not logically absurd, e.g. 'on a planet of Sirius there is a mountain composed of cheese' or 'all rulers of states are experts in mathematical logic'. Not by noting that people do not make any statements which resemble *in form* 'the thing is both red and green all over', for in linguistic form at least this statement resembles the legitimate statement that a thing is both smooth and hard all over, and if we are to differentiate the form we must go far beyond linguistic considerations to the kind of qualities meant and see that different colours in the same thing at the same time are incompatible, while smoothness and hardness, different qualities given by the tactual sense, are not so. Not because they were constantly drilled into us at school, because the statements that were impressed on us most then are not necessarily by any means always the statements which we are inclined to regard as *a priori*. Most English children have been pressed far more strenuously to say that the Battle of Hastings was fought in 1066 than they have been to say that the same thing cannot be both red and green all over.

But I have other arguments besides the difficulty of seeing how these *a priori* propositions were learnt, if they were merely rules of language, and how we are to explain the fact that, unlike other rules of language, they at least appear to be necessary. In the first place it is surely plain that some *a priori* propositions, e.g. everything which has shape has size, a thing cannot be both red and green, if one thing is above another and the second is above a third the first is above the third, all three-sided rectilinear figures have three angles, could be seen to be true without the use of language. A person who was capable of forming visual images might quite well see the truth of any of these propositions without having to put them into words, and therefore their truth cannot possibly depend on the structure of language. It is true, no doubt, that the grasping of most *a priori* propositions requires language, because their content cannot be adequately represented by imagery, but this is not, as we have seen, the case with all, and the existence of any exceptions is sufficient to show that all apparent *a priori* necessity is not derivable from linguistic considerations.

Secondly, I do not know, e.g. any Chinese, Afghan or Malayan, yet I know quite certainly that the propositions, e.g. that a thing cannot be both red and green all over or that $5 + 7$ is equal to 12 will be true just as much when asserted in Chinese, Afghan or

Malayan as when asserted in English, French or German. It is conceivable that one or more of these languages might be incapable of expressing such a proposition, but if they can express it at all it must be true as expressed in them. I know this about all languages or systems of symbolism that ever have been or could be employed. How on the linguistic view could I possibly know any such thing? I have never been told by a scholar who knew all the languages there are, if there be any such person, that the contradictories of these expressions are meaningless in all languages. Indeed, I know what I have said to be true not only in all actual, but in all possible languages, so that, even if I could meet such a wonderful scholar, it would not help me at all. Surely, I could only know the truth of such propositions on linguistic grounds if I could know *a priori* that all languages must observe certain detailed rules of lexicography, grammar and syntax, and that is obviously the sort of thing no one would admit could be known *a priori*, least of all, I should have thought, a person who assigns to *a priori* knowledge the very restricted function which is assigned to it by the people I am criticizing.

The reply is made that, if the contradictories of *a priori* statements were not inadmissible in these languages as in English, the words used would not mean exactly the same and therefore the statements would not have been correctly translated. It would be said that if the word used in translating 'red' into a foreign language could be applied to a thing together with the word used in translating 'green', it would not be a correct translation of 'this is both red and green', since in English we cannot say this at all, and therefore the words used in the foreign language could not have the same sense as the words they are intended to translate. My answer to this is as follows. Let us distinguish the linguistic rules which no one would regard as *a priori*, e.g. that we must apply not 'red' but 'green' to things like grass in spring, from those of the kind which would generally be described as *a priori*, e.g. that we must not say of anything 'this is red and green all over'. Then we can see that for all languages any words which obey the former set of rules *must*, if they are to express anything true, also obey the latter *in any context in which they obey the former*. The point is that we can see that in any language, granted the use of certain rules, it follows necessarily that, if certain other rules are not observed while the first are at the same time observed, we shall not be making an admissible statement, and how we could see this of all possible languages that obey the first set of rules when we do not know all such languages is quite incomprehensible if the basis of this *a priori* proposition is linguistic. It is easy enough to explain if we see that the objective characteristic signified by 'green' is logically incompatible with the characteristic signified by 'red'. From this it would undoubtedly follow at once that anybody who in any language disobeyed the rule that the words for 'red' and 'green' must not be applied to the same object when used in the sense in which 'red' and 'green' are commonly used of colours in English would not be asserting a true proposition. For without any investigation of foreign languages we can say at once that in whatever language a false proposition was expressed it would always be false.

Again, I am well aware that even in English the words 'red' and 'green' can be employed in an unusual way, if the speaker desires, so that it may be true to say that a thing is both red and green all over at the same time, e.g. 'green' might be used to mean 'appearing green to some percipient' and 'red' to mean 'appearing red', but this would make it express something different. I still know that what I am expressing now when I say that a thing cannot be both red and green all over, using 'red' and 'green' in their normal sense, must be true in whatever language it is expressed, though in all languages that can express it the speaker could no doubt, if he chose, use the words in a different sense so as to express something false. I can even say it is false that $2 + 2 = 4$ if I choose to use '4' to mean 5. But all this does not alter the fact that the propositions of which I have been thinking would be true in whatever language they were expressed, though the same English words might also, by varying their meaning, be used to express propositions which would be false in whatever language they were expressed or propositions the truth of which was doubtful.

But the defects of the linguistic theory are perhaps exposed best if we try to work out its application to deductive reasoning. One account of the linguistic theory of reasoning, the one we should naturally expect, would be to say that in all valid deductive reasoning the conclusion is part of the premises restated in different words, or that all *a priori* propositions are 'analytic', a view which as usually understood entails the truth of the former proposition about deductive reasoning. Both these statements are, in fact, very often made. Before criticizing such a doctrine I must point out certain mistakes which, if made, give it a plausibility to which it is not entitled. In the first place, it is certainly quite a common and correct expression to say that the conclusion of a valid argument is always 'contained' in the premises, but we must remember that the word 'contained' here is ambiguous. It may be used to mean that the conclusion is just part of the premises, in which case it commits one to the view I am going to criticize, but it may also be employed merely as a semi-metaphorical expression for 'entailed by'. In that case, while it is obviously true that the conclusion of a valid argument must be 'contained in' (entailed by) its premises, this does not support any particular theory of entailment. Secondly, people are apt to conclude that, because an inference is extremely obvious, therefore the conclusion is necessarily nothing but simply part of the premises, but this does not follow. An inference might be most obvious and yet not be such that the conclusion was just a part of the premises. Thirdly, an *a priori* proposition undoubtedly depends on language in the sense that, when we pronounce it true, we always presuppose some proposition about language, i.e. one which either specifies the sense in which the words are being used or asserts that they are being used in the ordinary sense, but this is likewise the case with all empirical judgements. I cannot assert that I am sitting in a chair without in a sense assuming propositions about the meaning of 'I', 'sitting' and 'chair'. It must be shown that *a priori* propositions depend on language in a different sense from this if we are to establish the linguistic convention theory.

Having removed these possible sources of confusion, let us now proceed with criticism of what I shall call for short the 'analytic' view of inference, i.e. the view which may be expressed by saying that the conclusion of a deductive argument is always simply part of the meaning of the premises restated in different words. Now, if we took these words literally, we should have to take them as meaning, or at least implying, that in deductive inference a person who knows the premises always knows the conclusion at the same time. Otherwise how could it be part of what he knows? This, however, is certainly false. Beginners in Euclid are certainly not aware of Pythagoras' theorem although it follows logically from premisses known to them. When we know something we do not therefore know at once everything which it entails, e.g. if we know the primitive propositions of *Principia Mathematica*, we do not thereby know all at once the whole of the book which consists of propositions entailed by them. At the most, if we use words in a terribly 'Pickwickian' fashion, we could say that the conclusions were always already known in a confused form without our being explicitly aware of them. But if so, I am not, when I reach the conclusion, contemplating the same propositions as I was contemplating when I had the premisses before me but had not yet drawn the conclusion. If I think '*p*' confusedly I have not the same proposition in my mind as when I think '*p*' clearly. Our premisses are not the objective facts as such, but only what we know about these before making the inference, and in the case of a valid inference we do not, when we make it for the first time, know the conclusion till we have made the inference. The complex inferences of higher mathematics and the elementary syllogism do not differ in this respect except as regards quickness and simplicity. No doubt the philosopher may say that when we know the premisses we already know the conclusion in a sense, but we want to know—in what sense? Again, the philosopher may say that we know the conclusion 'implicitly' when we know the premisses, but what does this mean except that we know something which implies the conclusion? So much everyone will admit, but this is certainly not all that is meant by the philosophers who assert the conclusion to be part of the premisses or included in the premisses. We must insist then in any case that the conclusion of a valid inference can be new in the sense of involving a passage of thought to something of which we were not in the least thinking and which we had never accepted as true, though no doubt it could not be described as 'new' if 'new' means altogether unconnected with what went before. What I have said is so obvious that I hardly think any philosopher of repute can have meant to deny it, but it is certainly true that philosophers have spoken in a way which gives the impression that they ignored it.

Let us then try another formulation of what is meant by the analytic theory. We might, secondly, describe it as the theory that, whenever a proposition *p* entails another proposition *q*, *p* is analysable into *q* + *r* in such a sense of 'analysable' that to assert

p and deny q could be reduced to a verbal contradiction of the type that would be committed by anyone who said that B was A's brother and then denied that B was male. (We must understand this statement as covering the limiting case where r is zero and p and q coincide.) My own opinion is that this theory is not applicable to any cases of useful inference, but in order to refute the theory it is not of course necessary to show that it does not apply to any cases, but only that it does not apply to all. I shall take classes of cases where it seems specially easy to refute. First I shall have recourse to an argument used by Professor Broad at a meeting of the Cambridge Moral Science Club, though I shall state it in a slightly different fashion in order to fit the particular formulation of the opposing theory which I am discussing. Let $p =$ this has shape[1] and $q =$ this has size. Since we can infer q from p, p on the view in question must be reducible to $q + r_1$, and since we can infer p from q, q must $= p + r_2$. Therefore, effecting a substitution, $q = q + r_1 + r_2$ and $p = p + r_1 + r_2$. Therefore $p = q$,[2] and so 'this has size' and 'this has shape' mean exactly the same thing, which is certainly not true. So there is at least one case in which p entails q or q entails p without the theory I am discussing being applicable to it.

I am assuming here that analysis does give a strict equivalent of the proposition analysed as regards content (though not necessarily as regard its 'point' or its entire effect). If 'analysis' is not understood as doing this but as merely giving a proposition which would entail the same propositions as the proposition analysed, the view that, if p entails q, p must be analysed as $q + r$, would not necessarily imply that all deductive inference was verbal but would be compatible with any theory of entailment and inference.

Now secondly, let us take some cases where the entailment is not reciprocal so that p entails q without q entailing p. According to the holders of the view I am criticizing the premisses of a valid deductive inference must always be complex, and whether this is true or not, it is certain at any rate that it is very often complex and can be split up into two propositions, neither of which by itself entails the conclusion. In fact it is a commonplace that most

---

[1] I am using 'shape' in the sense in which a geometrical point could not be said to have shape. This is certainly the usual sense of the word.

[2] Because $r_1 + r_2$ must then $=$ zero.

inferences we make require two premisses, it being immaterial whether we call the premisses two different propositions or say that together they form one complex proposition. Now call one premiss a, the other b, and the conclusion c. Then, if the theory of inference which I am discussing is true, $a + b$ must be analysable into $c + $ some other proposition, x. Now neither a by itself nor b by itself can be identical with c or analysable as $c + $ some other proposition, because if so only one of the premisses would be needed for the inference. So how can $a + b$ be analysable as $c + x$? Only two alternatives are left: (1) c might be analysable into two propositions, one of which was included in a in the sense in which 'he is male' is included in 'he is a brother', and the other likewise included in b. But this is clearly not always the case. It is arguable, though I think not true, that syllogisms can be treated in this way, but I defy anyone to reduce 'Glasgow is north of London' to two propositions one of which is included in 'Glasgow is north of Cambridge' and the other in 'Cambridge is north of London', or 'A is cleverer than C' to two propositions one of which is thus included in 'A is cleverer than B' and the other in 'B is cleverer than C'. (2) It might be held that, though c was neither itself included in a or b nor analysable into two propositions thus included, yet a and b when combined could still include c. But in that case there would be something new added by combining a and b and if we can make a valid argument by combining premisses which we come to know separately, as we certainly can, this new element must be entailed by and, on the theory of inference I am criticizing, therefore included in a and b taken separately, which contradicts the hypothesis. (No doubt there might occur linguistic usages such that in some cases 'a and b' stated in one sentence meant something different from 'a' and 'b' in different sentences, but in such a case we could not validly infer c, the conclusion of 'a and b', from 'a' and 'b' as known separately, unless the proposition for which 'a and b' stands was entailed by the propositions represented by 'a' and 'b'.)

Thirdly, it is plain that, on the one hand, Socrates is a philosopher entails, e.g., that if all philosophers live to the age of 150, or have corns on the little toe of their left foot, Socrates lived to the age of 150, or had corns on the little toe of his left foot, but nobody could possibly maintain that these hypothetical propositions and the other more or less far-fetched ones I might cite are included in the analysis of 'Socrates is a philosopher'.

If the view that all *a priori* propositions and deductive inferences are analytic is to be established, what is required is a detailed investigation of all the main types of *a priori* propositions and deductive inferences with a view to showing that their rejection would involve a verbal contradiction. This has certainly not yet been shown, and the *onus probandi* is on the person who claims to establish it. I am not putting forward a rival theory of the *a priori* which has to be proved, but claiming that his theory has not been established. The arguments I have given satisfy me indeed that his theory cannot be true, but if some of you are not so convinced by these arguments as I am, it is important that you should still remember that the verbal theory requires proof and be aware of the kind of proof it requires. For it cannot from the nature of the case admit of an *a priori* proof, since that would involve what it claims to be impossible, i.e. an *a priori* synthetic proposition, and it could therefore only be justified as an empirical generalization based on an examination of representative instances of all the different kinds of *a priori* propositions and deductive inferences leading to the conclusion that, since they had all been shown to be verbal, probably all *a priori* propositions and valid deductive inferences were verbal. And to show that a particular *a priori* proposition or a particular inference is verbal, what is required is surely to show that as a matter of formal logic there would be a strictly verbal contradiction in denying it. Without showing this it is surely useless to say just vaguely that it is dependent on the conventions of language.[1]

But there now arises a more general difficulty for the theory. I distinguished provisionally two forms or senses of the analytic theory of inference, one which would involve the obviously false view that we could not know the premises of a valid argument without at the same time knowing the conclusion, and one which would not involve this, but only the apparently less incredible consequence that, whenever a proposition p entails another q, p is analysable into $q + r$ in such a way that to assert p and deny q could be reduced to a verbal contradiction like that which would be incurred by saying that A is the brother of B and then denying that A is male. But I find it very difficult to separate the two

[1] Broad, *Proceedings of the Aristotelian Society Supp. Vol.* XV, p. 116.

senses, and to see how the analysis of a proposition p could be $q + r$ if people could assert p intelligently without having the least idea of q and r, unless indeed, when we are said to be analysing a proposition, we are really not analysing it itself but analysing, e.g., the criteria for its truth, or the propositions entailed by it. If q is not included in the meaning of 'p', how could there possibly be a verbal contradiction in asserting 'p' and denying 'q', and how could q be included in the meaning of 'p' without being part of what we know when we know 'p'? This remains the root difficulty of the analytic theory. (As I have pointed out, there are difficulties about the phrase 'q is included in the meaning of p', but (1) it is quite clear that we can understand what is meant by saying, e.g., that 'A is male' is included in the meaning of 'A is a brother', and what the advocate of the analytic theory is holding is that conclusions of valid deductive arguments are always included in their premises in just this sense; (2) if we cannot say that one proposition is included in another or that the meaning of one statement is included in the meaning of another the analytic theory, since it does say this, itself falls to the ground.) So the second form of the analytic theory seems to reduce itself to the first, and thus obviously to contradict the facts, since we clearly in the case of a complicated inference at least can know the premises without knowing at the same time the conclusion.

No doubt we may in some cases of valid and useful inference hold that the conclusion, which I will represent by 'q', and the premiss, which I will represent by 'p', are 'equivalent', for 'equivalence' commonly only signifies mutual entailment, but this is not to say that 'p' and 'q' mean the same unless we assume already the view of inference which I am criticizing. If it is retorted that 'p' and 'q' mean the same when they function in the same way in thought and all logically equivalent propositions function in the same way, we must reply that the latter statement is not true. 'This is 27 feet long' and 'the length of this is the cube root of 19,683 feet' are logically equivalent propositions, but they do not function in the same way in thought; the second is much less effective for giving a quick idea of the length of the thing to be measured than the first and stimulates a whole process of thought—finding the cube root—which the first does not. But it may be said, they have at any rate the same 'content', though, if you include in the notion of meaning a reference to such notions as emphasis, practical point and emotive effect, they have not the same 'meaning'. But since it is quite clear that a person may know that a line is 27 feet long without at the same time being at all conscious that it is $\sqrt[3]{19,683}$ feet long, what criterion have you for saying that the two statements have the same content except that they entail each other? And the point at issue is just whether two propositions which entail each other must have the same content or not. If it is said that they must have the same content because you can always substitute one expression for the other without change of meaning, I deny that you can. If in $27 = \sqrt[3]{19,683}$ you substitute 27 for $\sqrt[3]{19,683}$ the proposition becomes $27 = 27$, which is obviously either not a proposition at all, because it does not say anything, or at any rate a different proposition from the original one. It would be likewise impossible to substitute 27 for $\sqrt[3]{19,683}$ in 'the value of $\sqrt[3]{19,683}$ must be obtained by a process involving division or multiplication'. We cannot even always substitute $2 + 2$ for 4, since, if we say $2 + 2 = 4$, we are not saying exactly the same as $2 + 2 = 2 + 2$.

Finally, if a person maintained that we can only infer, e.g., 'A is not green' from 'A is red' or 'the number is 12' from 'the number is $7 + 5$' because 'not green' is included in the meaning of 'red' and '$7 + 5$' is included in the meaning of '12', then I should ask him whether he thinks $9489650 - 9489638$ and $\sqrt[4]{20736}$ and all the infinite numerical functions to which it is equal are also included in the meaning of '12', and whether not yellow, not black, not virtuous, etc., are also included in the meaning of 'red'. I might further use my liberty to invent new symbols 'rad', 'gran', '12+', '5+', '7+', the use of which was covered by exactly the same rules as that of 'red', 'green', '12', '5', '7', except that the rules that 'rad' and 'gran' must not be used of the same thing and that '5+ + 7+' must not be negated of anything of which '12+' was asserted did not occur. This would make it impossible to say that 'not gran' was included in the meaning of 'rad' or '5+ + 7+' in the meaning of '12+', yet it is perfectly clear that we should still see that it is logically impossible for the same thing to be 'rad' and yet 'gran' and '12+' and yet not '5+ + 7+'. Our insight into this therefore cannot be dependent on the inclusion of it in the language rules governing the meaning of red, etc.

But, thirdly, it is possible that a person who says all *a priori* propositions are analytic or that the conclusion is included in the premisses in all deductive reasoning may simply mean to say that it is self-contradictory to deny an *a priori* proposition or to deny the conclusion of a valid deductive inference while accepting its premisses. If that is all I agree with him. For if p entails q it follows logically that not-q entails not-p, so that to assert p and deny q may quite properly be said to be self-contradictory, but this is not saying anything more than that the denial of the second entails the denial of the first, and leaves it an open question what the nature of entailment is. One should indeed distinguish here between verbal and material contradiction.

I think one of the reasons which has led people to adopt the analytic view is because they confusedly thought that, if $p +$ non-q was self-contradictory, it could only be because p included q. But this is not the case. If we could say that it was self-contradictory to assert one proposition, p, without asserting another, q, this would indeed imply that q was part of p, but when p entails q there is not necessarily any self-contradiction in asserting p and *not asserting q*. We never draw all the possible conclusions from a proposition asserted by us, and why need we if they are not to the point? It is certainly not self-contradictory to assert something without also asserting everything that follows from it. What is self-contradictory is to assert p and *deny* its consequence, q, but to say this is self-contradictory is only to give the logical converse of 'p entails q', leaving it quite open whether we reduce entailment to inclusion or not.

The conventionalist, however, will often express his view by saying not that all *a priori* propositions are analytic, but that the truth of *a priori* propositions 'can be seen from a mere inspection of the meaning of the terms used' or 'depends wholly on the meaning of the terms used'. This is true in a sense, for an *a priori* proposition does follow necessarily if the meaning of the terms used is given, and therefore its truth, unlike that of an empirical proposition, does depend *wholly* on the meaning of the terms used, but this admission is compatible with my view as well as with the conventionalist view. If the terms used stand for characteristics one of which entails or logically excludes the other, the truth of the proposition must follow from their meaning, and if they do not stand for such characteristics the proposition is not *a priori*. It does not in the least follow that an *a priori* proposition is made true simply by the speaker or most educated people using words in a certain way. That the truth of an *a priori* proposition 'depends wholly on the meaning of the terms used' is indeed not inconsistent with any view about *a priori* propositions except the view of Mill that they are based on empirical generalizations concerning the objects to which they refer. The question is whether they depend on the meaning of the terms in the sense of being a necessary consequence of the nature of the characteristics for which the terms stand or whether they depend not on the objective nature of what they mean but on arbitrary rules of language which forbid us to combine certain words. The expression—*a priori* propositions depend on the meaning of the terms used—is therefore ambiguous in a very dangerous way. It expresses something that is undoubtedly true, but it suggests an arbitrariness and dependence on convention which is not in the least implied by the true proposition which it does express. Indeed, I think one of the causes why people have adopted a conventionalist view is because they confusedly regarded undoubtedly true statements such as '*a priori* propositions depend on the meaning of the terms used', as entailing the truth of their own views, when they do not do anything of the sort. What I have said of course applies also to the corresponding theory regarding deductive arguments.

Supposing the view that all *a priori* propositions are analytic and that the conclusion of a deductive inference is always part of the premisses is rejected, can the conventionalist view be retained in any form? The conventionalist will have now to admit that we can in inference pass to conclusions which go beyond the premisses and give something genuinely new, though not of course unconnected with what went before. Entailment is on any view a connexion of the most important kind. He can no longer say that the inference holds because the conclusion is part of the meaning of the words expressing the premiss. Therefore how can he maintain that the inference is verbal at all? He may say that, though the conclusion is not part of the meaning of the words expressing the premiss, the language rules fixing it are inferred from those fixing the meaning of the premiss-words, so that,

F

though the conclusion is new, it is still not a conclusion about anything objective but merely a conclusion about certain rules of language: e.g. 'Cambridge is to the north of Paris' is not part of the meaning of 'Cambridge is to the north of London and London is to the north of Paris', but, it may be said, we can deduce from the other rules governing the use of the words 'to the north of' that, if we can say 'Cambridge is to the north of London' and 'London is to the north of Paris', we ought not to say 'Cambridge is not to the north of Paris'.

But, if we admit that we can by inference pass from one set of rules about the use of language to a different one, why not admit that we can pass by inference from one fact to another regarding the things about which we are talking and not only our language? The linguistic convention theory seemed plausible because it seemed to provide a means of avoiding the admission, which seemed to many people so strange, that we could do anything by thinking but arrange and analyse what we knew by observation. But if we admit that thinking can do more than this in the case of rules of language, we have admitted that reasoning can arrive at new facts, for rules of language are facts, if a peculiar sort of facts, and if so, why not admit that we can attain other new facts by reasoning? The main ground for the theory has been abandoned by this admission.

But not only is there an absence of reasons for the view, there are positive objections to it of the most serious nature. In the first place it is simply not true that we can infer one rule of language from others, if we mean an actually observed rule, because there might always be anomalies. We cannot infer from any other rules of language that the words red and green are not as part of their normal usage applied to the same thing, because for anything we know *a priori* there might be a particular idiom by which, while 'red' and 'green' in other usages meant what they do now, the phase 'red and green' stood for, e.g., some shade of colour between red and green. We know empirically that there is not in fact such an idiom, but we cannot infer that there is not from any other rules. We could only know rules of language in the sense of actually observed rules *a priori* if we could know *a priori* how the members of a given nation will behave in a detailed matter, i.e. the use of particular words. It is true that there are certain rules of language which we can deduce by subsuming them as sub-cases of more universal rules, but that can only be done if we have first accepted the validity of these universal rules on authority, and even this is no guarantee that the rules will be actually obeyed. We certainly cannot tell *a priori* from examples which conform to a given rule, however numerous, that this rule will always be obeyed even by the majority of highly educated people. As every schoolboy knows, most linguistic rules have exceptions, and even if a rule has in fact no exceptions we could only establish the rule by examples, i.e. empirical generalization, and can never be sure that in the language as used there will not develop exceptions. We certainly cannot know that all people will speak grammatically, and at a certain point those who violate a grammatical usage may have become so numerous that it ceases to be the normal one.

Is what we infer then, not that a rule does actually hold, but that it ought to hold? But what reason can there be for saying a rule ought to hold in distinction from saying that it does hold? Even Kant does not claim to know any categorical imperatives about grammar. We might say a rule ought to be observed, though it was generally broken, on the ground that the people whom we thought most respectable observed it, but that is not a matter of *a priori* knowledge or of deducing it from other rules, but of empirical observation of behaviour. We might say that it ought to be observed because it was the rule stated in all books on grammar, but obviously this is not why we accept the *a priori* laws we are discussing today. Or again, we might urge the observance of a linguistic rule on the ground of convenience merely because its non-observance would be liable to lead to ambiguous and confusing expressions, but this again is obviously not how we know that we must obey the rule which forbids us to ascribe redness and greenness to the same object.

So, if we are talking about rules of language, it is just not true that we can know them *a priori* or validly infer them from other rules, except perhaps in the way in which we can be said to infer when we merely make empirical generalizations. What we do know *a priori* is that if we say, e.g., 'this is both red and green all over', these words being understood in their ordinary sense, we are not saying what is true, and how could we know that except by knowing that the qualities for which 'red' and 'green' stand are incompatible, which is not a proposition about language?

Besides, if all inference were merely from one linguistic rule to another, I do not see how there could be any possible arguments to show that it was this. Such arguments could clearly not be themselves arguments from one linguistic rule to another and therefore would be inconsistent with their own conclusion. Like the verification principle when taken as a dogma the linguistic theory turns out suicidal since any argument in its favour must result in its destruction.

If we cannot validly infer any linguistic rules from others and we can neither validly infer any other objective facts, there is no such thing as valid inference at all (except for purely empirical generalizations). Even holders of the linguistic view would be unlikely to admit this, but they sometimes do contend that 'valid inference' is simply the name for a certain kind of habit differing only from invalid inference in being generally followed, or being in accordance with the way in which most people, or the people one approves, use words. I should have thought this was itself a *reductio ad absurdum* even by itself quite adequate to refute the linguistic theory, and at any rate it takes away any possible justification for the theory. What arguments could there be for such a theory itself? It is not the case that most people maintain the theory, therefore it is not in accord with the way in which most people use words; and how could the fact, if it is a fact, that most people towards whom the conventionalist has a feeling of approval use words in this way be an argument that would or could rationally influence anybody who did not already hold the theory in question. If the conventionalist replies that his theory is not a statement of the way in which people actually use words but an inference from it to fresh rules of languages, I have already dealt with this point.

The conventionalist has been greatly encouraged by recent advances in mathematics and science, which at least suggest and perhaps prove that what we originally took as *a priori* axioms in geometry are not known *a priori*, but are rather of the nature of arbitrary postulates. But he forgets that, supposing we grant that the primary postulates are arbitrary, at least the inference of consequences from them cannot possibly also be arbitrary. If it were we might, given the same postulates, equally well draw totally different conclusions. If Euclid's presuppositions are arbitrary, still the hypothetical proposition that, *if* these are true, e.g. all triangles must have the sum of their angles equal to two right angles, is necessarily true *a priori*. Otherwise we could, while retaining as valid the whole proof down to the last step but one, still assert with no less justification, if we chose, that the sum was equal to a million right angles or to none. I do not suppose that the philosophers of considerable reputation who describe *a priori* inferences as arbitrary have really failed to see this simple fact, but they are at least open to the charge of having expressed themselves in a very misleading fashion. It has also been pointed out by conventionalists that, although the rules of a game, e.g. chess, are merely conventional, a good player can apply them in all sorts of new ways. But this is simply because deductive inference is possible in chess as well as in logic. Given a certain situation on the board a good player can deduce from the rules that it is possible to mate in two. He will in doing so go through a more or less complicated process of inference of the kind, e.g. if black moves his queen it follows from the rules governing bishops' moves that it can be taken by the white bishop, if he moves another piece something else will follow, etc. This is genuine inference, and no more analytic than the more serious deductive inferences to which I have referred, though it is based on postulates which are only rules of the game. The illustration is apposite as against a person who maintained that a deductive system always presupposed the truth of its initial postulates, but if used in favour of the view that all *a priori* propositions are conventional it ignores the fact that in order to infer q from p an *a priori* proposition, namely, if p then q, must be necessarily true and not just postulated or arbitrarily fixed by convention. Without some *a priori* propositions of that kind no deductive system would be possible at all because you could not deduce anything.

It is sometimes said that *a priori* propositions 'give no information' or 'do not say anything about the world' or are 'tautologies' simply on the ground that they are compatible with all possibilities, but surely it is a piece of information to be told that something is impossible. You are saying something about the world if you say that a certain state of affairs is impossible. Everybody, even the most hard-headed and tender-minded rationalist, agrees that *a priori* propositions are compatible with all possibilities, but they restrict the possibilities. Every defender of the *a priori* would admit that the kind of information they give is very different from the kind of information which empirical propositions give, but this is not to say it is not information, unless you choose to make 'information' by definition the same as 'empirical information', in which case you have said nothing whatever when you have said that *a priori* statements give no information. And, unless the analytic view of the *a priori* is established, to say that they are compatible with all possibilities is certainly not to say they are tautologies in the sense of being all of the same type as 'a brother is male'.

If we look at, e.g., the case of red and green again, to take one instance of many, surely what I see is just that these two characteristics simply cannot go together, not that the words are used in a certain way? If it was only a verbal connexion it would be a sheer mistake to think it impossible that the qualities could go together. All we should have a right to say would be that we do not know what could be meant by saying they go together, but that surely misreads our experience. We do not have the experience of failing to see what these words mean, but of understanding what they mean and seeing that it cannot be true. If I did not go behind the words to the qualities red and green, I should never know the proposition *a priori* at all. If our belief in the proposition is merely a result of the way in which we use words, this belief is only an illusion due to faulty language habits. The conventionalists are ready enough to say this about certain kinds of alleged *a priori* propositions, but if they were consistent they would have to condemn as illusory the whole of pure mathematics as well as the more speculative parts of the philosophy of Hegel and Spinoza. For with all *a priori* propositions that they recognized as true, everybody thought, till enlightened by the conventionalists, that they saw a relation of necessary connexion or logical exclusion between two real characteristics. If they did not see this they were simply suffering from an illusion, and in that case I do not see why they should be regarded as less culpable logically than the people who were deceived by the ontological argument for the existence of God because they were misled by the faulty language habit of treating 'exist' as an ordinary verb, though they were perhaps luckier in that their mistakes had useful practical results which the ontological argument did not have. It is a defect recognized as fatal in general if an argument has to be condemned as merely 'verbal', but the theory which makes all deductive arguments merely verbal has suggested no way of distinguishing between the sense of 'merely verbal' in which a good argument cannot be merely verbal and the sense in which all good deductive arguments are according to them merely verbal. To this objection must be added the difficulty of seeing how, if the linguistic view is true, inference could have the utility it admittedly does have.

Take again the humble and despised syllogism. Granted the truth of its premisses, the syllogism—the man who entered the house at midnight was the murderer of B, A was the man who entered the house at midnight—proves A's guilt, a fact sufficiently objective and non-verbal to hang a man, but on the linguistic theory could it prove anything more than that well-educated people will use the word 'murderer' of A under such circumstances? Why should A be hanged because of a linguistic convention?

What arguments could there be for the linguistic convention theory? It clearly cannot be established merely by empirical observation and generalization from observations. But the arguments for it, if valid, could not by their own showing be deductive unless they were themselves based merely on linguistic conventions, and it is difficult to see how the theory that all *a priori* propositions and deductive arguments are based on linguistic convention could be justified by arguments which were themselves based on linguistic convention. Even if the argument consisted in showing that all the main types of deductive argument and *a priori* propositions can be adequately explained as due to linguistic conventions, it is difficult to see how such an argument could be carried out in detail without asserting or presupposing some propositions which were not themselves based on linguistic convention. However, I have already dealt with this type of argument.

Conventionalists sometimes use an argument of the type which in another context and on another occasion I called 'the argument of the slippery slope'. It consists in enticing your opponent to admit that the view you wish to establish is true in some cases and then showing that there is no hard-and-fast demarcation line between these and other cases so that he ought consistently to admit it in the second class of cases if he does in the first, and so on till he finds there is no halting-ground short of admitting it in all cases. In this way once he has set his foot on the slippery slope he finds there is no stopping till he is dashed to philosophical destruction at the foot of the precipice below. In the present controversy this argument would take the form of showing an opponent that at any rate 'all brothers are male' or 'a black horse is a horse' are verbal, then inducing him to admit that other *a priori* propositions which he at first thought were not verbal were essentially the same in kind as the first examples, and suggesting the arbitrariness of halting at any point from then onwards till he had admitted that all *a priori* propositions were verbal. I think there are a good many possible halting-places on the way and therefore do not fear the precipice myself; but this paper is already too long and I should make it very much longer if I discussed the question at what exact point it was best to draw the line. But in any case the limits of the argument are obvious. (1) At the best it could only give some degree of probability to the linguistic view, while most of the arguments I have used against the view, unless vitiated by some fallacy on my part, would show it certainly false. (2) The same type of argument could be used to show, e.g., that all green is blue or that all animals are vegetables. With almost any terms we find difficult borderline cases. (3) The argument cuts both ways. In view of what we have said earlier it would be much more difficult to hold that some of the examples I gave are merely verbal than to hold that 'if A is a brother A is male' is not merely verbal, if we were absolutely forced, which I deny, to hold either that all deductive inferences and *a priori* propositions are verbal or that none are. After all even 'if A is a brother A is male' presupposes the law of contradiction, which is not dependent on linguistic convention.

I am not giving a rival explanation of *a priori* reasoning and deductive inference. I am only accepting facts. And the facts are that we can sometimes see that one characteristic entails or necessarily excludes another. It is not a question of going beyond our experience to postulate some mysterious faculty to account for this, but of noting that we do see this. I have no theory to account for the fact that we see it, for I do not think one is needed any more than it is needed to account for the fact that we have empirical knowledge, and the *onus probandi* is on my opponent who is putting forward a particular theory to account for or explain away the fact. People feel a peculiar difficulty about 'synthetic *a priori*' propositions because they are so unlike empirical propositions, but anyone who feels such a difficulty should realize that there can from the nature of the case be none sufficient to justify their rejection. For that there can be no synthetic *a priori* propositions would be itself synthetic *a priori*, and even if he only feels a difficulty about them and does not assert that he knows there cannot be any such propositions, he is, not indeed asserting, but at least entertaining as possible and wondering whether he ought not to accept the self-contradictory synthetic *a priori* proposition that there are no synthetic *a priori* propositions.

F*

CHAPTER VII

LANGUAGE AND REALITY[1]

Max Black
Sage Professor of Philosophy, Cornell University

Bertrand Russell once said, 'The study of grammar, in my opinion, is capable of throwing far more light on philosophical questions than is commonly supposed by philosophers. Although a grammatical distinction cannot be uncritically assumed to correspond to a genuine philosophical difference, yet the one is *prima facie* evidence of the other, and may often be most usefully employed as a source of discovery.'[2]

The grammatical distinctions that Russell proceeds to use as guides to philosophical discoveries are the familiar ones between nouns, adjectives and verbs. But he says that he hopes for 'a classification, not of words, but of ideas'[3] and adds, 'I shall therefore call adjectives or predicates all notions which are capable of being such, even in a form in which grammar would call them substantives'.[4] If we are ready to call adjectives nouns, in defiance of grammar, we can hardly expect the grammatical distinction between the two parts of speech to guide us towards what Russell calls a 'correct logic'.[5] If grammar is to teach us anything of philosophical importance, it must be treated with more respect.

My object in this paper is to clarify the character of philosophical inferences from grammar. By 'grammar' I shall understand a classification of meaningful units of speech (i.e. 'morphology'), together with rules for the correct arrangement of such units in sentences (i.e. 'syntax'). The conclusions of the kinds of inferences I have in mind will be propositions commonly called 'ontological'; they will be metaphysical statements about 'the

---

[1] Presidential address delivered before the Fifty-Fifth Annual Meeting of the Eastern Division of the American Philosophical Association at the University of Vermont, December 27–29, 1958. Published in *Proceedings and Addresses of the American Philosophical Association*, Vol. XXXII, and subsequently included in a volume of Professor Black's papers entitled *Morals and Metaphors*, Cornell University Press.

[2] *The Principles of Mathematics*, p. 42.

[3] *Loc. cit.*   [4] *Ibid.*   [5] *Ibid.*

ultimate nature of reality', like 'Relations exist', or 'The World is the totality of facts, not of things', or 'There exists one and only one substance'.

I

In seeking ontological conclusions from linguistic premises, our starting-point must be the grammar of some actual language, whether living or dead. From the standpoint of a language's capacity to express what is or what might be the case, it contains much that is superfluous, in grammar as well as in vocabulary. Grammatical propriety requires a German child to be indicated by a neuter expression ('*das* Kind'), a liability from which French children are exempt. If we are willing to speak ungrammatical German or French, so long as the fact-stating resources of the language are unimpaired, we can dispense with indications of gender. For to be told that the word '*Kind*' is neuter, is to be told nothing about children that would have been the case had the German language never existed. The indifference of the English language to the gender of nouns sufficiently demonstrates the superfluity of this particularly grammatical feature. For the purpose of eventual metaphysical inference, gender is an accidental, a non-essential, grammatical category.

In order to have any prospects of validity, positive philosophical inferences from grammar must be based upon essential, non-accidental, grammatical features, that is to say on features whose deletion would impair or render impossible the fact-stating functions of language. The essential grammatical features, if there are any, must therefore be present in all actual or possible languages that have the same fact-stating powers. They must be invariant under all possible transformations of a given language that conserve fact-stating resources. The system of all such invariant grammatical features would constitute a universal or philosophical grammar. Metaphysical inferences from grammar must be founded upon the constitution of a hypothetical universal grammar, in abstraction from the idiomatic peculiarities of the grammars of given languages.

There is little reason to suppose that the universal grammar, if there is such a thing, will closely resemble any conventional grammar. Contemporary linguists have made plain the 'formal' character of conventional grammatical classifications and the 'arbitrariness' of conventional rules of syntax. We shall need something other than grammarians' tools to uncover the universal grammar.

I assume, however, that philosophical grammar will still resemble conventional grammar in consisting of a morphology together with a syntax. I shall suppose throughout that we are considering the prospects of a certain kind of classification, coupled with a system of rules for admissible combinations of the things classified. I shall use the conveniently non-committal expression, 'linguistic features', to refer to the things classified.

Were it possible to construct a philosophical grammar, or any fragment of it, it would be very tempting to say that something would thereby have been revealed about the nature of ultimate reality. For what could be the reason for the presence of some grammatical feature in all conceivable fact-stating languages except the correspondence of every such language with reality? There is an inclination to say with the author of the *Tractatus* that the essence of language must be 'the essence of the World'.[1] Or, with a more recent writer, 'The universe is not a vain capricious customer of ours. If the shoe fits, this is a good clue to the size of the foot. If a language is adequate to describe it, this indicates something about its structure.'[2]

Of course, if metaphysical inferences from grammar are not to be circular, the construction of a universal grammar must proceed without prior ontological commitments. We shall need to consider whether the search for a universal grammar can be undertaken from a position of ontological neutrality.

It is obviously easier to show that some linguistic feature does not belong to universal grammar than the reverse; most of the examples I shall consider will have this negative character, that is to say, will be instances in which we argue that some feature of a given language is not essential to the fact-stating powers of the language. The corresponding ontological inference is the negative one that nothing in ultimate reality corresponds to the rejected linguistic feature.

[1] *Tractatus*, 5.4711.
[2] I. M. Copi, *The Review of Metaphysics*, vol. iv (1951), p. 436.

II

In the *Tractatus*, Wittgenstein says, 'In the proposition there must be exactly as much distinguishable (*gleich soviel zu unterscheiden*) as in the state of affairs that it represents'.[1] Let us read this to mean: 'In the particular utterance, there must be exactly as many different symbols as there are constituents in the state of affairs represented.' Following Wittgenstein, I shall assign two physically similar word-tokens to different symbols, when they have different senses or references.

Let us try to apply this plausible principle of invariance of the number of constituents to a concrete instance. Suppose I am riding in an automobile with somebody who is learning to drive, and I need some pre-arranged signals to tell him to start the car or to stop it. It is natural, and adequate, to use the words 'Stop' and 'Go'; but, of course, a tap on the shoulder would do just as well. Here we have a system of orders, not statements of fact; but similar considerations will apply in both cases, since the logical structure of the orders will be the same as that of the factual statements specifying the actions performed in response to those orders. An adherent of Wittgenstein's principle of isomorphism might point out that here the two actions to be performed are represented by exactly the same number of distinct symbols, 'Stop' and 'Go'. He might add that it would be logically impossible for the learner-driver to understand the two different orders, unless he were supplied with different and distinct symbols for the two cases. And he might add that every set of symbols that could serve the same purpose would necessarily exhibit the same duality. Whether the instructor spoke German, or Swahili, or anything else, he must necessarily use two symbols: here seems to be a perfect example of an essential feature, necessarily manifested in all the mutually equivalent notations.

But suppose the instructor used a whistle to signal 'Start' as well as to signal 'Stop'. This device would be just as effective as the conventional words, and we need not suppose the whistle blasts to be substitutes for the English sounds: their meanings might have been taught directly, by demonstration and training. Have we not here an exception to Wittgenstein's principle—one symbol (the blown whistle), but two represented actions?

[1] *Loc. cit.*, 4.04.

The retort is obvious: A whistle blown when the car is at rest means one thing ('Go'), but means another ('Stop') when the car is in motion. So the full symbol is whistle-plus-condition-of-car: there are two relevant states of the car, hence two symbols after all. But is this conclusive? Surely it would be just as easy to argue as follows: The whistle is one symbol, not two; but it also represents one action, not two: each time it means a *change-of-state*, whether from motion to rest or *vice versa*. To be consistent, an advocate of this view must be willing to say that the familiar orders 'Stop' and 'Go' mean one and the same thing; but a determined searcher for a depth grammar must accept consequences at least as strange as this.

In order to determine whether Wittgenstein's principle applies to the case in hand, we need criteria of identity for actions and criteria of identity for the corresponding symbols. We have to say whether starting the car and stopping it are to count as the same or as different actions; and we have to say whether blowing the whistle is to count as having the same or different meanings on various occasions. There are no definite criteria for identity in these cases. In ordinary life, in a particular setting, we might understand sufficiently well a request to say something different, or to do something different; but here we are not in an ordinary setting. We want to know whether there are *really* two actions and two symbols, and have no way of finding out. We are free to decide whether the symbols are the same or different; the relevant fragment of philosophical grammar must be stipulated. The philosophical questions lack determinate sense and depend for their answers upon how we choose to describe the relevant utterances.

It may be said that this disappointing outcome arises from the artificiality of the example. I shall therefore turn to other cases having greater intrinsic interest.

III

Nowadays, it is often said that the copula, that figures so prominently in traditional logic, is superfluous. Listen to this, for instance: 'There might certainly be various relations that the copula stood for, if it stood for any relation at all. But in fact no link is needed to join subject and predicate. . . . The grammatical copula is logically significant only when it serves as a sign of tense.'[1]

But here is a traditionalist speaking: 'The mode of connection of the subject and the predicate is symbolized in the standard formulation by the word "is", which is called the "copula" because it links subject and predicate together . . . some mode of connexion requires symbolization, and this function is performed by the copula.'[2]

The dispute is clearly about philosophical grammar: the question is whether the copula is, or is not, an essential feature of language. On the one side, a strong case can be presented for the dispensability of the copula. There are languages, like Hebrew or Japanese, which manage very well without a copula; and we ourselves do without it in such constructions as 'Peter loves Mary', in which the predicate, 'loves Mary', is attached to its subject, 'Peter', without benefit of any verbal link. Strongest of all is the argument that we could jettison the copula without in any way impairing the fact-stating resources of our language. Were we to say, 'Peter happy', as the Chinese are said to do, we would lose nothing in expressive and descriptive power. In any case, *some* words and expressions must be able to 'hang together' in a sentence without a symbolic link, for otherwise no completed sentence would be possible. So why not dispense with the copula altogether?

A defender of the copula's significance might reply as follows: 'You are right in claiming that we don't need the *word* "is" or any other word between the subject and the predicate of a sentence. But this is trivial and was never in dispute. Consider the pidgin English sentence, "Peter happy", that you offered as an adequate substitute for the conventional form. What is significant in this sentence is not merely the occurrence of the word-tokens, "Peter" and "happy", but the *relationship* between them. Separating the two words by others or by a sufficiently wide interval will disintegrate your sentence. It is the relationship of juxtaposition that here performs the function of linking subject and predicate. Similarly, in the conventional form, "Peter is happy", the union is effected by a relationship generated by writing the three words in correct order and in sufficiently close proximity. What is

[1] P. T. Geach, *Mind*, Vol. LIX (1950), p. 464.
[2] C. A. Mace, *The Principles of Logic*, pp. 77–8.

essential to the copula is not at all deleted by the translation into pidgin English, *Floreat copula!*'

What are we to say of this rebuttal? Its plausibility is undeniable, yet once again nothing compels us to accept it. For one thing, we may feel some reluctance to recognize 'juxtaposition' as a genuine relation. Do we really need to *bring* the words into any relationship? Isn't it enough that we use them both in making the statement in question? Here again, consideration of some non-verbal notation might rid us of certain initial prejudices. Could we not, perhaps, use a red disc to mean that Peter is happy, with the disc standing for the man and its colour for his condition of felicity? And what then would become of the alleged relationship between subject and predicate? Somebody might still insist, like A. E. Johnson in his *Logic*, that there would have to be a *characterizing relation* between the disc and its colour. But anybody who can confidently assert this must already be in a position to analyse reality directly, and has no need of the detour through language.

But indeed, an advocate of the no copula view can reaffirm his position without invoking a hypothetical notation of qualified objects. *His* analysis of the sentence-fact, 'Peter happy', might well be in terms of an 'object', the word-token, 'Peter', qualified by a certain property, that of having the word-token 'happy' in immediate proximity. If he conceives of properties as 'incomplete', i.e. as having the power to unite with objects without need of intermediaries, he will *see* the linguistic predicate in the same light. For such a neo-Fregean, learning how to *use* a predicate *is* learning how to attach it to subjects in complete statements, and there is no separate rule to be learned about the symbolic significance of the alleged relation of juxtaposition. For such a philosopher, a question about the relationship between subject and predicate of a statement is as otiose as a question about the relationship between a hand and the object it points at. Specification of the hand and the object indicated defines the gesture, without need for further specification; similarly, choice of a subject and an appropriate predicate uniquely determines a statement, without need for a further choice of a relationship between them.

Once again, we have a dispute which is inconclusive and threatens to be undecidable. What turns on the outcome? What difference will it make whether or not we recognize a characterizing relation? Well, a relation is conceived to hold between *terms*, so the traditional recognition of the copula goes with a classification of properties as special kinds of *things*. Admission of a characterizing relation allows questions to be asked about properties, so that predicates or their surrogates are sometimes permitted to function as subjects. The opposite point of view, that treats properties and their representing predicates as incomplete, forbids questions and assertions to be made about properties as subjects. The dispute about the copula, trifling as it may seem at first sight, is a focus of contention for full-blown alternative grammars.

IV

I pass on now to consider whether the ancient distinction between subject and predicate should be regarded as an essential feature of language that belongs to universal grammar.

How do we identify the subject and predicate of a given statement? A contemporary answers as follows: 'A predicate is an expression that gives us an assertion about something if we attach it to another expression that stands for what we are making the assertion about.'[1]

In order to apply this prescription to a particular instance, we have first to determine what a given assertion is 'about'. Should the assertion contain an expression standing for what the assertion is about, that expression will be the subject. According to the prescription, the remainder of the sentence will be the attached predicate.

This works well when applied to such a sentence as 'Peter is happy', in which there is reference to a person. It is natural to say that a statement using that sentence is about Peter; hence the word 'Peter' may be said to be a subject standing for Peter, and the remainder of the sentence, the expression, 'is happy', counts as the predicate.

But even in this paradigm case of the application of the distinction, an objection can be lodged. It may be plausibly argued that the statement in question is about happiness, no less than about Peter: the assertion, some would say, can be understood as a claim that happiness is instantiated in Peter. If it is per-

---

[1] P. T. Geach, *Mind*, Vol. LIX (1950), pp. 461–2.

missible to say that the word 'happy' stands for happiness, the rule we have adopted would lead us to say that 'happy' is the subject and 'Peter is' the predicate. The philosopher who formulated the rule I have cited would want to reject this inference.

Or, take the case of the statement, 'Happiness is desired by all men'. Here, it is still more plausible to say that the statement is about happiness, referred to by the word 'happiness'. But the author of our rule refuses to recognize 'happiness' as a subject, preferring to construe the sentence in question as being composed of two predicates.

I do not wish to suggest that a preference for this mode of analysis is wilful or capricious; yet I believe there is no rational method for persuading somebody who rejects it. The dispute, like others already reported in this paper, can be resolved only by fiat. It is an error to suppose that we can determine what a statement is 'about' by inspection of some extra-linguistic realm. No amount of observation or reflexion about non-verbal 'things' will show whether a given statement is about a person or about a quality. The answer must be sought in language itself.

We know that the statement 'Peter is happy' is about Peter, because we recognize 'Peter' as a proper name, without knowing whether there is such a person as Peter. The starting-point of the intended philosophical distinction between subject and predicate is conventional grammar, relying only upon formal criteria. But conventional grammar leaves us in the lurch as soon as we are asked to decide whether a statement using the word 'happiness' is 'really' about happiness.

v

I propose now to test the thesis of the universality of the subject-predicate form by applying it to the report of a move in chess. The case may be thought to have special peculiarities, but will serve to reveal the chief points in dispute.

A full verbal report of a chess move, such as might be found in nineteenth-century manuals, has the form, 'The King's pawn moved to the King's fourth square'. Here, there is no difficulty in identifying the grammatical subject, i.e. the expression, 'The King's pawn'. Hence, the remainder of the formula, the expression, 'moved to the King's fourth square', must be the predicate, and the report can be certified as being of the subject-predicate form.

Nowadays, English-speaking chess players commonly use the concise notation, '$P-K4$'. Reading this as a conventional abbreviation of the full English sentence previously cited, it is easy enough to discern a subject and a predicate in this fragment of symbolism: we might say that in '$P-K4$' the 'P' is the subject and the rest of the formula the predicate.

But other and equally adequate notations are in common use. In the so-called 'continental notation', a move is specified by giving only co-ordinates of the initial and terminal squares; thus the move already cited would be reported as '$e2-e4$'. In this version, there is no component homologous with the subject recognized in the other form of report. A last-ditch defender of the omnipresence of the subject-predicate form might still argue that in the formula '$e2-e4$' the first complex symbol, '$e2$', indirectly specifies the chessman moved. However, it would be equally correct to treat the initial symbol, 'P', of the English notation as being 'really' an indirect specification of the square from which the move started. Somebody familiar only with the continental notation can treat the English notations as having the square-to-square structure of his own paradigm; while a devotee of the English notation can treat the alternative symbolism as a disguised version of his own.

It becomes progressively harder to perceive the subject-predicate form in every conceivable chess notation as alternative notations are imagined. A given chess move might be represented by drawing a line on a square divided into 64 compartments, or by a set of two integers between 1 and 64, or by a single number less than 4096 ($= 64^2$), or by Morse code, or by suitably modulated electrical waves. Some of these possibilities might be handled by human beings, others might perhaps serve only to inform chess-playing computers; but all alike would have the requisite structure for representing every possible move in a game of chess. All of them, to use Wittgenstein's word, would have the same 'multiplicity'.[1] Now a determination to view all of these equivalent symbolic forms as having the subject-predicate structure would be quixotic in the extreme. Absurd loyalty to a preconception about logical form would be needed in order to view a line

[1] *Loc. cit.*, 4.04.

drawn on a chessboard as having a subject and a predicate. Long before this point was reached, most of us would prefer to abandon the dogma of the omnipresence of subject-predicate form.

The example may prepare us to expect similar conclusions about languages that are not restricted to the representation of an invented game. We are told, on good authority, that 'Chinese which is fully equipped for every sort of civilized communication, makes no use of the formal categories devised for the Indo-European languages'.[1] Another writer, after surveying the variety of grammars known to contemporary linguists, concludes that 'No grammatical concept seems to be *per se* sacred or universal, far less indispensable'.[2] In some languages, we are told, 'An isolated word is a sentence; a sequence of such sentence words is like a compound sentence . . . [and] the terms verb and noun in such a language are meaningless'.[3] If Whorf was right, the hope of finding the subject-predicate distinction exemplified in such 'polysynthetic' languages is doomed to frustration. For that distinction presupposes a way of distinguishing between nouns and other parts of speech. Yet 'polysynthetic' languages may be just as rich in fact-stating resources as our own relatively analytical English. I conclude that the subject-predicate distinction, valuable as it may be for analysing Indo-European languages, ought to find no place in a universal philosophical grammar.

VI

The three examples I have discussed sufficiently illustrate the difficulties that beset any serious effort to construct a universal grammar. We are now in a position to diagnose the source of these difficulties. In each case, we were assuming that the logical structure of certain statements ('Stop', 'Go', 'Peter is happy') must be identical with the structure of the situations or states-of-affairs represented. The search for what is presumed to be invariant in all statements having the same meaning, that is to say, those representing the same state of affairs, is a search for some way of presenting the common logical structure. In order to do this, we must be able to do at least the following: decide which

[1] W. J. Entwistle, *Aspects of Language*, p. 162.
[2] Mario Pei, *The Story of Language*, p. 129.
[3] B. L. Whorf, *Language, Thought and Reality*, pp. 98–9.

perceptible features of words or other signs can be treated as non-significant, recognize one and the same symbol behind its alternative manifestations (that is to say, recognize when signs mean the same thing), and assign different symbols to the same logical category or type, on the basis of identity of function. In order for the procedure to provide any ground for ontological inference, such recognition, individuation and classification of symbols must be performed without recourse to ontological premises, or to methods assuming the truth of such premises.

The chief difficulty arose from the need to count non-linguistic contextual features of statements as significant. So long as we confine ourselves to analysis of conventional verbal statements, in isolation from their settings, traditional grammar provides us with means of segmentation and classification that can subsequently be elaborated and refined in the service of philosophical insight. There is no question but that 'Stop' and 'Go' are different words; 'Peter' is clearly a noun and a grammatical subject in 'Peter is happy'. But immediately we recognize the non-verbal setting in which the words are pronounced as significant, we face formidable difficulties in identifying, distinguishing, counting and classifying the symbols that interest us. Are the situations in which a car is at rest and in motion to count as the same or as different? Are the actions of stopping and starting a car the same or different? These are not questions to be answered by looking at cars or their drivers. They are questions of philosophical grammar for which there are no decision procedures. We have criteria for deciding whether words are to be treated as the same or different; for rules to this end (superficial rules of grammar) are part of the language we speak and understand. But there are no adequate criteria for deciding whether contextual situations are to be counted as the same or different, for the purpose of determining identities and differences of meaning. It might be thought that we ought to examine the semantical *rules* governing the sounds and written marks in question. But this manœuvre achieves nothing. Were we assured that the rule governing 'Stop' must count as different from the rule governing 'Go', we should be entitled to conclude that there were indeed *two* symbols in question. But since the word 'Stop' and 'Go' or their synonyms will occur in the expressions of those semantical rules, individuation of the rules will raise the same troublesome questions. Nor will the case be altered by speaking about 'uses' instead of about 'rules'. For the purposes of philosophical grammar, descriptions in terms of 'symbols', 'rules' and 'uses' are mutually equivalent and generate the same problems. We can choose as we please, and our decisions about the points of philosophical grammar at issue will be determined by the choices we have made, not by any imposed analysis of the statements inspected.

Similarly in our illustrations of the copula and the subject-predicate form. At the level of surface grammar, there are crude criteria for deciding whether an expression is expendable without loss of meaning. But when we try to push on to a would-be 'deeper' level of analysis, we are embarrassed again by lack of criteria. Is the *relation* between 'Peter' and 'happy' 'really' significant? Is there 'really' a relationship there at all? It all depends upon how you choose to look at the statement. Nothing imposes an answer except the determination of the philosophical analyst to adhere to one mode of logical parsing rather than another. Seen through one pair of grammatical spectacles, there plainly is a significant relation of juxtaposition between subject and predicate; but we can wear another pair of lenses, and see nothing but subject and predicate, 'hanging in one another like the links of a chain'.

When we recognize that the fact-stating functions of language can be adequately performed by non-verbal symbolisms, the problems of detecting invariant logical structure become insuperable. If we represent states of affairs by configurations of physical objects, the task of discerning logical structure demands a capacity to determine the logical structure of certain physical facts. But if we can ever do this, we don't need the detour via language. If we can analyse a fact, we can in principle discover the logical structure of reality without prior recourse to language. On the other hand, if we face some obstacle of principle in dissecting reality, we shall meet the very same difficulties in trying to dissect language. For language, though it represents reality, is also a part of reality.

VII

In the light of the foregoing considerations, the prospects for a universal philosophical grammar seem most unpromising. I

believe the hope of finding *the* essential grammar to be as illusory
as that of finding the single true co-ordinate system for the
representation of space. We can pass from one systematic mode of
spatial representation to another by means of rules for transforming co-ordinates, and we can pass from one language to
another having the same fact-stating resources by means of rules
of translation. But rules for transformation of co-ordinates yield
no information about space; and translation rules for sets of
languages tell us nothing about the ultimate nature of reality.

It might perhaps be said that common logical structure is
shown in an invariant web of entailment relations. It is certainly
part of our concept of synonymity that statements of the same
meaning shall have parallel consequences: if one statement has
an entailment that is not synonymous with some entailment of a
second statement, that proves that the two original statements
have different meanings. To put the matter differently, we shall
not regard two languages as having the same fact-stating resources
unless we can trace corresponding patterns of transformation rules
in both. But we shall never arrive at a philosophical grammar
by this road: correspondence of sets of entailments is compatible
with the widest divergences of morphology and of syntax.

If we abandon the vain hope of finding the true philosophical
grammar, we may still hope to use its by-products. Schoolroom
grammar is coarse-grained for philosophical purposes, and the
refinements of latter-day linguists are impressive without being
philosophically useful. We shall do well to continue classifying
words and expressions according to their uses and functions,
inventing whatever labels will help us to remember our discoveries. It is not my intention to deprecate the received grammatical categories of 'quality', 'relation', 'function', 'class' and
the rest, or the finer classifications invented by contemporaries. I
would urge, however, that our attitude to such grammatical sieves
should be pragmatic. If reality leaves us free to choose our
grammars as convenience and utility dictate, we shall properly
regard them as speculative instruments to be sharpened, improved,
and, where necessary, discarded when they have served their
turn.

To anybody who still feels that there *must* be an identity of
logical form between language and reality, I can only plead that
the conception of language as a mirror of reality is radically

mistaken. We find out soon enough that the universe is not capricious: the child who learns that fire burns and knife-edges cut knows that there are inexorable limits set upon his desires. Language must conform to the discovered regularities of experience. But in order to do so, it is enough that it should be apt for the expression of everything that is or might be the case. To be content with less would be to be satisfied to be inarticulate; to ask for more is to desire the impossible. No roads lead from grammar to metaphysics.

CHAPTER VIII

THE APPEAL TO ORDINARY LANGUAGE[1]

P. L. Heath

Professor of Philosophy at The University of Virginia

Belief in the philosophic efficacy of ordinary language is a recurrent habit in British Philosophy, and can be regarded, according to taste, as a redeeming virtue or a besetting vice. Whichever view we take, there is no denying the importance of the matter; for if the belief is correct it provides a very simple way of disposing of immense quantities of metaphysical and other argument, without the smallest trouble or exertion; whereas if it is wrong, then preoccupation with it is largely a waste of time and ought not to be taken seriously. This paper argues for the latter alternative; but it only attempts to rebut the appeal to ordinary language as a (or the) method of doing philosophy, and is not itself intended to endorse any particular conception of the true subject-matter of philosophy or of the proper way to pursue it. That it is primarily a question of method can be seen from this, that though, traditionally, the appeal has been used to counter the claims of metaphysicians of all persuasions, its present revival is at least partly directed against theories, such as Analysis and Phenomenalism, which are not at all metaphysical, at least in intention. No doubt there are other reasons for this particular dispute, but I have no concern with them here; nor am I anxious to express disagreement (or agreement) with the general opinions of any of the authors referred to in what follows; I simply try to show that some of the arguments that they use are not good arguments, that they depend on assumptions which are not reasonable, and that attempts to put forward a studied colloquialism as the sole and sufficient touchstone of philosophical propriety have therefore little to recommend them.

The thesis I have in mind to criticize can be formulated somewhat as follows: 'Philosophical problems are generally, if not always, due to unnoticed or unadvertised departures from

[1] A paper read at a meeting of the Scots Philosophical Club, Aberdeen, May 1951 and published in *The Philosophical Quarterly*, January 1952.

Standard English, and are to be solved, or cured, as the case may be, by pointing out the normal usage of the words employed and the normal grammatical form of the sentences in which they appear. For ordinary language is correct language.' I hope this is reasonably fair. The reference to 'Standard English' comes from the introduction to a recent *réchauffé* of essays on this theme,[1] and suggests the passing remark that many writers who have descanted upon it, there and elsewhere, seem to take little account of the existence of other languages whose structure and idiom are very different from English (Standard or otherwise), but which seem to be equally, if not more, capable of engendering metaphysical confusion. Whether we are to conclude from this that philosophical theories are relative to the languages in which they are enunciated, is by no means clear. There is little to be said for such a view, and much against it, but I do not intend to say it here.[2]

A second, and rather less trivial point is that the expression 'Standard English' suggests that the uses of the language are uniform and well-established. Though little or nothing has been done to verify this empirically, writers who appeal to Standard English display a surprising confidence and authority in pronouncing upon the proper, normal, literal, primary, true, correct, or dominant meanings of words and phrases. It is surprising, because if you look up what the linguists have to say on the subject,[3] you find that this strictly normative conception of vocabulary and grammar is completely out of date, and has been for centuries. To the vast majority of modern linguists, 'Standard English' is no more than a trade-label annexed to a particular dialect, and has no special status or authority, apart from the (irrelevant) social approval accorded to those who happen to speak it. 'Correctness', if it means anything at all, means conformity with the prevailing mode of some specified group; it has no reference to any set of absolute rules, for there are none such. All that the modern grammarian looks for are the prevailing

[1] *Logic and Language*, ed. A. G. N. Flew (Oxford, 1951).

[2] Cf. L. J. Cohen 'Are Philosophical Theses Relative to Language?' *Analysis*, April 1949.

[3] Cf. among many others, L. Bloomfield: *Language* (London, 1935) and O. Jespersen: *The Philosophy of Grammar* (London, 1924). The latter's *Mankind, Nation and Individual* (London, 1946) concedes rather more to the normative view.

patterns and regularities within a language as it is actually used; except where conventional uniformities have been imposed by earlier grammarians, these patterns are mainly due to the natural tendency of speech forms to accommodate themselves to one another, owing to analogies of sound, shape or sense. Save *per accidens* there is no logic in the matter, no privilege, and no permanency. People talk as it suits them—primarily, one imagines, to be understood, and it is the task of the grammarian to describe and classify these activities, not to judge them. Belief to the contrary is merely an obstructive superstition, surviving mainly among schoolmasters and formal logicians, whose excuse, like that of most other Tories, amounts to no more than a vested interest in, or reverence for, the *status quo*. Why it should have been thought to deserve consideration as a philosophical principle, it is by no means easy to imagine.

This is not, of course, meant to imply that there is nothing to be said for ordinary language as a philosophical model; but it does bring out certain weaknesses in the attempt to construe it as a standard. It shows, I fancy, that the familiar and overworked analogy between logical and grammatical rules is about due for retirement, and that the fashionable conception of ordinary language as a static field of signs in a fixed or fixable relationship to a rigid structure of concepts and linguistic rules is, to say the least, an hypothesis. It shows also that the attempt to convict perfectly respectable philosophers of illiteracy, or of the perpetration of ungrammatical gibberish, is either naïve or disingenuous; for what is complained of is not lack of grammar, even in the textbook sense, but incoherence or absence of meaning, resulting (it is said), from the juxtaposition of terms which are incapable of being brought into intelligible relation with one another. Such crimes may have been committed, but it cannot possibly be correct to construe them as breaches of grammatical or linguistic 'laws', if these are merely descriptive in character. If recourse be had at this point to the 'logic' of language, we may reply that this notion is itself exceedingly obscure, and that offhand references to the man-in-the-street, John Doe, Bertie Wooster or the *Strand Magazine*, or the retailing of illustrative anecdotes and charades, or, again, appeals to a hitherto undetected 'sense of linguistic propriety' are not really very impressive methods of establishing the 'correct' or 'normal' usage of given words and phrases. So far as they serve any purpose at all, it is the opposite one, of bringing out the variety and fluidity of these usages, and the arbitrary character of any proposal to select and grade them by reference to 'dominance' or 'propriety'. And this is confirmed by the disputes which commonly break out, even among exponents of the method, when attempts at armchair lexicography are made in this way.

It is by no means uncommon for a philosopher, in expounding his views, to make use of academic or technical terms; but in doing so he falls an easy prey to the devices of an opponent who employs the vernacular method. By exposing such technicalities in contrast to more homely expressions it is easy for the latter to make them look absurd, and ultimately meaningless, so that the whole argument in which they occur is compromised or discredited. Thus Mr Toulmin, arguing recently against Ethical Intuitionism,[1] picks on the admittedly hideous expression 'Rational Faculty of Immediate Apprehension'. He then quotes Bertie Wooster, to the effect that 'we Woosters have a fine sense of what is fitting', and goes on to affirm that ' "Rational Faculty of Immediate Apprehension" would make Bertie's jaw drop a mile'. It would indeed. But what does this prove? Nothing whatever, so far as I can see, except that Bertie is a moron, not a moral philosopher, and that we knew anyway. But it *suggests* that since the offending phrase is unknown to (let us waive the point) common sense, it therefore stands for nothing recognizable to common sense; that it is therefore improper, as a description of whatever Bertie was talking about, and so, in the absence of any plausible alternative designatum, meaningless. Now there is no need to deny that the phrase is verbiage, a 'theorist's solemnity' of the first water, and doubtless misleading in its own associations; it is not even necessary to maintain that it *does* stand for anything. All that wants pointing out here is that this alleged meaninglessness does not follow automatically from the fact that the Woosters of this world have never heard of it—nor, for that matter, would anything of consequence follow if they had. Mr Toulmin, needless to say, has other and better arguments than this—indeed I hardly care to accuse him of using it *as* an argument, but it is an easy and common assumption, that because many technical

[1] 'Knowledge of Right and Wrong', in *Proceedings of the Aristotelian Society*, 1949–50.

expressions *are* used vacuously, therefore any sesquipedalian and unfamiliar locution must necessarily fall into the category of nonsense. It is a mistake. And it obscures the fact that technicalities are sometimes very useful.

There is a further temptation, when one is engaged in black-balling a technicality, to use the material instead of the formal mode of speech. This lends an agreeable gusto to the proceedings, but it is apt to alarm people unnecessarily. 'There are no such things as volitions!' seems startling intelligence—until one later finds the author (Professor Ryle, of course) talking unconcernedly about 'efforts of will'.[1] As who should say 'There are no such things as railway accidents!' only to add in a whisper, 'They all occur according to the laws of physics'.

From those who object to a technical term in place of an everyday one, it is no long step to those who cannot abide plain words used in technical or recondite senses. An example of this, and one which is, again, incidental to the main argument, may be found in a recent article by Mr K. E. M. Baier.[2] Referring to the (correct) usage of the word 'assert', he claims, on no less authority than his own, that it implies a doubt as to the truth and/or sincerity of what was said by the person described as asserting it. And 'thus, contrary to a popular view, "asserting something" does not mean the same as "expressing one's views about something" or "contending that something is the case" or, "making an utterance which is capable of being true or false" '. Here again, it is neither necessary nor worth while to argue that 'asserting' *does* mean the same as any of these (though if Mr Baier's interpretation is correct, it is hard to see why anyone should want to use the verb in the first person singular, present tense). The point is simply that if these other usages represent 'a popular view', neither Mr Baier nor anyone else can have any reason for objecting to them. And even if they do not (supposing that 'popular' means 'popular amongst an incapable minority of philosophers'), there is no way of showing them to be positively erroneous; the worst that can be said is that they are 'loose', 'extended', or 'specialized' applications of a vague term in com-

[1] *The Concept of Mind* (London, 1949), ch. iii.
[2] 'Decisions and Descriptions' in *Mind*, LX, 238. For a rather similar case, cf. the controversy over the word 'selves' between Mr J. R. Jones and Mr A. G. N. Flew (*Mind*, LVIII, 229, 231 and LIX, 234).

mon use. Which is to say nothing in the least reprehensible or extraordinary about them.

Now what is at the bottom of all this terminological hyper-aesthesia, and all the whistle-blowing and knuckle-rapping and scolding that goes along with it? Aside from its uses as a technique of controversy, it appears to depend on no more substantial a foundation than the egregious Fido—'Fido' fallacy, newly emerged from the kennel to which it was but recently (and rightly) consigned by Professor Ryle himself; on the one hand we are told that no dog is to have more than one name, and that a plain one; on the other, that once a name has been assigned to a dog it is never to be used, even as a nickname, for any other one. Any departure from this is to be instantly prosecuted as a misuse of language, breach of good grammar or wilful deviation from Standard English; and ignorance of the law is not to be accepted as an excuse.

Within certain limits this programme is a perfectly rational one; for the application of logic to discourse it is, indeed, essential that the terms should be well defined and univocal in their reference, and so far as the practice of philosophy depends upon logical procedures a similar exactness is, in principle, desirable. Where this theory goes entirely off the rails is in supposing that the casual and irregular speech-habits of everyday intercourse are somehow able to furnish unique and authoritative criteria for the interpretation of terms in common use amongst philosphers. It is just because they do *not* do this, that so many philosophers have felt obliged to employ technical terms and neologisms, even where this has made it difficult for other people to understand what they were talking about. The point of such philosophical rigmaroles is the same as that of legal rigmaroles. Both may look to be unintelligible, and often needlessly so, but properly handled they do enable something precise and testable to be said.[1] The danger, in both cases, is the creation of fictions; the advantage, that 'correctness' does mean something definite, in relation to the self-made rules and definitions adopted; it is not, of course, reasonable to complain of departures from the ordinary use of terms, since this is done deliberately, and can be judged only according to its adequacy, or necessity, for the purpose in hand.

[1] This point seems to have escaped Mr G. J. Warnock ('Metaphysics in Logic', in *Proceedings of the Aristotelian Society*, 1950–51).

There is a good deal more reason to complain of those who, by *not* using a specialized terminology, muddle themselves and other people quite as effectively as the man who makes his own will. Philosophers cannot avoid technical distinctions, and so if they will not use technical terms, they are obliged to follow the example of Locke and Hume, and press non-technical ones into the same service. This creates more trouble than it is worth, since the fixed and the fluid senses get hopelessly mixed. Look at the ruin which has come, in consequence, upon the word 'idea', and many others. The same thing is already happening with many of the happy colloquialisms launched into currency by Professor Ryle; as their copyright expires and they pass into general circulation, they come to operate as technical jargon-words of a misleadingly informal and concrete kind; misleading, because while it is not only permissible but essential to provide regulations for the correct use of technical terms, it is not justified in the case of non-technical ones, which have to be understood in context. Where the same words are used for both, confusion follows. The writer is apt to persuade himself that he is expounding the true, proper, or correct meaning of the words in question, and the reader gets the impression that he is being given arbitrary and unsought directions on how he ought to use them. The belief in a 'logical geography' of concepts, capable of being accurately mapped out by reference to the ordinary uses of language, with appeals to 'correctness', 'dominance', etc., seems to originate, in part at least, from this desire to use a precise terminology without employing explicitly technical terms; the assumption being that the necessary rules and regulations are *already* embodied in ordinary parlance, requiring only inspection, or the production of a few trivial examples, to make clear what is allowable and what is not.[1]

Granted, as I hope it may be, that there is no general warrant for this assumption, or for the preposterous restrictions upon free speech which its acceptance would entail, it may still be felt unreasonable to maintain that it is impossible to misuse language, and that apart from its technical employment it is subject to no rules at all. To hold that all words are inherently vague, and that grammar represents a merely social adjustment of the otherwise untrammelled possibilities of combination amongst them, is like-

[1] Cf. Baier, art. cit.

wise a paradox, and one which, by threatening to abolish the boundaries of sense and nonsense, merely compels us to redraw, within the postulated flux, the moderately restrictive limits which we do normally observe. So much may, I think, be urged in mitigation of the position lately adopted by Mr Haas,[1] in holding that in what he calls their expressive use, the potential range of meaning of words is infinite. It seems to be more in line with the facts to admit that in practice there *are* restrictions, limits to transgression, even where the use of language is almost purely expressive. But they are *a posteriori*, and cannot be laid down or legislated for in advance, since they depend on which words are used, and the context, verbal *and* social, in which they occur. Thus, in poetry, one may be prepared to tolerate a good deal, but there comes a point at which a line of a poem becomes merely a concatenation of words chosen at random. Similarly, with the more rhapsodic kinds of philosophic prose, there comes a point at which you can get nothing out of the stuff, and begin to suspect that you are being imposed upon. That is the time to start calling upon such epithets as 'meaningless' and 'nonsense'— terms of judgement, be it noted, which are much abused in being applied by rote, and hastily invoked whenever somebody slips on some minor, and usually fictitious, linguistic banana-skin.[2]

Mr Haas's valuable distinction between terminology and expression, between bond and free in the use of language, is, as he admits, an abstract one, since for most purposes it is customary to employ a mixture of the two. Philosophers, in particular, disport themselves mainly in the no-man's-land between these regions of discourse, so that unless there is a declared intention to abide by some particular set of regulations, accusations of impropriety cannot be sustained, except in the grossest cases. There is, admittedly, a sort of common-law stability and exactness attaching to *some* terms in ordinary use, for instance, the names of familiar objects—and to that extent they approximate to the statutory requirements of a terminology. Thus, when

[1] 'On Speaking a Language', in *Proceedings of the Aristotelian Society*, 1950–51; a paper to which my obligations are many and manifest.

[2] One is reminded of the prosaic gentleman (was it Babbage?) who sought to put Tennyson right on the Population Question:
'Every moment dies a man,
Every moment *one and one-sixteenth* is born.'

'Beachcomber' finds it necessary to announce: 'In my article on Milk Production yesterday, for "horse" read "cow" throughout', it is obvious to everybody that there has been a hideous mistake. But philosophers do not commonly drop that kind of brick. *Their* terms, the mental-conduct verbs, for example, belong in a meteorological rather than a geographical setting, and operate within much wider tolerances—*ex officio*, one might say, for if they were uniformly clear and distinct they would have little claim on the notice of philosophers.

Attempts to chart such a region are therefore unusually difficult; in the absence of an established technical vocabulary, they can hardly proceed otherwise than by borrowing the more appropriate informal terms and treating them rigorously. There can be no occasion to complain of this, in principle—but the temptation to father the result upon the man-in-the-street is one which ought to be resisted. Appeals to 'correct' language, in this context, must always be disguised definitions, having no unanimous support from ordinary usage, because such usage is just not sufficiently established to be able to decide what is correct and what is not. The same applies to Professor Ryle's *reductio ad absurdum* method of constructing allegedly impossible locutions to exhibit type-distinctions, and to show up type-mistakes. They are just not sufficiently absurd. Given a terminology, as in the case of the Sense-Datum Theory, it is possible and legitimate to point, as Professor Ryle does, to confusion, incorrectness and self-contradiction in the use made of it, either by its inventors or by those who, in adopting the jargon, commit themselves to the conventions it entails. But to issue general decrees for the governance of a range of expressions in common use is another matter; Mrs Partington's efforts to control the Atlantic would promise well by comparison. For whatever usages be laid down as correct, it is nearly always possible to produce counter-examples of an unimpeachable ordinariness and legitimacy. Nor is it by any means in order, as Mr Hampshire has emphasized,[1] to dismiss these as corruptions introduced by philosophers. For apart from the fact that philosophers have no such influence, baneful or otherwise, upon vulgar parlance, the very fact that these 'illegitimate' locutions have taken root there means that they are part of the standard to which appeal is being made. If it is a corrupted

[1] In his review of *The Concept of Mind* (*Mind*, LIX, 234).

G

standard, such appeals are either valueless or not *bona fide*, since they evidently involve undisclosed principles of selection, namely, the very theory which the favoured locutions are supposed, independently, to endorse. Where, as in Professor Ryle's case, the theory is not, perhaps, one which commends itself as obvious to common sense, it is inevitable that language should let him down in places. To give but one example, he states, in a recent article,[1] that 'it is not easy or difficult to believe things'. It seems fair to reply that this is itself *extremely* difficult to believe. Not that that does anything to refute Professor Ryle's point, that believing, in *his* preferred sense, is dispositional. But it brings out the fact that language recognizes other senses, such as that of assenting, which are equally legitimate, and closely related. Indeed, at the risk of seeming to countenance obscurity for its own sake, I am inclined to think that the whole business of distinguishing 'senses' of words in this connexion is perhaps misguided. Many of them have an almost intentional vagueness and ambiguity of reference, which, if evaporated under analysis, deprives them of their essential content, and leaves the world looking tidier but less recognizable than before. To select one sense as dominant is, as we have seen, to perform covertly a technical delimitation of 'proper' meaning, so as to fit the term in question into a pre-ordained scheme. There is nothing to stop anyone doing this, so long as there is no attempt to palm off the definition as a necessary one—as the only one sanctioned by 'ordinary' or 'correct' usage. Then, I should say, there *is* a legitimate appeal to ordinary language. To those who proclaim that 'We don't say this' or 'We do say that', it is proper to reply: 'Oh yes we do' or 'Yes, but we also say . . .'. General linguistic ordinances can be rebutted by reference to ordinary language; they cannot be safely erected upon it.

My main object, in the foregoing, has been to give reasons for dissenting from the opinion that there are 'correct' forms of language in any sense which is philosophically useful or interesting, and more particularly, to discountenance the idea that 'ordinary language', in the prevailingly vague acceptance of that term, has anything to offer in the way of authoritative guidance in this

[1] 'Feelings', in *The Philosophical Quarterly*, April 1951.

connexion. The discussion has centred on the use and meaning of individual terms, but I have no doubt that similar considerations could be shown to apply in the case of syntactical structure as well. Supposing this is so, what is left of the contention with which we began, namely that philosophical problems, paradoxes and errors in general, all originate at the point of departure from ordinary language? Not very much, perhaps, in so far as most of the specific arguments to this effect start off by assuming that ordinary language *is* the standard of correctness. Even if this be allowed for the moment, such arguments are not particularly convincing. Their chief begetter has been Mr Norman Malcolm,[1] and his views have met with so many criticisms from so many quarters,[2] that it would be tedious to recount their details, and difficult, if not superflous, to add to their number. Mr Malcolm himself has lately declined to defend the earliest statement of his position, though it does not yet appear how far he has actually vacated it *in toto*. In this situation, any criticism of Mr Malcolm's published opinions may well prove to be obsolete; so what follows had best be regarded simply as a retrospect of some points in the earlier stages of the controversy, which seem to bear upon what has been said already.

Mr Malcolm has endeavoured to state the argument from ordinary language in such a way that it can be used against *any* undomesticated utterance on the part of philosophers. In doing so he is, on his own showing, generalizing upon a procedure employed by Professor G. E. Moore in his famous, if somewhat mystifying argument against Scepticism in 'The Defence of Common Sense' and 'Proof of an External World'.[3] Mr Malcolm

[1] 'Moore and Ordinary Language', in *The Philosophy of G. E. Moore* (Evanston, 1942): 'Defending Common Sense', in *The Philosophical Review*, May 1949; and 'Philosophy for Philosophers', *ibid.*, July 1951. The latter appeared after the present paper was written and is not discussed here.

[2] E.g. C. A. Campbell, 'Common-sense Propositions and Philosophical Paradoxes' in *Proceedings of the Aristotelian Society*, 1944–5; Max Black, 'On Speaking with the Vulgar', in *The Philosophical Review*, November 1949; J. L. Cobitz, 'The Appeal to Ordinary Language', in *Analysis*, October 1950; C. D. Rollins, 'Ordinary Language and Procrustean Beds', in *Mind*, LX, 238, April 1951; R. M. Chisholm, 'Philosophy and Ordinary Language', in *The Philosophical Review*, July 1951.

[3] In *Contemporary British Philosophy* (1925), and *Proceedings of the British Academy* (1939).

interprets the notion of ordinary language in such a way as to entail that philosophical statements, however plainly expressed, *must* turn out to be either false, illiterate, futile, or senseless. It is therefore, as he recognizes, an *a priori* proof of our original thesis. The method is as follows: An expression, he says, is an ordinary expression if it has a commonly accepted use—not that it is necessarily in frequent use, but that it is such as *would* be used to describe a certain sort of situation, if it arose. Ordinary language is correct language—that is, a situation is correctly described if it is described in ordinary language, and *not otherwise* (this point is essential to the entire argument). Philosophers' expressions are not ordinary—*ex hypothesi*, for if they were they would be commonplace, without philosophic interest. What is characteristic of such expressions, therefore, is that they 'go against ordinary language'. They allege, for instance, that no line is really straight, that no empirical statements are absolutely certain, and so on. Now if such statements are to be taken as literal and factual, they are either false (i.e. contradict the ordinary statements which do have descriptive use in the situation), or else they are incorrect (i.e. refer to or describe the situation after a fashion, but only by grossly misusing the ordinary terms they employ). If they are not factual, then the only alternatives open to the philosopher who makes them are to admit that they are disguised terminological proposals, or else that they are moonshine. As linguistic proposals they are, to say the least, pointless, since they obliterate distinctions which it would at once be necessary to restore, e.g. between the evidently crooked and the apparently straight; as moonshine they are, of course, negligible anyway. The effect of this is that philosophers who deny the imputation that their statements are meaningless or merely verbal, and who wish to be understood as saying something about facts which is not (as Moore seems to have supposed) just literally and obviously false, are automatically convicting themselves under Section Two. They can only be misusing ordinary language, and talking about what is obvious to everybody in a grotesque and illegitimate way. Indeed, whatever category they ultimately fall into, they get there in the first place by going against ordinary language, thereby implying that its expressions are false, or improper, or self-contradictory; which is itself a false, improper and self-contradictory thing to say.

To see through this argument, it is only necessary to consider how the terms 'ordinary expression' and 'correct' are used in it. What follows, in the first place, from the definition of an ordinary expression as one having an accepted descriptive use? If we take 'expression' here to mean 'sentence', the statement does no more than equate 'ordinary expression' with 'verifiable (or falsifiable) sentence', thereby creating the not very plausible impression that the plain man is a verificationist, and, equally naïvely, that his use of language is invariably descriptive. If under 'expression' we include words and phrases occurring *in* sentences, all we do then is to restrict the 'ordinary' vocabulary to descriptive terms and predicates; but as Mr Malcolm is aware, this will not by itself be sufficient to prevent plain-speaking philosophers (such as Russell) from uttering the sort of sentence he wishes to exclude. For so long as their individual expressions are 'ordinary', and so long as they do not depart from grammatical orthodoxy, there will be nothing extraordinary in the actual sentence as it stands, but only in what it purports to say. So we must conclude that Mr Malcolm really wishes 'ordinary expression' to stand for 'verifiable sentence', i.e. a sentence with a certain sort of *meaning*, not a sentence of any particular linguistic form.

For full correctness, the sentence must also have an accepted use, and this means, I imagine, that it is the sort of sentence which all or most people would make use of when confronted with the situation in question. This, if it is not completely vague, is to introduce the objectionable supposition referred to earlier, that to any thing or class of things, situation or class of situations, there corresponds one, or at most a limited number of assignable formulae appropriate thereto, and equally, that any given expression is predetermined in respect of the range of situations to which it can properly be applied. Needless to say, no method is given for deciding what would or would not be said in any given situation, nor for predicting that a situation could not arise which might justify the use of almost any given expression you please.[1] (I add 'almost', to allow for the case of self-contradictory, or (possibly) type-transgressing expressions—but even about these there are questions to be raised and qualms to be had; for some

[1] Cf. Dr Waismann's stress upon the 'open texture' of empirical concepts; in 'Verifiability', *Proceedings of the Aristotelian Society, Supplementary Volume* XIX, (reprinted in Flew, *op. cit.*).

such expressions, as Mr Malcolm points out, do have accepted uses.) In default of any further explanation, one can only suppose that, here as elsewhere, Mr Malcolm is relying upon his 'sense of linguistic propriety' to tell him what would be an an 'accepted' use, and what not.

However, the main objection to all this is that, despite appearances, we are not being given any information about *language*, as such, at all. No grammatical or other linguistic criterion has been introduced to distinguish sense from nonsense, or philosophical utterances from any other kind: for 'verifiable sentence' is clearly not a grammatical or linguistic category. All that Mr Malcolm shows is that philosophical utterances go against ordinary language in that they do not say exactly what common sense would say; like Professor Moore, he gives the impression that they are intended to *contradict* common sense, but this, as Professor Campbell has pointed out,[1] is a gratuitous assumption, since they may be intended to amplify it, or to place emphasis on points which are commonly neglected, but not commonly denied. Nevertheless, by employing terms such as 'incorrect', 'misuse' and so on to express the way in which such utterances differ, in so far as they appear paradoxical, from commonplace ones, Mr Malcolm contrives to suggest that they violate language in exhibiting grammatical deformities, or an illiterate use of terms. Besides invoking the groundless normative conception of language already referred to, this description is plainly a mere polemical device, whose partiality becomes quite obvious when we consider other cases—poetical expressions, for instance, or statements to the effect that the soul is immortal, or the will free; these are certainly not 'ordinary' in Mr Malcolm's sense, but only the slave of a theory would be equal to describing them as 'incorrect', as 'going against ordinary language', or as 'deviations from Standard English'. The additional equivocation by which Mr Malcolm slides from 'incorrect' to 'senseless' (i.e. having no established descriptive use) is almost too obvious to be worth mention, except to show the parallel with the more inadvertent example provided earlier by Mr Toulmin.

If proof of the essential perversity of Mr Malcolm's procedure be needed, he has himself supplied it, in offering to return this technique upon its own chief inventor. For he has argued that

[1] C. A. Campbell, art. cit.

Professor Moore's insistence upon sticking to the 'ordinary' use of the word 'know', as applied to empirical propositions, is so far from defending this use as to constitute an 'enormous departure' from ordinary language. For when Professor Moore held up his hand to the British Academy and declared that he *knew* it was a hand, and so forth, he was doing so, according to Mr Malcolm, in an artificial and theatrical context, where nobody, least of all Professor Moore, had any real doubts about the matter. (Philosophic doubts which may have been felt on that occasion are not real doubts, and so do not count.) Now since, in Mr Malcolm's opinion, the correct and ordinary use of the word 'know' applies only in situations where there has been a genuine (e.g. perceptual) doubt, with subsequent conviction, after reasons or other evidence shown, it follows that the use of 'know' which Professor Moore was defending was non-ordinary, and therefore as incorrect and senseless as the one he attacked. From so arch an enemy of paradox, this has been too much to bear, and it has rained rejoinders ever since. Mr Malcolm deserves them all; he is hoist with his own petard, for by this argument, *all* use, even of ordinary language, in a philosophical context, would appear to be at least as artificial as Professor Moore's, which did, after all, involve a quasi-descriptive paradigm-situation. Mr Malcolm, who retails a number of anecdotes to illustrate what *he* conceives to be the 'proper' use of 'know', is himself guilty of using it 'incorrectly', since he, no less than Professor Moore, is talking about the *use* of the word, not employing it in a genuine context. Moreover, if, as Mr Malcolm might allow, the type of argument here employed by him against Professor Moore is parallel to that used by Professor Moore himself against the sceptic, the odd conclusion follows, that if Mr Malcolm is right, Professor Moore is wrong; if (as I suspect), he is wrong, then Professor Moore is still wrong—for they use the same argument. Contrariwise, if Professor Moore is right, Mr. Malcolm must be wrong in denying it, whereas if Professor Moore is wrong, Mr Malcolm must again be wrong, for his argument is certainly no better than Professor Moore's. What this proves, I do not profess to know, unless it be that those who appeal to ordinary language are likely to perish by it in the long run.

A final disclaimer: in railing thus against the prophets of a new language, and care in its use, are not of the utmost importance in philosophy. More, I should agree that the many obscure pressures and obstacles which one encounters in everyday commerce with language are undeniable, interesting, and possibly significant. My point is merely that, failing a systematic study of these peculiarities, there is no profit in treating them as a campaign-platform in the propagation of some philosophical theory. Such a study would be most unlikely to endorse any one theory beyond all others as the 'natural metaphysic'—or anti-metaphysic, embodied in language; and it certainly should not be undertaken with that idea in mind.

CHAPTER IX

MISLEADING ANALYSES[1]

Errol E. Harris
Professor of Philosophy, Connecticut College

The view that 'the sole and whole function of philosophy' is 'the detection of the sources in linguistic idioms of recurrent misconstructions and absurd theories' has, in the past twenty years, become widespread among practising philosophers in England. The absurd theories are, of course, metaphysical, for among these philosophers absurdity has come to be regarded more or less as the hallmark of metaphysics. And as the scope of philosophical investigation is limited to linguistic analysis, any other sort of philosophy is classed as metaphysics, so that, as the movement has advanced and linguistic analysis has been more widely practised, every other sort of philosophy has become discredited. In the words of Mr Antony Flew, 'enterprises of metaphysical construction have seemed less and less practicable, less and less respectable. For anyone who has seen how much muddle and perplexity, how much paradox and absurdity, has already been traced back to its tainted sources in misleading idiom, or in unexplained and unnoticed distortions of standard English, must suspect that any further metaphysical construction which he might be tempted to erect would soon meet with a similar humiliating and embarrassing débâcle under the assaults of the new "logic and critic".'[2]

One is led to reflect that English is not the only language in which metaphysics has been known to flourish, and it is surely remarkable that the uncritical use of languages differing widely in idiom and standard forms should have given rise to the same absurdities and to similar metaphysical theories, or that metaphysical doctrines propounded in one language should so frequently appear plausible in another. Further, if the temptation to erect metaphysical constructions results from a conviction which has not been shaken by such linguistic analysis as has already been undertaken, the philosopher who is deterred from

[1] *The Philosophical Quarterly*, October 1953.
[2] *Logic and Language* (Oxford, 1952), p. 9.

G*

it by fear of humiliation under the attacks of the new criticism is surely lacking both in moral courage and in intellectual integrity. If and in so far as we really do, as a result of our *façons de parler*, commit the sort of errors alleged and fall into the sort of muddles exhibited, linguistic analysis is performing a valuable and indeed a necessary service. If its method is sound and does not itself suffer from errors and confusions, we may pursue it with confidence. But are these conditions fulfilled? So devastating have the effects of the new 'logic and critic' upon the old type of philosophizing seemed to be (even though, for the most part, the actually expounded theories of the older philosophers have not been directly subjected to it) that the new method has itself largely escaped criticism. Yet the more effective it is, the more important it is that it should not be accepted lightly or without critical examination.

In order to avoid the accusation of basing my criticism upon assumptions which the exponents of the new method would reject, I shall confine myself to particular examples of it and shall choose for this purpose some of the papers re-published in Mr Flew's book, *Logic and Language*, noting his warning that his authors do not all claim to be in mutual agreement and that many of them would not today stand by all they have written in these essays. This will not matter so long as we criticize each on its own merits. For if subsequent changes in the authors' opinions are such as to correct errors and nullify criticism, they are to be welcomed (and should be published); but if they do not so modify the position as to make the criticism inapplicable, they do not affect the issue. Moreover, it would be readily admitted that all these essays have in common the claim to reveal ways in which linguistic forms can mislead us into propounding metaphysical doctrines which are disreputable, and in so far as any criticism affects this claim it touches them all.

I. Analysis of Misleading Expressions

I shall begin with what Professor Ryle calls 'systematically misleading expressions', taking them in the order in which he deals with them. First, quasi-ontological statements, such as 'God exists', 'Satan does not exist', 'Mr Pickwick is a fiction or figment', 'Mr Baldwin is a genuine entity', are said to be systematically misleading because they do not assert or deny genuine characters of genuine subjects or record genuine facts, though they resemble in grammatical form statements which do (such as 'Capone is not a philosopher'). ' ". . . is an existent", ". . . is an entity" are only bogus predicates, and that of which (in grammar) they are asserted is only a bogus subject.'[1]

How then do we distinguish genuine subjects? Merely by the fact that we assert of them genuine predicates? If so, and if 'real', 'existent', and the like, are not genuine predicates, only that is a genuine subject of which reality, existence, or genuine being is *not* asserted. The case of Mr Baldwin is significant (to be more up to date let us take Mr Churchill). If I say 'Mr Churchill is a famous person', he is a genuine subject; but if I say 'Mr Churchill is a genuine entity', he ceases to be one. But 'genuine subject', if it means anything, means 'genuine entity'. Professor Ryle's protest is against the multiplication of bogus entities by the hypostatization of bogus subjects,[2] so by genuine subjects he must mean to refer to genuine entities. It would seem, therefore, that a genuine entity is only genuine when it is not stated to be so and becomes bogus as soon as it is identified as a genuine existent. But this is absurd.

This conclusion cannot be avoided by saying that, in the propositions quoted above, it is not Mr Churchill himself who is either a genuine or a bogus subject, but the name 'Mr Churchill', for in neither case is the assertion made of the name, but, in both, of the person. But we are told that this is not so, that 'Mr Churchill is a genuine entity' is not about Mr Churchill. But it is about something, for we are also explicitly warned that it is 'not only significant but true', that it does not mislead its naïve user and *need* not mislead the philosopher. Accordingly, it may be paraphrased somewhat like this: 'There is somebody called Mr Churchill.' But this is only an oblique way of saying that somebody (who is called Mr Churchill) is a genuine entity, since that is the whole force of the phrase, 'there is'. The somebody in question is no other than Mr Churchill and it must, therefore, be he who is the logical subject of the proposition. If the statement that he is a genuine entity were not about Mr Churchill, we could not truly assert real predicates of him, for the ascription of real characters to a bogus entity must result in a false statement. But

[1] *Logic and Language* (Oxford, 1952), p. 17.   [2] Cf. *ibid.*, p. 32.

as we can ascribe real characters to Mr Churchill, it must be about Mr Churchill that we say he is a real entity, just as it is about him that we say he (and not merely his name) is a genuine logical subject whenever we predicate such characters of him.

The basis of any analysis like that made by Professor Ryle is that we can truly ascribe genuine characters to certain objects in propositions with genuine logical subjects and predicates. These are the standards for recognizing genuineness in subjects and predicates. And, if this be so, the true ascription of genuine being or reality to some objects must be possible, for unless it were there would be neither genuine subjects nor genuine predicates— and so no bogus ones either. The condition of the distinction between genuine and bogus subjects is the possibility of predicating reality, or existence, or genuine being, of certain subjects. It is, therefore, ridiculous to maintain that such predication is bogus. It consequently transpires that the analysis of existence-propositions itself presupposes the logical priority to all genuine subject-predicate statements of existence-propositions, and it is therefore seriously misleading to allege that, because existence predicates are not characters, their subjects are not genuine subjects.

Now let us consider 'Mr Pickwick is a fiction'. This statement also is said not to be about Mr Pickwick—for if it is true there is no such person for it to be about. Then what am I denying when I say that Mr Pickwick is not a real person? It cannot be that I am denying that 'Mr Pickwick' is a proper name, for grammatically it certainly is, and if in logic proper names are by definition restricted to actually existing entities (which are not for that reason bogus), it may well be false that nobody is or ever has been called Pickwick, and it is certainly not *that* which I am asserting when I say that Dickens's Mr Pickwick is a fiction. Am I then saying: 'There was and is nobody called Mr Pickwick identical with the character of that name in Dickens's novel?' No doubt I am, but this statement is not about 'nobody', nor (despite what Professor Ryle says) about Dickens, nor primarily about his novel, but about a certain character in the novel, namely, Mr Pickwick.

But it is alleged that, if we say this, we may systematically mislead some philosopher into thinking that a fiction is some curious kind of entity. Yet, if 'entity' means 'existent' that is what, in the statement, 'Mr Pickwick is a fiction', is explicitly being denied, and it must surely be a queer sort of wisdom which is beloved by the philosopher who is misled by not-p to believe p. 'The world', says Ryle, 'does not contain fictions in the way in which it contains statesmen.' True indeed, and that is why I say, and what is presupposed when I say, that Mr Pickwick is a fiction. If, then, I understand the statement in the least I cannot be misled into believing that the world contains fictions in the same way as it contains statesmen (and other things which are not fictions). And I submit that no sane person ever has believed any such thing. Whether the world contains fictions in some other way is a different question. If it did not, I suppose that there could be no novels.

It is clear, then, that ontological statements do not systematically mislead, for either they assert what must be presupposed if any genuine predicates are to be asserted of any genuine subjects, or else they deny of fictions and other nonentities that they are among the things contained in the world in the way in which actually existing things are contained in it. Only the insane or the hopelessly stupid could both understand them and believe that they deny what they assert or assert what they deny. And with all this Professor Ryle is substantially in agreement for he says that these statements are not only significant but true and that they do not mislead those who use and understand them, nor do I believe that he underestimates the intelligence either of his colleagues or of his predecessors. It is, therefore, difficult to understand who the philosophers may be that are so apt to be misled by innocent statements. On the other hand, we should be gravely misled if we believed 'that those metaphysical philosophers are the greatest sinners who, as if they were saying something of importance, make "Reality" or "Being" the subject of their propositions, or "real" the predicate', because these philosophers are attending to and are drawing our attention to just what makes any subject or any predicate a genuine one.

The analysis of 'quasi-Platonic' statements is in like case. Philosophers (again it is not stated which) are said to take such statements as 'Unpunctuality is reprehensible' or 'Virtue is its own reward' to be 'precisely analogous' to statements like 'Jones merits reproof' or 'Smith has given himself a prize', and accordingly to believe that 'universals' are 'objects in the way that Mt. Everest is an object'. But no philosopher has ever thought anything of the kind. No sane person who at all understands the difference between universals and particulars could think that one was the same as the other. No sane person ever imagines that Unpunctuality or Virtue is a person like Jones or Smith, even though some allegorists and artists have so depicted them. If we are not apt to be misled by allegories, why should we be by the grammar of ordinary language? There is no 'fraudulent pretence' in statements about universals that they are statements about particulars. This is precisely why the plain man is not deceived by them and philosophers in the past have been so far from being deceived that the precise nature of the difference between universals and particulars has occupied much of their thought. Plato, in particular, was concerned with this difference (was, perhaps, the first to see its importance), and so great was his anxiety that the two should not be confused that he committed the error of assigning 'ideas' to an altogether separate world of their own. But even that he did metaphorically, in a series of confessedly allegorical parables. Every serious discussion of the subject in the Dialogues is designed to emphasize the utter disparity between 'ideas' and particular, sensible things and there is nothing whatever in Plato's manner of speaking and of arguing about the 'ideas' to lead us to think that he assumed, even unconsciously, that because so-called general words can be made subjects in sentences they therefore denote particular objects. And there is no sort of object like a particular which is not a particular. It is true that there are defects in the Theory of Ideas which led Plato into serious difficulties (of which he was not entirely unaware), but what misled him was not linguistic idiom but the tendency to identify the universal with the common property of a class.

Other expressions which are recommended to our attention as systematically misleading are non-referential 'the'-phrases of various kinds. I shall confine my discussion to the three kinds which seem to give rise to the most serious philosophical errors.

(i) Spatio-temporal 'the'-phrases, such as 'the top of the tree', 'the centre of the bush', are said to mislead us into thinking that they refer to a material part of the tree or the bush, whereas they indicate no more than relative position. Hence other such phrases—'the region occupied by x', 'the path followed by y', 'the moment or date at which z happened'—become the source of certain unspecified 'Cartesian and perhaps Newtonian blunders about Space and Time'. In 'the top of the tree' there is some ambiguity, for in common parlance 'the top' is sometimes used to refer to a part of the tree[1] and sometimes merely to a relative position. But this cannot be said of 'the region occupied by' or 'the moment at which'. We are not normally tempted to think that these are material things or parts of them. When the phrase is ambiguous and there is a genuine sense in which it is used referentially, we can avoid error by clearly distinguishing the different usages. If we fail to do so we shall be misled but not *systematically* misled. But where there is no ambiguity it is difficult to see what sort of error could arise; for who would ever imagine that (except in special cases) 'the region occupied by x' referred to a tract of country, or 'the path followed by y' to some kind of roadway? It would be as apt to allege that it is a real garden path up which we are being led when it is suggested that Descartes or Newton made errors of this sort.

It is, of course, quite another matter to assert that Newton or Descartes may have paid too much attention, in framing their theories, to the perceptual appearance of material things and to recommend a more Leibnizian doctrine which would treat that appearance as merely phenomenal though founded upon actual relations between immaterial substances. But this is by no means what the linguistic analyst wishes to do, and what he is doing is misleading—perhaps systematically misleading.

(ii) Phrases like 'the thought of . . .', 'the idea of . . .', are held to have misled philosophers into believing in the existence of such entities as 'thoughts', 'ideas', 'conceptions' and 'judgements', all of which, like the members of 'the Lockean demonology' are condemned as bogus. These 'the'-phrases can be paraphrased into others which are not supposed to suggest any such entities. 'Jones hates the thought of going to hospital' becomes 'Jones is distressed whenever he thinks of what he will undergo if he goes to hospital'; 'the idea of having a holiday has just occurred to me' becomes 'I have just been thinking that I might take a holiday'. But presumably when Jones thinks of what he will undergo and when I think that I might take a holiday, we both

---

[1] As when we speak of cutting off the top of (or 'topping') a tree, and in 'Hush-a-bye baby in the tree-top'.

have something before our minds as what we are thinking about. It is to these somethings that philosophers have referred by the words 'ideas', 'thoughts', 'judgements', and the like, and the objects of our thought are not necessarily always bogus entities any more than the objects of perception. Locke may well have been mistaken in thinking that such objects were always mental images or something like them, but what misled him was not language but faulty introspection.

(iii) Some philosophers, it is alleged, falsely imagine that 'the meaning of x' refers to 'a queer new entity'—presumably neither x nor what x means, but something other than these. But whatever could mislead any reasonable person to think any such thing? 'The meaning of x' refers to precisely what 'x' refers to, and nobody ever would or ever has thought otherwise. Meanings, as such, therefore, may quite legitimately occupy the minds of philosophers who try to understand just what is involved when any symbol, like x, refers us to something else—in fact, it is usually held that this is the proper subject of Semantics. In the course of this study it would be quite legitimate to inquire whether, for x to have a meaning, something or other must be 'subjectively' entertained by the person for whom it has that meaning, and whether there must necessarily exist some 'objective' thing to which it refers. So that it may not be at all 'pointless to discuss whether word-meanings are subjective or objective', so long as we understand what we are about.

Accordingly, there is, after all, nothing specially seductive about these phrases and the danger of being misled by them is a mere bogey. But this bogey has been dangerously used to discredit philosophers who have made important contributions to their subject, by the pretence that they have been misled and have made blunders in ways which they have never dreamed of. Philosophers make errors enough, and important ones too, which it is vital to discover and expose, but this makes it all the more necessary not to be led astray by a hunt for imaginary sins.

II. Treatment of Time-Puzzles

Professor Findlay states with admirable lucidity many of the familiar problems about time,[1] and it will not be necessary to

---

[1] *Logic and Language*, pp. 44, 48–9, and 51.

re-state them here. I shall deal with his treatment of only two of them which really underlie the rest. The first is the consequence of the infinite divisibility of the continuum: How can events which take time be made up of instants which do not? The second is the problem of understanding the passage of time: How can what is now present fade away into the past, what is now future emerge into the present, so that what is now true becomes false with the passage of time, and what is now false becomes true?

Professor Findlay says that these puzzles arise 'not because there is anything genuinely problematic in our experience, but because the ways in which we speak of that experience are lacking in harmony or otherwise unsatisfactory'.[1] They can, therefore, be avoided by applying linguistic remedies. It is, however, not difficult to show that the suggested remedies do not remove the problems. And this is not surprising if, as I maintain, it is not in language that these problems have their source.

(i) The demand for consistency in the use of 'now' and 'present', if pressed to an extreme, results in the admission that 'the present' has no duration; yet all events must occur in some present (or 'now') and it is only through the present that future events can be related to those of the past. Accordingly, we conclude that all events must be made up of successive 'nows', none of which has any duration, and the question arises, How can events which take time be made up of 'presents' or 'nows' which do not? The suggested remedy is to realize that the facts themselves give us no trouble—'the facts are there', writes Findlay, 'we can see and show them, and it is for us to talk of them in ways which will neither perplex nor embarrass us'.[2] Moreover, we do not ordinarily use the words 'now' and 'present' with the extreme strictness the demand for which creates the problem. All we need do, therefore, is decide how we shall use them and to say of very brief events either that they take no time and then 'simply rule that events which take time *are* made up of events which take no time',[3] or that they are short time-lapses which cannot be further divided.

But will these decisions really remove the problem? Is this way of talking one which will neither perplex nor embarrass? We are exhorted by Findlay to avoid misleading pictures, but how is

---

[1] *Logic and Language*, p. 39.   [2] *Ibid.*, p. 46.
[3] *Ibid.*, p. 47.

this to be done? If we are to rule that an event which takes time is made up of events which take none, we must assume either that there is a lapse between the timeless events, or that there is not. If there is no lapse, then it takes no time to pass from one timeless event to the next and it will be impossible to understand how events which take time can be so constituted. If, on the other hand, there is a lapse between timeless events, that lapse will itself be made up of events which take no time. Between each of these there will be a lapse similarly made up of timeless instants, and again between each of these. So we should have our infinite regress and should still fail to 'picture' the way in which timeless events could add up to make those which filled some duration. But if we cannot understand how this comes about, how are we to understand the idiom by which we speak of the facts? The idiom, in fact, conflicts with our experience and could only cause perplexity and embarrassment to those who make the effort to understand what they are talking about.

Alternatively, if we decide to say that the present includes an indivisible brief period of time, are we to say also that between one 'present' and the next there is a lapse, or not? If we do, then between any two 'presents' there will be other 'presents' and again we have the infinite regress. If we do not, the transition from one 'present' to the next must be timeless. But unless there is temporal change from one 'present' to the next, there is no intelligible succession, and if there is temporal change then it must occur in time. Again, therefore, our linguistic ruling has failed to save us from insoluble puzzles.

(ii) The second problem to be resolved is: How is it possible 'for all the solid objects and people around us to melt away into the past, and for a new order of objects and persons to emerge mysteriously from the future', so that what is true of present facts ceases to be true when they have passed away and what is now false becomes true when new events have occurred? Confused thinking is fairly obvious in the statement of this problem, but it is not removed simply by recommending a linguistic convention. Findlay points out that our ordinary system of tenses precludes confusion and leaves no room for puzzlement,[1] but the fact that we use a well developed and precise system of tenses only records the passing away and coming to be of events, it does

[1] Cf. *Logic and Language*, p. 52.

not explain how it comes about;[1] and the adoption of a different linguistic system purged of tenses and of subjectively relative adverbs and pronouns[2] would be beset by the difficulty of determining some impersonal points of reference from which to date and place events. Not even the physicist can do this, for he always retains 'the observer' in his scheme. It is not true, therefore, that if we adopted this impersonal way of talking we should never be involved in difficulties. And there is good reason why we both try to talk in this way (as Findlay points out) and yet are uneasy in doing so. The nature of time is not altered by the way we speak about temporal events, and what is difficult to understand about it remains difficult whatever linguistic convention we adopt. In fact, philosophers in the past have tried all the suggested 'forms of locution', and just because these have been found wanting the puzzles have persisted.

It does not help us to point out that we are quite familiar with temporal changes and habitually speak about them without confusion. Practical difficulties are not the same as difficulties of understanding. The difficulties which Professor Findlay describes, of being desperately immobilized (because we cannot pass on to a future event before we have passed through an intervening one, and so on *ad infinitum*), or of casting about desperately for means to pass on to the next stage (for a similar reason), would be practical difficulties; and, of course, we never experience them. But that fact does not remove the intellectual difficulties, which are neither caused nor relieved by linguistic usage. Mere familiarity with certain types of experiences does not render them intelligible. We are nowadays all familiar with radio and television and have no difficulty in turning the knobs to get our entertainment, but it does not follow that we understand how the results are brought about. It is true that, in this case, some of the difficulties can be removed by the study of observable phenomena—but not all the difficulties. Complete understanding of the phenomena of radiation demands the interpretation of facts even where observation is frustrated by the nature of the facts

---

[1] It can be more easily explained as soon as we realize that it is not the passage of time that causes things to change, but something in the nature of the things themselves, and it is more nearly true that the changes cause the passage of time.

[2] Cf. *Logic and Language*, p. 53.

themselves. It is the function of theory to explain observed facts; observation is not, by itself, explanation. Similarly, though we may all be familiar with changing and persistent objects, it does not follow that we easily understand what is presupposed in dating and relating them, in temporal continuity and succession, in distinguishing the permanent from the changing.

III. *Dissipation of Doubts About Induction*

Many contemporary philosophers seem to be afflicted with a persistent blindness to the crucial point of the problem about induction which the empiricist is bound to face. Yet this crucial point is not difficult to make clear. The inductive argument reaches a general conclusion about matter of fact from a number of particular premises. Or, what amounts to the same thing, from a number (taken to be sufficient) of occurrences of a certain phenomenon, it draws the conclusion that in similar circumstances that phenomenon will recur. In other words, the occurrence of a number of cases satisfying a rule is taken as evidence that the rule holds universally. That such an argument is not deductively valid is generally admitted and nobody requires that it should be. Nor does anybody deny—neither the most radical of empiricists nor the most die-hard of rationalists—that we do, in inductive reasoning, accept as sufficient evidence of a universal rule the fact that it has been fulfilled in the past in a large number of (or in all known) cases. This has not been called in question. But the empiricist, who wants to admit no factual knowledge that cannot be empirically derived, is faced by the problem that the principle of induction cannot be so derived, because it cannot, without question-begging, be *inductively* proved that a large number of favourable instances is evidence of the universal validity of a rule. To repeat: it is admitted by everybody that no deductively cogent reason can be given validating the inductive procedure; it is admitted likewise that in induction we do accept as sufficient evidence a large number of favourable instances; but what Hume and Russell and others have stressed is that this acceptance of favourable instances as sufficient evidence is arbitrary, that it is not and cannot be the result of an inductive argument. It is, in fact, the generally accepted principle of inductive reasoning and cannot *for that reason* be inductively proved.

Mr Paul Edwards, in his paper on the subject, accuses Russell of seeking unnecessarily for a deductive 'justification' of inductive argument.[1] But the accusation is false. Russell is most emphatic that no such justification is possible. Further, Edwards asserts with much emphasis and repetition that we commonly do accept inductive evidence as sufficient reason for drawing conclusions and that *that* is all we commonly mean by the phrase 'good and sufficient reason'. And this nobody contests. But he goes further and claims to show that, 'without in any way invoking a non-empirical principle, numbers of observed positive instances do frequently afford us evidence that unobserved instances . . . are also positive'; and this claim he never makes good. For his argument is no more than that what we ordinarily mean by 'good and sufficient reason' for predicting the occurrence of a phenomenon is precisely that we have observed this or an analogous phenomenon frequently in the past. But, of course, our giving the phrase this meaning is precisely our acceptance of the non-empirical (because not empirically or inductively demonstrable) principle that frequent past instances are evidence for future instances. The principle cannot be empirical because it is inevitably presupposed in all inductive proof. The fact that consideration of a number of examples of inductive argument reveals our habitual acceptance as evidence of past favourable instances, is not the reason why we do accept past instances as evidence. Such an empirical investigation of inductive arguments is, therefore, not an empirical proof that numbers of observed favourable instances do afford us evidence of unobserved favourable instances, but only that they are habitually *taken* to do so.

Once this point is firmly grasped it becomes plain that Mr Edwards's appeal to the ordinary usage of the phrase, 'good reason', is misleading because it confuses the *fact* that we habitually accept past instances as evidence with our *reason* for accepting them. Only this confusion makes the contention seem plausible that inductive argument is not dependent on a non-empirical principle and consequently presents no problem for the empiricist. He castigates Russell for asserting the contrary—yet his whole argument is evidence in favour of Russell's case, and he has created the appearance that the problem has been disposed of merely by failing to see what it is.

[1] *Logic and Language*, p. 66.

IV. Disposal of Sense-Data

The linguistic analyst suggests that the question whether or not there are sense-data is misleading because it seems to refer to a peculiar kind of entity distinguished from, yet specially related to, material objects, whereas it is really a question about the terminology we intend to use for describing perceptual experiences. Here again, it is held, we are all familiar with and all clearly understand the facts, but we argue whether we should say, 'I see a round penny which looks elliptical to me', or 'I see an elliptical sense-datum "of" a round penny'. These reports of the same fact are said to be equally good, and each useful for different purposes, but the second is misleading because it makes us think that there are peculiar things called sense-data, like material things in that they are sensible, but unlike them in that they cannot appear to be other than they are.

It is hardly for one who disbelieves in the existence of sense-data to come to the assistance of sense-data theories when attacked, but it is one thing to reject a particular view of perception because it is based on an untenable assumption and quite another to allege that perception and the knowledge it gives us of material things presents no problem whatsoever. Those who postulate the existence of sense-data do at least draw attention to the fact that the perceptual act is not so simple as it appears to common sense to be. They are at least aware that to be apprised of the existence of a material object by direct perception is not just a matter of looking, or feeling, or listening; that what we become directly aware of in this way is not by itself sufficient to acquaint us even with the actual presence, let alone inform us of the nature, of a material object. But it does make us aware of something, and the sense-datum is one answer to the question, aware of what?

Mr G. A. Paul (not the only one who has done so) suggests by his analysis that this is not the case. He does not actually say, but he leaves us with the strong impression, that in every perceptual act we know quite plainly exactly what it is that we immediately perceive and that this is always some material object; but that we do not know, and no amount of experiment (or consideration?) will help us to discover, what sort of thing we directly perceive when we see a material thing 'by means of' a sense-datum which differs from that thing in appearance. The talk of sense-data is said to be just a special way of saying what we all and always clearly understand, that we are perceiving a so-and-so which looks (feels, or sounds) such-like to us.

Now this is very misleading because it overlooks the facts that (i) if we were always so clearly and easily familiar with what actually occurs in sense-perception, nothing would ever have induced philosophers to invent the sense-datum vocabulary, and (ii) if I know that I am perceiving a so-and-so (e.g. a round, brown penny) and that it appears such-like (e.g. elliptical and red) to me, I know far more than I ever directly sense. It is the attempt to analyse such a situation into what I know or assume about what I directly sense, and what I do actually and directly sense, that has led some philosophers to use the sense-datum terminology. They may or may not be right to contend that sense-data are special entities specially related to material things, but they do not mislead us about the nature of the problem they are tackling so much as those who suggest that it is the illusory effect of our peculiar use of words.

V. Conclusion

First, the allegation that philosophers (and possibly even others) are confused by the forms of ordinary language and misled into the formulation of absurd theories is not proven. In fact, the errors imputed to the philosophers are errors they have not made and are such as would be committed only by the intellectually deficient.

Secondly, the imputation of these errors to the allegedly misleading character of language forms is itself the result of confusions, such as the mistaken belief that we can assign a status in language to words without assigning a corresponding status to the things for which they stand: that we can, for instance, identify, either in language or in logic, a genuine subject of attributes without claiming for it a status in the actual world as 'a substance', or 'a real thing', or 'a reality'.

Thirdly, the attempt to show that some traditional philosophical problems are only apparent, and arise only from the way in which we talk about certain matters, fails because the problems remain however we choose to alter our way of speaking, so long as we continue by our words to refer to the same subjects.

Fourthly, at least some attempts by linguistic analysts to deny linguistic dispensation, I would not dispute that attention to the existence of philosophical problems are the result of *ignoratio elenchi*—as when the fact that we commonly accept empirical evidence as sufficient to establish a general conclusion is taken to show that the empirical justification of induction presents no problem.

CHAPTER X

COMMON-SENSE PROPOSITIONS AND PHILOSOPHICAL PARADOXES[1]

C. A. Campbell

Professor of Logic and Rhetoric, Glasgow University: 1938–61

I

Like many, perhaps most, students of philosophy in this country, I have long been troubled by a number of points in Moore's famous paper, 'A Defence of Common Sense', in the Second Series of *Contemporary British Philosophy*. Just why is Moore so certain that he 'knows' the common-sense propositions listed? Just what is it he thinks he is knowing when he knows them? Just how does he conceive the bearing of what is thus known upon the solution of philosophical problems? These are some of the questions to which it has seemed to me hard to find satisfactory answers in the paper. Nor did much real help appear to be forthcoming from the commentators. These philosophers, despite the close acquaintance which most of them enjoyed with the technique of Moore's philosophical thinking, were hardly less ready than one's self to confess perplexity. Moreover, these philosophers, however puzzled they might declare themselves to be about Moore's meaning, almost all seemed to feel in their bones that he was saying something of extraordinary importance —a circumstance which made one's failure to understand the more disquieting.

From the state of intellectual frustration thus induced, the recent volume on Moore[2] by nineteen eminent students of his philosophy naturally held out good promise of relief. Somewhere in this massive work one might surely hope to discover at least some of the missing clues. And, certainly, I do not think that anyone can read this stimulating set of essays with attention and

[1] *Proceedings of the Aristotelian Society*, 1944–5, Vol. XLV.
[2] *The Philosophy of G. E. Moore.* Except where otherwise stated, all page references in my paper will be to this work.

not gain a much clearer insight into many aspects of Moore's thought. I am bound to confess, however, that on the particular points upon which I especially desired enlightenment, such enlightenment as has ensued has in the main been evoked indirectly, through the medium of rather violent disagreement with contentions of the essayists. And as this has been most conspicuously the case with regard to the very contribution which Dr Nagel, in his review in *Mind*,[1] judges to be 'the best and most rewarding in the final group of papers, if not in the whole volume' exhibiting 'a penetrating grasp of Moore's method of philosophizing' and giving 'a most persuasive and illuminating account of the rationale behind his defence of "common sense" '—the essay by Mr Norman Malcolm entitled 'Moore and Ordinary Language'—I think it may be of some interest to others besides myself to attempt a rather detailed study of this ingenious but, as I think, misguided composition. I shall hope to show that, although Malcolm may conceivably be giving a valid *account* of Moore's thought,[2] he is certainly not, as he and apparently Dr Nagel believe, giving a valid *justification* of that thought. The criticisms I have to offer will pave the way for some final reflexions of a rather more positive character upon the relationship between common-sense propositions, language, and analysis.

II

In this Section I propose to describe the way in which Malcolm envisages the problem of his paper and the general line of argument which he adopts for its solution. Criticism will be deferred to the two following sections.

Malcolm begins with a series of twelve philosophical statements, whose common character is that they are all paradoxical to common sense. They are such propositions as 'There are no material things' (1); 'Time is unreal' (4); 'There are no other minds—my sensations are the only sensations that exist' (7); 'We

---

[1] *Mind*, January 1944. Quotations are from p. 70.

[2] The fact that, in his *Reply to My Critics* at the end of the volume, Moore does not expressly dissent from Malcolm's suggested 'rationale', cannot be taken as conclusive evidence of acceptance: but it does suggest that Moore has not felt that Malcolm misinterprets his mind very seriously.

do not know for *certain* the truth of any statement about material things'. (10)[1]

To each of these propositions in turn Malcolm then opposes a very short common-sense argument which in his opinion is the sort of argument *Moore* would give, 'or at least which he would approve'.[2] Thus (to take the two propositions about which there will be most to say in the sequel) the reply to Prop. 1 is 'You are certainly wrong, for here's one hand and here's another; and so there are at least two material things'.[3] The reply to Prop. 10 is 'Both of us know for *certain* that there are several chairs in this room, and how absurd it would be to suggest that we do not know it, but only believe it, and that perhaps it is not the case'.[4]

Malcolm's problem is, are these common-sense arguments valid refutations of the philosophical paradoxes they attack, and if so, why? Malcolm believes that they are, and that he can show why.

I hold that what Moore says in reply to the philosophical statements in our list is in each case perfectly true; and furthermore, I wish to maintain that what he says is in each case a good *refutation*, a refutation that shows the falsity of the statement in question. To explain this is the main purpose of my paper.[5]

The next paragraph indicates what is to be the cardinal principle in Malcolm's explanation, and the two stages which will be involved in the full development of the argument.

The essence of Moore's technique of refuting philosophical statements consists in pointing out that these statements *go against ordinary language*. We need to consider, first, in what way these statements do go against ordinary language; and, secondly, how does it refute a philosophical statement to show that it goes against ordinary language?[6]

At this point we may be said to have reached the beginning of the argument proper. Malcolm is undertaking to show us that the philosopher in uttering his paradoxes is using words and phrases

---

[1] Pp. 435–6.   [2] P. 346.   [3] *Ibid.*
[4] P. 347. It may be mentioned that Malcolm's opinion that his common-sense arguments would be approved by Moore is substantially borne out by Moore himself. In his *Reply to My Critics*, p. 669, he accepts all twelve arguments as *good* arguments; qualifying his approval only by the remark that in one case (Prop. 8) he would hesitate to say that the argument, though good, *proves* the falsity of the proposition against which it is directed.   [5] P. 349.   [6] *Ibid.*

in a way which conflicts with ordinary usage, and that in denying certain common-sense propositions what he is really doing is 'asserting the impropriety of an ordinary form of speech'. If this can be shown, the second stage of the argument will give little difficulty. It is an easy matter to show that *ordinary* language is *correct* language. It will then follow that the paradoxes of the philosopher are without justification.

In what way, then, do these philosophical statements 'go against ordinary language'? Malcolm develops his argument in greatest detail in connection with Prop. 10—'We do not know for *certain* the truth of any statement about material things'. In giving this argument, I shall quote Malcolm's own words as fully as regard to limitations of space will permit.

This paradox, Malcolm notes, has been a particularly popular one among philosophers. He chooses to concentrate, however, upon the version of it given by Mr Ayer in his *Foundations of Empirical Knowledge*; presumably because 'Mr Ayer is one who realizes that when he makes this statement he is not making an empirical judgement, but is condemning a certain form of expression as improper'.[1]

In that work, from which Malcolm quotes at length, Ayer gives as the ground of the paradox the fact that material-thing statements can never be fully verified, 'since the series of relevant tests, being infinite, can never be exhausted'.[2] Ayer goes on to contend that since the state of 'being sure' about a material-thing statement is one the attainment of which would require us to have completed an infinite series of verifications, and since the conception of such a state is self-contradictory, to say that 'we can never be sure'—a statement which suggests that the state of 'being sure' is in this context conceivable—may be objected to on the ground that it is misleading. 'What we should say', Ayer decides, 'if we wish to avoid misunderstanding, is not that we can never be certain that any of the propositions in which we express our perceptual judgements are true, but rather that the notion of certainty does not apply to propositions of this kind.'[3]

At this point Malcolm steps in. What Ayer has said, he thinks, is tantamount to an admission that the disagreement between the philosopher and the plain man is only about the use of language.

[1] P. 353.   [2] Quoted by Malcolm, p. 454.
[3] Quoted by Malcolm, p. 353. Italics Malcolm's.

'He [Mr Ayer] thinks that the phrase "known for certain" is properly applied only to *a priori* statements, and not to empirical statements. The philosophical statement "We do not know for certain the truth of any material-thing statement" is a misleading way of expressing the proposition "The phrase 'known for certain' is not properly applied to material-thing statements". Now Moore's reply "Both of us know for certain that there are several chairs in this room, and how absurd it would be to suggest that we do not know it, but only believe it, or that it is highly probable but not really certain!" is a misleading way of saying "It is a proper way of speaking to say that we know for certain that there are several chairs in this room, and it would be an improper way of speaking to say that we only believe it, or that it is highly probable". Both the philosophical statement and Moore's reply to it are disguised linguistic statements.'[1]

And it is Moore, Malcolm argues, who is right 'in this as in all the other cases'.[2]

'By reminding us of how we ordinarily use the expressions "know for certain", and "highly probable", Moore's reply constitutes a refutation of the philosophical statement that we can never have certain knowledge of material-thing statements. It reminds us that there *is* an ordinary use of the phrase "know for certain" in which it is applied to empirical statements; and so shows us that Ayer is wrong when he says that, "the notion of certainty does not apply to propositions of this kind".'[3]

In this last paragraph Malcolm is anticipating the second stage of his argument—that *ordinary* language is *correct* language—and as the second stage will be irrelevant if the first stage breaks down, we had better pause here to examine the first stage—that philosophical paradoxes 'go against ordinary language'.

III

No one can look after Mr Ayer's interests one half so well as Mr Ayer, and I do not propose to try to anticipate what his reply might be to Malcolm's criticism. Ayer's argument (which I accept) can quite well be treated in detachment from his general philosophical position—as indeed Malcolm has treated it. When so regarded, it seems to me not at all difficult to show that it is

[1] P. 354.   [2] *Ibid.*   [3] P. 355.

merely perverse to suggest that the implication of this argument is that the dispute between the philosopher and the plain man, between paradox and common-sense statement, is a matter of 'linguistics'.

For, consider. Certainly it follows from Ayer's argument that 'the phrase "known for certain" is properly applied only to *a priori* statements, and not to empirical statements'. So too we could say, if we liked, that from some argument designed, let us say, to demonstrate the internal activity of physical bodies, it follows that 'the phrase "internal immobility" does not apply to physical bodies'. But surely this would be an altogether inept and unnatural way to express the consequence of the argument in the one case as in the other? For it seems perfectly clear that what each argument is concerned with is the proper understanding of the *facts* of the situation, and not with any problem of linguistics: and that there is a 'disagreement about language' with the plain man *only because* there is a disagreement about the correct reading of the facts. The plain man thinks that in certain situations there is no possible room for doubting the truth of such and such a material-thing statement: he therefore, very properly, applies the phrase "known for certain' to that statement. The philosopher thinks that when we bear in mind certain considerations which the plain man has not taken into account, more particularly the never wholly eradicable possibility of hallucinations and dreams, we can see that there *must* always be room—however slight—for doubt: and he therefore, equally properly, says that we can *not* apply the phrase 'known for certain' to material-thing statements. In short, the 'disagreement about language' is wholly consequential upon a 'disagreement about the facts'. So that instead of it being the case, as Malcolm contends, that the philosophical statement, 'We do not know for certain the truth of any material-thing statement' is a misleading way of expressing the proposition 'The phrase "known for certain" is not properly applied to material-thing statements', precisely the *reverse* is true. The latter proposition is a misleading, a *highly* misleading, way of expressing the former proposition.

Let us get quite clear about this business of 'disagreement about the use of language'.

A small child, just learning the use of simple words, points to a cow close by, clearly outlined in the sunlight, and says, 'Look at the horse!' We say to him 'That's not a horse, it's a cow'. Here it is natural and proper to say that the disagreement is 'linguistic'. There is no difference, or none of substance, in the facts apprehended. The child sees much the same features as the adult, the features characteristic of the cow. He simply 'applies the wrong label', having mistakenly assigned to the name 'horse' characteristics which he should have assigned to the name 'cow'.

Suppose, on the other hand, two adults walking in the fields by night, and confronted by a dark shape, dimly silhouetted against the grass. One says 'There's a horse!' The other replies 'No, it's a cow', and he may add 'I can see its horns'. Here we would regard it as quite ridiculous to speak of the disagreement as 'linguistic'. The two men attach precisely the same meaning to the terms 'cow' and 'horse'. Their disagreement is about the facts: and naturally a different form of words is required to express differently apprehended facts.

The principle seems perfectly plain. A difference between statements is properly attributable to a disagreement about the use of language only in so far as that difference is *not* determined by a different reading of the facts of the situation and *is* determined by the assignment of different meanings to constituent words or phrases.

Let us apply this principle to the difference between the philosopher's paradox and the common-sense proposition. Is there, in the first place, no difference in the 'reading of the facts'? Of course there is. I have already indicated what it is. The philosopher's reading of the facts includes the apprehension of what he regards as a legitimate ground for doubt ignored by the plain man. So far as I can see, there is only one expedient by which it could be maintained, as Malcolm wants to maintain, that there is no disagreement about the facts. That is, by confining 'the facts' to the sensory presentations which occasion the statements. But Malcolm does not explicitly resort to that expedient, and it is not difficult to understand his reluctance. For if *that* is what we are going to mean by 'the facts', then 'the facts' are properly expressed *neither* by the statement 'We know for certain that . . .' *nor* by the statement 'We cannot know for certain that . . .' but only by some quite different statement such as 'We have a sensory presentation of . . .'.

In the second place, *is* there a difference between the philosopher and the plain man about the meaning assigned to constituent words and phrases? It seems to me equally clear that there is *not*. The plain man understands just as well as the philosopher that knowing for *certain* means knowing in a way that excludes the possibility of doubt. It is only because on his reading of the facts there is no possibility of doubt—or else for another reason, to be discussed in a moment, equally consistent with acceptance of the philosopher's meaning of 'knowing for certain'—that he is content to use the phrase he uses.

If anyone should feel the need of a proof that the plain man really understands that 'knowing for certain' means 'knowing in a way that excludes the possibility of doubt', I don't think he will need to search far to obtain it. Let him show the plain man hitherto unsuspected grounds for doubt in the case of any proposition at all which the plain man has been in the habit of thinking, and saying, he 'knew for certain'. If the plain man appreciates these grounds, he will at once confess that he does not, after all, know for *certain*; though he may very well add, should the ground suggested be ground for only a very faint degree of doubt, that he is still '*practically* certain'. Indeed, there must surely be very few, if any, teachers of philosophy who have not performed this kind of 'experiment' upon beginners in the subject; and performed it, moreover, in relation to precisely the kind of common-sense propositions here in dispute. I should be profoundly surprised to learn that the results of their 'experiments' differ significantly from mine. Almost universally, in my experience, the student recognizes that he is mistaken in saying that he 'knows for *certain*'; though he may, as I have said, go on to insist that the ground for doubt is so clearly negligible that he remains 'practically' certain. But 'practically certain' is *not* 'certain': and nothing but confusion can result in philosophy from their identification.

This notion of 'practical certainty', however, calls for a closer consideration. Examination of it will point to the need of a qualification to the general statement that the plain man always means by 'knowing for certain', 'knowing in a way that excludes all possibility of doubt'.

I think it would probably be agreed that what we normally mean by a proposition being 'practically certain'—at least where we use the phrase with any degree of care—is that the proposition is one about which the ground for doubt is so slight that it may safely be ignored in our actual behaviour, i.e. in 'practice'. Now, if a proposition is such that any doubt about its truth may be legitimately ignored 'for all practical purposes', then, *should we be speaking in a context in which it is clear that the sole interest of the proposition to us is its practical interest,* it would be by no means unnatural to *drop* the word 'practically'—since it would be taken as understood—and to speak simply of the proposition as 'certain'. The ellipse seems a perfectly justifiable one, and the practice of it is exceedingly common. Thus the philosopher himself is quite ready to say, in the ordinary traffic of life, 'I am certain there are several chairs in this room'. He *is* certain—for all practical purposes. And since it is quite evidently in the context of practical purposes that the proposition is uttered, he does not deem it necessary to make explicit this qualification to his certainty.

Malcolm's treatment of our problem seems to me to suffer rather seriously from his omission to take any account of this notion of 'practical' certainty. Had he done so, and had he observed how natural it is in certain circumstances to elide the word 'practical', it would, I think, have made a difference to some of the inferences he thinks it legitimate to draw from common speech. Thus he tells us that 'Moore's reply (to Prop. 10) reminds us of the fact that if a child who was learning the language were to say, in a situation where we were sitting in a room with chairs about, that it was "highly probable" that there were chairs there, we should smile, and *correct his language*'.[1] So we should. We should no doubt say to him that it was 'certain'. Not, however, because we believe it to be *absolutely* certain, but because we believe it to be *practically* certain, and because we consider that practical certainty is all that matters to the child—or indeed to the adult—in that practical context.

It follows from this discussion that a trifling modification must be admitted to the principle that the phrase 'knowing for certain' has the same meaning in common-sense propositions as in philosophical paradoxes. In the former case we *may* be meaning by 'certainty' only 'practical certainty'. But it must be insisted that the modification *is* only a trifling one, which in no way prejudices our criticism of Malcolm's argument. For in the common-sense

[1] Pp. 354–6.

propositions which Moore and Malcolm are interested to defend, 'certainty' is taken in the sense of 'absolute', not 'practical', certainty. Were it otherwise, indeed, *cadit quaestio*. For no philosopher that I know of has ever seriously disputed that these common-sense propositions have 'practical certainty'. The propounders of the 'paradox' that we do not know for certain the truth of any statements about material things assuredly have no thought of denying that in numberless cases the ground for doubt may safely be ignored 'for all practical purposes'.

IV

We have, I hope, seen adequate reasons for rejecting, at least in the case of the example to which Malcolm has chosen to give most attention, the view that philosophical paradoxes 'go against ordinary language'. If that stage of his argument fails, it becomes, strictly speaking, a work of supererogation to consider the second stage—the demonstration of how a philosophical statement is refuted by showing that it goes against ordinary language.

Nevertheless, I think it will be profitable to give a good deal of attention to this stage of Malcolm's argument also. And this for two reasons. First, because it may with some justice be felt that we have so far concentrated too much upon a single example; and we shall have an opportunity in 'stage two' of widening the field. And secondly, because in formulating the key proposition of 'stage two', the proposition that 'ordinary language is correct language', Malcolm seems to me to slip into the acceptance of a criterion of 'ordinary language' which makes that proposition not true but false. And I rather fancy that it is largely *because* he is thinking in terms of this criterion of ordinary language that he finds it so easy to persuade himself that philosophical paradoxes go against ordinary language.

The suspect criterion first makes its appearance in a passage designed to show how absurd it is for a man knowingly to use language in a way contrary to established custom. Malcolm supposes the case of two men (we shall call them A and B) looking at an animal. A says it is a fox: B says it is a wolf. Yet B, according to the hypothesis, agrees with A not only 'as to what the characteristics of the animal are, but furthermore *agrees that that sort of animal is ordinarily called a fox*'.[1] If B were to continue to

[1] P. 357.

insist that it is a wolf, Malcolm goes on, 'we can see how absurd would be his position. He would be saying that, although the other man was using an expression to describe a certain situation which was the expression ordinarily used to describe that sort of situation, nevertheless the other man was using incorrect language. What makes his statement absurd is that ordinary language is correct language'.[1]

I agree about the absurdity of B's statement. But I am not at all happy about the criterion of 'ordinary language' which seems to be implied in Malcolm's formulation of this absurdity. It looks as though Malcolm is saying that in any given situation the mark of 'ordinary language' is that the expression used to describe it should be 'the expression ordinarily used to describe that sort of situation'. Now, if this implies that language is being used in a sense *out of* the ordinary wherever a *different* expression is used from that ordinarily used to describe the situation, it seems to be plainly false. Suppose a situation X, ordinarily believed to have the characteristics *abcd*, and therefore ordinarily described by the expression which symbolizes the characteristics *abcd*. Does it follow that anyone who describes X by the expression which symbolizes the characteristics *abfg* is using language out of its ordinary sense? Not at all. For it may well be that this person disagrees with ordinary opinion in his analysis of X, and is convinced that it has the characteristics *abfg*. If so, his use of the expression symbolizing *abfg* is the ordinary and correct use of language.

B's position, of course, remains absurd. For B, *ex hypothesi*, agrees with A that the situation is characterized by *abcd*, and yet rejects as incorrect the ordinary expression, symbolizing *abcd*, used to describe that sort of situation. What I am anxious to make clear, in view of what immediately follows in Malcolm's paper, is that the use of language may be ordinary and correct even if it describes by an expression symbolizing *abfg* a situation *ordinarily* described by an expression symbolizing *abcd*.

What 'immediately follows' in Malcolm's paper is an attempt to show that the philosopher who says that we can never really perceive material things is committing the very same absurdity as B, 'though in a subtle and disguised way'. It will be best to give the crucial passage in full:

[1] P. 357.

But the philosopher who says that the ordinary person is mistaken when he says that he sees the cat in the tree, does not mean that he sees a squirrel rather than a cat; does not mean that it is a mirage; does not mean that it is a hallucination. He will agree that the facts of the situation are what we should ordinarily describe as 'seeing a cat in a tree'. Nevertheless, he says that the man does not *really* see a cat; he sees only some sense-data of a cat. Now, if it gives the philosopher pleasure always to substitute the expression 'I see some sense-data of my wife', for the expression 'I see my wife', etc., then he is at liberty thus to express himself, *providing* he warns people beforehand so that they will understand him. But when he says that the man does not *really* see a cat, he commits a great absurdity; for he implies that a person can use an expression to describe a certain state of affairs, which is the expression ordinarily used to describe just such a state of affairs, and yet be using incorrect language.[1]

Is our sceptical philosopher really as foolish as all that? I am quite sure he is not.

Does the philosopher agree 'that the facts of the situation are what we should ordinarily describe as "seeing a cat in a tree" '? In a sense, yes. He agrees that here is a situation X ordinarily described by the expression symbolizing *abcd* ('I see a cat in the tree'). But this does not in the very least imply, as it would have to imply for Malcolm's argument to be effective, that he agrees that X has in fact the characteristics *abcd*. On the contrary, the sceptical philosopher's analysis of the situation leads him to believe that X is characterized by *abfg*, not *abcd*. He therefore, very rightly, uses the expression symbolizing *abfg* to describe it. And of course he does *not* go on to say, or to imply, that the ordinary man is using incorrect language. For he knows that the disagreement is not about language at all, but about the facts. The philosopher would agree that the plain man is using perfectly correct language to describe the facts as he apprehends them.

It is worth while pointing out also that the philosopher would not demur in the indiscriminate and unqualified way that the passage quoted suggests to the statement of the plain man who says 'I see a cat'. On ordinary occasions the philosopher will freely make such statements himself. He objects to them only *in the context of philosophical discourse*, where it is vital that our words should *accurately* describe the facts. If our sceptical philosopher

[1] Pp. 357-8.

chose to make a detailed reply to Malcolm's criticism, incorporating this point, I think it might run somewhat as follows:

No doubt we do ordinarily describe this situation by saying 'I see a cat'. In ordinary life no harm is done thereby. For practical purposes this expression serves very well to secure the desired behaviour-adjustments—much better, indeed, than the technical statement of the philosopher, which would certainly be cumbrous and probably be unintelligible.[1] So I take no objection to the ordinary statement in the context of ordinary discourse. But if we are talking *philosophy*, if our interest is in the accurate and precise description of the real facts, and not in mere practical effectiveness, then I must demur. For I cannot agree that the statement 'I see a cat' does accurately and precisely describe the facts as these appear on an analysis of them more thorough than is appropriate to everyday life. The ordinary statement suggests, e.g. that through visual sensing alone we cognize the cat. And this seems not to be the case. There are good grounds for holding that several factors besides visual sensing (though precisely what they are is admittedly controversial) enter essentially into cognition of the cat. There are good grounds for holding that visual sensing gives us at most certain 'sense-data' of colour, shape and size, and that the sense-data seen at any one time are not only not identical with the cat (since there is much in what we mean by a 'cat' which these sense-data do not cover), but may not even be identical with the surface of the cat. In short, the real 'facts of the situation' are very different from anything that can be said to be accurately described by the statement 'I see a cat': and we must not therefore allow the practical convenience of this kind of statement to beguile us into supposing that it is other than inept in philosophy.

Is there any valid reply to this defence of his 'paradox' by the philosopher? I can only say that I cannot find one in Malcolm's pages.

v

In the light of what has been urged in the last two sections, I venture to conclude that Malcolm has failed in the main purpose of his paper. If Moore's defence of common-sense propositions

[1] Berkeley has said about all that needs to be said on this matter. 'In the ordinary affairs of life, any phrases may be retained, so long as they excite in us proper sentiments, or dispositions to act in such a manner as is necessary for our well-being, how false soever they may be, if taken in a strict and speculative sense.' (*Principles of Human Knowledge*, 1st Ed., Para. 52.)

against the paradoxes of philosophy is to be justified at all, it cannot be done on the ground that philosophical paradoxes 'go against ordinary language'. The division is far deeper than one of 'linguistics'.

In this final section I want to pass from Malcolm's paper in order to give attention to a very important type of common-sense proposition which plays a prominent part in Moore's writings. The statement 'I see a cat' may be said, in virtue of its form, positively to clamour for philosophical correction if it is made within the context of philosophical discourse. This is not, or not so obviously, the case if the perceptual judgement is for-mulated in the statement 'This is a cat'. Has the philosopher anything to condemn here? I gather that a good many persons think that the sceptical (which we may here take as including the immaterialist) philosopher *has* something to condemn; and that this proposition contradicts, by implication if not directly, such propositions as 'There are no material things', and 'It is doubtful whether there are any material things'. I believe this view to be mistaken. In what follows I shall attempt a brief analysis of the proposition in question designed to bring this out, and also to bring out certain other important facts about this type of proposition.

Let me indicate in advance the general ground upon which I hold that the sceptical philosopher has no reason to quarrel with the proposition 'This is a cat'. It is that in this (and in any similar) proposition, as asserted in common speech, nothing what-ever is asserted or implied as to the being or not-being of material things in any sense of 'material things' in which their existence has been a subject of philosophical controversy. Berkeley would not have considered it in the least way inconsistent with his immaterialism to assert 'This is a cat': and he would only have objected to the assertion of the proposition by others if he had some special reason to suspect from the context that the speaker intended his words to imply that the cat was a 'material thing' in a sense not resolvable into a cluster of 'ideas'. In ordinary contexts, it seems to me, there is no such implication. Nor, of course, is there a contrary implication. The specific point of the proposition is, as I see it, quite neutral towards the philosophical issue. I do not doubt, indeed, that if the plain man were asked, after he had uttered his statement, whether he means by the cat a cluster of ideas (in some sort of relationship) or a non-mental entity, he would reply unhesitatingly that he meant the latter. But that does not imply that the 'materiality' of the cat was any part of what he asserted in his original proposition. All the plain man would mean, I think, would be, that *had* the question been raised at the time he made his assertion, that is how he would have answered it. But he would agree that neither question nor answer was at that time in his mind at all.

I have said that the specific point of this type of proposition is neutral towards the philosophical issue. This I believe to be true, and to be the real justification of the contention of ·Moore and his school that propositions of this sort are proof against any of the paradoxes of the philosopher. But to see that, and in what exact sense, it is true, we must now examine more closely what precisely it is that is being asserted, whether by the plain man or by the philosopher in the ordinary context of life, in the proposition 'This is a cat'.

First, as to the 'this'. At first glance it might seem as though the 'this' were what is presented in sense. But a moment's reflection suffices to show that such is not the case. The sensory presentation contains a certain complex of sensible features, but the speaker assuredly does not believe that the 'cat', which he identifies with the 'this', is exhaustively characterized by the limited features in this complex. The meaning which the term 'cat' has for him includes many more constituents than can be presented in any single sensory apprehension. Evidently, then, the 'this', though it 'has' these sensibly presented features, is taken to be an entity of wider scope, which 'has' also many other features.

The importance for the proposition of the sensibly presented complex is, of course, that the speaker recognizes therein certain features which are characteristic, in a more or less central way, of what is ordinarily meant by a 'cat'. He recognizes, perhaps, a characteristic shape, size, and mode of movement, and a colour that falls within the rather wide range characteristic of cats. And he apprehends in the complex no features which he recognizes as incompatible with the characteristics of cats. Then, having reason to believe, either from experience or from hearsay, or from both, that an entity which sensibly presents this particular group of features is almost, or almost always, an entity which in the appropriate empirical situations exhibits all the other features characteristic of what we mean by a 'cat', he proceeds to identify the 'this' with the 'cat' in the proposition 'This is a cat'.

If, then, we attempt to articulate the precise meaning which the proposition 'This is a cat' has for the speaker who asserts it, we might do so in some such form as this: 'The entity which I sensibly apprehend as having certain of the features characteristic of what is meant by the term 'cat' is an entity so constituted that it will exhibit in the appropriate situations all the other features characteristic of what is meant by the term "cat".' This statement, so far as I can see, includes everything that the speaker intends, and nothing that he does not intend, when he asserts 'This is a cat'.

Two omissions from the statement call for special notice. Nothing appears there as to *how* the entity is supposed to 'have' these features. This is as it should be. The speaker, in asserting the proposition, holds no view as to 'how'. The entity may 'have' these features as real constituents of a 'thing', or as members of a 'family' of sense-data, or as 'representations' of real constituents of a thing—in what way is a matter of complete indifference from the point of view of the proposition being asserted. The proposition's truth or falsity is not affected by the truth or falsity of any view about 'sense-data' and 'things'. The speaker regards his proposition as verified or falsified according as the entity which somehow 'has' these sensible features does or does not exhibit in the appropriate empirical situations the other features characteristic of a 'cat'. Nothing else matters. That is the 'point' of the proposition. There is no reference, implied or otherwise, to *how* precisely the entity has the sensibly apprehended features.

Much the same has to be said about the second omission. Nothing appears about the relationship supposed to hold between the 'other features' and either the entity judged to have them or the sensibly presented features which the entity also has. Again it seems to me that nothing *should* appear, that the speaker has no views on the matter. That the entity should exhibit these 'other features' on the occasion of the appropriate empirical tests—that is all the speaker is concerned to assert. These empirical tests are recognized by the speaker as sufficient to verify or falsify his proposition. But it is clear that they cannot verify or falsify any view as to how these other 'features' are related to the 'entity' on the one hand or to the sensibly presented features on the other. What the truth may be about these matters is irrelevant to the truth or otherwise of the proposition.

Now, if this analysis be accepted as sound in substance, there are a number of comments which seem worth making as to its bearing upon contemporary philosophical controversies.

1. We have established our view that the sceptical philosopher has no quarrel with propositions of the type 'This is a cat'. The proposition 'There are, or at least may be, no material things', and the proposition 'This is a cat', are not contradictory of one another. It follows that no appeal can be made to propositions of the latter kind (in so far as they are true) in order to disprove propositions of the former kind. Of course, if the plain man were to say not just 'This is a cat', but 'This is a cat: and a cat is a material thing',[1] then his proposition *would* be in contradiction with that of the sceptic. But on this situation two remarks fall to be made.

(*a*) The contradiction *may* be only verbal. The plain man may very well be meaning, when he calls the cat a material thing, merely that under certain appropriate conditions relating to the entity he and others will have certain definite sensible experiences, primarily of a tactual character: that, in fact, it is a 'tangible' as distinct from an 'intangible' entity. If that *is* all the plain man means, the sceptic has no reason for dissent. Their respective propositions are only in verbal, not in real, contradiction. And certainly the plain man seems to think, with Dr Johnson, that a thing's materiality is at least *established* by the possibility of tactual sensations with regard to it.

(*b*) I agree, however, that the plain man may mean more than this. He may mean that the cat is a material thing in a sense of 'material thing' in which its existence *is* in dispute among philosophers. In that case his proposition is in real contradiction with that of the sceptic. But in that case I really fail to see why we should regard his proposition as a *common-sense* proposition, and entitled on that account to claim special authority. For if a common-sense proposition is entitled to special authority at all

---

[1] Malcolm's 'common-sense reply' to his Prop. 1 is of this general character, but it is only given by him by way of illustration, and not developed. Moore appears to approve it.

H*

it is surely only in virtue of the great mass of past experience through which it is supposed to have established and sustained itself. But the proposition which the plain man is now asserting is not established or sustained by anything of the sort. There seems no reason to suppose that the 'mass of past experience' is either more, or less, consistent with his proposition than with that of the sceptic. If we are going to prefer it to that of the sceptic, it ought therefore to be only because it is more capable of being supported by philosophical argument—not because of some peculiar authority enjoyed by common-sense propositions.

2. I want to say something now about the relationship between the kind of analysis attempted above and the kind of analysis which Moore gives of the same type of proposition in his 'Defence of Common Sense'.

There is, I think, no great mystery as to how our own kind of analysis is connected with the proposition it analyses. Its aim is, keeping consistently within the mental orbit of the speaker, to unfold, and give detailed expression to, what the speaker himself means when he asserts the proposition. It is of the essence of this kind of analysis that the speaker should be able to recognize that this *is* what he meant by his assertion. There was no reason, of course, why he should himself trouble to say it in this elaborate way. The simple words 'This is a cat' are the accepted way of expressing the meaning in question, and give rise to no misunderstanding. But in so far as the analysis is a sound one, it will contain nothing which the speaker cannot recognize, and everything which the speaker can recognize as relevant constituents of his proposition.

In some respects this is very similar to Moore's kind of analysis. And in point of fact the analysis of 'This is a cat' given above seems to fulfil pretty completely the conditions of analysis in his own sense which Moore lays down in his most recent statement on the subject.[1]

On the other hand, it does differ in at least one important respect from analysis as Moore actually practises it in the context referred to. This becomes manifest when we remind ourselves of the special difficulty in the analysis of common-sense propositions which led Moore to declare that although we know these

---

[1] P. 663, and later on p. 666.

propositions for certain, 'no philosopher, hitherto, has succeeded in suggesting an analysis of them, as regards certain important points, which comes anywhere near to being certainly true'.[1] When we try to analyse a proposition such as 'This is a hand' Moore finds, we are able to say some things about it with tolerable certainty. But one particularly obstinate problem holds us up. What is it in such propositions that we are knowing with regard to the 'sense-datum', and more particularly with regard to its relation to that of which it is a sense-datum? Moore examines what he believes to be the only possible alternative types of solution of this problem: but to each of them he finds objections which seem to him sufficiently grave to warrant him in saying that 'no philosopher has hitherto suggested an answer which comes anywhere near to being certainly true'.[2]

But it is clear that this kind of difficulty can arise only for a kind of analysis which refuses to confine itself to what the speaker himself means in his assertion of the proposition. No such difficulty arose for us; because (so it seemed to us) the speaker is not, in asserting the proposition, in the least way concerned with the nature of the relationship between the sense-datum and that of which it is the sense-datum. The speaker is of course aware of presented sensible features and of an entity which somehow 'has' them. But as to the special nature of the 'how', he has no view. For no view on this subject is relevant to what he is concerned to assert. The truth or falsity of what he is concerned to assert does not depend in the smallest degree upon the truth or falsity of any view about the relationship of the sense-datum to that of which it is the sense-datum.

It seems to me, therefore, that Moore's analysis is not, in this instance at any rate, an analysis of what the speaker means in asserting the proposition. This conclusion would still hold even if I am mistaken in my view that the speaker is asserting nothing about the relation of the sense-datum to that of which it is a sense-datum. For suppose he *is* asserting something about this. If he is, then, if he really is a plain man, there is only one kind of relationship he *could* be asserting; for there is only one kind of relationship the possibility of which has ever entered his head, viz. the inherence of the sense-datum as a real constituent in that of which it is a sense-datum. Hence if Moore's analysis were

---

[1] *Contemporary British Philosophy*, p. 216.   [2] *Ibid.*, p. 219.

really analysing common-sense propositions of plain men from the point of view of what plain men assert in them, he would have to rule out *ab initio* all other alternative answers about this relationship. That he in fact is far from doing this confirms our view that he is not, or not consistently, concerned to bring out what the speaker himself means in asserting his propositions.

I must confess that it seems to me difficult to hold that an analysis which makes problems of this sort central can be called, in any intelligible sense, an analysis of 'common-sense' propositions. This kind of problem, I should have said, belongs essentially to the metaphysics of perception. The question to which an answer is being sought in the discussion of this problem is, at bottom, 'What is the true nature of the sensory presentation which occurs in perception of objects and how is it related to the object that is perceived?' That is a question of first-rate interest and importance: but I cannot think that the answer to it is capable of throwing any light upon the problem of what is being asserted in 'common-sense' propositions.

3. I should like, finally, to stress, though it must be briefly, a main element of value in our kind of analysis, which remains consistently at the point of view of the speaker himself.

This kind of analysis, in elucidating for us precisely what we are asserting, and thus what precisely we are claiming to know, seems to me to be an indispensable condition of our forming a worthwhile judgement as to whether we really *do* know what we claim to know. It is a commonplace that people frequently think they know with certainty all sorts of propositions which are in fact false, and which they therefore cannot 'know': and that this failing is not confined to the plain man, but extends even to philosophers gifted beyond the ordinary with powers of self-criticism—Descartes, for example—the history of philosophy amply attests. Fairly early in the Modern era, however, philosophers (largely through the influence of Descartes himself, despite the occasional aberrations of that philosopher's practice) learned to view with acute, and wholesome, suspicion propositions backed by nothing more substantial than strong personal conviction. That lesson seems to me to be in danger of being unlearned. Perhaps the pendulum had swung too far in the direction of scepticism. Certainly it is swinging back now with a vengeance.[1] I think it is a good deal more than time to call a halt. When, for example, Moore says to us, in answer to his own question whether it isn't possible that he merely *believes* common-sense propositions, or knows them to be *highly probable*, 'I think I have nothing better to say than that it seems to me that I *do* know them with certainty',[2] I could wish that philosophers would have the courage to retort, with all respect, 'If indeed you have nothing better to say, we are not interested. For this is a matter upon which there obviously *is* something better to say.' For surely there is something a *great deal* better to say: first and foremost, what precisely is being asserted in the proposition claimed as known. Once we are clear about *that*, we shall generally (perhaps always) be in a position to see the kind of evidence that is relevant to the verification of the proposition. Then, and only then, we shall be able to form a critical judgement as to whether the evidence in our possession really does entitle us to claim that we know the proposition 'for certain'.[3] But to insist that we know for certain the truth of a proposition before we have even tried to make clear to ourselves what is being asserted in the proposition —that is an attitude for which no defence seems to me possible.

Let me illustrate by reverting, in a last word, to our old proposition 'This is a cat'. Are we entitled to say that we know for certain a proposition of this sort? It is evident that analysis can assist us enormously towards giving the correct answer. It enables us to appreciate that at least some of the objections which philosophers have directed against the possibility of knowing such a proposition are groundless. We can see the irrelevance of objecting that there are, or at least may be, no material things; or again of objecting that nobody yet knows how a sense-datum

[1] Consider, e.g., the favour now so widely accorded to 'intuition'— not so long ago, for excellent reasons, the bogey-word of philosophy.

[2] *Contemporary British Philosophy*, p. 206.

[3] The view expressed in this paragraph is not meant to imply the view that there is no rational certainty without 'proof', or that where we cannot prove a thing acceptance of it becomes a mere matter of faith—a view which Moore justly condemns in the concluding paragraph of his British Academy Lecture. I at least should agree that proof presupposes something known without proof. My point in this paragraph is that we cannot know whether or not the proposition in question is the kind of proposition for which grounds are needed until we analyse it and find out what precisely it is that is being asserted in it.

is related to that of which it is a sense-datum. On the other hand, in revealing to us the kind of evidence that *is* relevant to the truth or falsity of the proposition, analysis seems to me to make it clear that even under the most favourable conditions absolute certainty is impossible. I at least cannot see any way of evading the force of Ayer's contention that the series of relevant tests is infinite, and can thus never be exhausted. Doubtless we can in certain cases attain to a degree of probability that is quite fantastically high. But the distinction between even fantastically high probability and *certainty* remains. And though such distinctions are of little interest to 'common sense', I do not think they can be slurred over in philosophy without disaster.

CHAPTER XI

ORDINARY LANGUAGE AND PERCEPTION[1]

W. F. R. Hardie
President, Corpus Christi College, Oxford

It is a commonly held view, and a view which inspires much contemporary philosophical practice, that the investigation of the uses of words in ordinary speech is at least an important part of the philosopher's task. It is claimed that, if we adopt this approach, we shall find, if not the answers to old questions, at least ways of reformulating these questions which will bring us nearer to answers. Sometimes too we shall find that the questions which have puzzled philosophers are not real questions at all; they have only seemed to be questions because philosophers have misunderstood words, and in particular have failed to distinguish the different kinds of jobs done by apparently similar words or by the same word in different uses. No one denies that such misunderstanding is one source of philosophical perplexity; but opinions may well differ on the question how much help and benefit is to be expected from the linguistic treatment of problems. There are two ways of testing the claim of a new method or new approach in philosophy. One is by considering in general how far it is new and what fruits it might be expected to yield. The other is by sampling the fruits themselves. In this paper I shall try to do the latter. I shall discuss some arguments, concerned with perception and our knowledge of the external world, which have been used by recent or contemporary philosophers. These arguments have in common that they base their conclusions on uses of ordinary, or at least non-philosophical, language and that they claim to solve, or dissolve, problems which have for centuries been found perplexing. I shall maintain that these arguments are unsuccessful. I do not wish to draw any sweeping conclusions from this. But anyone who agrees with my criticisms will tend to become less hopeful of important results from the linguistic approach at least to this group of problems.

[1] *The Philosophical Quarterly*, Vol. V, No. 19, April 1955.

I

I shall begin with a well-known argument used by the late Miss Stebbing in criticizing an assertion made by Eddington that, when we step on a plank, we do not step on something solid. 'The plank has no solidity of substance. To step on it is like stepping on a swarm of flies. Shall I not slip through? No, if I make the venture one of the flies hits me and gives me a boost up again; I fall again and am knocked upwards by another fly; and so on.'[1] Miss Stebbing replies in her *Philosophy and the Physicists* that this denial of solidity is 'nonsensical'.[2] It is nonsensical because we define solidity by pointing to things like planks. 'But we can understand "solidity" only if we can truly say that the plank is solid. For "solid" just is the word we use to describe a certain respect in which a plank of wood resembles a block of marble, a piece of paper, and a cricket ball, and in which each of them differs from a sponge, from the interior of a soap-bubble, and from the holes in a net.'[3] This pattern of argument has recently been referred to by Mr J. O. Urmson as 'the argument from standard examples'. The following is his generalized account of its form. 'By it the philosophical doubt whether something is really an X is exposed as being in some way improper or absurd by means of a demonstration that the thing in question is a standard case by reference to which the expression "X" has to be understood, or a doubt whether anything is X is exposed by showing that certain things are standard cases of what the term in question is designed to describe.'[4] Mr Urmson refers to Miss Stebbing's argument against Eddington as an example of this form of argument. By means of it, he says, 'she showed conclusively that the novelty of scientific theory does not consist, as had been unfortunately suggested, in showing the inappropriateness of ordinary descriptive language'.

Before I comment on Miss Stebbing's argument against Eddington, I wish to make one general remark about the argument from standard examples. It is not true without qualification that

---

[1] *The Nature of the Physical World*, p. 342.

[2] *Philosophy and the Physicists*, p. 53.

[3] *Op. cit.*, pp. 51, 52.

[4] *Revue Internationale de Philosophie*, No. 25, 1953 ('Some Questions Concerning Validity').

a doubt whether something, or anything, is really X can be removed by producing standard cases of what 'X' is designed to describe. For 'X' might mis-describe the standard cases. Thus if, in some language, the word designed to describe insane persons were 'moonstruck' or 'devil-possessed', this fact would not make it absurd to doubt the existence of a connexion between insanity and the moon or devils. For the assertion that no one is really moonstruck or devil-possessed to become nonsensical it would be necessary for 'moonstruck' and 'devil-possessed' to shed their first meanings and cease to be theory-laden. As soon as 'moonstruck' ceases to convey a theory the assertion that no one is moonstruck is shown to be nonsensical by producing a standard example of the behaviour which 'moonstruck' is used to describe. This non-philosophical case helps us to estimate the use of the argument from standard examples to discredit philosophical paradoxes. If a philosopher who uttered the paradox that tomatoes and pillar-boxes are not really red were using 'red' as part of what Mr Urmson calls 'ordinary descriptive language', then he would be saying that the things which look red to a normal percipient in daylight do not so look red. Thus his paradox is only not nonsense if, when he utters it, he means 'red' to convey a theory, this time not a causal hypothesis, but an analysis of the admitted fact that tomatoes are red. Here two questions arise. First, can the philosopher state, and state clearly, the theory the rejection of which he means to convey by asserting his paradox? If he can, his paradox is a piece of philosophy, not of nonsense. Secondly, is the vocabulary of actual non-philosophic utterances merely 'ordinary' and 'descriptive', in the sense of not being laden with questionable theory? If not, then the mode of statement used by the philosopher in propounding his thesis, though it may be misleading and excessively dramatic, is yet not sheerly perverse.

Miss Stebbing's contention that there is no sense in Eddington's denial that a plank is solid rests on her view that 'solid' has a certain assigned meaning and that no other meaning is assignable. The kind of nonsense to which she seeks to reduce Eddington's paradox is that of asserting that something which is X is also not X. The plank has no visible holes; it can hold water; it is not porous. If you cut through it anywhere, you find that it is not hollow. But what is neither hollow nor porous is by definition solid. Hence to suggest that the plank is not solid is to suggest that it is a non-solid solid; the suggestion is nonsensical. But it is surely false that there is no sense in the question whether a plank which, under all the tests we can apply, appears solid, really is solid. First, how can we know that new and more refined tests will not be devised which would yield evidence that the plank is after all not solid? A drop of blood, we are told, looks white with red spots when seen through a microscope. Perhaps a new kind of microscope would reveal holes in the plank. Receptacles which are mercury-tight or treacle-tight are not necessarily water-tight. Perhaps scientists could make a liquid which, being as much less viscous than water as water is than treacle, would ooze through the as yet undetected holes in the plank. But, secondly, even if it could be shown that no tests could yield evidence that the plank is not solid, this would not show that the plank is solid. We know that there are surfaces the gaps in which are too small to be detected without optical instruments or experimental techniques. Why should there not be gaps much smaller still, too small to be detected by any instrument or any technique? To the question whether the plank is quite certainly solid the natural answer is not that the question is nonsensical but that the plank is at least, so far as we can see, as solid as anything we know. Miss Stebbing fails to see how much acuteness and sophistication is needed in order to detect any difficulty in giving a meaning to 'solid' such that it makes sense to say that what, under all tests, appears to be solid may yet not be solid.

It may be objected that the above answer to Miss Stebbing is invalid, and based on misunderstanding, since it assumes that it makes sense to speak, by an analogical extension from observed gaps and discontinuities, of gaps and discontinuities too small to be detected by the most powerful microscope. But this extension is only possible if sub-microscopic entities exist, and are not merely devices for representing the connexions between observable events. This retort, however, puts the burden of proof in the wrong place. The question I am discussing is not the question what is the status of the minute entities of which physicists seem to speak but the question what is the force of Miss Stebbing's use of the argument from standard examples. Miss Stebbing is obviously trying to persuade us that, when Eddington speaks about atoms and electrons in terms designed to fit flies and bullets, he commits a philosophical howler. If, when her argu-

ment is attacked, the defence assumes that electrons are convenient fictions or links in a system of notation, then the defence
is assuming what the argument under criticism is designed to
prove. Hence this objection to my criticism of Miss Stebbing's
argument admits and confirms the contention that her argument
is a failure.

Miss Stebbing wishes to save us from thinking that, if we accept
the findings of scientists about the ultimate constituents of
material things, we must think that our perceptions are illusory,
that the sights, sounds, feels, tastes and smells with which we
are familiar are a curtain concealing from us what really happens.
Many contemporary philosophers agree with her in repudiating
what used to be called the 'representative' theory of perception,
the theory that we do not 'directly perceive' the thing itself.
Professor Ryle, for example, rejects as spurious the question how
a person gets 'beyond his sensations to apprehension of external
realities',[1] and seeks to reduce to absurdity the implied theory by
repeated application of the argument from standard examples.
He attacks the suggestion that 'we can observe our visual and
other sensations, but cannot, unfortunately, observe robins'.[2] 'But
this is doubly to abuse the notion of observation. As has been
shown, on the one hand, it is nonsense to speak of a person
witnessing a sensation, and, on the other, the ordinary use of
verbs like "observe", "espy", "peer at", and so on is in just such
contexts as "observe a robin", "espy a lady-bird" and "peer at
a book". Football matches are just the sorts of things of which
we do catch glimpses; and sensations are the sorts of things of
which it would be absurd to say that anyone caught glimpses.'[3]
It is sometimes held that our beliefs about material things require
to be justified by inferring them from directly known facts of
sense-experience. The existence of a thing is required, or made
probable, by the occurrence of the sensations which it causes.
Professor Ryle denounces this view: 'But having sensations is not
discovering clues. We discover clues by listening to conversations
and looking at finger-prints. If we could not observe some things,
we should not have clues for other things, and conversations are
just the sorts of things to which we do listen, as finger-prints and
gateposts are just the sorts of things at which we do look.'[4]

[1] *The Concept of Mind*, p. 223.   [2] *Op. cit.*, 224.
[3] *Op. cit.*, 224.   [4] *Op. cit.*, p. 232, cf. p. 236.

Professor Ryle is correct in insisting that at least many of the verbs which we use in connexion with our perception of material things and events cannot, without a violation of usage, have for their objects nouns which do not mention material things or events: we do not peer at our visual sensations or listen to our auditory experiences. But we can notice them and report that we are having them. It is a well-known fact that it is not easy to find, or invent, the right idioms for making such reports, and that any general account of what the reports are about is liable to convey or suggest mistaken assumptions. But a philosopher who thinks that statements about material things need to be justified, and can be justified, on the basis of statements about personal sensations need not yield any ground that matters to the argument from standard examples as applied by Professor Ryle. For Professor Ryle has not tried to show that the basic premisses from which it is proposed to prove, or make probable, statements about material objects cannot be formulated. He has shown only that certain words and expressions are unavailable for this purpose.

I hope that what I have said will not be understood as an attempt to resuscitate, or to defend, a doctrine of 'representative perception'. My present object is only to discuss the validity and scope of the appeal to ordinary language in the argument from standard examples. I am sure that 'representative' theories have sometimes been stated, even by their friends, in ways which are logically vicious. In the days when Representationism was seriously discussed it was customary to argue that, if we cannot perceive a chair without perceiving a copy of a chair, then we cannot perceive the copy without perceiving a copy of the copy. A perceiver confined in some sense to private objects is unlike a prisoner in a cave who sees flashes and listens to taps; for flashes and taps are themselves public objects. It is vicious, unless as a suggestive metaphor, to speak of the sensuous curtain as if it were a barrier. But it is also and in the same way vicious, unless as a suggestive metaphor, to speak as if the barriers were down, to say that in perception we 'directly confront' material objects or apprehend them 'face to face'. When we are speaking of ordinary sight, touch and hearing, it is nonsense, although *perhaps* suggestive nonsense, to say that there is always a screen between us and the object, and nonsense, although not *necessarily* misleading, to say that there is never anything between us and the object. The physical world does not lurk coyly or modestly behind a screen; but neither does it frankly or wantonly expose itself. If we wish to have a name for the former kind of nonsense, say Occultism, we should have a name for the latter also, say Nudism. These names describe myths rather than doctrines; for doctrines cannot be explicitly nonsensical. But Locke, when he suggests that things themselves are for ever concealed behind layer upon layer of 'ideas' and 'qualities', is crypto-occultist. Berkeley, when he suggests that we have only to open our eyes to see all Nature's goods displayed in her shopless shop-window, is crypto-nudist. It is worth making the point that Nudism is as bad as Occultism because philosophers have often thought that to reject the latter, in the shape of Representationism, was to accept the former, disguised as Realism. In fact, as we have seen, it is impossible to reject either for the right reasons without rejecting the other. When we have seen that both are strictly nonsensical, we can make a fresh start by considering in what ways either, or both, convey true and helpful suggestions about the nature and scope of our knowledge and ignorance of the things which we perceive. I think that those who agree with the views and arguments I have been criticizing have something to learn from Occultism, and that there is a suggestion of Nudism in the use made by Miss Stebbing and Professor Ryle of the argument from standard examples and in the eagerness of these philosophers to deny that the sciences can teach anything which should lead us to reconsider or reject what we believe as plain perceivers and idiomatic talkers.[1]

[1] Since the date at which I wrote these comments on the argument from standard examples, Professor Flew has referred to this form of argument in the concluding paragraphs of his interesting article, 'Philosophy and Language' (*The Philosophical Quarterly*, January 1955, pp. 35–6). He claims that The Argument of the Paradigm Case 'can be deployed against many philosophical paradoxes'. His statement of the argument is—'Crudely: if there is any word the meaning of which can be taught by reference to paradigm cases, then no argument whatever could ever prove that there are *no cases whatever* of whatever it is' (35). The concluding sentence (and paragraph) of his article is: 'To see the power, and the limitations, of The Argument of the Paradigm Case is to realize how much of common sense can, and how much cannot, be defended against philosophical paradoxes by simple appeal to the ordinary use of words; and why' (36). The limitations which, following

II

The argument from standard examples is a technique of refutation: it attacks statements made by philosophers by means of the contention, not that these statements are false or unproved, but that they are without sense. It is a method of deflation and doubtless often salutary. The philosopher is invited to reflect on the natural meaning, the informal logic, of the words he is using,

Mr Urmson (*loc. cit.*), he finds in arguments of this form is that what by themselves they 'will certainly *not* do is to establish any matter of value, moral or otherwise' (35). Professor Flew's claim that this pattern of argument 'demands special attention', that it has numerous and important uses against philosophical positions which to common sense sound paradoxical, rouses a keen expectation that he will give us some convincing examples of its use. In fact he gives only one, while telling us that 'a moment's reflexion' will assure us that there are many others. The philosophical paradox against which he shows the argument in action is the denial of 'freewill': 'Thus, since the meaning of "of his own freewill" can be taught by reference to such paradigm cases as that in which a man, under no social pressure, marries the girl he wants to marry (how else *could* it be taught?): it cannot be right, on any grounds whatsoever, to say that no one *ever* acts of his own freewill' (35).

Now the problem, or set of problems, in the formulation of which it has been traditional to use the words 'free', 'will' and 'freewill' is a natural example to take when commending The Argument of the Paradigm Case. For the argument has certainly helped to clarify the problem, and it is not unplausible to claim that it exposes the principle of the definitive solution. The claim would be justified if the solution sketched by Hume were acceptable. Professor Flew has commented on Hume's solution in an earlier passage of his article: 'But the skeleton solution he suggested depended, fairly explicitly, upon recalling to mind with the help of simple concrete examples, just what the ordinary use of the word "free" actually is: and that it is not its ordinary job (not what it ordinarily means) nor yet any part of its ordinary job (nor yet part of what it implies) to attribute to actions unpredictability in principle. If this is so then it is not contradictory to say that some action was both predictable and performed of the agent's own freewill: always assuming of course that the key words are being used in their ordinary senses' (30, 31). Hume unduly depreciated his own conceptual solution when he said that the controversy had 'turned merely upon words'. (Of course it did. But on what else could it have turned?) He also tended to conceal the merit of his own contribution 'by the aggressive way in which he misrepresented a good start as the end of the affair' (31).

Professor Flew does not state explicitly that he accepts Hume's thesis; but I think that he implies such acceptance when he takes the problem of the freedom of the will as his example of the successful use and to admit that, even if there is something which he is trying to say, it cannot be said in these words. The practice of many contemporary philosophers implies that, in their view, the scrutiny of ordinary language is a large part, if not the whole, of what philosophers should be doing when they discuss perception and our knowledge of the external world. This view is stated explicitly

of The Argument of the Paradigm Case. By 'Hume's thesis' I mean the contention that we should call off the dispute between those who assert and those who deny 'freewill' because to see that, unless 'freewill' is being used with a meaning or implication which is not part of its meaning or implication in its ordinary sense, there can be no real dispute is to see that there is no real dispute. It must, no doubt, be allowed that the alleged question whether the will is free or not is not a debatable question unless 'freewill' can be, and is, given an extraordinary implication. For the libertarian does not mean to maintain the truism that not all actions are done under coercion or social pressure; and the determinist does not mean to deny this truism. But Professor Flew's deployment of The Argument of the Paradigm Case against what he takes as the thesis of determinism is inconclusive unless the extra implication given to 'freewill' by the disputants can be dismissed as senseless, as a philosophers' *misuse*. How, then, can Professor Flew expect to be understood when he alludes to this misuse as the attribution to actions of 'unpredictability in principle'? The thesis of the libertarian, as he here implies, is that a free action makes a break in the order of causal determination, or in whatever looser kind of orderliness modern science has substituted for causal determination; the thesis of the determinist is the contradictory of this thesis of the libertarian. Professor Flew has not begun to prove that The Argument of the Paradigm Case proves that the use of 'freewill' with this implication is a mere misuse. Moreover, he has himself observed that 'no one has asked to be excused from dealing with whatever arguments may be deployed in support of any philosophers' misuses' (31). This admission implies that his own appeal to The Argument of the Paradigm Case in order to reduce to absurd paradox the thesis of the determinist and to empty platitude the thesis of the libertarian is a deceptively short short-cut which cannot be taken, in this (his only) instance, without begging the only interesting questions. The argument which claims to settle the dispute assumes that the dispute is settled when it is shown that, if the words in which it is formulated are used in their ordinary senses, the thesis is a platitude and its denial an absurdity. But what is needed is an argument for this assumption. The assumption is not plausible. For everyone who studies the literature of the problem, including the most recent additions to it alluded to by Professor Flew (p. 31, n. 54), can see that the temptation to assert that free actions are 'contra-causal' or 'unpredictable in principle' is not removed by the recognition that, in its everyday uses, the expression 'of his own freewill' does not carry this implication.

by Mr Warnock at the end of his admirable Pelican Book on Berkeley. He remarks that, since the time of Locke and Berkeley, philosophical discussion of perception 'has been prosecuted with enormous industry and ingenuity, but also with a certain lack of originality—a lack which is itself a striking tribute to the power of our seventeenth- and eighteenth-century predecessors'.[1] The 'lack of originality' shows itself in the failure to 'break the dead-lock between Locke and Berkeley': 'philosophers were found, well into the present century, discussing perception as if the only possibilities were versions of Locke's position, or of Berkeley's'.[2] He suggests that philosophers should desist from the attempt to repair these positions and from the elaboration of revised versions. 'Perhaps it is time . . . to undertake instead the proper investiga-tion of the immensely complex vocabulary of perception in ordinary language. At the very least we shall thus be able to ensure that no time is wasted on problems due *merely* to imperfect understanding of language; and this would be, if not the end of the whole matter, at least a by no means inconsiderable gain. . . .'[3]

But perhaps it is optimistic to expect that such an investigation could be more than the beginning of the whole matter. For the vocabulary of perception is complex not simply, it may be sug-gested, because it conveys delicately differentiated nuances of meaning, but because it often reflects confusions between incon-sistent views. If this is so, it seems unlikely that ordinary language itself could be adequately understood and justly estimated except as part of an inquiry with wider terms of reference. But I do not propose to discuss *a priori* the prospects of the investigation which Mr Warnock desires to see carried out. I prefer to examine actual arguments which exhibit the linguistic approach, and to see whether any general morals can be drawn from their success or failure. I shall examine first Mr Warnock's own interesting attempt to 'break the deadlock between Locke and Berkeley', and, secondly, an argument developed by Professor Ryle in his recently published Tarner Lectures.

According to Mr Warnock there is a 'deadlock between Locke and Berkeley' in the sense that while their theories of perception and the material world are both fundamentally wrong, it has for centuries been found difficult to see how anyone who rejects one of these theories can avoid accepting some version of the other.

[1] *Berkeley*, p. 236.   [2] *Op. cit.*, p. 182.   [3] *Op. cit.*, pp. 246, 247.

For it has seemed plausible to think that statements about material things must be understood *either*, with Berkeley and modern Phenomenalism, as being statements, mainly hypothetical, about 'ideas' or sense-experiences *or*, with Locke, as statements about 'a mysterious realm whose nature we can discover only, if at all, by risky inference or elaborate construction'.[1] In order to understand how formidable this impasse is in Mr Warnock's opinion, it is necessary to make clear what the fundamental errors are which he finds in both views.

Mr Warnock's main criticism of Berkeley and of Phenomenalism starts from his clarification of what is meant by a 'statement of immediate perception', a statement in making which we assume nothing except that we are using words correctly.[2] By a process of reduction, carried out in a series of approximations, he reaches the following typical formulation: 'it seems to me as if I were hearing a sort of purring noise'.[3] Berkeley's view that a thing is a 'collection of ideas' may be expressed by saying that reality is consistent seeming; the inference from immediate perceptions to material objects is an inference to other immediate perceptions. But reality cannot be consistent seeming, since it is not self-contradictory to say that it seems to everyone, including God, as if there were a sort of purring noise but there is in fact no such noise.[4] I entirely agree with Mr Warnock in thinking that, for the reason which he states so persuasively, Berkeley's view is fundamentally wrong.

The objection to Locke which Mr Warnock takes to be 'wholly conclusive'[5] is a form of the familiar puzzle as to how Locke, on his premises, can know what he claims to know about the similarities and non-similarities between bodies and the sensations (ideas) which they produce in us. The knowledge is not obtained by comparing the two, since bodies are taken for granted or inferred and not perceived. But the inference to bodies could not be valid. In one place Mr Warnock makes this point, or represents Berkeley as making it, in a very mild form, by saying that 'it is not *necessary* that ideas be caused by objects', since 'ideas may occur (for example in dreams or hallucinations) "though no bodies exist without, resembling them" '.[6] This way of stating

[1] *Op. cit.*, p. 98.   [2] *Op. cit.*, pp. 163 ff.   [3] *Op. cit.*, p. 168.
[4] *Op. cit.*, cf. pp. 181, 182.   [5] *Op. cit.*, p. 101.
[6] *Op. cit.*, pp. 101, 102.

the objection leaves open the possibility that ideas might be *good evidence for* objects; the inference might be a probable inference, not a demonstration. But this lesser claim is rejected by Mr Warnock in a later passage in which he says that the inference to bodies, since it 'could never conceivably be checked', 'would be invalid and is indeed not intelligible at all'.[1] The justification which, if I follow him, Mr Warnock offers for maintaining the objection in this very strong and sweeping form lies in the contrast which he proceeds to draw between the kind of inference which can be checked and may be valid and the inference from ideas to objects which Locke's theory requires. When I see an angular bulge in a Christmas stocking I may validly infer that there is a model boat in the stocking, and, in principle at least, my inference can be checked—by pulling the model boat out of the stocking. The inference required by Locke's theory is from my idea of an orange on the mantelpiece, i.e. according to Warnock's analysis, from the fact that it seems to me as if I were seeing an orange on the mantelpiece, to the existence of an orange on the mantelpiece. The contrast, in short—this way of putting it is mine, not Mr Warnock's—is between an inference from a bulge which I see to a boat which I can come to see and an inference from an 'idea-of-an-orange' which I 'see' to an orange which I can never come to 'see' (although I am already seeing it). I agree with Mr Warnock that there is this contrast. But it is not clear to me that, by drawing our attention to the contrast, he has *proved*, as he thinks he has, that an inference from seeming to real existence must be invalid and unintelligible. All that he seems to me to have *proved* is that there will be important differences between such an inference and the inference in the anecdote about the Christmas stocking. This comment on Mr Warnock's argument is similar to the comment I made earlier on Professor Ryle's contention that sensations are not 'clues'.

We are now in a position to state shortly, with the help of Mr Warnock's symbolism, the 'deadlock' which he finds between the views of Locke and Berkeley. S_1, S_2 . . . S_n are to represent a set of 'statements about ideas' or 'statements of immediate perception' (such a set of statements may be referred to as an 'S-set') and M a 'statement about a material object'. We have to reject Locke's view that we can reach an M by causal inference from

[1] *Op. cit.*, p. 176.

an S-set, but accept his view that no S-set can be equivalent to an M. We have to reject Berkeley's view that any M can be analysed in terms of an S-set, but accept his view that from an S-set only another S, or another S-set, can be inferred. Mr Warnock maintains that, if we understand what we are doing when we pass from an S-set to an M, we can see that this eclectic position is not, as it at first appears to be, internally inconsistent. For, although we can validly infer from an S-set only to another S, it is also true that, when the accumulation of an S-set has reached a certain point, 'it is *reasonable to stop* talking in the "S-language" and to assert M instead'.[1] But to say all this is *not* to say that we *infer* an M from an S-set. Mr Warnock adduces an analogy from the law-courts to support this contention. The analogy is stated in one place as follows: 'Statements about material objects are no more *unconnected* with statements about "ideas", than verdicts are unconnected with evidence; but statements about ideas are no more the *same* as statements about material objects, than statements of evidence are the same as verdicts'.[2] But what is the connexion between the evidence and the verdict? Does not the connexion at least include the relation of premisses to conclusion? Mr Warnock denies this, and this denial is essential to the point on which the analogy is designed to throw light, that M is not *inferred* from an S-set. But he can deny this only by treating the statement that the evidence points to the prisoner's guilt as if it were itself a 'statement of evidence'. That he falls into this confusion is clear from the following passage: 'If the foreman says "we are all quite sure that all the evidence supports the view that the accused committed the offence", then he has, simply in that he has not said "Guilty", *not* pronounced a verdict. He has stated an excellent, indeed a complete, *reason* for pronouncing a verdict, but he has not yet pronounced it. In order to get this done he must be asked, not to make up his mind or collect new evidence or go beyond the evidence, but simply to *say* something different —to pronounce a verdict, by saying "Guilty".'[3]

We have to distinguish three stages, not two: (*a*) stating what the evidence is, (*b*) stating that the evidence supports the view that the accused committed the offence, (*c*) saying 'Guilty'. In his exposition of the analogy Mr Warnock wobbles between saying that the passage from an S-set to an M is analogous to the tran-

[1] *Op. cit.*, p. 192.   [2] *Op. cit.*, p. 189.   [3] *Op. cit.*, pp. 184, 185.

sition from (*a*) to (*b*), (*c*) and saying that it is analogous to the transition from (*a*), (*b*) to (*c*). If the analogy were with the latter transition, it would support the idea that the transition from an S-set to an M is not inferential. But in fact the analogy is with the former transition. Hence the whole comparison fails to illuminate or to commend the paradox that the transition from an S-set to an M is not an inference. If my criticism has not been unfair to Mr Warnock's elaborate discussion of 'the central puzzle of Berkeley's philosophy',[1] we must, I think, conclude that he has not here given us a convincing example of the way in which the linguistic approach may be expected to solve or dissolve problems about perception and our knowledge of the external world.

The argument of Professor Ryle on which I wish to comment occurs in the chapter on Perception in his *Dilemmas* (pp. 99 ff.). It seems to me that in this passage a claim is made to solve, or partially solve, an epistemological problem, or set of problems, by the application of a linguistic observation or discovery, and that this claim is unplausible and unproved. The discovery in question, which is linguistic in the sense that it is a discovery about the uses of words, is that a large number of verbs which are important in discussions about perception and knowledge fall into one or other of two classes called by Professor Ryle 'task verbs' and 'achievement verbs'. Thus 'listen', 'look', 'argue', 'investigate', like 'search', 'treat', 'travel', are task verbs; 'hear', 'see', 'prove', 'know', like 'find', 'cure', 'arrive', are achievement verbs.

In a section of *The Concept of Mind* Professor Ryle claims that the failure to notice in particular cases the difference between these two classes of 'episodic verbs' 'has been the source of some gratuitous puzzles and, accordingly, of some mystery-mongering theories'.[2] He gives two examples of such puzzles. (1) The first is the puzzle raised by the fact that 'epistemologists have sometimes confessed to finding the supposed cognitive activities of seeing, hearing and inferring oddly elusive'.[3] Professor Ryle claims that 'the mystery dissolves when we realize that "see", "descry" and "find" are not process words, experience words or activity words. They do not stand for perplexingly undetectable actions or reactions, any more than "win" stands for a perplexingly

---

[1] *Op. cit.*, p. 176.   [2] *The Concept of Mind*, p. 151.
[3] *Op. cit.*, p. 152.

undetectable bit of running. . . .'[1] It is this claim, developed more fully in the later book, on which I shall comment. (2) The second puzzle to which the distinction between task and achievement verbs is applied in this passage of *The Concept of Mind* arises from a misunderstanding of the fact that adverbs like 'erroneously' cannot qualify achievement verbs. This fact has given rise to the idea that there are certain faculties or procedures which cannot go wrong. 'The logical impossibility of a discovery being fruitless, or of a proof being invalid, has been misconstrued as a quasi-causal impossibility of going astray.'[2] On this point I agree with Professor Ryle; a good deal of what has been said and thought by some philosophers about the infallibility of memory and knowledge can be cleared up by noticing that 'remember' and 'know' are achievement verbs. I mention this point, without discussing it, because I do not wish to be understood as suggesting that the investigation of the everyday uses of words can never contribute in an important way to the solution of the problems which have been discussed by philosophers.

What is difficult in Professor Ryle's treatment of perceptual achievement verbs in *Dilemmas* is to understand what he thinks is the relevance of the point to the problems which he is ostensibly trying to solve, or at least to alleviate. These are described as being problems which arise when we reflect upon the answers given by physiological psychology to questions like 'How do we perceive?' and 'Of what is seeing the effect?'[3] Towards the end of his discussion Professor Ryle describes as follows the kind of 'dilemmas about perceptions' which he has had in mind: 'From some well-known facts of optics, acoustics and physiology it seemed to follow that what we see, hear or smell cannot be, as we ordinarily suppose, things and happenings outside us, but are, on the contrary, things and happenings inside us. When we ordinarily speak confidently of seeing other people's faces, we ought, apparently, to speak instead of seeing some things going on behind our own faces, or else, more guardedly, inside our own minds.'[4] This description might cover a considerable variety of familiar difficulties: problems about the apparent fact of body-mind interaction, the puzzles raised by illusions and hallucinations and by the time-lag between the event said to be perceived

[1] *Op. cit.*, p. 152.   [2] *Op. cit.*, p. 152.

[3] *Dilemmas*, p. 100.   [4] *Op. cit.*, p. 109.

and our perception of it. Professor Ryle seems to tell us that we can solve these problems, or dissolve them, by removing the misconceptions which make them seem to be problems, when we realize that 'seeing a tree' is not the 'psychological end-state' of a process.[1] Seeing is 'not a state or process at all'.[2] 'See' stands for an achievement and not for an experience—any more than 'win' stands for 'a perplexingly undetectable bit of running'.

My objection to this argument is that the account given of the class of verbs to which 'see', 'hear', etc., belongs is *prima facie* irrelevant, and certainly not clearly relevant, to the 'dilemmas about perception' with which the chapter is concerned. In view of this major difficulty it seems superfluous to raise the question whether there is not some overstatement in Professor Ryle's treatment of 'see' and 'hear' as achievement words which never signify an experience, 'a sub-stretch of my life-story'.[3] A man whose sight was restored by an operation might say that from the time of the operation he began to see; here beginning to see seems more like beginning to walk than like beginning to win races. But, even if we concede that 'see' is always, and without qualification, an achievement word, so to class it does not banish out of existence the process of visual experience. On the contrary, seeing, like any other successful termination, presupposes the process which it terminates: a race to be won must be run. Nor is there anything 'elusive' about the experience or process which stands (according to Professor Ryle's analogy) to seeing and hearing as running a race stands to winning it. If epistemologists have seemed to find it elusive, what they have been looking for must have been, not the process itself, but something, for example an act, which would be an element in the process if, but only if, some philosopher's analysis or description of the process were correct. Thus, if I am right, Professor Ryle's negative answer to the question whether 'see' and 'hear' stand for processes is irrelevant to the problems which arise from reflexion on the physical and physiological conditions of perception. For the problems arise from the existence of perceptual processes which have to be distinguished from their physical conditions and not from an injudicious choice of a vocabulary to be used in mentioning them.

[1] *Op. cit.*, p. 101.   [2] *Op. cit.*, p. 102.   [3] *Op. cit.*, p. 103.

CHAPTER XII

POLAR CONCEPTS AND METAPHYSICAL ARGUMENTS[1]

C. K. Grant

Professor of Philosophy in the University of Durham

In these remarks I propose to examine the credentials of an argument that enjoys a considerable vogue in contemporary philosophy. I shall be concerned with a logical principle about the nature of polar concepts, which for the sake of brevity I shall call the polar principle. It is not so much an argument as a dogma that is employed in discussing and, I hope to show, distorting different kinds of philosophical problems. I shall therefore first say something about the principle itself, and then consider how it has been applied to three philosophical issues, for it is only by examining how the principle operates in detail that its shortcomings can be detected.

The earliest and clearest formulation of the polar principle with which I am acquainted has been made by Mr N. Malcolm as follows: 'Certain words of our language operate in pairs, e.g. "large" and "small", "animate" and "inanimate", "vague" and "clear", "certain" and "probable". In their use in ordinary language a member of a pair *requires* its opposite—for animate is *contrasted* with inanimate, probability with certainty, vagueness with clearness. Now there are certain features about the criteria for the use of the words in these pairs which tempt philosophers to wish to remove from use one member of the pair. When the philosopher says that all words are really vague, he is proposing that we never apply the word "clear" any more, i.e. he is proposing that we abolish its use. But suppose that we did *change* our language in such a way that we made the philosophical statements true—that is, made it true that it was no longer correct to call any empirical statement certain, no longer correct to say of any word that its meaning is clear. Would this be an improvement? It is important to see that by such a move we should have gained nothing whatever. The word in our revised language

[1] *Proceedings of the Aristotelian Society*, 1955–6, Vol. LVI.

would have to do double duty. The word "vague" would have to perform the function previously performed by two words, "vague" and "clear". But it could not perform this function. For it was essential to the meaning of the word "vague" in its previous use, that vagueness was *contrasted* with clearness. In the revised language vagueness could be contrasted with nothing. The word "vague" would simply be dropped as a useless word. And we should be compelled to adopt into the revised language a new pair of words with which to express the same distinctions formerly expressed by the words "clear" and "vague". The revision of our language would have accomplished nothing.'[1]

There are two serious weaknesses in this argument. I shall summarize them now, and consider them in greater detail when we consider the three uses of the polar principle.

I. It is clear that Malcolm holds that the only purpose a philosopher can have in generalizing a polar term in the way that he describes (e.g. by saying 'All words are vague') is that he wishes to alter our use of language in order to make it more 'precise' or 'accurate'. Malcolm has no difficulty in showing that the philosopher's statement, so interpreted, achieves nothing. But we must ask why Malcolm is so confident that the philosophical observation is intended to be taken as a linguistic recommendation. In fact no philosopher who made a statement of this kind would accept Malcolm's account of what he is attempting to do; hence he does not feel abashed when Malcolm points out that he fails. Perhaps Malcolm is right and the philosopher wrong; how can this be decided? Before vexing ourselves with this question we should consider the following two points.

(*a*) The two standpoints can perhaps be reconciled in this way. A polar generalization, although not itself a rule of language, entails a modification of language rules. Certainly Malcolm is right in saying that if we accept the truth of 'All words are vague', then we are committed to a language in which there is no use for the expression 'a word with a clear (or vague) meaning'.

In parenthesis, I should point out that there are ambiguities in the expression 'use of an expression'. This may refer merely to

[1] N. Malcolm: *Moore and Ordinary Language* in *The Philosophy of G. E. Moore* (Living Philosophers Library), pp. 364-5.

the place of a symbolic form within a language system of some kind; this notion is rather like that of an uninterpreted proposition in mathematics. On the other hand 'use' may mean '*actual*' rather than 'possible' use; in this case we are referring to the specific role, not necessarily descriptive, of an expression within a natural language. Failure to notice this ambiguity can lead to trouble, especially if it is coupled with an uncritical adherence to what may be called an extensional theory of meaning. The following quotation illustrates this. 'For an *established* linguistic practice is one which we know to be taught, so to speak, and learned, and used accordingly, and which must therefore have at least *some* occurrences in which it is free from error. . . .'[1] Since the phrase 'honest broker' is part of an 'established linguistic practice', as presumably it is, it follows from Rollins's argument that there *must be* honest brokers, i.e. there must be some occasions on which 'honest broker' is correctly applied. This is a rather perverse form of the ontological argument.

Nevertheless the possibility remains open that the polar generalization may be important and illuminating, even though it should entail redundant verbal reforms in the way that Malcolm describes.

(*b*) The significance of polar generalizations is partly explained by some further remarks of Malcolm, which are difficult to reconcile with those already quoted. He points out quite rightly that philosophical paradoxes of this kind arise from a 'desire to emphasize similarities or differences between the criteria for applying the phrases "absolutely certain" and "highly probable" to empirical propositions; and also from the desire to stress the difference between the criteria for applying "certain" to empirical statements, and for applying it to *a priori* statements'. Malcolm is now saying that a polar generalization is not just a suggestion about changing language, but is essentially a statement about an *analogy*; and since presumably the question of whether an analogy is helpful and illuminating is logically independent of the question whether or not it entails pointless syntactic changes of

[1] C. D. Rollins, 'Ordinary Language and Procrustean Beds, *Mind*, 1951, p. 230. Author's italics. Rollins goes on to say that this point is well known and refers to its formulation in Malcolm's article *Moore and Ordinary Language*.

I

the kind illustrated, it follows that Malcolm's original linguistic criticisms are beside the point.

II. There is a more obvious and more serious objection to Malcolm's formulation of the polar principle; we shall see that this applies to various applications of the principle that have been made. The relevant sentence here is as follows: 'When the philosopher says that all words are really vague, he is proposing that we never apply the word "clear" any more, i.e. he is proposing that we abolish its use'. Now even if the philosopher *is* making a linguistic proposal, which we have seen to be very doubtful, it is certain that he is not making the one that Malcolm ascribes to him. Even if we accept 'All words are really vague', all that follows is that we cannot use 'vague' and 'clear' *to qualify words*; all the other manifold uses of these polar terms remain unaffected. For example, we can still significantly say things like 'I saw the vague outline of a figure', 'The water in the brook is clearer than that in the pond', etc. Now the importance of this resides in the fact that because there are accepted uses of the polar terms 'clear' and 'vague' for describing things other than words, then a generalization of one of the terms that is restricted to a certain class, e.g. words, is meaningful in so far as there is an analogy between the generalized polar concept and its other uses where it functions to point a certain contrast. Hence the legitimacy of polar generalizations is to be determined by whether or not they indicate a genuine resemblance between the whole of a certain class that is qualified by a generalized polar term, and other classes to which the term applies as a contrast. It may appear from this that a polar generalization is legitimate only in a restricted sense, i.e. as applied to a class, and that it acquires its significance from the fact that there are other familiar and established uses of the polar term. Certain metaphysical arguments contrast a generalized and familiar polar term with a definition of the contrasted term that does not correspond to an accepted usage. The first two applications of the polar principle that we shall consider are to arguments of this type. The first of these is as follows:

A. Descartes believed that his methodological innovations would rescue him from a number of vexatious puzzles, amongst them the possibility that we may be always dreaming. This is not, according to the polar principle, a genuine problem, for its very formulation is without sense. The word 'dream' refers to a state that is the opposite of waking, its function is to point a certain contrast. The Cartesian generalization robs the word of this function and therefore of its meaning. A further consequence, as Malcolm indicates, is that the familiar and important distinction between dreaming and waking cannot be drawn, for we no longer have a terminology in which to do so. If in the metaphysical Cartesian sense I was dreaming while I ate my breakfast this morning, then I cannot describe my experiences while I slept as dreams in that same sense. Thus the only thing achieved is that a perfectly good word is deprived of its familiar meaning without being assigned any other.

Here, we must note for later consideration an assumption that underlies this argument. It is that if it has been shown that the *proposition* 'We are always dreaming' is meaningless, then it follows that it must also be senseless to raise the *question* 'Are we always dreaming?'

A propos Malcolm's formulation of the polar principle, I argued that a generalization of a polar concept is to be interpreted as an implicit statement of an analogy. It may of course be a good or a bad analogy, but the chief point that I wish to establish is that it is as an analogy that a metaphysical assertion of this kind must be considered—to dismiss it in cavalier fashion by invoking the polar principle is entirely to miss the point. Let us then re-state Descartes' problem along these lines.

In the first place it must be recognized that this metaphysical worry is not about dreams in the ordinary familiar sense of the word 'dream'; thus any argument that relies on the assumption that Descartes *is* using the word in this sense will be irrelevant. Nor is it the case that in order to state the problem it is necessary to use the word 'dream' in an extraordinary, meaningless sense. The question at stake may be put in this way: is there a kind of consciousness which stands to our normal waking experience in an identical (or similar) relation to that in which these waking experiences stand to our dreams? The problem is not whether we are perpetually dreaming in the ordinary sense of the word, but whether there is a resemblance or analogy between our waking life and our dream life *vis-à-vis* another sort of awareness. It is by contrast with this order of consciousness that Descartes gives a metaphysical definition of 'dream' that embraces waking experience. In this way the Cartesian difficulty can be stated without employing any verbal formulae in which a polar concept is generalized. Thus the polar principle does not 'dissolve' the problem at all; it is merely a not very well founded objection to a certain way of stating it.

My reformulation is open to a number of objections. For example, it may be urged that the notion of a more 'real' or profound kind of consciousness is nonsensical because it is unverifiable. This is not convincing. In the first place the verification principle itself is by no means beyond question, as is now generally recognized. Moreover, it is not self-evident that the Cartesian problem is empirically untestable. We might say that it is verifiable on death; if it should be objected that this condition itself is nonsensical, then we can specify various operations that could give the problem an empirical significance. Prayer, fasting, meditation and the consumption of mescaline may separately or together give rise to states of consciousness of such an intensity that in comparison with them ordinary waking experience is vague, disjointed—in fact, dreamlike. Again, it may be objected that the problem is a pointless one; there are no elements in human experience that give rise to it. This is surely to beg the question, for presumably a mystic would claim that he has experiences of illumination incomparably more vivid and intense than ordinary waking consciousness—and who is to gainsay him? If he does have these experiences, by what right is he denied a language with which to compare them with more familiar ones? It is worth remembering, I think, that Descartes himself had such an experience in November 1619.

Nothing that has been said here has anything to do with the empirical issue of whether or not there is a more profound or ultimate sort of knowledge accessible to all or some human beings, although I am taking for granted the fact that people sometimes have peculiar experiences that seem to them profoundly or perhaps supernaturally illuminating. I am concerned to show only that it is not necessarily unintelligible to attempt to characterize such experiences by generalizing the polar term 'dream'.

Polar terms, and generalizations of them, may occur in hypothetical as well as categorical sentences. (I am using 'hypothetical' here rather loosely.) Philosophers are perplexed by the supposition that we *may* be always dreaming, as well as by the positive assertion that we are. Even if the polar principle were successful in demonstrating the meaninglessness of assertions that generalize polar concepts, it would not follow that suppositions of a similar form were also meaningless. It is a confusion of modalities to assume that the logical rules which govern polar terms in indicative sentences are identical with those that apply to these terms in suppositions or questions, where the inapplicability of one of the terms is raised only as a possibility. The most important logical difference between propositions and suppositions is this: if a polar term is generalized in the former, then the whole expression can be given a meaning only if it is interpreted an an analogy, while a supposition may be meaningful even if it is taken in its literal, i.e. familiar, sense. To make the *assertion* 'We are always dreaming' is to commit oneself to a use of "dream" which is different from, though not unrelated to, its ordinary use, while to consider perpetual dreaming as a *possibility* is not necessarily to use the word 'dream' in any unusual sense.

This distinction between suppositions and assertions indicates that it is important further to analyse suppositions in which a polar term is generalized, for as we shall see these sentences can bear different constructions. I shall illustrate the salient ambiguities of these by reference to the sentence 'We may be always dreaming'. This may be interpreted as raising issues that are primarily either epistemological, empirical or logical. They will be discussed in that order.

(A) The expression may be interpreted as raising the epistemological question of the nature of the tests and criteria by reference to which we answer the question 'Am I dreaming?' The particular point at stake here is whether or not there is a *decisive* test for determining which of two polar terms is to be applied to a given subject-matter, in this case a certain state of consciousness. Many philosophers (perhaps Descartes amongst them) have mistakenly thought that if there is no decisive test, then the distinction in question is in some way 'unreal' or 'irrational' or 'illegitimate'. As Malcolm points out, the question here is essentially the same as that involved in the notion that we can never be completely certain of the truth of any empirical proposition, for theoretically such a proposition is testable by an infinite number of operations and is liable to be falsified by any one of them. This consideration does not entail, in either this case or that of Descartes, that the validity of the distinction is in any way impugned, for not all tests are acid tests. There is no standard criterion for baldness, yet the familiar differences between men who are bald and those who are not remain unaffected, even though it follows from the lack of a decisive criterion that there may be borderline cases which cannot be classified *tout court*.

(B) From an empirical standpoint a supposition of this kind should be regarded as a statement either to the effect that there is no known empirical obstacle to the non-existence of one side of the polar distinction, or that the distinction is a factual and contingent one, so that either of the polar terms may be empirically inapplicable.

These suppositions may refer to either the present or the future. In the former case it is being stated that it is an empirical possibility that everyone is now dreaming. If so, then our present so-called waking experiences will be dreams in the same sense as are our so-called dreams. I am inclined to think that this possibility is untestable and strictly meaningless, but I suggest that it arises naturally from an experience which, though odd, is not uncommon—namely, dreaming that one is dreaming.

As applied to the future, the supposition may be taken to state, falsely, that there are no known empirical reasons why everyone should not in the next moment or later fall asleep and immediately begin to dream.

(C) Alternatively it could be taken to illustrate a logical point, viz. that there is no logical contradiction in any expression that generalizes a polar term. The proposition 'All conscious beings are dreaming' is not logically absurd; although a *statement* to this effect may well involve a pragmatic paradox, the sentence gives rise to no difficulty from a formal point of view.

This brings us to the question: what is the logical status of polar terms? It is not adequate to say simply, as does Malcolm, that certain words in our language operate in pairs, because this covers different logical relations, e.g. those between contrary and correlative terms. Let us first consider a general definition of 'opposite' terms, and then examine the different cases that it covers. A and B are 'opposed' terms when: 'X is B' entails 'X is not A', and 'X is A' entails 'X is not B'.[1] This definition applies to the following:

(1) Philosophically puzzling polar concepts such as 'material' and 'mental', 'dreaming' and 'waking', 'absolute', and relative'.

(2) Contrary terms that have, as Aristotle[2] puts it, an 'intermediate' or 'mean', e.g. 'concave' and 'convex' (intermediate 'flat'), and 'past' and 'future' (intermediate 'present').

(3) Contrary terms that do not have a mean, i.e. contradictories, e.g. 'husband' and 'wife', 'brother' and 'sister', 'necessary' and 'contingent', 'male' and 'female', and 'true' and 'false'. (In these last two examples I am observing the ordinary rules for the use of these expressions; in a more elaborate language, such as that of biology where the phenomenon of hermaphroditism is of importance, the 'male-female' distinction may come under heading (2). Similarly in a 3-valued logic the distinction between 'true' and 'false' would come into that category.)

The definition is a highly general one, since it applies to contrariety considered simply as incompatibility, that is, the view that 'contrary' should be so used that 'blue' and 'black' are contraries of each other. A more restricted definition of 'contrary', which rules out this case, is the following: A and B are contrary when 'X is B' entails 'X is not A', and 'X is not B' entails 'X is A'. The generality of the first definition makes it preferable for our purposes.

'Opposite term' is an expression that is not applicable to all predicates. Influenced by examples from formal logic we may be tempted to say that any predicate P is a contrary term of some kind, on the ground that we can construct its opposite by using some such symbol as 'not'. This logical triviality is of no

---

[1] These two conditions are interdependent.

[2] Aristotle. *Categories* 11b. Cf. also *Categories* 6b. 'By the term "slave" we mean the slave *of a master*; by the term "master", the master *of a slave*.' According to the polar principle it should follow that no meaning whatever can be attached to 'All men are slaves'; yet this could have the perfectly good analogical meaning that all men (including masters and slaves in the ordinary sense) are in servitude to their passions—or perhaps to God.

importance here; what makes a term an opposite is whether it is
in fact used as such, either in ordinary language or in a metaphysical system. Thus there are not, in ordinary discourse, any
opposites of predicates like 'jealous' or 'green', while there are
opposites of 'fast' and 'intelligent'. It is not always easy to distinguish between those predicates that have opposites and those
that do not. Thus should we say that 'angry' is a polar concept?
If so, is its opposite 'good-tempered', 'amiable', or what? These
difficult cases do not, however, invalidate the general distinction.

Some polar concepts are used not to point a contrast within
a certain subject-matter, e.g. words or states of consciousness, etc.,
but to indicate a universal distinction, for example 'mental' and
'material'. Various theorists employ these expressions as exhaustive
categories; it is supposed that anything you may care to name
must fit into one or other of these pigeon-holes. Highly general
terms of this kind are employed univocally; that is, the sense in
which a tree is 'material' is the same as that in which a brick is
'material'.[1] Now the polar concepts that we have so far considered
mark similar distinctions within different but analogically related
classes of entities, so that a generalization of one of the terms as
it applies in one region is meaningful because its opposite still
retains a use elsewhere. As we have seen, this is not the case with
distinctions like 'material' and 'mental', hence it may seem that
the polar principle applies to them.

It is certainly meaningless to say 'Everything is material' in
the ordinary sense of 'material', and for the reason adduced by
the polar principle—namely that here 'material' can be contrasted with nothing. Having conceded this, I must point out
that very little follows from it. We cannot, for example, conclude
that the 'mental-material' distinction is in any mysterious way
'ultimate' or 'irreducible'. Some have tried to put the polar
principle in the service of metaphysics in this way; but from such
a starting-point we cannot reach an ontological terminus. Let us
ask: what is it to affirm or deny that a certain distinction is 'irreducible'? This may refer to many different things. One of them
which is relevant here is the kind of theory represented by
epiphenomenalism. This doctrine denies the irreducibility of the
distinction between mental and physical processes by claiming,
roughly speaking, that the laws of psychology are special cases of

[1] Cf. Aristotle, *Categories* 1.

the laws of chemistry and physics. It is conceivable that one day this may be demonstrated, so that when the epiphenomenalist says 'Everything is matter' he is making a logically respectable assertion that may one day be shown to be empirically true. He is not, of course, denying that there are mental events in the ordinary sense, for his thesis presupposes their existence; and no one but a very literal-minded philosopher bemused by the polar principle would suppose that he was denying this.

This example of universal polar concepts illustrates a further point, which is that the polar principle is not confined to predicates. The temptation to think of all polar concepts as predicates arises from the fact that alleged irreducible ontological distinctions between kinds of substances can be expressed in the form of propositions about the applicability of certain predicates. Thus 'Matter (or mind) is the only reality' is equivalent to 'Everything is really material (or mental)'. This shows nothing, for neither form of expression is more 'fundamental' than the other. In any event, as we have seen, it would be extremely difficult to translate Descartes' problem into the terms of either of these formulae. From these considerations, then, we can draw only the conclusion that polar terms are non-sentential expressions, not necessarily predicates, that are used in a certain way, i.e. as opposites, either in ordinary discourse or in the artificial language of a metaphysical system. This does not take us far, and indeed is not intended to, for one of the theses I wish to maintain is that there are important differences between polar concepts which are obscured if the polar principle is applied to them blanket-fashion. This consideration is independent of the criticisms that I advance against particular uses of the principle.

As we have seen the polar principle expresses a theory about meaning, namely that the significance of a term that is used as an opposite depends upon a *contrast*. It is often supposed not only that this is clear but that it is clearly true. I wish to cast suspicion on these notions, which I propose to do by considering an example of two opposed terms which give rise to no philosophical difficulties. The distinction between 'concave' and 'convex' is sometimes cited as a paradigm of opposition. Let us imagine a world in which only one of these two kinds of surfaces is to be found in nature, say 'concave'. The polar principle entails that no inhabitant of such a world could have a name for this sort of

I*

surface. This is false. Admittedly if a certain word has a meaning its use must be contrasted with another word; i.e. the rules for its use must differ from those governing the use of related expressions. But this is not to say that its use must be distinguishable from that of another *particular* word, in this case 'convex'. Suppose that in the hypothetical world all physical surfaces are either flat or concave; all surfaces are 'concavo-plane'. In the language of the inhabitants 'concave' would have a meaning because it is contrasted with 'flat'; here 'flat' and 'concave' are contradictories and not, as in our language, contraries. (It is not difficult to imagine different states of affairs; to describe some of these we would need a language with more complicated logical rules. Imagine that there are only flat and concave surfaces, and further that all—and only—flat surfaces are white while all the other colours are encountered only in concave surfaces. Then, presumably, 'flat' could be used as the contradictory of 'coloured', and 'white' as the contradictory of 'concave'. This is on the supposition that the language in question would be capable of doing the describing jobs that ordinary English does. There is no *necessity* that in this imaginary empirical situation the grammar of 'flat' and 'coloured', etc., would be as I have suggested, any more than there is any compelling philosophical reason why we should use the 'concave-convex' distinction to describe the world that we know. There are reasons for this, of course, but they are scientific and perhaps biological ones. If we were interested only or primarily in the texture of surfaces there would be nothing in our language corresponding to the concave-convex distinction. In fact English is very poorly equipped for discriminating between differences in texture.)

It might now be objected that in my hypothetical language 'concave' could not have the same meaning as it does in ordinary English. But what does this mean? It may be simply a reiteration of the fact that in the imaginary language 'concave' is contrasted with 'flat' and not, as in ours, with 'convex'. This is true but trivial. If, on the other hand, it is taken to mean that in the language 'concave' *must* be used in accordance with rules that differ from those of English, then it is false. We would use the word to refer to precisely the same kinds of surfaces as it describes in ordinary English. To use a somewhat unhelpful idiom, semantic rules are not always logically dependent upon syntactic rules.

This discussion of the logical grammar of 'concave' has shown that its familiar meaning is not conditional upon its being used to point a particular contrast, for it retains this meaning if used as the contradictory of 'flat' or even 'coloured'. Hence this meaning is not, as the polar principle states, dependent upon its use as a contrast to 'convex'. It is true, but merely as a matter of definition, that a polar term is used as the opposite of *some* other expression; but its significance is not dependent upon its being contrasted with any other particular expression. The error here arises from confusing the definition of 'polar term' with a false theory about the meaning of these terms.

Our consideration of the 'concave-convex' distinction has shown also that what are incompatible properties in one world (or opposed terms in one language) are not necessarily so in another world or language. (Many-valued systems have made this a familiar notion in formal logic.) Hence we cannot allow the claim, which is implicit in the polar principle, that any rule to the effect that one term is the opposite of another can possess *a priori* universal validity. There is nothing *wrong* with a language in which 'concave' is used as the contradictory of 'flat', for it might describe perfectly well a certain sort of world. In this world philosophers who held the polar principle would presumably argue that there *could not be* a *tertium quid*, an idea that we know to be false because in our world physical surfaces can be concave or flat or convex. A language that can describe these differences is richer than the former; yet from the standpoint of the imaginary language the polar principle would lead us to the conclusion that the richer language was a logical impossibility.

I now wish to make two points to guard against possible misunderstanding of the philosophical moral that I wish to draw from the discussion of the 'concave-convex' distinction.

1. I have used the distinction as a purely empirical, descriptive one. It is quite possible, *pace* Rollins, that in a world which has only concave or concavo-plane surfaces the inhabitants would be able to imagine, define and name convexity. In that case they would be able to contrast empirical concavity with the *a priori* concept of convexity. This case therefore is easily covered by the polar principle, hence I have interpreted the distinction as an entirely empirical one.

From this an interesting question arises. Suppose an inhabitant of the concavo-plane world, who has not envisaged convexity and who therefore uses 'concave' and 'flat' descriptively, is confronted with a convex surface. Will he say 'This is a flat surface', i.e. a 'non-concave surface', or will he be at a loss, knowing that he has no vocabulary to describe it? What happens will depend entirely upon the meaning that he has attached to the expressions 'concave' and 'flat'; if he uses 'flat' as simply the equivalent of 'not concave' then he is likely to say the former, while if he has discriminated between the two kinds of surface he will know that he does not know what to say.

Compare this with teaching a child the use of 'blue' and 'red' by confining it in a room that contains only red and blue objects.[1] The child is brought out, shown a yellow object and asked to name its colour. He will say 'blue' if he has defined this as 'not red' and 'red' if he has defined this as 'not blue'. If discrimination has taken place he will have no expression for yellow. But what is one to understand by 'discrimination' here? Simply the ability to use 'red' and 'blue' not merely as the contraries of each other but of other colours also; *ex hypothesi* this ability cannot be demonstrated while the child is confined in the room.[2]

2. It may be thought that I have misrepresented the ordinary idea of the relations between 'concave' and 'convex' on the ground that any object which is concave on one side (such as a lens) *must be* convex on the other. Convexity is concavity looked at from the other side, as it were. But how are we to regard the 'must' here? It certainly refers to no logical necessity, and indeed this notion is empirically true only provided that we are thinking of an object like a lens. There is no reason at all why objects that are concave on one side should be convex on the other, which might be flat. And an object might be concave on one side without having another side at all, e.g. a cliff. My question, then, was: in a world without empirical instances of 'convex', what

---

[1] This example was suggested to me by Mr J. L. Ackrill.

[2] This is connected with a problem raised by Wittgenstein: 'Could we define "red" by pointing to something that was *not red*? That would be as if one were supposed to explain the word "modest" to someone whose English was weak, and one pointed to an arrogant man and said "That man is *not* modest" '. *Philosophical Investigations*, p. 14.

would be the logical rules governing the relation between 'flat' and 'concave' in the language which describes this world? In answer to this I argued that although the logical relations between the expressions would be altered, their meaning would be unaffected. Hence as a doctrine of meaning the polar principle is false.

B.[1] Certain arguments which do not explicitly invoke the polar principle are based upon an essentially similar theory of meaning. A sophisticated example of this is to be found in Chapter VII of Professor Ryle's book *Dilemmas*, where he deals with the general inference from 'the notorious limitations and fallibilities of our senses to the impossibility of our getting to know anything at all by looking, listening and touching'.[2] We shall soon see that with little alteration Ryle's argument could be re-stated in terms of the polarity of 'true' and 'erroneous' (or related expressions) as applied to propositions that embody sensory observations. However, Ryle employs an original analogy to make this point, so that his treatment of the topic requires separate consideration.

Ryle considers the notion of the systematic delusiveness of the senses in the light of this analogy. 'A country which had no coinage would offer no scope to counterfeiters. There would be nothing for them to manufacture or pass counterfeits of.'[3] He develops this idea in the following way. 'In a country where there is a coinage, false coins can be manufactured and passed; and counterfeiting might be so efficient that an ordinary citizen, unable to tell which are false and which were genuine coins, might become suspicious of the genuineness of any particular coin that he received. But however general his suspicions might be, there remains one proposition that he cannot entertain, the proposition, namely, that it is possible that all coins are counterfeits. For there must be an answer to the question "Counterfeits of what?" '[4]

Is Ryle here denying that we can *always* be mistaken on the ground that if this were the case we could never *find out* that we were mistaken? If he is maintaining this, we might object that it

---

[1] This is the second example of a metaphysical argument which contrasts a familiar polar term with a novel definition of the contrasted term. For A, see p. 258 *supra*.

[2] *Loc. cit.*, p. 94. [3] *Loc. cit.*, p. 94. [4] *Loc. cit.*, pp. 94–5.

is a common experience to discover, in retrospect, that we have made a mistake in observation, although at the time of making the error we were not able to avoid or correct the mistake. Indeed, if knowing how to correct a mistake is a necessary condition of making it, we would presumably commit fewer errors than we do. This criticism is without foundation, for it rests on a confusion about the concept of 'finding out a mistake'. Ryle is saying nothing about the particular cases where we make an error of observation and are at the same time in ignorance of how to rectify it. What is being maintained is that a mistake is to be defined, in part, as something that is in principle detectable. Detection is ruled out by the notion of universal and perpetual error, so that in these circumstances a mistake is a logical impossibility. An *in principle* undiscoverable mistake is not a mistake at all.

With this conclusion one must agree; yet we shall see that the parable about counterfeiting is not as immediately relevant to establishing it as Ryle supposes. I shall try to show that this analogy throws no light on general scepticism about the senses, and furthermore that it leads Ryle to misrepresent the philosophical issue that is at stake.

The sceptic's statement 'The senses always deceive us' is more like 'All the paintings attributed to Vermeer are false' than it is like 'All coins are counterfeits'. In my proposed analogy I do not mean by 'false', 'fake', i.e. a forgery intended to deceive experts and the public about their authorship, for in that case Ryle's question 'Fakes of what?' would arise. I am envisaging the possibility that art historians might discover that the individual Vermeer painted none of the 'Vermeer' pictures. In that case the phrase 'genuine Vermeer' would lack any empirical application. The following line of argument is now relevant. Since it is the function of the phrase 'genuine Vermeer' to mark off a certain class of paintings from another class (the works of all other artists and in particular the forgeries of Van Meegeren), it therefore follows from the polar principle that the expression 'false Vermeer' is without significance and *a fortiori* that the sentence 'All Vermeers are false' is meaningless. This is absurd, for it was with precisely this supposition that we constructed our imaginary case. And as we have seen, this sentence is a perfectly good description of an empirically possible state of affairs. What has gone wrong? How is it that the phrase 'genuine Vermeer' can retain its meaning even when it points to no contrast?

The explanation is simple. It is that the contrast between 'false' and 'genuine' is highly general, and is relevant to a vast number of contexts other than that of the paintings of Vermeer. These polar terms indicate contrasts elsewhere, and in fact many different kinds of contrasts. Compare 'a genuine (or false) bank-note' with 'a genuine antique', 'a genuine aristocrat', 'a genuine person', 'genuine craftsmanship'. Because the polar terms have these manifold other uses, the phrase 'genuine Vermeer' remains significant even when it is deprived of possible descriptive employment.

How is this relevant to Ryle's treatment of the sentence 'The senses always deceive us'? The connexion is this. Ryle assumes, quite naturally but, as I hope to show, unjustifiably, that the verbs 'to know' and 'to make a mistake' as applied to our experience of material objects, refer always to our having sensations of some kind. Thus he is restricting the empirical uses of 'know' and 'make a mistake' to the level of sense experience in a way that is in important respects similar to that in which 'genuine' and 'false' were confined in our example to the paintings attributed to Vermeer.

In order to clarify this we should first recall that Ryle describes the sceptical philosopher's problem as whether we can get to know anything at all by 'looking, listening and touching'. If this is denied, says Ryle, there follows the absurd consequence that we are continually making in principle undiscoverable mistakes. But these mistakes are undiscoverable only if it is tacitly assumed that the only way of disclosing and correcting observational errors is by making further observations. Now there is no doubt at all that this is how we in fact detect and rectify errors of perception, and therefore Ryle is quite correct in his analysis of ordinary perceptual judgements. Nevertheless, those philosophers who cast doubt on the reliability of all sense experience do so in order to question this very notion. Hence the counterfeiting analogy, which rests upon it, is a *petitio principii*. Descartes doubted all empirical propositions based on sense perception. He came to this conclusion, and was logically entitled to state it, only because he held (no doubt wrongly) that we can acquire knowledge about material things by the clear and distinct ideas of reason.

This is the burden of the well-known discussion concerning the piece of wax. If, for the moment, we grant this to Descartes, it is clear that he is entitled to cast general doubt on the senses because he holds that there is a non-sensuous source of empirical knowledge by reference to which the deceptiveness of sense experience is exposed. He is thus advocating a use of 'know' and 'discover a mistake' which, though empirical, does not refer to sensations. Thus, although Descartes denies that we can find out anything by looking, listening and touching, he is not committed, as Ryle believes, to the idea that we can never find out anything by any means at all. Because the deliverances of sense perception are contrasted with the knowledge obtained by clear and distinct ideas, it makes sense for Descartes to argue that sense experience is systematically deceptive.

In a similar way to that in which the meaningfulness of 'genuine Vermeer' is guaranteed by the fact that the 'genuine-false' distinction can be drawn elsewhere, so for Descartes the sentence 'The senses always deceive us' is significant because he is contrasting deception with self-evident, clear and distinct ideas. The important difference between these two cases is that in the Vermeer example there are numerous familiar and established other uses of the 'genuine-false' distinction, but there is no corresponding use of 'know' to refer to an empirical but non-sensuous cognition, hence Descartes is compelled to make this innovation. There are no parallel uses of 'counterfeit' which could give the expression 'universal counterfeiting' a meaning because counterfeiting is defined *simpliciter* as copying coins.

Therefore the counterfeiting analogy does not, in my submission, do the job that Ryle gives to it. I am not, of course, defending Descartes' general scepticism, but attempting only to clarify its nature and to show that it is not vulnerable to Ryle's form of attack. Descartes does not make the logical blunder of defining a perceptual mistake as something in principle undiscoverable, but he does commit the epistemological error of supposing that there can be non-sensuous knowledge of facts. This epistemological mistake undermines his proposed alteration in the logical grammar of 'know', but it does not render logically inappropriate his doubt of the senses because it is the very purpose of the appeal to clear and distinct ideas to specify a form of knowledge that shows up the illusions of sense experience.

This consideration applies, I think, to all metaphysical and religious systems in which the *general* trustworthiness of the senses is impugned; in all these doctrines sense experience is contrasted with another alleged type of knowledge or awareness.

If I am correct, the conclusion to be drawn from this discussion is that the complexity of the rules for the use of philosophically puzzling expressions like 'know' and 'mistake' is sufficiently great to render analogies like 'counterfeit' (and other popular ones such as those drawn from games like chess and poker) as dangerous as they are on occasion illuminating. Under the influence of an over-simple analogy Ryle has been led not only to misrepresent philosophical scepticism concerning the senses but also to give a false diagnosis of the error upon which it is based.

Mr I. Berlin has invoked the polar principle on various occasions. Let us examine briefly one use that he makes of it.

'Propositions about the past were required by the more uncompromising among the early positivists to become ("in some sense") propositions about the future—or else to be eliminated. Propositions about the present underwent the same drastic treatment, and this, incidentally, was soon seen to provide two senses of "about the future"—the normal sense in which propositions about the future were distinguished from those about the present and past, and an abnormal sense in which all propositions were "in some sense" or "for methodological purposes" propositions about the future; in this sense "the future" could no longer be contrasted with the past or present, or indeed with anything else, and so in the end turned out to be devoid of meaning.'[1]

If the preceding argument has been on the right lines, enough has been said to show that this argument is a misleading oversimplification. Here I wish to draw attention only to Berlin's account of the view which he is criticizing. He asserts that early positivists held that *all* propositions are in an abnormal sense 'about the future', with the result that 'the future' can be contrasted with nothing and is therefore meaningless. No positivist, to my knowledge, has ever believed this; what has been maintained is that all *empirical* propositions are 'about the future'.

---

[1] This quotation is from: Berlin, 'Logical Translation', *Proceedings of the Aristotelian Society*, 1950, pp. 167–8. The principle is employed again on p. 186. See also Berlin's Auguste Comte Memorial Lecture, *Historical Inevitability*, pp. 61–2.

The point behind this paradox is that all factual propositions, even historical ones, are liable to falsification by empirical information that may become available in the future, unlike logical and mathematical propositions that are not empirically falsifiable—or verifiable either. There is thus a contrast between propositions that are 'about the future' in this sense, and propositions that are not about facts at all. The positivist thesis is thus far from meaningless. It is simply a legitimate but not very clearly expressed attempt to stress the analogy between 'The sun is shining' and 'The Battle of Waterloo was fought in 1815', and the difference between both of these and '7 plus 5 = 12'.

In conclusion let us try to tie the threads of this paper together by asking why it is that philosophical problems arise from only certain 'opposed terms' (i.e. 'polar terms' as we have called them) such as 'dreaming' and 'waking', 'clear' and vague', 'mental' and 'material', while no such puzzles arise from opposites like 'concave' and 'convex', 'husband' and 'wife', and 'hot' and 'cold'. I have argued that the polar principle is based on a misunderstanding of the nature of polar concepts and that it leads to a misrepresentation of the philosophical problems to which they give rise. If this is correct it becomes important to see why these difficulties are occasioned only by certain sorts of opposites.

The clue to this is given by Malcolm in the quotation with which we began. He there says 'There are certain features about the criteria for the use of words in these pairs which tempt philosophers to wish to remove from use one member of the pair'. Malcolm does not explain what it is about the criteria for the use of polar terms which tempts philosophers in this way. Let us try to repair this omission. The most obvious characteristic of polar terms, as distinct from non-puzzling opposites, is their abstractness and the consequent generality of their application. Such terms are thus applied to many different sorts of entities; furthermore, there is not one but many 'criteria' or, as I should prefer to say, rules, for their use. A polar distinction changes to a greater or lesser extent according to the phenomena which it is employed to classify. Consider, for example, the senses of 'genuine' and 'false' illustrated on p. 271 *supra*, or the many different distinctions marked by 'real' in expressions like 'a real friend' (not a sycophant), 'a real mountain' (not a cloud), 'a real tiger' (not a stuffed one), 'a real oasis' (not a mirage), etc. (These shifts in the meaning of a polar distinction are not a consequence of the generality and abstractness of the terms. 'Concave' and 'convex' are abstract terms which refer to properties shared by many different sorts of things, but they are simple and univocal opposed terms.) It could be misleading to lay great stress on the differences between the manifold senses of a polar distinction—to say, for instance, that 'real' or 'genuine' is used *ambiguously*. On the other hand it is a mistake to think of such expressions as univocal, i.e. invariably used in precisely the same sense. Ordinary opposed terms are, with certain exceptions like 'concave' and 'convex', not only relatively restricted in their range of application, but none of them shift their meaning as do polar concepts. There is one fairly clear condition or set of conditions that must be fulfilled if an entity is to be described as 'a husband' or 'concave'.

From the shifts in the meaning of polar distinctions some philosophers derive an impression of logical confusion and untidiness. The commonest method of rectifying this is somehow to show that polar terms are employed in accordance with rules similar to those that govern the use of univocal terms. This is one of the chief motives behind what I have called the 'generalization' of a polar term, i.e. its extension to cover its opposite. At the same time it must be remembered that propositions of this kind are by no means invariably nonsensical, and can be illuminating if they draw attention to an important or neglected analogy. I am not claiming that philosophical statements of this kind are the clearest or the best ways of bringing out analogies, but only that they are sometimes meaningful and sometimes helpful.

This consideration brings out further difficulties in the view that metaphysical propositions are disguised linguistic recommendations. This doctrine postulates a very heavy disguise indeed, for metaphysical statements are *prima facie* entirely different from suggestions that we change our language in certain ways, although as I have pointed out, literally to accept such a proposition is also to adopt new linguistic rules. It is not, however, correct to assume that metaphysical statements are to be understood, or intended to be understood, literally. It is also wrong to suppose that if p, a metaphysical proposition, entails q, a new rule of language, this relation can be adequately described by saying that p is really a disguised (or 'covert' or 'implicit') formulation of q.

The view that the purpose of metaphysics is to modify language habits leaves the matter obscure, because it then appears that the metaphysician is trying to alter our ways of talking *for no reason whatsoever*. If the analogical foundation of metaphysical statements is ignored, it throws little light to say that they are recommendations about language; to adopt, and *a fortiori* to advise the adoption of, new rules of language is to do something for or against which reasons can be given. Frequently these reasons consist in good or bad analogies, both positive and negative, between various concepts or, if preferred, types of expression. (An adherent of the disguised linguistic recommendation theory has recently maintained[1] that philosophers advocate their linguistic reforms not on rational or objective grounds but as a consequence of predisposing psychological causes such as hidden fears and anxieties. There is doubtless something in this, though it seems premature to search for the psychological causes behind the statements of philosophers before we have investigated whether there are any reasons, e.g. tacit analogies, for what they say. In any event, this view is compatible with mine, for it could be argued that a psychological quirk can help as well as hinder a philosopher in recognizing a certain analogy.)

It may be objected that although metaphysical propositions are not like proposals to reform language, neither are they like statements of analogies, so that my position is no improvement on the one that I have been criticizing. The answer to this is that metaphysical arguments do not state, but rather *draw attention to*, analogies. They do this in many different ways, as Professor Wisdom has shown. I have been considering only a certain class of metaphysical propositions, namely those that generalize polar terms. In so far as these are linguistic recommendations they rest on, and thus attract attention to, the analogies that are the reasons for advocating the linguistic innovation. The proposal about language is thus made on the strength of an unstated but not necessarily unstatable analogy of some kind. It follows that it is plausible to describe a metaphysical proposition which generalizes polar terms as a linguistic recommendation only if it is further admitted that reasons (i.e. analogies) good or bad can be given for it. If this is conceded, and the analogical foundation of the state-

---

[1] M. Lazerowitz: *The Structure of Metaphysics*, Chapter Two. See especially pages 64 to 79.

ment exposed, it is no longer necessary to regard it as a linguistic proposal at all, still less one that is pointless and redundant, as the polar principle claims.

Further, the polar principle itself represents an attempt to reduce the complexity of polar distinctions to the simplicity of straightforward opposites like 'husband' and 'wife'. But it is precisely because polar terms are not used in accordance with rules of this kind that they are philosophically puzzling in the first place, so that when devotees of the polar principle refuse to see certain problems about these concepts it is because they hold a theory which not only does not allow the difficulties to be stated, but which rests upon an over-simplified notion of the concepts that give rise to them. Furthermore, even if the programme of interpreting polar terms like ordinary univocal opposites were feasible, it still would not lead to the desired conclusion. As our discussion of the very simple distinction between 'concave' and 'convex' showed, the significance of either term does not depend upon its use as a contrast to the other.

It is no longer fashionable for philosophers to try to fix the limits of thought, but dogmatism is still at work in the form of some recent attempts to lay down *a priori* the boundaries of significant language. I hope I have exposed, or at least cast doubt upon, one of the crudest of these.

CHAPTER XIII

RYLE ON THE INTELLECT[1]

C. A. Campbell

Professor of Logic and Rhetoric, Glasgow University: 1938-61

As this paper is, I fear, in the nature of a sustained assault upon the central teaching of *The Concept of Mind*, I should like to preface it by saying that I share the opinion, from which I imagine very few dissent, that the author of that work is one of the most powerful, original and ingenious thinkers in contemporary philosophy. But, as history amply testifies, it is from powerful, original and ingenious thinkers that the queerest aberrations of philosophic theory often emanate. Indeed it may be said to *require* a thinker exceptionally endowed in these respects if the more paradoxical type of theory is to be expounded in a way which will make it seem tenable even to its author—let alone to the general philosophic public. That Professor Ryle has succeeded to admiration in expounding his theory persuasively, there can be no possible doubt. Few if any philosophical works of recent years have been greeted in this country with a comparable enthusiasm. But though I could myself applaud with sincerity many of the penetrating incidental discussions in which the book abounds, it seems to me a good deal more useful, in the present state of philosophic opinion, to draw attention to the truly mortal weakness (as I see it) of the general position which it is the concern of the book to establish. The 'one-world theory' (to use a convenient title) is in my opinion totally unable to survive a serious examination of the arguments upon which it is based. In the present paper I shall review one major field of its application, and I shall try to show that even so skilful an advocate as Professor Ryle can 'make a case' only by resorting to arguments that are invariably inadequate, frequently flimsy, and at times almost openly fallacious. It will be best to begin, however, with some brief observations about the character of the work as a whole.

The Concept of Mind is, as everyone knows, in its main purport an attack upon the traditional dualism of mind and matter.

[1] *The Philosophical Quarterly*, Vol. III, 1953.

According to the traditional 'two-world' theory, the material and the mental are irreducibly different from one another; so different, indeed, as to be in some respects polar opposites, since extendedness and divisibility are commonly regarded as definitory characteristics of the one, and unextendedness and indivisibility as definitory characteristics of the other. Moreover, the two realms are known to us in sharply contrasting ways. In respect of the material, there is direct access of a 'public' nature, through the medium of the senses common to all of us. But in respect of mental happenings, direct access is a privilege reserved for the individual being in whom they happen. Apart from the possibility of telepathic information, the mental states and processes of others can be apprehended only inferentially on the basis of certain physical 'signs'. In this sense, then, and to use Ryle's terminology, mental happenings on the traditional theory are 'occult', and only material happenings are 'overt', or 'publicly observable'.

This dualism, Ryle wants to show, is radically false. The correct way to overcome it, however, is not (we are told) by reducing one side to the other side. 'The hallowed contrast between Mind and Matter', he claims in his opening chapter, 'will be dissipated, but dissipated not by either of the equally hallowed absorptions of Mind by Matter or of Matter by Mind, but in quite a different way.'[1]

What is this 'different way'? I think it turns out in the end to be not so *very* different. The mental and the material would appear to be for Ryle denizens of 'one world' of overt bodily behaviour, amenable to public observation by the ordinary senses: and the only ground I can discover for his denial that this involves the absorption of Mind by Matter is the surely insufficient one that the bodily behaviour to which we apply the term 'mental' has certain typical differences from other forms of bodily behaviour. Now of course if we choose to limit the term 'material' to *certain forms only* of bodily behaviour—e.g. to the 'mechanical' form—we can certainly say that Mind, even as Ryle understands it, is not 'absorbed by Matter'. But we shall be guilty of a departure, and one not easy to justify, from the ordinary use of words. For 'material' is a term which is ordinarily applied to whatever can be described as 'bodily', not merely to certain *specific* bodily forms. It would seem, therefore, that the claim

[1] *The Concept of Mind*, p. 22.

that Mind is not being absorbed by Matter really rests upon a rather esoteric use of language.

That *Concept of Mind* is, at bottom, a thinly disguised form of Materialism comes out perhaps most clearly in the final chapter, where Ryle devotes a short section to the relation of his view to Behaviourism. For the only distinction he is there able to point to is that the Behaviourist is in the habit of interpreting mental happenings in terms of a *mechanistic* view of matter. The behaviourist is right in denying the supposed 'inner life'. But (Ryle says) 'Man need not be degraded to a machine by being denied to be a ghost in a machine. He might, after all, be a sort of animal, namely, a higher mammal. There has yet to be ventured the hazardous leap to the hypothesis that perhaps he is a man'.[1] The implication is that the behaviourist has gone wrong only in so far as he interprets such processes as, e.g. those commonly called 'intellectual', in terms of physical categories that are too narrowly conceived. There is nothing wrong in principle in his confining himself to *physical* categories. And this is surely materialism, though not *mechanistic* materialism. Perhaps, adapting a term used elsewhere by Ryle himself, we ought to call it 'polymorphic' materialism.

But perhaps it will be objected that Ryle's materialism is, after all, of a very different sort from ordinary materialism: so different that it is more misleading to say that he is a materialist than to say that he is not. Ordinary materialism, in recognizing only mechanical and chemical forms of bodily behaviour, or at most these *plus* an 'organic' form, finds no room for intelligent purpose. And it is precisely this omission which by reason of its implication for human values, is felt by most people to constitute the real 'sting' of materialistic philosophies. Now Ryle, it may be urged, *does* find room for intelligent purpose. There is for him, over and above even the organic form of bodily behaviour, the further form that is characteristic of distinctively *human* conduct: and of this 'further form', 'intelligent purpose' would seem to be of the very essence. But if Ryle thus repudiates that in materialism which constitutes its real sting (viz. the denial of intelligent purpose), the mere fact that he is at one with the materialist in denying an 'inner life' of 'consciousness' does not suffice to make appropriate the description of his philosophy as 'materialist'.

[1] *Op. cit.*, p. 328.

This rejoinder would be reasonable enough on one assumption —that it is possible for what is ordinarily meant by 'intelligent purpose' to survive when 'consciousness' is eliminated. But this assumption is surely false. 'Intelligent purpose' without 'consciousness of an end' seems to be about as near a self-contradiction as makes no difference. Later I shall be criticizing at length Ryle's attempt to give an account of 'intellectual acts' without reference to consciousness. But so far as 'intelligent purpose' is concerned, it is very hard not to feel that argument is sheer waste of time. Anyone who supposes that an act can be intelligently purposive in the total absence of consciousness of an end must just be using words in some queer way of his own. But if what is ordinarily meant by 'intelligent purpose' is not reducible to bodily behaviour, there is, after all, no room in Ryle's scheme for what is ordinarily meant by intelligent purpose. And if that be so, Ryle's materialism would appear to differ from ordinary materialism in none of the respects which would commonly be regarded as important.

To avert misunderstanding, let me add that if I have seemed somewhat to labour Ryle's 'materialism', it has been by no means with the object of enlisting against him the unfriendly emotions which that term is apt to evoke. My motive is merely to clarify a situation which it is certain that a good many of Ryle's readers have found obscure.

There is one further preliminary point upon which I must dwell for a little. I assume in this paper that at least part of the object of *The Concept of Mind* is to make a contribution to our knowledge of the nature of mind; or at any rate of the nature of mental operations. When it is contended, for example, that (contrary to the orthodox view) mental operations are exhaustively describable in terms of overt behaviour, one can hardly suppose that a claim is not being made to enhance our knowledge of the nature of mental operations. We are being invited to substitute a true view of their nature for a false one. Yet there are prominent passages in Ryle's book, particularly in the early stages, which must give one pause. A disturbing contrast appears to be being drawn between knowledge of mental operations on the one hand, and knowledge of the 'logic' of mental-conduct concepts on the other; and Ryle seems to be saying that it is *only* with the latter that he is concerned. Thus he tells us in his *Introduction* that

'This book . . . does not give new information about minds', and that 'The philosophic arguments which constitute this book are intended not to increase what we know about minds, but to rectify the logical geography of the knowledge we already possess'.[1] A little later, speaking of the 'myth' of the official doctrine which 'represents the facts of mental life as if they belonged to one logical type or category (or range of types or categories), when they actually belong to another', he goes on to say:

In attempting to explode this myth, I shall probably be taken to be denying well-known facts about the mental life of human beings, and my plea that I aim at doing nothing more than rectify the logic of mental-conduct concepts will probably be disallowed as mere subterfuge.[2]

This seems to me very puzzling. *Can* the 'rectification of the logic of mental-conduct concepts' be divorced in this way from the knowledge of mental operations? 'Mental-conduct concepts' are, presumably, thoughts about mental operations. To 'rectify the logic' of them is therefore, presumably, to expose certain false ways of thinking about mental operations, and to expound the true way—to tell us how we *ought* to think about them. But knowledge of the true way of thinking about mental operations is surely inseparable from knowledge of the real nature of mental operations? If so, can the rectification of the logic of mental-conduct concepts fail to 'give us new information about minds', or to 'increase what we know about minds'?

Or again, from the other side, what is the procedure for 'rectifying the logic of mental-conduct concepts'? If (as I have suggested) the phrase quoted can only mean determining how we *ought* to think (i.e. how to think *truly*) about mental operations, there would seem to be no procedure of any sort of promise that does not involve the patient, critical and untendentious examination of the mental operations themselves. We all of us want, just as Ryle does, to assign mental operations to their proper logical categories. But it seems to me clear that we cannot do this until we know the nature of mental operations, and that we cannot know the nature of mental operations without directing attention upon them.

But here, I suspect, the myth that bedevils so much of the

[1] *Op. cit.*, p. 7.　　　　　　　　　　　[2] *Op. cit.*, p. 16.

thinking of the linguistic philosophers is at its baneful work again. Is it possible that Ryle thinks we can 'rectify the logic of mental-conduct concepts' by discovering what is the 'correct' way of *talking* about mental operations; the 'correct' way of *talking* about them being itself discoverable by appeal to 'accepted linguistic usage'? If so (and it is hard to deny that we do have here one of the many strands of Ryle's thought), it seems sufficient to reply, first, that there is *no* 'accepted linguistic usage' in respect of most mental operations (accepted by *whom*, anyway?): and secondly, that even if there *were*, a 'correct way of talking' about something in the sense of a 'generally accepted' way of talking about it, must be distinguished from a correct way of talking about something in the sense of a way of talking about it *which describes it as it really is*; and that the *latter* is the *only* sense in which the 'correct way of talking' has any relevance to the aim of 'rectifying the logic of mental-conduct concepts'. But on this whole question of the philosopher's appeal to 'ordinary language' I would refer to Mr Heath's article in the *Philosophical Quarterly* (January 1952)[1] which says incomparably well a number of things that have needed saying for a very long time.

I come now to the specific aim of this paper. To avoid the danger of vagueness which is always attendant upon generalized criticism, I have chosen to attack upon a limited front. But a break-through on this sector must, I think, have the effect of turning the whole enemy line. To drop metaphor, I shall be criticizing in some detail Ryle's application of his general thesis to a single, but central, topic, viz. the character of those happenings in our so-called 'mental' life which it is customary to group under the title of 'intellectual'. There is the more need to examine Ryle's treatment of this topic since it has so far, to the best of my knowledge, evoked singularly little critical reaction from those who have published comments upon his book: very much less, e.g., than his accounts of Will and Imagination. Yet it does not appear to me that his account of Intellect is in any degree less vulnerable.

Chapter IX of *The Concept of Mind*, it will be remembered, is devoted expressly, and exclusively, to 'The Intellect'; and to this chapter, in the main, I shall confine myself. There is, of course, material relevant to this question in the earlier parts of

[1] See above, chapter VIII [Ed.].

the book also, notably in the famous second chapter on 'Knowing how' and 'Knowing that'. But although this earlier chapter makes perfectly clear Ryle's view that 'knowing how' is neither preceded nor accompanied by a 'knowing that', and also his view that 'knowing how' is fully describable in terms of overt behaviour, his precise view of the nature of 'knowing that' is—reasonably enough—left somewhat in the air. And it is with 'knowing that' rather than with 'knowing how' that 'intellectual activity' is, as a rule, primarily identified. It seems best that we should concentrate, therefore, upon Chapter IX, where most of the doubts the reader may have entertained earlier about just how Ryle understands 'knowing that' are resolved. But I shall occasionally find it necessary to draw upon, and I shall constantly have in mind, the discussions which precede it.

Let us then now address ourselves directly to the content of the chapter in question.

The purpose of the chapter is to show that there are no 'intellectual acts' in the sense given to that expression by orthodox epistemologists. Judging, inferring, and the like are not 'occult' happenings to which the person judging or inferring can alone have direct cognitive access, nor have they a special status in some sphere of their own totally different from that in which physical happenings occur. Properly interpreted, they will be seen to consist, as 'physical' happenings consist, of publicly observable behaviour through and through: though, as is to be expected, the behaviour of which they consist will turn out to be of a pattern different from that of the happenings we are accustomed to distinguish as 'merely physical'.

Now the intellect is usually taken to be concerned primarily with the discovery of *truth*. This suggests to Ryle that we shall be most likely to get a good view of 'intellectual acts' if we fix our attention upon the operation in which 'truth' is systematically sought; i.e. the operation of 'theorizing'.

Within 'theorizing', however, there is, he tells us, a very important distinction to be drawn. There is the process of *building* the theory; and there is the quite different process of *didactically expounding* the theory after it has been built. And here comes the first of the many surprising things that Ryle says in this chapter. Epistemologists, we are informed, constantly confuse these two processes. They very frequently describe the labours of building theories in terms appropriate only to the business of going over or teaching a theory that one already has; as if, for example, the chains of propositions which constitute Euclid's *Elements* mirrored a parallel succession of theorizing moves made by Euclid in his original labours of making his geometrical discoveries; as if, that is, what Euclid was equipped to do when he had his theory, he was already equipped to do when constructing it. But this is absurd.[1]

It *is* absurd; but I confess I find myself quite unable to identify the peccant, though unnamed, epistemologists who have (apparently in considerable strength) committed the absurdity. I should have thought myself that, so far from this confusion being widespread, the distinction between 'the order of discovery' and 'the order of exposition' was something of a commonplace among reputable epistemologists.

However, to this alleged, but I think totally imaginary, confusion among the epistemologists Ryle attributes certain grave consequences. The importance of the distinction in our present context, he tells us, is that, once it is recognized, we see that we ought to raise the question, in *which* of the two sides of theorizing, the exploratory or the expository, are so-called intellectual acts like judging and inferring to be found? Traditional epistemologists have omitted to ask this for the obvious reason, so Ryle believes, that they have failed to make the above distinction. They therefore 'tend not to realize that such a question exists'.[2] What they commonly do, he continues,

is to classify the elements of doctrines didactically expounded by theorists already at home in them, and to postulate that counterpart elements must have occurred as episodes in the work of building those theories. Finding premisses and conclusions among the elements of published theories, they postulate separate, antecedent, 'cognitive acts' of judging; and finding arguments among the elements of published theories, they postulate separate antecedent processes of moving to the 'cognizing' of conclusions from the 'cognizing' of premisses. I hope to show that these separate intellectual processes postulated by epistemologists are para-mechanical dramatizations of the classified elements of achieved and expounded theories.[3]

The relevance of Ryle's argument here to his main thesis I take to be as follows. Epistemologists have not *really* found direct

1 *The Concept of Mind*, p. 289.   2 *Op. cit.*, p. 291.   3 *Op. cit.*, p. 291.

evidence of 'occult' intellectual acts. They have *assumed* them in order to account for certain elements which they do find in the exposition of 'achieved theories'. If, therefore, it can be shown that the *exposition* of theories does not in fact imply the said intellectual acts, the whole case for their existence disappears. And Ryle believes, of course, as we shall see in detail later, that this *can* be shown.

But surely, in the first place, this story of how epistemologists have come to believe in 'cognitive acts' of judging and inferring is the sheerest fiction. It is perfectly true that epistemologists have not, as a rule, asked whether these acts are to be found in the building of theories or in their exposition. But the reason for that is simple; just that it has seemed obvious to them that such acts are to be found in *both* phases of theorizing, and not at all that they have failed to recognize any distinction between the two phases. It is certainly false that 'what they commonly do' is to postulate cognitive acts in the building process as 'counterparts' to elements discovered and classified in 'achieved and expounded theories'. Rightly or wrongly, they have at least *supposed* that there is no difficulty in finding any number of judgements and inferences quite directly in the building operation itself. Almost any textbook account[1] of how we set about solving a theoretical problem will testify to this. The usual account, very briefly, runs somewhat as follows. Firstly, we specify our problem as precisely as possible. Secondly, we look for likely hypotheses, guided by our knowledge of the relevant facts and of the laws and patterns pertaining to the given field. Thirdly, we consider in the case of each hypothesis what would follow if it were true. Fourthly, we test the hypotheses by observation of, and it may

[1] Citation of instances, unless so voluminous as to be here impracticable, could prove little. But I may mention in passing that reference to the chapters on induction in a random half-dozen of popular textbooks has discovered none that does not describe 'problem-solving' (generally under such heads as 'Explanation', 'Hypothesis', or 'Scientific Method') in the manner here summarized. All of the authors—Stebbing, Mace, Joseph, Latta and Macbeath, Welton and Monahan, Mellone— devote much space to the cognitive processes involved in the exploratory or building phase of scientific theory, and they manifestly believe that they are directly finding in that phase the judgements and inferences which they describe as constituent of it. I can see no trace of evidence to support the suggestion of 'postulation' (conscious or unconscious) of 'counterpart elements'.

be experiment upon, the facts. Now such a procedure cannot possibly be described in any detail without constant reference to judging and inferring: inferring, e.g., in the consideration of what will follow from the alternative hypotheses; judging, e.g., in noting what facts are, and what facts are not, in accordance with the hypotheses.

There is, then, I submit, no mystery about where the traditional epistemologists have found their 'intellectual acts'. They have found them in *both* phases of theorizing, the exploratory and the expository. Moreover, so far from its being the case that they are exclusively concerned with the *latter*, I think that any survey of their actual writings[1] will show that it is to the *former* that they preferably turn for the clearest examples of intellectual acts. And naturally so. For it is evident that in exposition of a finished theory, especially when one has become very familiar with it, the mental activity involved is normally a good deal less intense, and its features, in consequence, are a good deal less easily distinguishable, than when we are still 'straining our minds' to discover a tenable theory.

This contention of Ryle's, that it is obviously to the expository, not the exploratory, phase of theorizing that we must look (if anywhere) for intellectual acts, is on the face of it so surprising that it is natural to ask whether he nowhere offers better justification of it than has so far appeared. In point of fact he does later in the chapter return to the topic and attempt some argument in its favour. The argument seems to be patently fallacious, but on this the reader must be given the opportunity to make up his own mind.

In this later part of the chapter, then, Ryle asks once more at *which* stage of theorizing are a man's acts of judging, inferring and the like supposed to be manifested, 'in his saying things when

---

[1] I find it as hard here as in the case dealt with in the previous footnote to name any instance to the contrary. Cook Wilson, Stebbing and Mace are only among the more conspicuous of those who focus their account of 'inferring' upon the constructive, exploratory phase of mental operations. (Incidentally, each of these shows explicit awareness of the distinction between the exploratory and the expository phases.) Most notable of all, perhaps, is Blanshard, who in his *The Nature of Thought* (Part III especially) has studied the exploratory phase with a care and skill and completeness not equalled in any other work with which I am acquainted.

he knows what to say, or in his travailings, when he does not yet know what to say, since he is still trying to get this knowledge'.[1] Ryle's answer, of course, is that it is in the expository phase. He takes the case of the detective investigating the death of the squire and reaching the conclusion that he has been killed by the gamekeeper.

If we are to use at all the odd expression 'making a judgement', we must say that the detective makes the judgement that the gamekeeper killed the squire, only when he is putting into indicative prose a piece of the theory that he now has, and that he keeps on making this judgement as often as he is called upon to tell this part of his theory, whether to himself, to the reporters or to Scotland Yard.[2]

But the answer to this is surely obvious. Who would ever have thought of claiming that *this* judgement ('the gamekeeper killed the squire') was among the judgements belonging to the exploratory stage? No one ever supposed that we should find in the exploratory phase the *self-same* judgements and inferences that appear in the finished theory. The kind of judgement one has in mind as belonging to the exploratory phase of the detective's work is 'there is a small round hole in the squire's forehead': the kind of inference, 'this hole must, in view of its size and character, have been made by a bullet from a Service revolver'. To argue that the judgement 'the gamekeeper killed the squire' does not belong to the exploratory phase seems to me a clear case of *ignoratio elenchi*.

Actually Ryle seems to realize this himself. He seems to see that it is upon quite different judgements that the real issue turns. And in the very next paragraph he admits that in the 'preparatory ponderings' that precede there *may*, after all, be some thinking 'consisting of, or containing, the making of some judgements'. *But*—and here is the ingenious device he adopts to reconcile this admission with his thesis—these judgements which occur 'en route' to the theory are just 'interim reports of sub-theories' which the investigation has already established. And so, despite appearances, they *really* belong to the expository stage after all!

This is clever; but it will surely convince nobody. One would have to use language in a very odd way to say that, e.g., the detective's observational judgement that there is a small round

[1] *Op. cit.*, p. 297.   [2] *Op. cit.*, p. 298.

hole in the squire's skull is the 'exposition of a theory'—even of a 'sub-theory'. Not only is this a most unnatural meaning for the phrase, but it is not at all the sort of meaning that Ryle himself seemed to be attaching to it in the early part of the chapter.

However, the question of terminology is of little importance. Let Ryle call the judgements involved in the 'preparatory pondering' interim reports of sub-theories if he chooses. What *really* matters is that he has found himself forced to recognize at least the appearance of intellectual acts in a realm which he had seemingly hoped to be allowed to ignore, i.e. in the realm of what *most* people would regard as 'theory-building'. It follows that his initial programme must suffer some revision. It can no longer be adequate to the disproof of 'occult' intellectual acts to concentrate upon 'the didactic exposition of established theory' and show that there is no evidence of them *there*. Ryle is now obliged to attend also to those ostensible judgements and inferences that occur *en route*, and to show that they too involve no occult acts. This development is not unimportant. For although Ryle cannot by any means, in my opinion, show that even the didactic exposition of established theory is describable in terms of publicly observable behaviour alone, it is distinctly easier to make a case of sorts here than it is with regard to the more conspicuous manifestation of intellectual activity in the actual *constructing* of theories.

So far we have been considering little more than the framework within which Ryle's arguments against 'occult' intellectual acts are set. We turn now to the arguments themselves.

The argument which first emerges, however, is one upon which I shall not dwell at length; for although it is given some prominence by Ryle, I find it difficult to suppose that he can really attach much importance to it.

Ryle's view is, it will be remembered, that the terms 'judgement', 'inference', etc., are only by confusion taken to designate recordable acts of any kind—let alone occult intellectual acts. The 'reality', as it were, whose significance traditional epistemology misinterprets, is the *published theory*, classifiable into certain elements: and the 'misinterpretation' consists in postulating 'counterpart' elements in the mind (acts of judgement, inference, etc.) which 'must have occurred as episodes in the work of

K

building those theories'.[1] In support of his contention that such episodes do not in fact occur, Ryle thinks it worth while to call to the witness-box Citizen John Doe. And John Doe, it appears, knows nothing of such happenings in his own life-history. He just 'cannot answer at all' if he is asked such questions as:

... How many cognitive acts did he perform before breakfast, and what did it feel like to do them? Were they tiring? Did he enjoy his passage from his premisses to his conclusion, and did he make it cautiously or recklessly? Did the breakfast bell make him stop half-way between his premisses and his conclusion? Just when did he last make a judgement . . ., etc. etc. etc.

Now I submit that John Doe's bewilderment before this formidable array of psychological posers offers not the slightest presumption against the occurrence of the psychical events referred to. John Doe may be an admirable citizen, but there is no reason whatever why he should be any good at introspection. *Nothing* follows from his inability to answer questions which, in so far as they are answerable at all, could be answered only by a person highly skilled in introspective technique.

But, in the second place, the questions in almost every case are either virtually or absolutely unanswerable even by an expert introspectionist, *not* because the mental acts at issue do not occur, but because of the way in which the questions are framed. 'How many cognitive acts did he perform before breakfast?'—as if, without the prior acceptance of some convention as to what is to count as a cognitive 'unit', anyone could even begin to answer such a question; or as if, waiving this difficulty, even an expert introspectionist could have had any conceivable interest in keeping a numerical tally of all the thoughts that had occurred to him, and all the routine and other observations he had made of his surroundings, between waking up and beginning his breakfast! As well ask John Doe how many *breaths* he drew between waking and breakfast; and then, because he cannot tell us, conclude that he must really have been dead! Certain others of the questions are unanswerable absolutely, because they are asked about non-existent features of mental acts. 'Did the breakfast bell make him stop half-way between his premisses and his conclusion?' A question like this has no significance save on the assumption that, within inference, there is a time-interval between apprehension

[1] *Op. cit.*, p. 291.   [2] *Op. cit.*, pp. 292–3.

of the premises and apprehension of the conclusion. But this assumption is false (as indeed Ryle himself later has occasion to stress). The question asked, then, is unanswerable, not because there are no intellectual acts of inference, but because inference is not characterized in the way that the question implies.

I think we need analyse this passage no further. It is an entertaining sample of its author's wit, but its function is perhaps better regarded as one of light relief than of serious philosophic argument.

Let us hasten on, then, to Ryle's more important arguments. They can, I think, be reduced to three. The first two (which are closely connected) are concerned with the expository phase of theorizing, and try to show that this supplies no evidence of occult intellectual acts. The third is directed to what would normally be called the exploratory phase, or the phase of discovery, and tries to show that what admittedly *looks* like 'acts of inferring' can and should be otherwise interpreted. We shall deal with each of these three arguments in turn.

It is Ryle's view, as we know, that in the finished and delivered theory there can be distinguished 'arguments which can be called inferences or reasonings'; but that it is an error to suppose that there are something called thoughts *in addition to* the written or oral form in which the theory is overtly presented. Traditional epistemologists, of course, have been guilty of this error. They have been tempted to suppose that

there must be mental acts of passing from premises to conclusions, since the 'because' and 'so' sentences which feature in the statements of theories are significant and therefore express counterpart cogitative operations in the theorist's mind. Every significant expression has a meaning, so when an expression is actually used, the meaning of it must have been occurring somewhere, and it can have been occurring only in the form of a thought that took place in the speaker's or writer's private stream of consciousness.[1]

Ryle's first argument against this view is, in effect, that the implication of an expression's 'having significance' has been misunderstood by the epistemologists. Certainly, he agrees, significant expressions have *meaning*. This is a tautology from which nothing follows. But

this does not warrant us in asking, 'When and where do these meanings occur?' A bear may be now being led about by a bear-leader . . . but

[1] *Op. cit.*, pp. 294-5.

to say that an expression has a meaning is not to say that the expression
is on a lead held by a ghostly leader called a 'meaning' or a 'thought'. . .
The very fact that an expression is made to be understood by anyone
shows that the meaning of the expression is not to be described as
being, or belonging to, an event that at most one person could know
anything about.[1]

The last sentence, I think, contains the essence of the argument.
The fact that an expression is made to be understood by *anyone*,
Ryle suggests, implies that the meaning which an expression
expresses is not something belonging to 'the speaker's or writer's
private stream of consciousness'.

The argument has some plausibility. I agree that the fact
alluded to does entail that an expression's 'meaning' must, in
some sense at least, be regarded as a 'public' rather than a 'private'
phenomenon. What we must ask, however, is whether the sense
in which an expression's meaning is 'public' is not compatible with
an equally valid sense in which an expression's meaning is 'private'.
It seems to me that it is not very difficult to see that the two *are*
compatible. But in order to show this, a brief analysis of the
ambiguous phrase 'the meaning of an expression' is indispensable.
I shall conduct the analysis from the standpoint of common
sense and ordinary linguistic usage, which is (I think) the standpoint from which Ryle is himself arguing.

Consider such an expression as 'The Theory of Evolution has
been established'. What is its 'meaning'? It is a commonplace
(is it not?) that it may mean one thing to the speaker and another,
significantly different, thing to the hearer. Thus the meaning
which the words 'the Theory of Evolution' carry may include
for the hearer, but not for the speaker, a mechanistic view about
the origin of the variations which make evolution possible, and
the hearer may on that account (and in fact often does) vigorously
dispute the statement, supposing himself, quite erroneously, to
be in disagreement with the speaker. And that, of course, is only
one of the many significant differences which might obtain
between what the speaker meant by the expression and what the
hearer takes it to mean. Obviously not only the words 'the Theory
of Evolution' but also the word 'established' can be understood
in a variety of partially conflicting ways.

[1] *Op. cit.*, p. 295.

There is, then, the speaker's meaning, and there is also the hearer's meaning. And to these we should add what might be called (not perhaps very happily) the 'conventional' meaning. This may be described, sufficiently for present purposes, as the meaning which the expression would carry for a hearer who interpreted its constituent terms in as strict accordance as possible with the accepted usage of the words in the operative language, and, in the case of specialist terms like 'Theory of Evolution', in accordance with the accepted usage of the appropriate specialists.

Now this analysis of 'the meaning of an expression', conducted at a common-sense level, may well be defective. It may be that it ought to be rejected in favour of a much more sophisticated and esoteric analysis. But *any* analysis, no matter how sophisticated or esoteric, has got to give *some* account of the commonly recognized distinctions to which our simple analysis draws attention. I do not find any account of them given by Ryle. Yet until he tells us how he interprets what I have called 'the speaker's meaning', this item at least of the analysis stands out in unresolved contradiction with his thesis.

On the simple analysis we have here offered there is, of course, no difficulty at all in seeing how 'the fact that an expression is made to be understood by *anyone*' is compatible with the expression being the expression of a meaning in the speaker's private consciousness. The situation is that the speaker chooses the particular pattern of words which he hopes will excite the hearer (assuming him to be conversant with the language) to think substantially the same thought as *he* is thinking. To that extent the meaning is, or is intended to be, 'public'. But even where the speaker's intention is wholly successful, there is the speaker's thinking of his thought and the hearer's thinking of his thought, and the two 'thinkings' remain separate private episodes in the respective individuals' histories none the less because the objective content of the thinking is identical in the two cases.

It will be worth while to look also, in terms of our analysis, at Ryle's contention that 'to say that an expression has a meaning is not to say that the expression is on a lead held by a ghostly leader called a "meaning" or a "thought" '. This contention seems true or false according to which of the three senses of the term 'meaning' distinguished above we happen to have in mind. It is defensible if we have in mind the meaning for the hearer—what

hearing the words excites the hearer to think; or if we have in
mind the 'conventional' meaning—what certain hypothetical
hearers would be excited to think. In these cases, evidently, the
meaning of the expression pertains to events posterior to the
utterance of the expression, and cannot, therefore, 'lead' the
expression. But (at least at our present level of common-sense
analysis) it seems equally evident that if we have in mind the
meaning for the *speaker*—what the speaker thought, and sought
to convey by the expression—the meaning does precede (though
it may also accompany) the expression. And that it also (in a
manner) *directs* the expression, so that it is a valid, if not specially
helpful, metaphor that the expression is 'on a lead' held by a
'meaning', seems sufficiently established by the fact that what the
speaker is aiming to express in the expression is precisely his
'meaning', or 'what he thinks'.

Ryle's first argument, then, would not appear to have much
force against the orthodox view that the use of significant expression in the exposition of a theory indicates a meaning present in
some form in the speaker's or writer's private stream of consciousness. The 'facts' to which he draws attention in our ordinary
intelligent usage of the phrase 'what an expression means' are
facts which comport perfectly well with the orthodox view.
Evidently a new line of attack is required: in particular, one
which will impugn the validity of that common-sense analysis of
'the meaning of an expression' which seemed adequate to rebut
the first line of attack. And that is, in fact, what we now get.

This second argument (the most crucial, I think, in the whole
chapter) seeks to establish that the so-called thought in the
speaker's mind—what we have identified with 'the speaker's
meaning'—turns out, when we attempt to give a description of
it, to be indistinguishable in principle from the expression itself.
It may, indeed, be a 'covert', rather than an 'overt', expression:
for the overt expression may be preceded by a rehearsal of the
words in the speaker's head—'silent speech', as Ryle often calls
it. But that, for Ryle, makes no theoretical difference, since silent
speech (so he appears to think) is in principle, if not in practice,
publicly observable just as audible speech is.

I quote the key sentences of this second argument:

When descriptions are proffered (of 'the thought that corresponds
with the word, phrase or sentence'), they seem to be descriptions of

ghostly doubles of the words, phrases or sentences themselves. The
'thought' is described as if it were just another more shadowy naming,
asserting or arguing. The thought that is supposed to bear-lead the
overt announcement 'tomorrow cannot be Sunday, unless today is
Saturday' turns out to be just the announcement to oneself that tomorrow cannot be Sunday without today being Saturday, i.e. just a
soliloquized or muttered rehearsal of the overt statement itself.[1]

Up to this point Ryle's position would seem to be that the
speaker's 'thought' in significant expression cannot be distinguished from the utterance, audible or inaudible, of the words
themselves. This is a simple and straightforward enough theory;
but almost immediately Ryle goes on to add a qualification about
which it is really rather difficult to know what to say. To express
oneself significantly, it now appears, it is not enough merely to
utter words in a certain order. One must utter them '*in a certain
frame of mind*', viz. 'on purpose, with a method, carefully, seriously,
and on the *qui vive*'.[2] Now this at least *looks* like readmitting by
a back door the 'separate' intellectual activity just ejected from the
front door. I think it will be best, therefore, to defer discussion
of this seemingly suicidal development, and to ask first how far
the theory can stand *without* the qualification as an intelligible
account of the 'thought' commonly supposed to 'underlie' significant speech.

The theory as thus understood seems to be open to many
criticisms:

1. It should be noted that by 'silent speech' or 'soliloquizing'
Ryle means something more than the 'sub-vocal talking' which
the behaviourist identifies with thinking. Ryle remarks earlier
(p. 35) on 'the technical trick of conducting our thinking in
auditory word-images, instead of in spoken words'; and it is
imaging—no doubt visual and kinaesthetic as well as auditory—
which I think Ryle has primarily in mind rather than the concealed operation of linguistic mechanisms. In what follows I shall
assume that this is the case. It is, I think, at least a more plausible
doctrine that we mean *this* by thinking than that we mean sub-
vocal talking. On the other hand, if the straight behaviourist
account be abandoned, and thinking identified with 'word-
imaginings', the inclusion of thinking within the category of the
publicly observable is surely very hard to defend.

---

[1] *Op. cit.*, pp. 295–6. [2] *Op. cit.*, p. 296.

2. The mere fact that, if asked to describe the 'thought' to which a sentence corresponds, we tend to reply by repeating the words of the sentence, does not at all entail that we cannot distinguish the thought from the words. To reply in this way would admittedly be natural if we could not make that distinction; but it would also be natural if we *could*. For suppose that we *could* make the distinction—that our thought *is* for us something different from the words. This thought will have two aspects; the psychical occurrence which is the 'thinking', and the objective content which is 'what we think'. Now it is the *latter*, or 'what' aspect, not the *former*, or 'that' aspect, in terms of which the specific character of a thought is determined. Hence if we are asked to describe some *specific* thought (not 'thought in general'), such as the thought corresponding to the sentence, 'Tomorrow cannot be Sunday unless today is Saturday', we shall naturally tend to reply with a description of the 'what' aspect of our thought. But to 'describe' the 'what' aspect is just to put into words 'what we thought'. And as this is precisely what we were already doing in our original sentence, it is inevitable that our description should more or less repeat the sentence itself.

I suggest, therefore, that the fact that our proffered description of a thought 'seems to be a ghostly double' of the words of the sentence tells us nothing one way or the other about the identity of the thought with the sentence.

3. Admittedly, all that our second criticism establishes is that a man's inclination to describe a specific thought in terms of the words of a sentence does not *entail* that he recognizes no distinction between the thought and the sentence. It is still *compatible with* his recognizing no distinction. But it seems clear that if the ordinary person, having given an answer in such terms to the request for a description of his 'thought', had the question actually put to him, 'Do you then agree that your "thought" was simply the words (perhaps the soliloquized words) of your sentence?', he would most emphatically dissent. No doubt he would find it far from easy to explain clearly just what it was, other than the words, that he *did* mean by the 'thought' that tomorrow cannot be Sunday unless today is Saturday. But he would not, I think, be wholly at a loss. I think a very little Socratic interrogation would speedily elicit his agreement that the 'thought' was *the apprehension of a certain relationship*: of a certain relationship,

moreover, not between words or groups of words (such as might interest the grammarian), but between what the words or groups of words *mean*; a relationship, namely, between what we mean by 'the tomorrowness of Sunday' and what we mean by 'the todayness of Saturday'. Now the saying (or imaging) of words, in whatever pattern, includes nothing that can be even remotely identified with this 'apprehension of a relationship'; not even if the 'relationship' apprehended were a relationship between words, which (in this instance at any rate) it certainly is not.

4. Perhaps the clearest proof that the 'thought' or 'meaning' in a speaker's mind cannot be identified with the verbal expression is the fact that the self-same thought can be expressed in different languages. 'The king is dead.' 'Le roi est mort.' How is this possible on the hypothesis that the thought and the verbal expression are indistinguishable?

The odd thing is that Ryle does *notice* this very familiar objection to the kind of view he is holding, but apparently does not think it worthy of examination. He admits that a man 'might have uttered a sentence to the same effect in a different language, or in a different form of words in the same language'.[1] I quote the reply—the *sole* reply—which he gives:

Knocking in a nail is not doing two things, one with a hammer and another without a hammer . . . for all that the carpenter could have knocked in his nail with another hammer instead of with this one.[2]

This seems to call for a comment of equal brevity. I shall only observe that a single sentence of a rather obscure metaphor is hardly an appropriate form of reply to a criticism so determinate in character, so frequently advanced by reputable philosophers, and, at least in appearance, so utterly deadly to the theory criticized.

5. The words of a sentence, whether uttered audibly, soliloquized inaudibly, or imaged in auditory imagining, succeed one another in time. But in a thought which is, as here, the seeing of an implication, there can be *no* time interval between the apprehension of the premisses and the apprehension of the conclusion. The seeing that the 'tomorrowness of Sunday' entails the 'Saturdayness of today' cannot be divided into a stage in which we apprehend the tomorrowness of Sunday and a tem-

---

[1] *Op. cit.*, p. 296.   [2] *Ibid.*

K*

porally later stage at which we apprehend the Saturdayness of today. We should not under these conditions be 'seeing the implication' at all. We may, of course, in an *earlier* phase of our reflexions, apprehend *simply* the tomorrowness of Sunday. But that is *before* we 'see the implication'—not a constituent *in* the 'seeing the implication'. At any point at which the apprehension of the premisses and the apprehension of the conclusion are temporally external to one another, there can be no seeing that the premisses *entail* the conclusion. How this fact is to be reconciled with the temporal sequence in which the words of the sentence occur, on the hypothesis that the thought and the words are identical, it is hard to see.

The above criticisms seem to me more than sufficient to refute the doctrine that a speaker's 'thought', in 'significant expression', is indistinguishable from his 'words'. There is no obligation upon the critic, *qua* critic, to go on to develop his own view of the nature of the 'inner act'—of the thought on its 'that' side as well as on its 'what' side. And I shall not attempt this here. It may be worth while, however, to point out in passing the special difficulty which the traditionalist must always have in giving a description of thought that will satisfy a 'last-ditch' opponent. The fundamental reason is that consciousness is indefinable. We can go some way towards describing cognition, as a specifically directed *mode* of consciousness, distinguished in certain ways from other modes of consciousness. But if anyone likes to say, 'This means nothing to me, for I don't know what "consciousness" is', I doubt whether one can do very much about it. One cannot force a man to become aware of the direct experience or 'enjoyment' through which consciousness is known to almost everyone but himself. Perhaps the most one can do is to show him that attempts to interpret the states and processes to which 'consciousness' and its derivatives are normally applied in terms of some *other* notion break down in intolerable paradox. But the fact is that in the case of ultimates and indefinables generally, the last and most important step in understanding cannot be initiated from without. The final appeal must be to the sceptic's own experience.

We must now take notice of the rather puzzling qualification, already mentioned, which Ryle makes to the straightforward theory which identifies thinking with the use of words. When we are told that the 'thought' which we think we 'express' in significant speech is 'just a soliloquized or muttered rehearsal of the overt statement itself', we know pretty well where we are. I think we find it difficult to know where we are when Ryle goes on to describe saying something significant, in awareness of its significance, as saying it 'on purpose, with a method, carefully, seriously and on the *qui vive*'.[1] 'Saying something in this frame of mind,' he proceeds, 'whether aloud or in one's head, *is* thinking the thought.' What are we to make of these adverbial qualifications—'on purpose', 'carefully' and the like—all of which seem to get their ordinary meaning from the very thing they are here supposed to be helping to define, viz. thinking? Indeed, when one considers the generic character of these adverbs and adverbial expressions one feels that Ryle might just as well have added the adverb 'thoughtfully' to the list while he was about it. But to define thinking a thought as 'saying something thoughtfully' might have been too obviously unhelpful.

But Ryle is not to be caught out so easily as this. The ultimate question at issue is evidently whether these adverbial qualifications can be understood as denoting only publicly observable features of behaviour, or whether they must be taken, as on the common view, to denote 'occult' processes of 'thinking'. And Ryle has prepared the way for acceptance of his present paradox by a systematic attempt in an earlier chapter to establish the former of these alternatives. I refer to Section 4 of Chapter V, which is concerned primarily with the analysis of what Ryle calls 'heed concepts'. Ryle is aware that such concepts—e.g. of 'noticing', 'taking care', 'attending' and the like—at least *seem* especially difficult to reconcile with the theory that there is nothing going on in our so-called 'minds' save publicly observable happenings; and he addresses himself to the task of showing that a reconciliation is nevertheless attainable.

The problem which the 'heed concepts' set for the 'one-world' theory is that they appear to designate something more than is capable of inclusion in what we sensibly observe in the activities qualified by heed adverbs. As Ryle puts it, 'When a man is described as driving carefully, whistling with concentration or eating absent-mindedly, the special character of his activity seems

[1] *Op. cit.*, p. 296.

to elude the observer, the camera, and the dictaphone'.[1] Hence we seem at first sight

forced to say either that it is some hidden concomitant of the operation to which it is ascribed, or that it is some merely dispositional property of the agent.[2]

But either alternative seems untenable. For

to accept the former suggestion would be to relapse into the two-worlds legend. It would also involve us in the special difficulty that since minding would then be a different activity from the overt activity said to be minded, it would be impossible to explain why that minding could not go on by itself as humming can go on without walking. On the other hand, to accept the dispositional account would apparently involve us in saying that though a person may properly be described as whistling now, he cannot be properly described as concentrating or taking care now; and we know quite well that such descriptions are legitimate.[3]

Before going on to consider how Ryle seeks to escape from this dilemma, let me pause for a moment to point out the inadequacy of the two reasons he has given for rejecting the former of the two alternatives (that minding is a 'hidden concomitant of the overt process').

The first reason is that it involves 'relapse into the two-worlds legend'. But of course that the two-worlds theory *is* a legend is an *hypothesis*, the tenability of which must largely depend upon whether a satisfactory account can be given in terms of a one-world theory of just such refractory phenomena as set the problem of this section. This reason, therefore, does not seem to carry much weight.

The second reason, that it would then be 'impossible to explain why that minding could not go on by itself', carries, in my judgement, even less. It is not at all clear why the acceptance of two processes as enjoying a different ontological status should entail the rejection of any intrinsic connexion between them. Surely we can perfectly well, and frequently do, mean by 'minding', something of different ontological status from what is being minded, and *yet* recognize that, since 'minding' necessarily has for its object something that is being minded, the minding 'could not go on by itself'. Indeed, this is to understate

---

[1] *Op. cit.*, p. 138.   [2] *Op. cit.*, p. 139.   [3] *Ibid.*

the case. Since on the traditional view, mind, *qua* consciousness, is of its very essence 'intentional', it does not make sense to ask why on *this* view minding cannot go on by itself—without an 'object'. It is precisely on *this* view of mind that the inseparability of minding and what is minded is *not* open to question. Admittedly we do not know *how* the two are connected; least of all, perhaps, where what is being minded is a 'physical' process. That is just the Mind-Body problem. But we do not require to *understand* a connexion in order to be satisfied that a connexion exists. So far as I can see, only on one supposition would the 'two-worlds' theory support the suggestion that, where what is being minded is a physical process, 'the minding could go on by itself'; the supposition, namely, that we understand by 'two worlds' (with some of the early rationalists) two absolutely self-subsistent entities. But who among all the philosophers of the last 200 years and more who have insisted upon the different ontological status of 'mind and matter' have had any interest in sponsoring a dualism of that kind?

Let us see, however, how the *one*-world theory fares with heedful operations. How does Ryle meet the admitted difficulty of bringing these within the orbit of a 'one-world' theory?

His solution consists essentially in a development of the 'dispositional' interpretation. According to the 'straight' dispositional interpretation, to say that a person is 'reading carefully' is to mention one overt occurrence (reading), and to 'make some open hypothetical statement' about the person reading. This account, Ryle contends, has obviously *some* truth. For one of the tests that a person is reading carefully is that certain true hypothetical statements can be made about him; as, e.g., that if he is asked to give the gist of what he has read he will be able to satisfy us. But the trouble is that heed concepts seem to have something *episodic* as well as something dispositional in their reference. As Ryle frankly points out, 'it is proper to order or request someone to apply his mind, as it is not proper to order him to be able or likely to do things'.[1] How is this 'episodic' aspect of the situation to be incorporated in the analysis?

The following passage gives (I think) the clearest statement of Ryle's solution:

---

[1] *Op. cit.*, p. 140.

To say that someone has done something, paying some heed to what he was doing, is not only to say that he was, e.g., ready for any of a variety of associated tasks and tests which might have cropped up but perhaps did not; it is also to say that he was ready for the task with which he actually coped. He was in the mood or frame of mind to do, if required, lots of things which may not have been actually required; and he was, *ipso facto*, in the mood or frame of mind to do at least this one thing which was actually required.[1]

That is to say (if I understand the passage aright), the requirement that the episodic reference of heed concepts be recognized as well as the dispositional is met by locating the dispositional factor *not only* in those *other*, associated acts of the agent to which the appropriate hypothetical statements will refer, *but also* in the actual doing of the act under immediate observation. To say that someone has done something 'heedfully' is 'not only to say that he was, e.g., ready for any of a variety of associated tasks . . .; it is also to say that he was *ready for the task with which he actually coped*'.

Now my quarrel with this solution of the problem is, in a sense, not with its analysis of heedful action at all. The analysis seems to me, on the contrary, most instructive. My whole trouble is that I cannot see how the analysis is to be understood in terms of the 'one-world' theory which it is Ryle's concern here to justify. The crux, of course, lies in the interpretation of that 'readiness', or 'ready frame of mind' which is declared (rightly, I think) to find expression in the heedful act itself. Ought this not to be something publicly observable if the one-world theory is to be saved? And how *can* it be? There are, admittedly, certain sensibly observable physical signs which we have all come to associate more or less closely with heed, care, concentration and the like. But Ryle has himself earlier agreed that these do not constitute what we *mean* by the 'heed-terms' in question. They are not even conclusive *evidence for* it. As he puts it, 'Perhaps knitted brows, taciturnity and fixity of gaze may be evidence of intentness; but these can be simulated, or they can be purely habitual'.[2] Yet if we rule out these physical signs, what is there sensibly observable left of which 'readiness of mind' can consist?

---

[1] *Op. cit.*, p. 141. See also p. 147 ('To describe someone . . . called on to do').

[2] *Op. cit.*, p. 138.

So far as I can see, Ryle has given no answer: and certainly I cannot supply one.

From the ordinary standpoint, of course, there is no need whatsoever for all this mystery. Puzzles arise only if our preconceptions compel the attempt to interpret 'readiness of mind' in terms which exclude 'inner' happenings directly knowable only by the subject of them. Lift this gratuitous ban on the so-called 'occult', and everything is plain sailing.

The simple, natural interpretation of heedful acts in terms of the *two*-world theory—or as I should much prefer to call it, less tendentiously, the *different-status* theory—ought perhaps to be briefly illustrated. Let us take as example a heedful act of one's own; since it is only in respect of one's own acts that there can be any claim to be directly aware of constituents of *each* of the two worlds. Suppose, then, I am set to transcribe from a long list of names prefixed by 'Mr', 'Mrs', or 'Miss' the names *only* of persons of the female sex. After a little my attention 'wanders', and I write the next three names 'automatically'. By sheer good fortune, however, they happen to be the names of females; the same, therefore, as they would have been if I had been paying heed. Now in my overt action there is nothing whatever to show that I was not acting heedfully, in 'a ready frame of mind'. But if someone should come along and say to me at this juncture, 'I hope you're taking proper care', I should of course at once realize that I was *not* heeding what I was doing. How can I know this if there is no discernible difference in my overt activity? Quite easily, because what I mean by 'heeding' is not an 'overt' activity, but an inner, 'occult' activity which is known to me in introspection; and I am aware that it is, and for some moments has been, lacking. I am aware that my overt acts had temporarily ceased to be consciously directed towards the end to be accomplished—the transcription of the names of females only. By noting the presence or absence from my mind of such a process of conscious direction I have no difficulty in distinguishing my 'heedful' from my 'heedless' activity. Without this clue the distinction would, I think, be altogether baffling.

In the case of other persons, of course, I do not enjoy the direct access to the mind which would enable me to determine in the same way (or, very significantly, with anything like the same confidence) whether they are acting heedfully or not. I am obliged to be content with the evidence of their overt behaviour. But I am certainly *not* obliged on that account to *mean* by the term 'heedful', when I apply it to others, characteristics of their overt behaviour. (That would be to confuse 'evidence for' with 'meaning of'—a confusion of which it is difficult to satisfy oneself that Ryle is always guiltless.) Indeed, so far from my being *obliged* to mean this, the truth is that I am obliged *not* to mean this, on pain of being convicted of using the term 'heedful' with one meaning in its application to myself and with another meaning in its application to other people. And it must surely be agreed that we at least *intend* that our use of the term should be univocal when used of ourselves and when used of others.

I venture to conclude, therefore, that we are amply justified in dismissing as a failure Ryle's attempt to interpret heed concepts in terms of his 'one-world' theory. It follows that Ryle's qualified account of thinking as using words 'heedfully'—apart from other grounds for criticism—must be rejected on the ground that while his adverbial suffix does make the theory rather more plausible as an account of thinking, it destroys the claim of the theory to be an account of it in terms of 'one world'.

I turn now to the third and last of the three main arguments which Ryle advances against 'intellectual acts' as ordinarily understood. This argument (it will be remembered) is directed against intellectual acts in the *exploratory* phase of theorizing. It is (ostensible) acts of *inferring* that give him especial concern. Ryle seems confident that he has already disposed of acts of *judging* in this phase to the satisfaction of the reader, but is evidently apprehensive that the reader will prove less docile about acts of inferring. For according to the traditional view, he recognizes, it seems, 'part of the very notion of a rational being that his thoughts sometimes progress by passages from premises to conclusions'.[1] It is necessary to take some pains over the rebuttal of a dogma so strongly entrenched.

I think it may be helpful to begin by getting better acquainted with the 'one-world' account of inference in favour of which Ryle asks us to jettison the traditional notion of intellectual acts of inferring. Such acts, it will be remembered, Ryle regards as gratuitously postulated by his *bêtes noires* the epistemologists to explain certain features discoverable in expounded theories.

[1] *Op. cit.*, p. 299.

'Finding arguments among the elements of published theories', this muddle-headed breed of men invent the fiction of separate, antecedent, 'counterpart' processes of 'inferring'; the only 'reality' to which the term 'inferring' bears witness, it would seem, is for Ryle the saying or writing of the words of the argument. As in his account of thinking in general, however, Ryle complicates what would otherwise be a very simple theory by a qualification which makes it look more plausible. Here, too, we discover, the operation is one of using words *in a certain frame of mind*.

An argument is used, or a conclusion drawn, when a person says or writes, for private or public consumption, 'this, so that', or 'because this, therefore that', or 'this involves that', provided that he says or writes it knowing that he is licensed to do so.[1]

Now the last clause of this passage tends to create the impression that Ryle *is*, after all, talking about something recognizably akin to what ordinary folk mean by 'inferring'. For to most of us a man 'knows that he is licensed' so to speak or write if, and *only* if, he sees the logical implication of conclusion with premisses. But of course this cannot be the way in which Ryle is understanding the clause. On Ryle's principles, a man's 'knowing that he is licensed' to make the transition in question must *itself* be something 'publicly observable'. We must therefore ask what features of overt behaviour Ryle is prepared to identify with 'knowing that one is licensed' to say or write 'because this, therefore that'. And to this question Ryle's answer is, to say the least of it, inexplicit. It is possible, however, that the following passage may contain the clue:

If he [any 'thinker'] is to merit the description of having deduced a consequence from premisses, he must know that acceptance of those premisses gives him the right to accept that conclusion; and the *tests* of whether he does know this would be *other applications of the principle of the argument*, though he would not, of course, be expected to name or to formulate that principle *in abstracto*.[2]

Now we may freely grant that the *test* of whether a man knows that acceptance of certain premisses gives him the right to accept a certain conclusion lies in the way in which he deals with problems involving the same ratiocinative principles. And this will mainly be manifest in the 'overt behaviour' of speech or

[1] *Op. cit.*, p. 301. [2] *Op. cit.*, p. 300.

writing. But the fact that the evidence for another person's 'knowing' is some form of overt behaviour does not, of course, entail that his 'knowing' is itself a form of overt behaviour. One is hesitant, once again, to impute to Ryle a confusion of 'evidence for' with 'meaning of': but it is very hard to see how otherwise he supposes himself able to identify the mode of 'knowing' that is here at issue with publicly observable behaviour.

However, the unconvincing character of Ryle's own 'one-world' account of inference does not of itself invalidate, though it may fairly raise a presumption against, his criticisms of the orthodox account. The orthodox account is, roughly, that 'inferring' is a datable, and frequently occurrent, intellectual act, the essence of which is the seeing of a logical implication between premisses and conclusion. What does Ryle find so mistaken about this notion?

The first point he makes is that inference does not involve *discovery*.[1] For we still call an inference an *inference* even though it is being made for the twentieth time, by which time, obviously, there can no longer be any question of 'discovery'.

This contention seems to me to be sound. One's difficulty with it is merely to appreciate its relevance as criticism of the orthodox view. Granted that inference is not necessarily discovery, what then? If it followed that inference is therefore not 'the seeing of a logical implication', that *would* be helpful for Ryle's critical purpose. But this does not follow, unless on the assumption that the seeing of a logical implication is held by those who believe in such acts always to involve 'discovery'. And this assumption is surely false. Certainly I should not myself hold, and I fancy few 'traditional' epistemologists would hold, that seeing a logical implication involves discovery, save on the occasion when one 'sees' it for the first time.

And in any event, what about this 'first time'? How does Ryle deal with the case when 'the light first bursts' upon a thinker? Is there not the seeing of a logical implication, which is likewise 'discovery', on *this* occasion? Must he not admit an 'act of inferring' here at least?

At this point Ryle becomes more than usually elusive. He first tells us that there *need* not 'have been any occasion on which the light first burst upon him'.[2] It may only have 'dawned' upon him.

[1] *Op. cit.*, p. 299.   [2] *Op. cit.*, p. 299.

'Need not', however, suggests that Ryle agrees that there are
some occasions upon which the light *does* 'burst', and one feels he
is merely postponing the evil day when he will have to tell us
what in his view happens *then*, if it is not to be the 'seeing of an
implication'. But as Ryle's argument proceeds, and no special
account emerges of light 'bursting', one is gradually forced to the
conclusion that he really wants to say that the light *never* 'bursts'
upon the thinker. It is *always* a case of 'dawning'. Now if *that*
is his view, we must look more closely at his account of the light
'dawning'. We must ask especially whether the process so described is in fact, as Ryle appears to suppose, one in which
the 'seeing of implications' is absent. Here is the relevant
passage:

Nor need there have been any occasion on which the light burst upon
him. It might well be that the idea that the gamekeeper was the murderer had already occurred to him and that the new clues seemed at first
to have only a slight pertinence to the case. Perhaps during some
minutes or days he considered and reconsidered these clues, and found
that the loopholes they seemed to leave became gradually smaller and
smaller until, at no specifiable moment, they dwindled away altogether.
In such a situation, which was the situation of all of us when we began
to study the proof of Euclid's first theorem, the force of the argument
does not flash, but only dawn, upon the thinker, much as the meaning
of a stiff piece of Latin unseen does not flash, but only dawns, upon the
translator. Here we cannot say that at such and such a moment the
thinker first drew his conclusion, but only that, after such and such a
period of chewing and digesting, he was at last ready to draw it in the
knowledge that he was entitled to do so. . . .[1]

Now what does all this add up to?

In the example which Ryle has taken (and I do not quarrel
with it) of a comparatively complex problem, it is of course true
that we do not reach in a single, sudden, inspired flash the conclusion that is sufficiently strongly supported by evidence to be
deemed the 'solution'. Before that final stage is reached, we have
gone through a long, laborious process; searching for clues,
testing the several alternative hypotheses suggested by freshly
discovered facts, and so on. These preliminary steps prepare the
way for, and (positively or negatively) contribute towards the
logical force of, the culminating insight. In that sense the process

---

[1] *Op. cit.*, pp. 299–300.

as a whole may fairly enough be described as one in which the light 'dawns' rather than 'flashes' upon the investigator. But surely this has no tendency to show that the process is one that is devoid of definite, datable acts of seeing implications, whether *en route* or at the finish? All that it shows is something that no one disputes, that the detective's ultimate solution did not arrive 'out of the blue'. If the light *as a whole* 'dawns' rather than 'flashes', this is perfectly compatible with countless individual *shafts* of light flashing upon the detective in the course of the inquiry, and contributing each its quota to the final illumination. And that is surely what normally happens? The whole prior process, impartially surveyed, would seem literally to abound in the 'seeing of implications'; and even in the seeing of them for the first time. How, for example, can the testing of the alternative hypotheses be carried out save in terms of 'seeing implications'? When we test an hypothesis X by observations directed to discovering whether a state of affairs *a* is a fact, this can only be in virtue of our seeing, or thinking we see, that if X is true *a* must be, or cannot be, the case. We are 'seeing implications' like this from beginning to end of any complicated investigation. Many of them are doubtless very simple implications, such as that if the gamekeeper killed the squire he must have been in the vicinity at the time the crime was committed: but the ease with which we may see an implication does not make this any the less an 'act of inferring'.

This seems to me a plain, straightforward description of what does actually happen in a typical case of seeking a solution to a comparatively complex problem, a description which anyone may verify for himself from his own experience. And I would emphasize that it is quite guiltless of the paradox which Ryle would apparently like to fasten upon all accounts of theorizing which stress the 'seeing of implications'. Our account is *not* 'like describing a journey as constituted by arrivals, searching as constituted by findings. . . .'[1] What *is* maintained in our account is that there are normally many intermediate arrivals preceding the terminal arrival in the course of the 'journey', many intermediate findings preceding the terminal finding in the course of the 'searching'. There is no question, for us, of the journey being *constituted* by arrivals, the searching *constituted* by findings. That

[1] *Op. cit.*, p. 303.

would indeed be paradox; though whether anyone really holds a view which has this implication, I do not know.

Moreover, there would seem to be no reason whatever to suppose that these 'seeings of implications' throughout the course of an inquiry are not in principle 'datable' acts. Often enough they are datable in practice too. A detective narrating the progress of a case is surely sometimes able, and very willing, to tell us just when this or that important 'shaft of light' first flashed upon him. There seems even less reason to suppose that the detective's final insight, e.g., that the gamekeeper did definitely kill the squire, is reached, in Ryle's phrase, 'at no specifiable moment'. I should have thought it a commonplace occurrence for detectives, in fact and in fiction alike, to impart to suitably admiring audiences just what new fact, or what old fact viewed from a fresh angle, supplied the missing link to clinch his case, and at what point it did so. It seems to me that there is no better ground for asserting that the detective arrived at his final insight 'at no specifiable moment' than that the gamekeeper killed the squire 'at no specifiable moment'.

There is, I think, only one other point that need detain us in Ryle's polemic against datable acts of inferring; and it need not detain us long. Ryle takes some trouble over showing that inference is not the kind of thing that can be fast or slow. '. . . Reaching a conclusion . . . is not the sort of thing that can be described as gradual, quick or instantaneous.'[1] I entirely agree. I have indeed already had occasion to urge that if a conclusion is apprehended at a later time than the premises are apprehended, then the conclusion is not apprehended as *implied by* the premises, and the situation is therefore not one of 'inference' at all. But what follows from this that threatens the orthodox view? If I understand him rightly, what Ryle *thinks* follows from it is that 'datable acts' of inferring are a myth. But this is surely wrong. The fact that in inference there is no time occupied *between* apprehending the premises and apprehending the conclusion by no means entails that there is no time occupied by apprehending the premises *as implying* the conclusion; i.e. by the *inference*. There seems to me no more danger from this than from any other quarter to the orthodox view that inference occurs at a time and occupies a time.

[1] *Op. cit.*, p. 302.

Let me very briefly summarize. I have sought to show (*a*) that Ryle's attempt to discredit the orthodox belief in 'occult' intellectual acts which differ in status from publicly observable behaviour, breaks down all along the line; every one of the arguments he uses can be effectively rebutted; and (*b*) that Ryle's substitute account of intellectual acts, while adhering ostensibly to 'one world' of publicly observable behaviour, gets whatever plausibility it enjoys by introducing elements incompatible with that world. It not merely looks like, but is, giving the 'one-world' case away when thinking is described as using words *heedfully*, and when inference is described as proceeding from the verbal statement of premises to the verbal statement of a conclusion *knowing that one is licensed to do so*. Perhaps the ancient Mind-Matter dualism may some day be successfully resolved. But I make bold to assert that, if it is, it will not be along the lines of *The Concept of Mind*.

CHAPTER XIV

PROFESSOR RYLE'S ATTACK ON DUALISM[1]

A. C. Ewing
Reader in Philosophy, University of Cambridge

If there is one British work on philosophy in the last five years which has attracted attention more than any other, it is Professor Ryle's *The Concept of Mind*, and it is certain that we shall hear a great deal of this type of view in the near future. Now, when a new kind of philosophical view gains ascendancy, especially one presented in such winning terms as Professor Ryle's, there is great need of an opposition speaker to stress the other side, and I cannot help feeling qualified for this role, if not by my ability, at least by my convictions. So I think that I need make no apology for this paper, though the *Proceedings of the Aristotelian Society* have already been enriched by more than one on the same subject.[2]

Now there is what one might call both a minimum and a maximum interpretation of Professor Ryle's book. On the minimum interpretation it is no doubt justified on the whole. By this I mean that it is undeniably the case that many psychological terms are far more complex in their meaning than a naïve introspectionist would at first sight suppose. They do not just name events in such a manner that there is a single definite kind of mental event corresponding to each term, but are essentially dispositional in character, each disposition being manifested in a great variety of ways, many of which are accessible to public observation in the fashion in which bodily events are. They cover not only private events but physical behaviour, and intelligence or mind may be exemplified as directly in the latter as they are supposed to be in the former class of occurrences. In some cases the terms also have a reference not only to the actual or hypothetical occurrence of events or processes, whether mental or physical, but to the success of these processes (achievement-words). Thus, e.g., the term *know* or *remember* signifies not merely that the person to whom it is applied thinks that something is so-and-so, but that he is

---

[1] *Proceedings of the Aristotelian Society*, 1952–3, Vol. LIII.
[2] Professor Wisdom in Vol. L and Professor Aaron in Vol. LII.

right in so thinking. For such reasons a person who thinks, e.g., that to say A knows B is necessarily to say that a single psychological event of a well-marked kind open to introspection but not to public observation has taken place in A relatively to B is committing a sort of mistake which may appropriately be called a 'category mistake' with some analogy to that of a person who supposed that to say the average man is 5 ft. 6 in. is to specify a particular class of men who are all 5 ft. 6 in. tall and no taller, or who supposed that propositions about Britain are propositions about a particular entity over and above all British people.

Professor Ryle's book is thus certainly very illuminating on the usage of particular psychological terms, but he only claims to examine these as part of the process of establishing a conclusion of a far more sweeping and revolutionary character. He wishes to show not only that many psychological terms do not stand for definite introspectible entities, but that 'the official theories of consciousness and introspection are logical muddles' and their supposed objects 'myths'.[1] He wishes to deny that there is a mental world at all over and above our bodily behaviour. 'The radical objection to the theory that minds must know what they are about, because mental happenings are by definition conscious, is that there are no such happenings; there are no occurrences taking place in a second-status world, since there is no such status and no such world and consequently no need for special modes of acquainting ourselves with the denizens of such a world.'[2] 'I try to show that when we describe people as exercising qualities of mind we are not referring to occult episodes of which their overt acts and utterances are effects; we are referring to those overt acts and utterances themselves.'[3] He is concerned to demolish altogether the dualism between mental and material with what he calls 'the privileged access' view, i.e. the view that there are certain events discoverable only by consciousness and introspection, and to maintain that 'the sorts of things that I can find out about myself are the same as the sorts of things that I can find out about other people, and the methods of finding them out are much the same'.[4] What are we to make of this wider conclusion? If it is true, it is certainly very important, but has it been in any way established?

[1] Ryle, *The Concept of Mind*, p. 155.
[2] *Op. cit.*, p. 161.   [3] *Op. cit.*, p. 25.   [4] *Op. cit.*, p. 155.

It is obvious that one might accept a very great deal of what Professor Ryle has to say, and yet stop far short of such drastic conclusions as those he draws. It may well be the case that most (or even conceivably all) of our psychological words are dispositional and yet that an account of them cannot be given merely in terms of outward behaviour but must invoke mental states observable only by the person who has them. Granted that 'believe' refers not to an actual state but to a disposition, it still may well be the case that the disposition referred to is not primarily a disposition to behave in a certain way, but a disposition to have private experiences of a certain kind. Again Professor Ryle may have succeeded in refuting the old view that we have a faculty, introspection, which tells us infallibly all about our own experiences and mental states. But the capacity may be fallible and yet real. After all we make mistakes in mathematics and mal-observe physical events. And against difficult cases of introspection and the mistakes about oneself pointed out by the psycho-analyst may be set the very numerous cases where we know so well what we are experiencing that in ordinary life no one but a madman would think of questioning it. I know Professor Ryle does not intend really to deny that I feel pain when I put my hand into the fire, but if so how is he able to deny the privileged access view and carry out his programme to the bitter end? He does not claim that he can feel my sensations of pain or observe my mental imagery. He has to admit that 'there are some things which I can find out only, or best, through being told of them by you. . . . If you do not divulge the contents of your silent soliloquies and other imaginings, I have no other sure way of finding out what you have been saying or picturing to yourself.'[1] Now a particular affirmative is sufficient to refute a universal negative, and therefore even if Professor Ryle has shown that there are not so many private mental predicates as we are apt to think, it is somewhat difficult to see how, if any remain, he can have overcome the dualism which he is attacking. He rightly insists that mind is sometimes displayed directly in physical happenings without a shadowy mental process necessarily intervening, but it is a big jump from never to only, and if he admits processes such as doing sums in one's head or reasoning privately at all, has he not reintroduced the dualism which he abhors?

[1] *Op. cit.*, p. 61.

It is not very clear what Professor Ryle's answer to this question would be. There are passages which suggest two alternative lines. One course is to say that it is a mere physiological accident that I cannot, e.g., feel your pain.[1] It is physically conceivable that, if it were worth doing, surgeons might discover a way of attaching my nerves to somebody else's teeth or brain, and then it might be argued that I could feel his toothache as well as mine. And there is good evidence that people sometimes know something of the experience of others by telepathy, and conceivable that this species of knowledge might be greatly extended and become attainable at will. In view of this it may be inferred that the distinction between private and public, mental and physical is not one of principle. After all, since no two persons can occupy the same position in space, they cannot obtain completely similar perceptions even of the same physical object at the same time.

The second course is to say that the privacy of my experiences is merely a verbal matter. 'There is a philosophically unexciting, though important, sense of "private" in which of course my sensations are private or proprietary to me. Namely, just as you cannot, in logic, hold my catches, win my races, eat my meals, frown my frowns, or dream my dreams, so you cannot have my twinges or my after-images. Nor can Venus have Neptune's satellites, or Poland have Bulgaria's history. This is simply a part of the logical force of those sentences in which the accusative to a transitive verb is a cognate accusative.'[2] We may, however, note that there is a certain point where the above analogies break down, suggesting that a combination of the two ways of defence is needed. Namely, I cannot hold somebody else's catches, but I can be aware of his catches in a way in which I cannot be aware of his pain. I think it is logically possible that I might, not have, but be aware of, his pain, but in practice I am not (at any rate if we exclude the relatively very rare cases of telepathy, of which I have had no conscious experience myself and which might after all be explained without supposing *direct* awareness of another person's experience as opposed to a veridical belief that he has a certain experience).

[1] *Vide* pp. 184–5, 'I can pay heed to what I overhear you saying as well as to what I overhear myself saying, though I cannot overhear your silent colloquies with yourself. Nor can I read your diary, if you write it in cipher, or keep it under lock and key.'   [2] *Op. cit.*, p. 209.

Against the view outlined we may set the moderately dualistic view which still commends itself to most thinkers. In order to reject Professor Ryle's conclusions it is not of course necessary to adopt the theory that body and mind are different 'substances'. All we need maintain is that besides the series of bodily events there is a series of mental events, whether the two belong to the same substance or not, and indeed whether or not this substance phraseology has any applicable meaning at all here. It may be admitted by the dualist that part of what many psychological words mean is to be analysed in terms of physical behaviour, but he will insist that over and above the physical behaviour and to a large extent determining it[1] there is all the time we are awake a continuous stream of mental events, the existence of which may be directly experienced only in ourselves, but inferred, at least with great probability, in the case of other human beings. The mental and the physical are very different qualitatively, a difference which can easily be recognized empirically when we compare a throb of pain felt by ourselves to a nervous reaction as observed by a physiologist or a thought in our mind to the movements of the larynx on which behaviourists enlarge. That these experiences are not to be identified with behaviour is no metaphysical hypothesis but a plain matter of fact empirically known. That thought or pain is not (though it may accompany) a nervous impulse, overt conversation or motion to withdraw, is as much an empirically observed fact as that a sight is different from a sound. As I have said, we can gladly admit very much in Professor Ryle's analysis of psychological terms, but even if we drop the view that to know anything is to perform or have performed a single mental act of a definite kind, we may still hold that there is a continuous stream of experience to which as well as to physical behaviour these terms normally, directly or indirectly, refer. If they are dispositional, mental as well as physical dispositions may be introduced into their analysis. And as for the general distinction between physical and mental, I should distinguish

[1] Strictly speaking, this involves the assumption that mental events can affect material events, a view which has been questioned by many who make a very sharp distinction between the two, but I may be pardoned for not dealing with the arguments (as I think, quite invalid) against causal interaction, since, apart from any general argument which would sweep away altogether one member of the interacting pair, they are not discussed by Professor Ryle.

them by saying that it is quite conceivable that the physical may exist apart from consciousness but inconceivable that the mental should do so. An idealist will not like this distinction, but he could substitute for it the distinction between subject and object of experience, a distinction the fundamental character of which is still more obvious. I cannot see that Professor Ryle has provided any refutation of the above outlined dualistic view. The distinction is not primarily between private and public but between experience and what is not an experience, between qualities which are modifications of consciousness and qualities which are at most objects of consciousness. On what I think is a logically possible theory of telepathy as analogous to the direct theory of perception any modifications of consciousness could conceivably be public, on the (at least possible) representative theory of physical perception every object of consciousness, and on a phenomenalist theory of physical objects which did not admit literal sharing of perceptions between different minds, everything whatever, would be private.

But whatever the truth about theories of perception and telepathy, we on the usual view have throughout our waking life a continuous train of experiences which are not, at least normally, observed by anybody else, even if it be arguable that they might be. It is not a case of just a few facts which cannot, owing to some physiological accident, be observed by others or of something which differs only from physical events in being by definition private, a merely verbal matter. Throughout our life there are two qualitatively quite different groups of processes taking place in us, one consisting of sensations, emotions, cognitions, conations as psychological events, the other of bodily movements. These two are generically different in character. The qualities of each are in the extreme dissimilar, and their relation to consciousness is quite different. Further, it is only through the mental that the physical is known, and all intrinsic value resides in the former, the latter being of value only as a means, not as an end in itself. This is the dualistic view in a form in which it is hard indeed to overcome.

But let us now examine seriatim the arguments by which Professor Ryle thinks he has got rid of dualism. I shall first take certain general arguments and then consider his attack on specific alleged mental phenomena. First, we may mention a subsidiary, but important, argument, namely the argument that, if dualism were true, and we identified other minds with the private side of their nature, nobody could ever know anything about anybody else's mind, a striking *reductio ad absurdum*. 'It would follow that no one has ever yet had the slightest understanding of what anyone else has ever said or done. We read the words which Euclid wrote and we are familiar with the things which Napoleon did, but we have not the slightest idea what they had in their minds.'[1] We could not, he holds, even make probable inferences.[2] Now we may retort that an argument for preferring one view *a* to another view *b* is never a success if it can be shown that the objection brought against view *b* is equally valid against view *a*, and it is plain that, if there are difficulties about claiming knowledge of other people's minds, there are equally difficulties about claiming knowledge of their bodies. Their bodies are physical objects, and all philosophers are familiar with the diffities about these. Yet Professor Ryle talks here as though these difficulties had never been heard of and all the difficulties were on the other side. Whatever we may think of Berkeley's criticism, we surely cannot treat the existence of physical objects or events as just established without further question by perception and the existence of other minds (in the non-Rylean sense) by contrast as an impossible inference from certainly known physical events. The common-sense notion of a physical object involves the notion of existing unperceived, and we obviously cannot perceive anything unperceived. Nor could we save the situation by a recourse to phenomenalism (which Professor Ryle incidentally rejects), for even on the phenomenalist view the notion of a physical object includes a great deal more than the assertion that I am perceiving something. It includes also a reference to what I cannot perceive directly, i.e. my possible future perceptions under different conditions and the perceptions of other human beings. Further, if we adopted phenomenalism in addition to Professor Ryle's view of the mind, we should be in a most curious position, for since we should then have to interpret all physical object propositions in terms of experience, the non-existent mythical ghost would have swallowed up the whole of solid reality. We cannot without a vicious circle interpret both propositions about mental states behaviouristically and propositions about physical objects experi-

[1] *Op. cit.*, p. 52.　　　　　[2] *Op. cit.*, p. 54.

entially. We cannot first reduce A to B and then reduce B to A.

Common sense and scientific beliefs about physical objects may indeed be justified, if we accept the ordinary criteria of induction and do not suppose something like a deceitful demon, by showing that our assumption of their truth enables us to predict successfully, explains our experience and makes it coherent in some wide sense of the term. But, if we make the same assumptions, our belief in other people's mental processes may be justified in a similar way.[1] A great deal in our experience is explained, and can only be explained by supposing the existence of mental processes other than our own. Professor Ryle attacks the argument for other minds from analogy with our body,[2] but he ignores the much stronger arguments from fulfilled predictions and the manifestations in our experience of purposes other than our own.[3] Of course the arguments do not give logical certainty, but neither do any scientific arguments. If, on the other hand, we admit scepticism as to the validity of induction or suppose a malicious demon, such doubts will affect beliefs about the bodies of others just as much as beliefs about their minds.

But more serious is the objection that mere knowledge of the physical behaviour of others does not give us what we mean by mind, unless it allows of an inference to something beyond itself, not observable in the same way. If I heard Professor Ryle screaming, why should I feel any sympathy with him or bother to try to remove the causes of his screaming, unless I on the strength of the screams supposed the existence of mental states not observable by me, states of pain? If 'pain' just means screaming and other physical behaviour, why is it so important to alleviate it? I do not think indeed that even Professor Ryle holds it only means this, but if I assert that anybody else feels pain in any other sense I am asserting something which according to his own words I can never know or even have any ground to think probable.

We shall now turn to Professor Ryle's general arguments against introspection. He is quite right for all practical purposes in attacking the old view that introspection is infallible. Anybody

---

[1] The justification of a belief must of course be distinguished from the account of its origin.

[2] *Op. cit.*, pp. 53–4.

[3] *Vide* Price, *Proceedings of the Aristotelian Society*, 1931–2.

who wished to defend that view might indeed theoretically escape by attributing the alleged mistakes of introspection to misuse of language, bad classification, defective memory, and inability or omission to observe what is present as opposed to observing it wrongly. In particular, alleged errors can always be ascribed to memory, not introspection of a present state, since the process of making introspective judgements, even to oneself, must always take time. But if we attempt a defence on these lines, we shall at least have to admit that we cannot in practice point to any pure introspective judgements untainted by these possible sources of error, and it becomes a merely academic question whether, if there were any such, they would be necessarily infallible. And it is quite wrong to assume that we are self-consciously aware of all our mental states and, even at moments when we deliberately introspect, of everything in these states.

Professor Ryle also uses the old argument that introspection would involve attending to two things at once, but admits that this is not conclusive in itself, though he thinks it would suffice to make many people doubtful whether they did introspect.[1] Coming from Professor Ryle, this is a peculiar argument, because he would hardly claim to know *a priori* that we cannot attend to two things at once, and the evidence against our being able to do so would have itself therefore to be based on introspection. And in any case what is meant by 'two things'? He does not mean two 'substances', and if our object of attention were never to have any discernible complexity, we could not attend to anything at all. If the difficulty is that we cannot attend to two *disconnected* objects at once, we may reply that there is surely a close enough connexion between the object of an act involving attention and the act, so that we might at the same time, e.g., resolve to get up early or to think of introspection and attend to our resolving or thinking. I certainly seem to be able to attend to these two at once, but it is theoretically possible that a period of time may have elapsed without my noticing its passage, and in that case the introspection would really be retrospection. But, as Professor Ryle admits,[2] there is no objection to retrospection, and that might be enough for our cognition of mental states, though we should have to agree with Professor Ryle that it is on principle fallible, which is not necessarily the same as saying that it can

[1] *The Concept of Mind*, pp. 164-5.   [2] *Op. cit.*, p. 166.

on no particular occasion give justified certainty, a distinction which Professor Ryle's philosophical associates have often made in regard to the perception of physical things. I may still claim to know with certainty that I feel warm or that I at least seem to myself to be writing in my study even if introspection is not as such always infallible, as contemporary philosophers have insisted *ad nauseum* that we can know some propositions about physical objects even though mistakes in science and illusions of perception are possible.

Professor Ryle also has recourse to the infinite regress argument both against the notion of introspection[1] as a separate cognitive operation or act of attention and against the notion of a self-consciousness supposed to be inherent in every mental state or process.[2] In either case the question arises whether I am thus conscious of my consciousness of my mental states. If I always am, we have a vicious infinite regress, and therefore we must admit that some elements in mental processes cannot be the object of consciousness. But in that case we can no longer maintain that what is mental necessarily carries with it the property of consciousness.

It seems to me that Professor Ryle in this argument has confused two senses of 'conscious'. All experiences must be conscious in the sense of 'felt', otherwise they would not be experiences, but it does not follow from this that we must be able to say to ourselves when they occur what they are like, still less that we discern all the elements present in them. So if I introspect or am in some way conscious of myself as resolving, both introspection and resolving will be part of my total felt state, but they need not both be objects of distinct consciousness, still less need my consciousness of my consciousness that I introspect (if there is such a consciousness at all). I can be conscious vaguely of a whole without being conscious of all its parts. It is important for the introspectionist to realize that there is no special difficulty or even paradox about elements in our experience which are unconscious in the sense of not being noticed as such, though they are still part of our total experience and therefore conscious in the sense of 'felt' (not indeed separately but as contributing to our total experience, as undiscriminated organic sensations or the background memory of a mishap may contribute to give it an

[1] *Op. cit.*, p. 165.   [2] *Op. cit.*, p. 163.

unpleasant feeling tone). Even the most introspective person is not introspecting all the time, and even when he does introspect he probably never picks out introspectively every theoretically distinguishable element in his experience. Mental events can only be *defined* as 'conscious events' if that word is understood to mean 'experienced' or 'felt'.

Professor Ryle lays an extraordinary stress on the fact or alleged fact that we do not use words like 'witness', 'observe', 'discover', 'listen to', of the alleged objects of introspection, making this the ground of a general argument against introspection.[1] Now it has been said that a person who is revolutionarily sceptical of certain things generally believed often makes up for his scepticism in one respect by undue credulity in another, and it seems to me that I have noted many instances, of which I believe this passage is one, where thinkers of Professor Ryle's type come dangerously near a verbal inspiration theory of common-sense language.[2] What becomes of this argument if, as may well have happened owing to multitudinous historical accidents, common sense is not consistent in its use of terms? At the very least it would need an investigation of several languages besides English before any conclusion could possibly be drawn from these linguistic facts. As a matter of fact, however, it is not necessary even to attribute any error to common-sense language in order to meet the argument. It would not be an inconsistency but merely a further specialization of language to apply different names to the same activity according to the kind of objects on which it is directed, even if the activity were in this case the same, but nobody, least of all the introspectionist, would deny that the process (or act?) of ascertaining what feelings, etc., one has is different from the process of observing physical objects, and therefore *a fortiori* may reasonably be given a different name. Professor Ryle, however, himself admits that we use the terms 'heed' and 'notice' not only about physical things but also in relation to our sensations.[3] So I do not see that the argument has

[1] *Op. cit.*, pp. 205 ff. Incidentally I should have said that the term 'observe' at least is used of sensations and other objects of introspection.

[2] Another example of this occurs where Professor Ryle objects to the use of the concept of sensation in philosophy and psychology because 'novelists, biographers, diarists or nursemaids' do not use the word 'sensation' (p. 201) in such contexts.

[3] *Op. cit.*, p. 206.

L

the faintest tendency to show that there are no mental entities, sharply different from physical, or to restrict the number or kinds of these mental entities in any way. Many introspectionists would no doubt agree with Professor Ryle that sensations, as opposed to their objects, 'do not have sizes, shapes, positions, temperatures, colours or smells',[1] but if this is so it only strengthens the dualist's position, unless we deny their existence altogether, and Professor Ryle does not deny headaches and other sensations but admits that, though we cannot witness or observe them, we can notice them. He points out that, while we need or at least know what it is like to need observational aids, like telescopes, stethoscopes and torches, for the observation of the physical, we do not need or even know what it would be like to need them for the observation of our own sensations, and that while we know what kinds of handicaps impair our observations of the physical we have no analogous knowledge as regards our sensations. But surely this could again only show that the way of knowing was different, which the introspectionist readily admits, and that the analogy between observation of the external world and introspection should not be pressed too far, which he ought also to admit. If 'dualism' is true, it is not to be expected that physical instruments other than our brain would be needed for introspection in the same way as for external observation, so the argument ought, if anything, to tell against Professor Ryle's own view which assimilates the way in which we know ourselves to the way in which we know the physical world. Further, we certainly do know some handicaps which impair our ability to notice accurately our sensations, as Professor Ryle himself has pointed out in other contexts, e.g. emotional excitement or a diversion of attention to some other topic. He again seems to confuse the fact that a certain kind of question is not usually asked because of lack of occasion or of general interest with the supposition that it is logically absurd to ask it. We do not usually ask people the question whether they have inspected their sensations closely or casually, carefully or carelessly,[2] but I imagine if Professor Ryle were teaching psychology to not very keen students he would often have occasion to ask it.

Turning from these more general criticisms of introspection to Professor Ryle's more specific treatment of particular alleged

[1] *Vide* p. 208.　　　　　　　　　[2] *Vide* p. 207.

mental characteristics, we find a great deal of interest, but no real disproof of the dualist position. It is interesting to note that Professor Ryle first publicized his present tendency of thought in a paper on 'Knowing How and Knowing That',[1] and that it is on this theme too that he starts his present work after a general introductory chapter. He is concerned to point out that the word 'know' may be used to signify ability to perform certain operations where it cannot be reduced to what we call a knowledge of propositions, and to try to treat all knowing on these lines. He argues that any view which opposes him in this involves an infinite regress. For if we hold that, in order to carry out any process intelligently, we have to go through a process of considering propositions about the process, the objection arises that by the same argument this process of considering propositions requires another such process and so on *ad infinitum*.[2] This argument is salutary as a safeguard against giving too large a part in our account of mental life to the consideration of propositions, but the introspectionist certainly need not take the view that we can never do anything intelligently except through a process of considering them. I think indeed that Professor Ryle has under-rated the role of propositions even in physical games which show skill, for merely to recall consciously in which court we ought to serve in tennis or what is the state of the score is to have a proposition in view; but it may be admitted that a man can play a game intelligently without considering propositions all the time he shows intelligence, and that he can select intelligently what propositions he is to consider without considering prior pro-positions about the question what propositions it would be best to consider. But since it does not follow that we never consider propositions, I do not see how this argument can be used to get rid of the view that there are some mental events or processes which consist in that considering. The consideration of propositions about a physical activity one is performing is not in general necessary as long as the activity goes on quite smoothly, but it occurs where there is a doubt about which of two steps to choose and there is any time to reflect on the subject. And similarly if our primary activity is at a given time dealing with propositions, we shall usually only want to consider secondary propositions

---

[1] *Proceedings of the Aristotelian Society*, Vol. XLVI, p. 1.
[2] *The Concept of Mind*, pp. 30-1.

about how to deal with them where there is some doubt as to whether we are doing so in the best way, where we have to decide what activity to start, or where an activity we have begun is somehow blocked. Thus before I started considering Professor Ryle's arguments I considered, and very quickly accepted, the proposition that it would be worth while doing so, but I have never needed to reconsider the proposition in question. If I am in doubt about certain arguments I may ask whether they conform to the rules of logic, but if I am not in doubt I shall not do so but just use them (unless I am interested in their logic for other reasons, as most people are not). I can even go on to consider third- or fourth-order propositions about the propositions with which I primarily deal. I might consider whether the proposition that Professor Ryle's arguments are worth considering is a logical or an ethical proposition (third-order), and might even go on to consider the fourth-order question what distinguishes logical from ethical propositions. But obviously I could not carry this process on *ad infinitum*. We must thus agree with Professor Ryle in rejecting the view that an intelligent activity always requires the considering of propositions about the activity, but we should not under-rate the extent to which consideration of propositions occurs, masked as it is by the fact that, when we consider them, we do not usually formulate them fully, as we should if we were communicating them to others. I do not say that we can even consider them without using words to ourselves except where we are dealing with a subject-matter which can be imaged, but where a whole sentence would be required when speaking to others a word or two suffices in our private thoughts. But our consideration is none the less real for all that. However, since Professor Ryle does not deny that we do consider propositions, presumably the argument is only intended as a warning against exaggerating their role. But in that case it cannot be used as an objection to the privileged access view. I can certainly know in many cases that I am considering a proposition when there is no overt sign by which anybody else would know that I am considering it.

I think indeed that Professor Ryle has said something important, which has very commonly been forgotten by philosophers, when he insists that cleverness may be shown directly in physical action without being first displayed in an intervening conscious process 'in the agent's mind'. If intelligence can be shown in doing sums in one's head, it can be shown equally directly by doing them on paper, and we applaud a skilful clown or sportsman for his physical skill, not for an extra hidden performance in his mind.[1] We need not suppose the occurrence of such a mental performance at all, and it is immaterial to our admiration whether it occurs or does not occur. All this is true, but one thing at least is omitted. We only applaud a man seriously for physical performances because we think they express his purpose, and purpose is surely a mental phenomenon not capable of direct observation by anybody else. We do not indeed admire his purposes as such—I might purpose to score a century till I was black in the face without being a good cricketer—but his execution of them. Or rather we only admire the man's performance on the assumption that it expresses a purpose. This need not take the form, before he does something, of reciting to himself words to the effect that he will do it, which recitation, as Professor Ryle points out, might itself like public conversation be carried out by habit without intelligence. Purpose is of course a very difficult thing to analyse and describe adequately, but at least it includes *consciousness* of what one is doing, and how are we to observe or, if Professor Ryle prefers it, *notice* the consciousness of another man? His consciousness is not his actions, and therefore to know of its existence we must, unless we have telepathic powers, infer it, explicitly or implicitly, from his actions. But if an effective stroke or an amusing antic is thought to be the result of accident our attitude is quite different. Professor Ryle points out that we can as outside observers tell whether it is the result of intelligence or accident by considering a more protracted series of movements, but there is an important difference to be noted. The person who performs it can without going beyond the one move itself tell you whether he purposed to do what he actually did. He can tell directly whether he intended to checkmate you by this move, but an outside observer, before he could answer this question, would have to take note of the man's other moves or at least of things he said, and his answer would be of the nature of an inference. This is not the case with the agent himself: he can at least tell you whether he did what he intended to do, though he may be very doubtful whether he could repeat it at will. You cannot, like him, know his intentions *directly*. He

---

[1] *Op. cit.*, p. 33.

knows without argument, but you have to use the *argument*: He was not a good enough player to have done it on purpose.

Professor Ryle has a similar infinite regress argument against the concept of volition. He asks whether volitions are themselves voluntary or involuntary. If the former it would seem that the theory he is criticizing leads to the conclusion that they must issue from a prior act of volition and so on *ad infinitum*; if the latter, the acts to which they lead could not themselves be voluntary. If, on the other hand, we say that they cannot be described as either voluntary or involuntary, we cannot describe volitions as 'virtuous' or 'wicked'.[1] But surely we might accept the third alternative without accepting Professor Ryle's *reductio ad absurdum* of it. Because it is the case that in order to be virtuous or wicked an action must be voluntary, need it follow that this is true of a volition? I have never heard people talking of voluntary or involuntary volitions. If 'a voluntary action' is defined in terms of volition, this would itself be a good reason for saying that the terms voluntary and involuntary could not be applied to volitions themselves. To be virtuous or wicked an action must be voluntary, I should say, because it would otherwise not be indicative of a good or bad will, and virtue or wickedness applies primarily to the will, but this is no reason why a volition could not be virtuous or wicked without being determined by a previous volition. It is itself an exemplification of good or evil will and does not need, like a physical act, to exemplify something further behind itself in order to be morally good or evil. (It seems to me that this answer is independent of what answer we give to the question whether the will is itself determined or not.)

But the infinite regress argument is only an episode in a more general and fundamental attack on volition. Professor Ryle contends that the concept is not used in ordinary life and has no empirical warrant but is merely the fruit of a philosophical theory. He supports his view by such remarks as these. 'No one ever says that at 10 a.m. he was occupied in willing this or that, or that he performed five quick and easy volitions and two slow and difficult volitions between midday and lunch time.' 'If ordinary men never report the occurrence of these acts (of will), for all that, according to the theory, they should be encountered vastly more frequently than headaches, or feelings of boredom; if

[1] P. 67.

ordinary vocabulary has no non-academic names for them; if we do not know how to settle simple questions about their frequency, duration or strength, then it is fair to conclude that their existence is not asserted on empirical grounds.'[1]

Now there is no doubt an element of truth in what Professor Ryle says: there is no need to suppose a specific act of will for every voluntary physical act. To call an act voluntary it is not necessary that it should have been specifically willed. In the case of a prolonged action like a speech which is specifically willed we need not suppose a separate act of volition for each distinguishable phase, say, each word. Yet in the latter case the uttering of each word may certainly be described as voluntary (except for involuntary slips). Indeed I should go further and say that the account in terms of acts is faulty in that it pictures our will as consisting in a set of quite discrete, almost instantaneous events interpolated at relatively rare points in a series of experiences which are not at all volitional in character. Volition, at least in one sense, should rather be viewed as a continuous striving present during all purposive activity. It is not a set of acts so much as one side of most of our mental life, more or less prominent. We are always aiming at something, vigorously or casually, except perhaps in a state of the merest day-dreaming, and even there, according to the psycho-analyst, purposes are very active indeed. Even when we neglect to attend to our work we do so in order to attend to something else, if only something in our idle imaginations or reminiscences which has a casual emotional or low-grade intellectual interest.

But of course there are volitional phenomena which are noticeable in a very special degree and have therefore excited the chief interest in discussions of volition, and it is at least arguable that it is best to reserve the term volition to cover these and use 'conation' in the wider sense indicated above. Of such there seem to me to be two kinds: (1) Decisions or choices. (2) Efforts of will. That the two classes are not identical is clear from the fact that the first may be separated by a very considerable time from the second. I may decide now to get up at 6 a.m. tomorrow or resolve not to be cross next time I am annoyed, and if the carrying out of these decisions was in no way repugnant to me that would be sufficient, provided I did not simply forget them,

[1] Pp. 64-5.

but when it comes to carrying them out it is probable that this will also require at the time a specific effort of volition. The effort need not be made now when I decide, but it will have to be made before I carry out what I have decided. I have spoken of the two phenomena as temporally separate, but they are not always so. Thus it costs a real effort of will to make an intellectually or morally hard decision even in advance of action, and when the time comes to carry it out the obstacles may be such that at the very time of action I have again to make the decision and not only try to carry it out as something already decided (not to mention the numerous cases where there is no time to decide—appreciably in advance of action). Decisions are not carried out for two different reasons: (1) because we, while not reversing our decision, simply do not make the effort required to carry it out, (2) because in face of difficulties we reverse our decision. It is these two phenomena chiefly: (1) decision, (2) volitional effort, which are covered by talk about the will. We must, however, still not think of volitions as single acts but rather as processes which may take up a long time. A decision is indeed not exactly a process, but then a 'decision' is not a separate event but only the terminal limit of the process of coming to a decision, and it is this in which the 'will' shows itself; and efforts may be continuous for a long period though oscillating very much in severity. At any rate there is no reason whatever to ascribe to these phenomena the merely instantaneous character often supposed to be connoted by 'mental acts'.

Now it is certain that we do sometimes talk about decisions and efforts of will. I may say—I decided to reply in this way as soon as I heard Professor A's argument or—Before going to bed I decided that I should return to Cambridge as soon as possible, and since the decision in cases like these precedes any overt action it obviously cannot be identified with carrying out the decision. I may also say—I was so worried by what had happened that I had to make a constant effort to attend to what I was doing, or When I touched the water with my foot and felt how cold it was, I had to make a great effort of will to go any farther. We certainly sometimes say such things, though most people do not say them very often because of a sense that they usually lack general interest. And we also talk about what I called 'conations' as opposed to 'volitions' in the less wide sense when we say things such as—Throughout this paper I am trying to show there is a place for introspection in philosophy, or My purpose in the game was to keep on the defensive till my opponent was tempted into making a rash move. I do not want volition in any further sense beyond these any more than Professor Ryle does. But I cannot see what on earth he means by denying that such processes are introspectible or asserting that they can be discovered by outside observers *in the same way* as they can be discovered by the man who experiences them himself. The fact that we cannot answer questions such as how many acts of volition we performed in a given time is partly due to the fact that owing to their lack of practical importance hardly anybody has got into the way of asking such questions, partly because owing largely to this very circumstance there is no agreed definition as to where one volition ends and another begins. Is to decide to ask somebody and his wife to come to tea at 4 p.m. tomorrow one decision or two, three or four? And how do we decide when one effort of will begins and another ends? We are practically without any ideas as to what constitutes *one* act of will at all. Neither do we remember how many times we got up from our chair during the morning, nor is it ever asked how many assertions were made in the newspaper leader we have just read, nor what was the total number of times during the day I noticed the mantelpiece or felt a headache. Professor Ryle asks 'By what sorts of predicates should they [volitions] be described? Can they be sudden or gradual, strong or weak, difficult or easy, enjoyable or disagreeable? Can they be accelerated, decelerated, interrupted or suspended? Can people be efficient or inefficient at them? Can we take lessons in executing them? Are they fatiguing or distracting?'[1] Well, surely we do talk about difficult or sudden or painful efforts or decisions, we are interrupted in making up our minds or in trying to do something, and we are strong-willed or weak-willed. It is obvious that frequent perplexing decisions and strong efforts of will are fatiguing, and moralists have constantly told us that we learn to will better in future by practice in willing to the best of our ability.

Let us now turn to the cognitive side of our nature. I must admit, and have indeed already admitted, that Professor Ryle has made valuable contributions here, especially in bringing out

---

[1] P. 64.

the dispositional character of psychological terms. In particular I think that the theory of knowing which Professor Ryle has apparently chiefly in mind in his attacks was very defective. It was supposed that there were certain acts of knowing (not processes, and therefore presumably instantaneous phenomena) by which we were infallibly aware of sense-data or propositions, and the suggestion conveyed was that to say I know A is to say that I have performed such an act in relation to A. Against this Professor Ryle has maintained the view that 'know' is a dispositional term and that the disposition referred to is not manifested in just one definite kind of act but in a manifold variety of behaviour. He has further maintained that besides being a dispositional term it is an achievement term, i.e. it signifies not merely that we have done something but that we have done it successfully, and that it is this and not the possession of a peculiar infallible faculty which makes it impossible to admit that we can ever be mistaken when we 'know'. The latter point does not hold of all psychological cognitive terms, but it does of some, and it is certainly true of many that they are dispositional in character. In this I should agree with Professor Ryle, if only he would include in the account of the disposition not only physical behaviour but its psychological manifestations in experience. 'I know' and 'I believe' might be dispositional, and yet in the actual events in terms of which the disposition must be realized might be included acts of knowing and mental events of coming to believe as well as the manifestations of the disposition in physical behaviour.

Professor Ryle uses against any psychological interpretation the same argument as he had used against volition as a mental phenomenon, namely, the argument that a man is not able to answer certain questions which, if the view were true, he should be able to answer. 'How many cognitive acts did he perform before breakfast, and what did it feel like to do them? Were they tiring? Did he enjoy his passage from his premises to his conclusion, and did he make it cautiously or recklessly? Did the breakfast bell make him stop short half-way between his premises and his conclusion? . . . Is conceiving a quick or a gradual process, an easy or difficult one, and can he dawdle over it or shirk doing it? About how long did it take him to consider the proposition and was the spectacle in the later stages of the consideration like or unlike that in the initial stages? Was it rather like gazing blankly at something or more like detailed scrutiny? He does not know how to begin to answer such questions.'[1] I admit these questions mostly sound rather odd, partly because Professor Ryle has not employed the terminology usual in relation to the subject and partly for reasons such as those I have mentioned in the case of volition.

The first pair of questions is perhaps unanswerable because there is no recognized criterion as to when one cognitive act begins and another ends, and because how they feel is indefinable as in the case of colours. But certainly we do see something to be true at some specifiable time. We enjoy drawing conclusions which refute our opponents, and we are well aware that considering a philosophical problem for long is tiring, though we should not ordinarily say of a single cognitive act any more than of a single step in a walk that it was tiring. We certainly can draw inferences cautiously or over-hastily, and when the inference is difficult the breakfast-bell may interrupt us at a time when we are only half decided as to its validity or even as to what follows at all. (If the inference is easy, as in a simple syllogism, it would usually be completed, breakfast-bell or no breakfast-bell, before we had time to respond to the stimulus from outside.) Conceiving is sometimes quick and sometimes gradual, sometimes easy and sometimes difficult. It is a very slow job to form a concept of what some philosophers are talking about, and a very quick job to form one of an easily distinguishable physical object definable by its shape. And to my regret I certainly know that it is possible to dawdle in carrying out the former operation or shirk the effort needed to do it to the best of my ability. I could, if I chose to take the trouble and remembered to look at the right moment, find by consulting my watch how long I spent considering a given proposition. If I am candid with myself I am well enough aware that I sometimes gaze blankly at propositions put forward by philosophers, and I can distinguish this from scrutinizing them in detail; and when the scrutiny is successful, the proposition commonly appears to me different in statable ways from what it did at the start.

But we certainly must not exaggerate the role of cognitive acts. It is a quite unwarranted assumption that there is an act of knowing for every piece of knowledge we possess, or that there

[1] Pp. 292–3.

is a specific, introspectively discoverable experience of believing
for everything we believe. When we say that A believes a proposition, not only do we not commit ourselves to any statement
about his actual state of mind or experience at the time we speak,
but we do not even commit ourselves to the statement that he has
ever had an experience of believing in respect of the proposition.
He may have just taken it for granted without consciousness of
what he was doing, and yet it may be correct to make the positive
statement that he believes it. Indeed 'believing', as commonly
understood, does not stand for an experience. However, 'coming
to believe', 'seeing to be true', 'thinking about with a feeling of
conviction' do; and the meaning of the dispositional words believe
and know should surely be analysed in terms of mental occurrences
like these as well as in terms of the physical behaviour to which
beliefs give rise. Take a case of belief which will suit Professor
Ryle's line of argument if any does. I venture to suggest that
you all believe that the roof of the building in which you are
sitting will not collapse, and that you believed this even before I
put the idea into your minds by my suggestion. Yet very probably
none of you were giving the matter a thought: you were not
considering at all the proposition that it would not collapse and
therefore were not having any actual experience of believing it.
It is therefore plausible to say, as Professor Ryle presumably
would, that this simply means that you *acted* as if the building
would not collapse. You did not hurry out of the room; you did
not even glance at the roof with anxious faces; you did not start
moving furniture into the street; you made plans which involved
remaining in the building; if you had been asked by a hysterical
person whether you thought the roof would collapse, you would
have said: 'No of course it won't, do not be silly', or something
like that. But it is surely just as correct to include possible mental
events as well as possible physical ones in the analysis. If the
analysis includes saying openly certain words when asked a
question, it should also include the saying them to oneself with a
feeling of conviction. It should include at least the liability to feel
very surprised if anybody questioned the proposition believed,
and mentally to make inferences which assumed its truth. It
should include the fact that you are not mentally disturbed by
any fears of being buried alive in the ruins and are not in the least
disposed to ask serious questions in your own mind relating to the

possibility in question. It is true, these facts are merely negative, but so were the facts included in the behaviouristic analysis such as that you do not rush out of the room. In cases like this at least, Professor Ryle seems to be right in holding that 'belief' stands for a disposition not analysable in terms of any one *specific* kind of mental event exclusively, but need its analysis therefore be limited to physical behaviour? It may be analysed in terms of a variety of possible conscious mental events as well as of possible publicly observable physical events, and, if we can supply an analysis in mental terms, the doubt is whether we really also need the physical terms in order to complete the analysis. Would it indeed be correct to say that we believed something if we acted as if it were true but did not do so with any conscious purpose in our mind and felt no mental inclination to assert the belief to ourselves when it was challenged nor any vestige of surprise when it turned out false? We can often, even if not always, know at once whether we believe or do not believe a proposition without having had occasion to act on it, and I do not see how a behaviouristic theory of believing could explain this at all. The same applies, I think, to 'know', except that this term, unlike 'believe', (1) excludes all lingering doubts, and (2) is verbally incompatible with error, so that it is self-contradictory to say A knows p, but p is not true, i.e. it is an 'achievement word'.

But the most formidable and influential argument against cognitive acts is constituted by the mere fact of the existing disagreement as to whether they occur. If there are such things, it is said, surely there should be no disagreement or doubt about them any more than about ordinary objects of observation in the physical world. If they occur at all, they must be very numerous indeed. But a defender of mental acts may legitimately reply as follows. He may say that the critic was looking for the wrong sort of thing in the wrong sort of way. The latter may have been looking for something such as extra sensibilia, and we need not be surprised that he failed, since knowing and willing are not that sort of thing at all. Or, even if he did not regard them as sensibilia, he may still have been expecting to know them as a sort of objects, while cognitive acts are not objects of awareness but the subject's awareness itself. When we know such, it may be argued, this is not because they have become objects, except in memory, which presupposes prior consciousness of them when they occurred, but because the very mental act carries with it an awareness of itself which was present before this retrospective introspection but is clarified and intensified in the latter. Further, it should be pointed out that, whatever doubts there may be about admitting that we can be aware of mental acts or attitudes as such, we can certainly be aware of ourselves as doubting or believing a specific proposition, if not doubting or believing in general. It may be that the trouble is largely that people assume that, if they occur at all, these mental acts or attitudes can be caught by themselves apart from their object, and this they cannot be because they necessarily imply an object. But to know what something is, one need not necessarily know it by itself, it may be enough to know it as it is in relation to an object. This is surely the best we can do if it cannot exist apart from some object. I cannot know what knowing or believing is like *per se,* because it does not exist *per se,* but I might still know what it was like to judge something or to know something to be true. There would indeed be similar difficulties about determining what the mental state of feeling pain is apart from the felt pain. Nobody would think of looking for pleasure or pain *in vacuo* apart from some experience which has other characteristics besides being merely pleasant or merely painful, similarly cognition can only occur in an experience which has the characteristic of being or including contemplation of some specific object or proposition. Just as it is a vicious abstraction to separate propositions from the cognizing or considering of them and regard them as subsistent entities independent of our thoughts, is it not also a vicious abstraction to suppose that we can contemplate knowing or believing *per se* in abstraction from the propositions known or believed?

The reply has been made by other philosophers to an argument of this kind that we cannot distinguish believing and not believing in the way suggested since exactly the same content is never both affirmed and doubted or affirmed and denied. If we use B for believe we never have both the experience $BA1$ and at a later time not-$BA1$, but only not-$BA2$, so that we cannot distinguish believing from other mental states by simply eliminating the constant element in two different experiences and noting the difference left. But surely, even if the above is true, we can distinguish two different kinds of differences, one in the more subjective, and the other in the more objective, side of the total process. We have certainly no noticeable tendency to confuse the distinction between believing confidently and doubting with a distinction between propositions entertained.

In general it may be suggested that what introspective psychology really suffers from is not inability to observe cognitive acts or events—we usually know well enough whether we believe something or not without having recourse to inference from our overt actions—but inability to analyse and describe them.

While in general accepting this line of reply about mental cognitive events and processes, I must, however, admit that I have for long thought 'act' to be a somewhat unfortunate term in this connexion as suggesting to us that we should look for something which is not there. As I have said already, it is certainly not clear that there is a definite act of knowing whenever I know anything. Indeed we may go further and say that what I observe introspectively is never knowing but either coming to know or coming to believe, or recapitulating the process by which I came to know or believe. This process will vary much according to the kind of thing I come to know, and as a conscious event may well itself not be present in the case of many things which I should quite ordinarily and properly be said to know or believe. It will be very different with pieces of knowledge or beliefs acquired by reasoning and those acquired by sense-perception. To notice the presence of a physical object, to find out that I am fond of or dislike somebody, consciously to infer q from p, to see something to be true *a priori*, to realize that it is my duty to do so and so are experiences the similarity of which is less conspicuous than the differences. Too much has been said about cognitive as about volitional 'acts', and as too little has been said about the conative process of continuous purposive striving, so too little has been said about the cognitive process of thinking about something. In these processes the 'acts' cannot be more than episodes, and the process should not be reduced to a mere series of such episodes, as walking is reducible to a series of steps or a book to a series of sentences. It is not merely that, as the latter illustration would suggest, the process is an organic unity with the acts as its components parts, but that there is a good deal in the process besides the acts, even if we apply the term *act* to coming to know or believe, i.e. seeing or judging something to be true. We should rather say of 'acts' what William James said of images. 'What must be admitted is that the definite images (acts) . . . form but the very smallest part of our minds as they actually live. The traditional psychology (old-fashioned philosophy of mind) talks like one who should say a river consists of nothing but pailsful, spoonsful, quartpotsful . . . of water. Even were the pails and the pots all actually standing in the stream, still between them the free water would continue to flow.'[1] The term, act, is objectionable also as suggesting that we decide directly what we are to know or believe and do not have it decided for us by the evidence as it appears to us.

Just as a theory in terms of 'acts' suggests too episodic a view of cognition and conation, so Professor Ryle himself takes far too episodic a view of pleasure and interest on the psychological side. He thinks that, apart from any analysis in terms of behaviour, they can only consist of very short-lived exciting 'thrills', and argues that a person may still be interested in or enjoy his pursuit in between the thrills. He argues that, if interest were reducible to a number of thrills,[2] it would follow that, since emotion is liable to distract one from a pursuit, it would be reasonable to say that a man could not get on with his work because he was so interested in it. No doubt a writer may well be so delighted in contemplating a brilliant paragraph he has just written that he wastes an appreciable time in getting on with the next, but surely pleasure is even on the introspective view a continuous feeling-tone qualifying a mental process, however absorbed in its object the person may be, rather than a second process or string of episodes besides the mental pursuit, which therefore necessarily interferes with the latter. As Aristotle long ago pointed out, one's work is not hindered by pleasure in the work, but only by pleasure in something other than the work. (This may of course be something quite closely connected with the work, or even one's own immediately past work.) The usual view has been that there is some degree of feeling-tone, pleasant or painful, attached to every or almost every state of mental activity, and that on the whole the activity is facilitated when the feeling-tone is pleasant and thwarted when it is painful, pleasure and pain being thus not separate processes or emotions but qualities which

[1] *Principles of Psychology*, Vol. I, p. 255.
The Concept of Mind, Pp. 93, 100.

may accompany any kind of experience.[1] Professor Ryle says that 'enjoying digging is not both digging and having a (pleasant) feeling',[2] but surely it is both physically digging and having a pleasant experience of the physical process. This experience is not just a feeling of pleasure—you cannot have pleasure without having pleasure in something—but a cognitive and conative experience pleasantly toned throughout or so toned with only slight interruptions. The person need not have been introspectively observing his pleasure all the time, but it may still have been present, and even without anything that would ordinarily be called introspection at the time he may when he recalls the experience have the general impression that it was enjoyed. Who would wish to indulge in any amusement for its own sake if he knew that he would feel no pleasure at all, but merely show all the physical symptoms of pursuing it with concentrated interest? Only a small part of one's pleasure is taken in exciting emotional thrills, but every experience we have will be in some respects agreeable or disagreeable, however slightly, perhaps both at once. Enjoyment cannot be reduced to physical behaviour plus a few sensations, which happen not to be observable by other men but are of no particular account; it qualifies a continuous mental process side by side with the physical. If I am not aware of what I am doing I am not enjoying it, and as long as I am aware of it I am continually experiencing more or less pleasure or its opposite. Totally indifferent experiences are at least rare, and it may even be doubted whether they occur at all, for a total lack of pleasure at any time would seem to involve boredom at that time and therefore pain.

The same account does not apply to words like desire which in most senses are dispositional, but I must insist that they include in their meaning not only potentialities of physical action but potentialities of feeling in a certain way.[3] Professor Ryle regards feelings (felt experiences) as very unimportant, but are they not what gives rise to action, and if we had no felt experiences would

[1] There is, of course, as Professor Ryle points out, another sense of 'pain' in which it stands for a specific kind of sensations.

[2] *Op. cit.*, p. 109.

[3] I do not say this applies to all the words which Professor Ryle discusses. Thus I agree that 'patriotic' and 'vain' are terms which do not refer to a liability to have feelings of patriotism and vanity but mainly to a liability to act in a certain way.

there be any point in action? Professor Ryle has to admit inconsistently that there are some things which a man can only observe about himself, but he seems to be trying the tactics of the woman who excused herself for an illegitimate baby by saying that it was a very little one. At any rate he speaks as though feelings were a rare and at any rate superfluous accompaniment of behaviour. But the baby is by no means a little one. Private feelings of one sort or another are there throughout waking life, and if nobody had these feelings and experiences, feelings and experiences which no other men but oneself can observe by normal perception of behaviour, there would be no value in existence. Nor should we learn anything about the behaviour of others, since we can only learn it through our experience, and our experience is not something that other men can observe. This holds even if a direct theory of perception of physical objects is maintained, for, even so, my experience of perceiving an object is not yours. We may be very grateful to Professor Ryle for his particular contributions to the linguistics of psychology, but I do not see how he has contributed to his more radical object, the removal of dualism. Whether or not we hold the mind and the body to be different 'substances' we must admit as an empirical fact a radical dualism between their qualities, which can be obscured only by confusing the psychological qualities themselves with the criteria we have for ascribing these qualities to other men.

CHAPTER XV

RECOMMENDATIONS REGARDING THE LANGUAGE OF INTROSPECTION[1]

J. N. Findlay

Professor of Philosophy, King's College, University of London

I

The aim of this paper is to make a few tentative recommendations in regard to our talk about the acts and processes that take place in our minds. There is a linguistic performance, very frequently practised, in which we give other people information about our own contemporary or past thoughts and feelings. And it would not be incorrect to say that people frequently understand this form of discourse, and that they reciprocate by telling us what *they* are thinking or feeling, or what they thought and felt on given occasions in the past. There is also a much less frequently practised game in which we are not content to say baldly *that* we thought this or that, or that we were having this or that sort of experience, but in which we try to say more specifically *how* we felt, or what the experiences in question were 'inwardly like'. In this latter kind of performance we are frequently at a loss for suitable words in which to clothe our meaning, and are forced to eke out the inadequacies of established usage by gestures and intonations, as well as by neologisms and figures of the most various kinds. While we are frequently unsuccessful in such a performance, and our auditors cannot be certain just what kind of experience we are talking of, there are cases where communication seems entirely successful, and our auditors exclaim: 'Yes, I know exactly how you felt at that time', 'How very well I can enter into your feelings', and so forth. There are also some

[1] *Journal of Philosophy and Phenomenological Research*, December 1948. The subject-matter of this paper is not merely introspective language but all language about inner experiences, whether belonging to ourselves or others. But since the term 'psychological' has acquired a new connotation, we have to content ourselves with the best brief term available.

occasions on which we try to give listeners elaborate analyses of
our inner experiences in terms that have currency only in small
groups of specially schooled people. While these attempts at
communication often end inconclusively in general confusion
and puzzlement, there are also occasions when results of some
value are achieved by them. But though these forms of linguistic
communication are commonly practised, and though their simpler
varieties are regarded as only a little more precarious than many
other communications about remote or hidden objects, yet their
existence nevertheless gives rise to various forms of deep puzzlement, so that we ask ourselves: 'How is it possible to tell other
people how we feel inwardly? How can we ever effect a comparison between the private feelings of different individuals? How
can we ever be sure that other people really feel as we think they
feel?' and so on. Furthermore, all the variable and unsettled
figures in which we try to describe our inner experiences also
give rise to such troublesome questions as: 'How is it possible
for the same object to be present in many minds?' or 'What is
the nature of the agent or factor within me that does my thinking
and feeling?' or 'How is it possible to think of something that
exists nowhere or exists no longer?' These and many other similar
questions leave us hesitant and tongue-tied, and without any clear
notion as to how to *begin* answering them. So that the whole
situation seems to demand a thorough examination of our introspective usages, an examination which will lay bare the sources
of our difficulties, and permit our talk about experiences to
achieve a maximal degree of smoothness and internal unity.

The first step in such an examination must, however, be to
ask how we manage to impart an understandable and agreed
meaning to our introspective terms and phrases. We must inquire
into those *sense-giving procedures* which enable us to *teach* others
what we actually mean by certain introspective ways of speaking,
or to reach agreement as to what we *shall* mean by them. For
only by gaining clearness in regard to such procedures can we
hope to discern where our difficulties lie, or make profitable
proposals for amending language. Here, at the outset, we must
deal with a widely current theoretical approach which connects
meaning very closely with processes of *proof* or *validation*, and
which likes to say that we know the *sense* of any verbal forms
occurring in statements when we know the circumstances in which

the statements in which they function are validated or proven true. Now this approach to the problems of sense-giving has at least one merit: that it fits a case which may be regarded as the ideal or best form of knowledge, the case in which one's reference may be said to be consummated by 'direct confrontation' with the things or circumstances referred to, in which the *same* things that show what one is saying also suffice to show that one is telling the truth. Thus if someone said that a signal light was showing green and if subsequently he were brought face to face with the signal light actually showing green, then he would have shown what he *meant* by his statement by the very same circumstance which proved it was a true one. But though there are indeed such happy coincidences between the things covered in the meaning of a statement and the things which help to prove it, we should nevertheless be flying in the face of established usage if we sought for them everywhere, or raised them to identities. For there are countless cases in which ordinary speech differentiates stubbornly between the meaning of some statement and the circumstances or procedures used in validating it. Thus the green signal light which serves to validate the statement that the line is clear, would not ordinarily be included in the meaning of this statement, and we might even say that a man *knew* that the statement was a true one, through connecting this truth with the colour of the signal light, though he hadn't the faintest inkling of its meaning. And there are also cases in which we recognize something which can only be called a 'systematic and necessary divergence' between the things covered in the meaning of some statement, and the circumstances or procedures which might serve to validate it. Thus statements in the past tense, to take only one obvious instance, might be said to be validated by such processes as taking testimony or consulting witnesses, which are all activities referred to the present or future, while the things covered in the meaning of such statements are just as unequivocally referred to the past. The techniques used for elucidating the meaning of such statements are likewise different from the techniques used in validating them: for in the former we should not make that appeal to documents and witnesses that we make in the latter, but should rather point to happenings in the present which *resemble* those we are speaking of, as well as to a few simple cases of passing or vanishing, as when a noise ceases or an act is over, in order to make plain the general sense of referring things and happenings to the past.[1]

In no case, however, do we find a more obvious discrepancy between meaning and validation than in the case of introspective statements. For here, very plainly, I can only prove or test the truth of *your* introspective utterances by paying heed to all those acts, gestures, intonations, and utterances, both now and at other times, which would ordinarily be called the 'outer manifestations' of your inner experiences. And if 'proving' means 'publicly demonstrating' (which many would take it to mean), then I cannot even prove *my own* introspective statements without calling attention to similar manifestations on my own part. Yet quite obviously we do not ordinarily conceive that such outward manifestations are covered in the *meaning* of our introspective statements, nor that knowledge of the former would necessarily involve an understanding of the latter. We are in fact ready to conceive that someone who either had not had certain experiences, or who was not gifted with the sympathetic capacity for divining them in others, might nevertheless take an exhaustive note of all the signs ordinarily regarded as indicative of certain inner states, and so be in a position to say exactly *when* such inner states were present, without having a notion of what those states were 'really like', nor consequently of what the terms used to designate them really meant. We likewise think it possible that someone who had been through certain experiences or was greatly gifted with intuitive sympathy, might form a *good notion* of the character of certain inner states, and might be able to understand descriptions which suggested them, although he had not paid any close or discriminating attention to their outer pantomime. Generally we say that it is possible to give a very full, intelligible, and accurate account of the outer manifestations of some inner experience without having said anything about its inner character, and that it is likewise possible to weave phrases together which 'hit off' this inner character, although they make no mention of such

---

[1] If I have any fault to find with Husserl's superb account of the phenomenology of knowledge in the last section of *Logische Untersuchungen*, it is that he couples every referential act with some 'fulfilling intuition' in which the object referred to is *itself* presented. Obviously there are some forms of knowledge in which this not only does not happen, but is essentially impossible.

outward manifestations. All these are ways of speaking which are not readily squared with our proposed identification of the matters covered in the meaning of some statement with the matters that would serve to prove it true. And we may indicate one further oddity or anomaly which would confront us if such an identification were adopted: we should have to say that introspective utterances were covered *in their own meaning*, and were therefore always covertly about themselves. For obviously one of the best reasons for believing that a man is having certain experiences is the fact that he says so: his statement therefore helps to prove itself, and must accordingly be covered in its own meaning. Here we should be faced with one of those curious reflexive situations, which, while not invariably involving absurdity or senselessness, are nevertheless not situations whose presence is suspected in any ordinary notion of introspective statements.

We might of course arbitrarily rule at this point that 'things covered in meaning' should *mean* things used in validation, and apply our ruling to the case of introspective statements. But this would involve, first of all, the somewhat absurd proceeding of making 'meaning' *mean* something in a sense in which it palpably did not mean that thing.[1] And, quite apart from this general difficulty, we could not fail to feel that our ruling tempted us to ignore something important or to confound it with something else. Its effect in practice would only be that we simply should not study those techniques through which what we *ordinarily* call a meaning is imparted to certain sorts of statements. These techniques *are* interesting, and particularly so in the case of introspective statements. We refuse, therefore, to adopt a convention which identifies what is covered in meaning with what is done or used in validation, and which in consequence virtually identifies our inner experiences with what would ordinarily be called their outer manifestations. We do this while freely admitting that such a simplification has been valuable for certain purposes, and important historically in the understanding of language. We proceed to ask how, in actual fact, sense can be given to our various introspective ways of speaking so as to result in a scheme of discourse which can be used and understood by several speakers.

[1] Since we are not obviously making the meaningless suggestion that 'things covered in meaning' should be *validated* by things used in validation.

We are here tempted to imagine that such a sense might be imparted to introspective expressions by the *ostensive* methods which are our main stand-by in linguistic dealings with 'external nature'. For there we remove incomprehension or establish new understandings by *showing* people the thing or sort of thing we are speaking of, by *pointing* to objects or situations illustrative of our meaning or covered by it. Thus a simple act of showing might suffice to make very plain what we understood by a 'spiral movement' or an 'aquiline nose' or a 'Gothic finial'. And though we often resort to verbal processes of elucidation in such matters, we do so in the confidence that all such verbal processes must have their roots somewhere in ostension, from which they derive whatever lucidity they possess. Now there certainly is something which might be called an ostensive method in introspective matters, and one might readily suppose that it was through such a method that sense was imparted to introspective expressions. Thus we often endeavour to *show* someone what a given sort of experience is like, by placing him in a situation where he actually *has* that sort of experience. Thus (to confine ourselves to cases studied in laboratories) we might confront a person with stereoscopic materials, or break down his temper with a series of senseless tasks, or ask him to carry out some difficult instruction in defiance of an ingrained habit, and then say to him: 'There, you see, that is what it is like to have stereoscopic vision, to experience intense anger, to live through the inner activity of willing.' We might then assume that he understood the terms referring to the experiences in question, so that his use of any of them was a sure sign that he was having some experience covered in their meaning. There is another less drastic form of ostension, generally referred to as 'emphatic' or 'sympathetic', in which we point to persons or animals behaving angrily, or boldly, or contentedly, or in some other manner, and then ask that a man should try to *realize* how they feel inwardly, to *put himself in their place*, and so forth. When a man assures us that he has performed the feat in question, and possibly shows a resultant capacity to foresee other actions of that person or animal, we assume that we have genuinely introduced him to the inner character of certain states, and expect that he will henceforth use correct terms when he *has* the experiences in question. But though we hope that ostensive methods will enable us to show each other what *sort* of experience we are speaking of, we never expect them to show us any *particular* experience as it occurs in someone's inner life. For while the general *character* of a man's experiences are thought of as a public matter, which can be shown by making people attend to *similar* experiences in themselves, we still think of anyone's actual experience as a private matter, which cannot be exhibited in this manner. Now the whole distinction of the public and the private is doubtless exposed to dialectical criticism, and is not by any means so hard and clear as many people have thought it; but it brings out the obvious difference between our very straight-forward and easy approach to outer things, and our correspond-ingly derivative, difficult, and hazy approach to experiences. As long as we sustain it for this obvious merit, we shall have to supplement our ostensive methods with a set of 'postulates' which lay down exactly *when* it is proper to say that different people are having similar experiences. Plainly these postulates will be more or less of the form that people acted on by similar outward influences are (with some probability) having similar experiences, and likewise that people responding similarly to such influences are (with some probability) having similar experiences. We should be in a happy position were we willing to accept such postulates as *definitive* of the meaning of 'similarity' in connexion with different people's experiences, or at least as telling us how to *prove* the presence of such a similarity. But that we *are not* willing to do this, comes out in our singular, haunting sense that people who behave similarly in similar circumstances may, after all, be having deeply different experiences. As long as such a possibility is genuinely conceded, we are resisting any attempt either to define or to validate an inner similarity of experience by means of the outer similarities we have mentioned; and this resistance means that we have to *justify* ostensive methods as applied to introspective materials, that we have to show that they really *are* ostensive, and that such methods cannot therefore be our primary sense-giving procedures in this field. We may note, further, that our whole procedure in asking someone to consider the *inward side* of a certain happening, or to try to realize what is happening in his own, or someone else's *bosom*, involves turning his attention in a direction which is not anywhere among the points of the compass, which is not, in the ordinary sense, a direction at all. So that the whole problem of giving sense to introspective talk remains unclarified on the methods we have mentioned.

How, then, if ostensive methods are so useless, can sense ever be given to our introspective expressions? The answer is extraordinarily simple. Introspective expressions arise *spontaneously* in the talk of various speakers, and *create their own sense* as this talk is developed. How this is possible is not hard to understand, for plainly we find in ourselves and others a spontaneous readiness to use expressions appropriate in public contexts in situations where there is nothing public that fits them: thus everyone has moments when he wants to say that he sees some person vividly before him (though he knows that this person is many miles away), or that the room is turning round and round (though he knows that nothing can be more stable), or that a certain figure is 'standing out' from a picture (though he knows that the picture is flat), or that he is collapsing with grief and shame (though he is actually maintaining an upright position and the calmest of bearings). And, recognizing the profound difference between such situations, in which we speak *as if* something were present for all to see, and situations where such a thing is actually present, we begin to seek words to cover this difference, and end up by saying (among many other possible ways of speaking) that the situations spoken of in such circumstances are 'ideal' and not real, that they merely represent 'inward changes' in ourselves, that they exist only 'in the mind', 'in thought', 'in a dream', 'in imagination', and so forth. We then start to characterize such situations by *modifying* the expressions applied to ordinary things, so as to indicate both a likeness and a difference. We thereby add to our world of references an indefinite set of realms, each private to a single speaker, and spoken of by *analogy* with external showable objects. It is easy to see how such talk in terms of analogies achieves genuine sense-giving and successful communication. For this may be held to happen whenever one person *accepts* another person's analogies, as descriptive of situations private to himself, and *caps* them with other analogies, which they in their turn accept as descriptive of their inner experiences. A typical pattern of such sense-giving might be sketched as follows: *A* may say to *B*: 'It is rather *as if* this or that happened to me' (where 'this' and 'that' are matters pertinent to their world of common objects). Whereupon *B* might reply: 'Yes, I understand you perfectly. Wouldn't you perhaps say that it was as if such and such had happened?' Whereupon *A* continues: 'Yes, I think we mean the same thing: the inner situation I am describing was rather similar to one that occurred previously, when it seemed as if so and so.' Or the pattern may develop by *B*'s saying that he cannot imagine what sort of inner situation *A* means, whereupon *A* varies his comparisons, until *B* says he knows inner situations that fit or nearly fit them, and then proceeds to sketch further features of such situations, using words *A* feels would be appropriate in describing the situations he was characterizing. Through such continued interchanges, a set of terms and ways of speaking finally arises, each of which gathers together a set of analogies recognized as equivalent (or nearly equivalent) by a certain body of speakers. In so far as such speakers use these terms and ways of speaking, they may be said to be speaking of the same or closely similar experiences, and to be giving their introspective expressions an agreed and uniform sense. There does not appear to be any other way through which such a sense could be given in the first instance, nor much point in asking whether such a sense has, after all, really been given by the method in question.

The language of introspection which arises in this manner has been called an *analogical* language, since it arises whenever men begin to *liken* something, which certainly *is not* 'there for all to see', with things that definitely have this public status. This act of likening itself only *resembles* ordinary acts of comparison, in that we do not look forward (as we do in ordinary comparisons) to any ultimate setting of likeness and original side by side, so as to bring out all their points of likeness and difference. The act of likening *brings* the 'inner situation' into the range of our common references, and the only ordinary, public resemblance of this inner situation to the situations now denominated 'outward' by contrast, is that we use the same or similar *words* in the two types of cases. The 'analogy' of introspective diction is, in fact, rather like the analogy of the Schoolmen, who sought to characterize God by likening Him to various earthly things, while rejecting any possibility of setting Him beside them, or finding any property genuinely common to Him and them. It also resembles the scholastic analogy, in that in it every predication of likeness goes together with a balancing predication of unlikeness. For, while the Schoolmen credited God with something *like* our intellect and will, they also added that it differed *toto caelo* from these faculties. And we, in the same manner, never liken inner to outer situations, without qualifying our likenesses with 'profound differences'. Though there are occasions when we go as far as saying that it is *just as if* a certain outward situation were before us, *just as if* we were surveying a blue circle projected on the wall in front of us, or *just as if* we were again taking coffee in a Swiss hotel where we formerly stayed, yet even here we could be made to admit that the 'inner' situation' in question differed from its outward original in many queer and ghostly ways. Other analogies are acknowledged to be much wider of the mark, and are explicitly spoken of as 'figures', as when we speak of judgement as an 'inner act of assertion', or speak (with James) of the 'slow, dead heave' of the will, or compare attention to some brilliant searchlight roving over objects. (Yet even such analogies are not figurative in the sense that any quite straight and perfectly literal manner of speaking could be substituted for them.) There are also occasions on which we insist so strongly on the utter unlikeness of an inner situation to external things, and speak of it in terms of so many 'uniques' and 'indescribables', that we might very well be emulating those theologians of the negative way who hope to speak of God least inadequately by dwelling on His complete lack of resemblance to earthly things. Much of the talk about imageless thought is, in fact, not very different from talk about the 'Divine Dark'; both ways of speaking achieve great appropriateness through a liberal use of negatives.

We may suggest, further, that an element of analogy is present even in the most commonplace use of introspective terms, of words such as 'thinking', 'wishing', 'loving' and the like. For it is plain that such words do not stand solely, nor even primarily, for inner qualities of experience, but that they also cover certain typical styles and policies of behaviour, so much so, indeed, that we frequently use them even in the case of actions classed as 'automatic', where we do not suppose any distinctive inner experiences to be present. It may also be conceded that many of our vividest experiences are *not* connected with a very pronounced or uninhibited outer pantomime, that they are in a manner *inversely* related to external expression, are in some sort *substitutes* for it, and that they flourish most intensely when the smooth sequence of our outer acts is halted, or reduced to gestures. And being, after a manner, *substitutes* for outward action, it is not surprising that we find it natural to characterize them by *analogy* with the kind of action they do duty for. Thus the inner sense of wanting something is naturally characterized as, in some manner, a 'condensed substitute' for the acts and gestures of purposive activity: it is *as if* we were endeavouring purposively, though we are not actually achieving anything. Our inner feeling of conviction may similarly be regarded as the last attenuation of the firm movements, ringing voice and other features of convinced behaviour: it is *as if* we were speaking or behaving confidently, though we may not overtly be doing or saying anything. And when we try to say how these experiences feel inwardly, we find ourselves inevitably having recourse to such analogies and comparisons (unless deterred by absurd 'existential' restrictions), so that there is abundant justification for saying that the introspective use of terms like 'thinking', 'wishing' and so forth is covertly analogical.

We maintain, accordingly, that the language of introspection is a language in which ranges of analogical description, each capable of indefinite extension, have come to be accepted, among a certain class of speakers, as more or less stating the meaning of various characteristic terms and verbal forms. And this account of the matter has the great advantage that it goes far toward disposing of the deep difficulties raised at the beginning of this article, when we wondered how we ever knew that different people were having similar experiences. For while we were not willing to dismiss the possibility of systematic error, if we took similarity of outward influences, and attendant similarity of behaviour, as criteria for the inward similarity of experiences, we do not feel we have to entertain such a possibility, if we take thoroughgoing agreement in analogical description as the criterion for such inward similarity. We even feel disposed to say that if people *persistently* compare 'inner situations' to the same range of outward situations, and never feel anything inappropriate in each other's analogies, that there *must* be a certain degree of similarity in their inner experiences. Our only hesitation would arise if we began to wonder whether different people really see outward things in the same manner, in other words, whether so-called outward things are not really private and inward, and whether inner acts of mind are not accordingly being compared to quite different originals. But such difficulties are general difficulties connected with the publicity of our common world, and have no special connexion with introspective statements; and recent thinkers who have stressed the impossibility of communicating the inner quality of experiences, have not generally seen any similar impossibility of speaking of a world of outward things. So that *if* we go on speaking of a world whose features can be *shown* to others—and so much seems involved in speaking at all—there is not much sense in doubting whether people are having similar experiences, when they persistently liken them to the same outward things.

And we may note further that in taking likeness of analogical description as a sufficient test for likeness of inner experience, we have gone far toward justifying the two problematic 'postulates' mentioned in a previous paragraph. For plainly the ordinary person tries to enlighten other people as to the inner quality of his sense-experiences (which are directly elicited by outer influences) by pointing to the public sights, sounds, smells, and other sensible phenomena, which *are* the influences which normally elicit them: he says, for instance, 'I was seeing a colour like that sample of red' or 'I was imagining a sound like the note of that instrument'. He would in fact have so little doubt of the likeness between his own and other normal sense-experiences and the outer states and changes which elicit them, that he would frequently fail to draw any distinction between them. It has often been pointed out how all the terms used by psychologists, in distinguishing the qualities of sensations and their correlated images, are always derived from terms which stand for the corresponding qualities of physical things. It is, in fact, only when people begin questioning whether there *is* a realm of public, showable matters, when they start entertaining pictures of themselves immured in worlds which are in part of their own manufacture, and in part the product of outer influences that cannot be seen or shown, that there comes to be some point in doubting whether people similarly affected have somewhat similar experiences. For since people inevitably describe their inner sensations by analogy with the public phenomena which normally produce them, and which they barely trouble to distinguish from them, there does not seem room, on our principles, for doubting that sense-experiences springing from the same outward sources have *some* degree of similarity.[1]

As regards our second 'postulate'—that similarity of outward action (in a like context) affords some reason for believing in an inner similarity of experience—we may recall our previous remark that all inner attitudes are (after a manner) substitutes for outward doing or undergoing, and can only be characterized by analogy with these. In one experience we say it is *as if* we were sinking through the floor, in another *as if* we were sweeping some irritant out of our path, in another *as if* we were caressing something, in another *as if* we were squirming uneasily, and so forth. Surely it is meaningless to maintain that experiences so characterized by a number of people, and whose inner nature comes out in the analogies in question, are nevertheless experienced in a totally different manner by those people? It seems obvious that such a suggestion could only be put forward by people who think of experiences as mysterious x's and y's, and who are forgetting entirely how we actually talk of them. And if there are gestures, expressive movements, and so forth, which may reasonably be regarded as abbreviations of certain styles and policies of behaviour, then they may also be used with quite as much reliability as evidences of inner experiences which likewise do duty for such outward lines of behaviour. On our principles, therefore, it is not merely gratuitous, but definitely absurd, to maintain that similarities of gesture and expression afford *no* evidence whatever of inner similarities of experience.

II

Having indicated, in a general manner, how we come to talk understandably of our inner states, we may now raise the more difficult question as to how we *should* talk about them. For, despite the current prejudice—oddly reminiscent of the eighteenth-century worship of the 'noble savage'—in favour of

[1] Even bodily feelings, which are ranked as peculiarly private, are connected in the closest manner with public phenomena, and can be characterized through these. For private chills and pressures in our fingers are said to 'mediate' our awareness of public properties like coldness and hardness. And if the former 'mediate' the latter, why should not the latter 'mediate' the former? They are certainly as close to each other as the convex is to the concave.

ordinary ways of speaking, as opposed to all forms of philosophical sophistication, we may nevertheless maintain that there is much that is deeply defective in these ordinary ways of speaking, which philosophical reforms in diction may remedy or alleviate. We inquire, accordingly into the *best* way of speaking of our inner experiences, in the hope of being able to make positive recommendations on the matter. Such an inquiry will not differ profoundly from one conducted with the professed aim of analysing or elucidating the 'real nature' of the mental. It is merely tautological to maintain that the best way of talking about something is also a way that comes closest to the real nature of the things it speaks of. But, while there is one approach, which may be called 'ontological', which first inquires into the real nature of something, and then lays down the best way of speaking about it, there is also another approach, which we may call 'linguistic', which first inquires into the best way of speaking about something, and then expresses, in the language thus built up, the 'real nature' of the thing it speaks of. And while the former approach would do justice to our inexpungable unwillingness to say that things are similar or related merely because *we* classify or connect them together—a way of speaking which would draw no proper distinction between such classifications and connexions as are *arbitrary*, and others that are not arbitrary at all[1]—the latter approach accords well with our willingness to be persuaded that there are many ways in which things may be similar or related, and that it is, to a very large extent, a matter of choice which of these we choose to 'bring out' in our talking. While the latter approach encourages us to look for the *best* way of talking about anything, it keeps us mindful that there may be many less good ways of speaking, which nevertheless serve to stress important aspects of our subject-matter, and that even a bad way of speaking may have some illuminating features.

The linguistic approach has this further advantage: that it encourages us to lay down plainly—in terms acceptable to the

---

[1] There is no need to speak in terms of Platonic realism to make plain the nature of this difference. If the word 'red' were applied, by a series of arbitrary choices, to a book, a lamp-post, a virtue, an equation, etc. etc., everyone would be hesitant before applying it to a *new* object, and would not agree with his neighbours, whereas this is not the case with 'red' as we actually use it.

majority of reflective speakers, as roughly covering 'ideals' for the refinement and reform of diction—those features of a way of speaking which will entitle us to call it *good*. And here we ourselves may briefly put forward, as items readily acceptable in such a list of 'good points', that a scheme of discourse should not leave us hesitant as to whether something should or should not have a certain name applied to it, or be described in certain terms,[1] that it should not leave us torn between linguistic impulses both to say and not to say something,[2] that it should not make us draw distinctions where we are not, even on reflexion, disposed to draw any,[3] and that it should not make it difficult or impossible for us to draw distinctions that we cannot help wanting to draw.[4] We may add, further, that it should be a way of speaking that brings the maximum of unity and perspicuity into the subject-matters we are dealing with, that it disposes us to say, for instance—without more than an initial shock of uttering something 'queer' or 'clumsy'—that things not previously regarded as having great affinity are 'really only different forms' of one thing, that things previously said to be casually or externally connected, are 'deeply bound together', and so on.[5] And a good way of speaking should also, plainly, be one that removes linguistic difficulties that are *general*, which most speakers feel when provoked by certain statements or questions.[6] It should be a way of speaking which removes difficulties *durably*, which does not

---

[1] We may speak of a requirement of 'definiteness'. The puzzles about the 'bald man' therefore depend on inevitable defects in language.

[2] We may here speak of a requirement of 'harmony' or 'non-contradiction'. This will not forbid us to say both 'p' and 'not-p' (as poets, Marxists and others have done) if we do so with a purpose, and with an easy mind, and *without wishing to withdraw either statement*.

[3] We may here speak of a requirement of 'non-redundancy'.

[4] We may here speak of a requirement of 'avoiding undue simplification and omission of essential elements'.

[5] We may here speak of a requirement of 'systematic unity'. Of course, the unity desiderated must not seem 'wanton' or 'forced', but illuminating and inevitable.

[6] We may here speak of a requirement of 'general acceptability'. Some think it hard to be sure that a linguistic reaction is general if we cannot conduct inquiries on the Gallup poll model. I personally think that our estimate of the general or typical character of reactions is of considerable value, a view confirmed by such protocol studies as that of Arne Ness on non-philosophical concepts of truth.

M

merely intoxicate us with a temporary sense of brilliant clarity which afterwards evaporates.[1] These, and a large number of less readily formulable characteristics, would readily recommend themselves to reflective speakers as 'good points' in a way of speaking. And, being clear in advance as to the meaning of a good way of speaking, we are much more likely to achieve a satisfactory introspective language, than if we set out simply to discover the 'real nature' of mentality.[2] In regard to mind, also, a linguistic approach has particular advantages. For since the 'inner quality' of mind is primarily approached through what we say of it, the analogical language used to characterize it, we are most likely to achieve a satisfactory way of talking of this inner quality, if all verbal schemes used in connexion with it are subjected to a long and careful examination, and are then deliberately simplified and amended.

In this article, however, we can only treat, illustratively and somewhat superficially, a few issues that might reasonably be called 'fundamental'. We shall inquire whether it is advisable to adopt a *personal* way of speaking of our inner experiences, a way of speaking which ascribes them to some more or less attenuated analogue of the human person, and tends to liken them to the deeds and sufferings of such a person in its intercourse with outer objects. In polar opposition to this way of speaking, we shall inquire whether we should not rather favour one of those queerer ways of talking in terms of mental 'elements', 'constituents', and 'processes', which assimilate our inner life to blind assemblages of *things* rubbing together, and eschew all reference to a central personal agent. We shall then consider whether some judicious combination of elements from both schemes of diction may not perhaps leave us more completely with the feeling of having 'done justice' to the inner nature of experience. We may note, at this point, that philosophical ways of speaking of our inner experiences are generally mere elaborations of certain comprehensive 'figures'—we call them 'figures'

---

[1] We may here speak of a requirement of 'lasting acceptability'.

[2] It would, of course, be possible to find ontological equivalents for many of the characteristics included in the above list. Thus we might say that the real nature of anything is wholly determinate, free from inner conflict, deeply unified, and so forth. But it might not be so easy to find ontological equivalents for general and lasting acceptability.

by courtesy, since there is no wholly *straight* way of speaking
of the mental—which occur confusedly in ordinary diction. We
speak of 'our minds' quite frequently as of personal agents, which
survey or work upon the things around them; we also speak of
them as rooms or boxes through which notions pass rapidly, or
in which they remain stored, or even as streams in which ideas
rush and eddy. And we also devise many selections of such
figures, some stark, and some exceedingly florid. Philosophers,
who have not been slow to criticize such 'metaphors', have
nevertheless often taken them so seriously as to frame questions
in terms of them, in the confident expectation of some ultimate
answer. Thus they have asked whether there was or was not an
ego in experience, whether this ego could or could not see itself
directly, whether there were or were not such things as 'conscious
acts', and whether the mind could or could not see them, whether
the objects of our thinking were *in* our minds or only stood *before*
them, and so forth. Whereas the analogies used in ordinary
diction are all so imperfectly elaborated that they afford no way
of answering such questions. It is for philosophers to make initial
decisions as to the way in which they propose to talk about their
minds, before they can conduct discussions in regard to them.
(Not that many philosophical discussions on such topics are not
really to be regarded as attempts to come to such decisions.)
And, in the framing of such initial decisions, they can be guided
by nothing but that 'ethics of speaking', some of whose principles
we have just tried to formulate.

We turn, accordingly, to the scheme of diction which consistently adopts the picture of the *person*, variously *active* in regard
to things outside it, and variously *affected* and *determined* by them.
It is not hard to see that this way of speaking derives from the
manner in which a living creature, whether animal or human,
concerns itself with things around it. We might, in fact, say that
the *subject* of our mental attitudes is always a more or less
attenuated analogue of an *organism*, whereas the *mental acts* with
which we credit it are all more or less attenuated analogues of
the active and passive ways in which that organism *busies itself*
with environing objects. We find that the most widely current
classification of our inner acts and attitudes is precisely one which
classifies these in analogical correspondence with the typical
relations of the living creature to external things. There is an

'ingoing' determination of a living creature by external objects, in so far as its changes mirror their structure, or its actions 'take account' of them: this, plainly, is the original of that purely inward registration of objects known as 'cognitive'. There is, likewise, an 'outgoing' relation of the living creature to external things, in which it either acts on them or performs gestures which seem rudiments of such action: this relation is the original of those inward poses called 'conative'. There are also those 'immanent' disturbances of a creature's rhythms and ways of doing things which form the original even for the most ethereal types of feeling. But though the relation of a living creature to environing things inspires this whole way of speaking, we should not be interested in the latter if it were a 'carry over' from the former. In particular, it is not the case that a person who speaks of *himself* in describing his inner experiences, is merely ascribing those experiences to a certain individual, whom other people would speak of in the third person: he is endeavouring to indicate analogically something in regard to their inner nature. The first person of introspection is, in short, not always—though it doubtless is sometimes—merely a suitably modified variant of the third person of our ordinary talk about people: it sometimes stands for what can only be called an 'inner moment' in experience. And the man who speaks of various kinds of doing and suffering in his inner life is likewise not merely labelling experiences extrinsically by the outer acts they are connected with: he is also trying to tell us something of their inner nature, through analogy with outward changes.

The analogy of the person dealing with environing objects, is obviously least remote in all those cases where we have the experience of some *physical* encounter with an object, whether of walking on ice, striking a tennis-ball, smelling a flower, shaking a friend's hand, and so forth. All these are experiences of *oneself*, of various outward *objects* which surround oneself, and also of a certain *transaction* between oneself and those environing objects. And we are sometimes even ready to *identify* the physical transaction in question with the experience connected with it: thus we say frequently that smelling a flower or shaking a friend's hand *are* agreeable experiences. But, on reflexion, we tend to think of such a way of speaking as 'naïve': we say that it is not the public, physical transaction which *is* the experience, but only that transaction *as it appears from the point of view of the man concerned in it.* But, even with this added qualification, there is not a large step from the physical transaction to the experience connected with it. For there is nothing essentially private in the appearance of an object *from* a given standpoint. We do not ordinarily consider it a whit more difficult to *show* someone how an object *looks* from this or that angle, or from this or that distance or direction, or even how it *sounds* through water, or *feels* through muslin, than simply to show him that object. It would in fact be paradoxical to say that we could show a man some object, and yet could not show him how it looked or felt, sounded, smelled, or tasted. And though we might show a man some object without drawing attention to any of its appearances, he would nevertheless, almost certainly, be able to tell us something about them, and would experience no particular verbal difficulties in doing so. There are, in short—if ordinary language is to be followed—public appearances or *phenomena* that many people can take note of and refer to, and there are public standpoints that many people can occupy. We are not, therefore, making any very large analogical jump when we pass from these appearances, and these standpoints, to others which are credited with the inevitable privacy of a given person's body. We may note that even the sense in which we readily say of our bodies, that they 'occupy the *centre* of our experienced world', is one readily paralleled by the way in which public objects can be shown to occupy the *foreground* of the world as viewed from public standpoints.

There are then, certain elementary experiences, closely connected with actual physical transactions between the living creature and environing things, which that creature inevitably describes in terms of its physical self, external objects, and some interchange between them. It is obviously by analogy with these elementary experiences that many of our more rarefied experiences are described, and hence these too are ultimately talked of in terms of a central organism and its relations to environing things. Thus we have experiences called 'imaginative', which are not experiences of an *actual* transaction between ourselves and outward objects, but which are nevertheless described by their likeness to this: it is *as if* we were standing in front of the Madeleine, *as if* we were boarding the boat at Dieppe, *as if* we were again throwing a hand grenade, and so forth (the words 'as if', in such contexts, indicating not only a likeness but also some unique unlikeness, which can itself at best be described analogically, e.g. by 'scrappiness', lack of 'vividness', and so forth). There are other types of experience, called 'purely notional', in in which the analogy is attenuated still further, and the gathering unlikeness is described by a welter of negatives: in these it is still *as if* we were doing or suffering something in regard to objects, though all vivid content has been 'telescoped' into signs of the most laughable irrelevance, or reduced still further to that pregnant emptiness in which the *skeleton* of a situation may be said to persist, though all the *flesh* has been stripped from it.[1] And there are many types of experience classified, on reflexion, as mixtures of the 'sensuous' and the 'notional': they are, on the one hand, experiences of ourselves involved in actual physical transactions with surrounding objects, but they also include much that lies at a considerable analogical distance from actual presence or execution. The experiences of dining with a celebrity, signing a document or giving notice to a servant, are cases in point. And, in this last mixed category, it will be profitable to put the experiences known as 'emotional' or 'conative', in which *we ourselves*, as acting and suffering organisms, are 'high-lighted' and emphasized. For these are experiences, on the one hand, of actual physical changes—of noddings, twitchings, clenchings, shudderings, and so forth—and they are also experiences in which it is *as if* we were performing (in a strange, condensed, preparatory manner) acts of timid withdrawal, open-armed welcome, agonized squirming, horrified collapse, and so forth. While such inner experiences are in some respects so *unlike* unfolded behavioural sequences, that we sometimes speak of them as 'simple and unanalysable', there are quite as many occasions on which we speak of them as a felt *readiness* for this or that type of action, treating them as in some manner an *implicit* form of such action. It is a far cry from such 'physical' experiences as that of walking on ice, to the rarefied experiences of seeing the truth of a theorem, or being satisfied with a fiscal policy. But, in every case, we cannot help discovering the same pattern—whether richly concrete or emptily formal—of a central

---

[1] All ways of talking about 'imageless thought' are highly paradoxical, and any attempt to reduce that paradox results in misdescription.

organism coping in varied fashion with a world of objects round it.

And it is easy to see how the central organism of our more elementary experiences is refined into the 'pure subject' of certain ways of speaking. Since in imagination, dreams, and other similar states, it is often *as if* a central organism stood in certain relations to external objects, the organism standing in these relations is obviously not our actual physical self which may be very differently situated. While we *might* say, in characterizing such situations, that the 'self' thus pictured is quite as imaginary as the situations it stands in, it is also possible to say that it is a *real* self capable of separation from the body. And since, in purely notional situations, we retain the antithesis of organism to cosmos without any concrete filling, it is possible, by a turn of speech, to pass from the fact that it is *as if* some wholly indeterminate central organism were present, to the *actual* presence of a pure *ego*. Since there are also emphatic experiences, in which it is *as if* things appeared from points of view wholly different from our own, it is possible to say, *not* that we are imagining what other real or hypothetical people *might* feel, but that we are projecting *ourselves* into the place of these people. Plainly the self which can be thus projected into countless people, becomes as void of concrete content as the universal Self of Oriental mysticism.

But though talk in terms of a pure ego arises in this manner by a perfectly natural series of exaggerations, there are nevertheless some good reasons why we should not adopt it. For talk in terms of a pure ego has an *indeterminateness* which cannot be removed, and which leads readily to unanswerable questions. For once we have made this pure self an ingredient in experience, we are readily led to ask what manner of thing it is, and yet we are precluded from answering such a question, since if we characterized the pure ego more concretely, we should not be sketching it 'in its purity'. It is likewise impossible to say whether this pure ego makes itself introspectively known, and is only incapable of being *disentangled* from the remaining contents of experience, or whether, on the other hand, it is a transcendental factor whose existence can at best be postulated. Ways of talking which lead to such quandaries are certainly not an improvement on the unsystematic variability of ordinary language. And there also seem to be experiences, certainly not common but by no means rare, which are not naturally described in terms of *any* antithesis of a central organism and surrounding objects. There are many experiences, particularly in the aesthetic sphere, in which, as we say, we forget ourselves and are absorbed in objects: these, obviously, are experiences not naturally described in terms of any central self or person. There are also experiences, generally of a relaxed or 'twilight' character, in which the line between what is and what is not ourself seems to be blurred or vanishes altogether.[1] We read of certain very distressing abnormal experiences, called experiences of 'depersonalization', in which it is as if the man *himself* is totally absent from the picture;[2] these are obviously not experiences naturally described in terms of oneself as principal agent or patient. Most people would admit, after a little imaginative effort, that *all* experience might assume this depersonalized form, that it might be *as if* objects were present, formed various pleasing or unpleasing combinations, were subject to certain tensions and relaxations, and yet seemed to have no bearing on any permanent or central person.[3] There does not accordingly seem any good reason to force all our introspective accounts into the linguistic mould in question, and if we are in quest of introspective usages that are both natural and of universal application, they *will not* be in terms of a central person and its deeds and sufferings.

We turn, accordingly, from personal ways of talking about experiences to ways of talking which assimilate them to impersonal *things*, whether these things be thought of with clear-cut contours, or with the melting boundaries of a march of clouds. The schemes of discourse under consideration may, on the one hand, build the mind out of things which do not differ significantly from the things of ordinary discourse, which the mind would ordinarily be said to make its *objects*, or on the other hand, they may seek to build it out of other novel constituents, such as are the pared and chastened elements of existential psychologies. We

---

[1] See Koffka, *Principles of Gestalt Psychology*, p. 323.

[2] See Oesterreich, *Phänomenologie des Ich*, chapter xvii.

[3] It may seem absurd to say that an object can seem pleasing without seeming to please someone. But objects, particularly beautiful objects, can certainly seem to have something of the harmonious, luxuriating, basking attitude characteristic of the pleased organism. The term 'smiling fields' describes something in experience which only external reflexion connects with a subject.

need not, however, devote great time to pointing to the weaknesses of such ways of speaking, as these have made themselves painfully evident in the course of philosophical controversy. If we say that our inner experiences are made up of the things that would ordinarily be called their objects, then at once we face the posers: How can the phoenix which does not exist anywhere, or the round square which cannot exist on account of an inner contradiction, or the triangle in general, which cannot exist because it is so wholly indeterminate, nevertheless be part and parcel of experiences, of which we should like to say that they exist, are free from contradiction, and are in all respects definite? How, likewise, is it possible for things remote in time and space to be elements in experiences that exist *now*, in close connexion with an organism that is *here*? And how can objects grossly palpable and solid be parts of something that we only liken to the most impalpable things? If we say that such objects *are* part and parcel of our inner life, how shall we also speak of them as present in purely physical contexts, or in other people's experiences? And if they are *not* present in these other contexts, shall we not find ourselves imprisoned in a private picture-gallery, from which we cannot even significantly pass to any outward series of originals? These time-worn difficulties could of course be met by saying that the sense in which an object is *in* experience is not the sense in which a man is *in* a regiment, but that it simply is a sense in which it is quite possible for non-existent, contradictory, indefinite, or solidly physical objects to be present in several people's experiences. Such rulings would accord with an ordinary tendency, which allows us to say practically *anything* of an object which is 'only in the mind'. But though we might speak in this manner, it would be hard to see what force it would leave in our original analogy, and what advantage this would still have over other ways of speaking. If, on the other hand, we preferred to speak in terms of mental elements which are *not* the objects of experience, then our main problem would become to construct bridges of equivalence between our new, queer statements about experiences, and the things we ordinarily want to say about them. For, without such bridges, we cannot help saying that our new talk is not *trying* to give a full description of our inner life, or that it is rather laughably failing to do justice to its subject. The task of bridge-building is not rendered any

M*

easier by the frank confession of the existential psychologist that practically *any* mental content can carry *any* meaning or mediate *any* reference, and that a 'noticeable sense of breathlessness' may be *all* that consciously represents what would ordinarily be called the thought of a bank crash or the thought of the Holy Trinity. If we say that 'meaning' reveals itself in what we do, or in our readiness for further sense-contents, we are still not doing justice to our ingrained unwillingness either to admit anything 'extrinsic' or merely 'dispositional' into our description of experiences, or to leave our concern with objects altogether out of it. The whole proposal to talk about experiences exclusively in terms of elements which are *not* the objects of experience is, in short, rather similar to proposing that we should try to describe a tragedy satisfactorily, by likening it to a bill-board advertisement or a ticket for the pit. We feel, in both cases, that the wildest tropes and metaphors could scarcely be less appropriate than a description so restricted.

We are led, accordingly, to propose a *via media* between the personal way of speaking of experiences, which did not cover *all* experiences satisfactorily, and the impersonal ways of speaking we have just considered and found wanting. We shall not liken experiences analogically to situations in which personal agents cope with environing objects, nor to situations in which those objects *themselves* are variously modified and organized, but shall choose, alternatively, to liken them to situations in which objects *show themselves* or *appear*. In this analogy we shall retain something of the 'point of view' and 'concern with objects', which are the merits of the personal way of speaking, while dropping out, as not of universal application, anything suggestive of an agent or its agency. There is nothing, as we indicated previously, of a peculiarly occult or private nature in the original of our analogy: *phenomena* or things apparent, and their varying modes of appearance, are as much a part of our common world of references as are the objects revealed in such *phenomena*. We can draw attention to a car *appearing* from behind a bend; we can *show* people that it at first appears to be a blurred speck with indistinguishable parts, that it then begins to *manifest* a definite colour and structure, that some of its sides *seem* fully projected while others *appear* variously foreshortened, and so on. The various appearances of the car are, in fact, so indefeasibly a public matter that they can be accurately recorded on a sound-film: any

sense in which they are not public but private, is also a metaphysical sense in which the car itself is 'only an idea in the mind'.
Now it seems obvious, once we have thought of it, that it is by
analogy with these public facts of appearance that we can and do
most conveniently and intelligibly describe our inner experiences
to each other. (Though sometimes the analogy is so close or so
remote as barely to be recognized as analogy.) Thus the simple
sense-experiences of the normal observer, might very well be
described as 'hardly differing at all' from certain public
appearances, if we ignore their foreground of bodily feeling,
which has to be approached in a much more indirect manner.
We undertake a remoter flight of analogy, when we deal with
such appearances as the yielding look of velvet, or the cold look
of snow, or the solid look of stereoscopic pictures, or the cross
look of certain faces, which require special training or 'set' in
the observer, though here some people would still say that we
were dealing with appearances that were perfectly public and
could be shown to anyone. We range yet further in analogy when
we speak of after-images appearing on a wall, or of absent things
and people appearing vividly before us. We move a step further
when we pass to those notional situations where it is *as if* certain
objects and situations were appearing, while yet, in another sense,
it is as if nothing at all were appearing, or at best fragmentary
signs and irrelevant pictures. And if we keep the term 'appearance'
(used simply) for those public appearances which are the original
of our whole series, we may use the term ' "appearance" '
(enclosed in quotation marks) for all the inner states characterized
by analogy with these. We may note further that, just as the
standpoint *from* which certain things appear publicly is irrelevant
to the description of the phenomena revealed from that standpoint, so the person or organism *to* whom this or that is 'appearing', is irrelevant to the description of these 'appearances' and
'apparent' things. No doubt it is clear that something 'appears'
in *most* experiences which either represents or is vaguely correlated with, the person who is having those experiences, but
we have seen that *some* experiences are not naturally described
in such terms. And we cannot think of any *a priori* reason why
all experience should not assume that depersonalized form in
which the rarefied spectator vanishes altogether. So that while
our account allows us to incorporate ourselves, and our ways of

acting, into *most* descriptions of experience, it does not demand that such matters should figure in every such description.

We may lay down, further, in clarification of the grammar of our term ' "appearance" ', that we are using it for a *process* of 'appearing', and not for any object or phenomenon that 'appears', though it is indeed part of the description of any process of 'appearing' that it is the 'appearance' of a given object. And we are proposing a grammar that will permit us to say that there may be many successive 'appearances' of the same object, which are all distinct experiences of the same person, and that it is also possible for the same object to 'appear' many times over, on the same occasion, each such 'appearance' being the experience of a different person. We may also rule, quite in harmony with ordinary usage, that the fact that there are 'appearances' of objects (or of objects as having certain properties and relationships) will not in any way entail that such objects (or their properties and relationships) *have reality*. And we may adopt this ruling quite as firmly in the case where some object, e.g. an after-image, 'appears' in vivid, sensuous guise, as in the case where objects 'appear' in some merely indicated or notional manner. For it is only our determination to force the grammar of ' "appearance" ' (or of its active equivalent 'awareness') into a mould appropriate to other outwardly similar words, which makes people say that after-images *must* exist since they 'appear' before us (or are seen by us), and which only avoids saying a similar thing in the case of griffins by such complexities as the Russellian 'theory of descriptions'.

Our suggested grammar of ' "appearances" ' will, however, make it both natural and convenient to say that, while the object 'appearing' enters into the description of a given 'appearance', the latter is nevertheless wholly independent and distinct from the former. For it may exist though its correlated phenomenon is non-existent, may be manifold when this phenomenon is single, and is always a mental event occurring at a certain date and place, whereas its phenomenon need not be a mental happening at all, and may occur at a totally different date and place.

Our proposed distinction of 'appearances' from 'apparent' things is further aided by the fact that we can easily direct men's notice (through analogical description) to certain variations in their inner experiences, which are much more readily regarded as variations in an object's manner of 'appearing', than in the character of the 'apparent' object. Thus everyone readily finds differences in his experiences which are described analogically as differences in 'clearness': this is not the public clearness of objects with well-defined contours, seen in good illumination or through transparent media, but it is something which is at once like it, and also quite unlike it. There are, in our experience, certain objects which 'appear' with maximum 'clearness', toward which we sometimes[1] 'appear' to be making what are called efforts of attention, and there are other objects which 'appear' in the background, or with much less 'clearness'. Now while we might elect to ascribe this 'clearness' to the thing 'appearing', as Titchener did when he made 'attensity' an attribute of sense-contents, we should then have no easy way of avoiding the awkward statement that *non-existent* objects frequently have an attribute of 'clearness'. It is much better, therefore, to say that 'clearness' characterizes the manner in which an object 'appears', than that it characterizes that object itself. We also find in our experience a dimension of variability, whose extremes are described analogically as the wholly 'empty', 'stripped', and 'formal', on the one hand, and the wholly 'fulfilled', 'clothed', or 'concrete', on the other. It is obviously much easier to ascribe these differences to the way in which objects 'appear', than to make them attributes of the objects themselves. Thus a musical note actually sounding, differs profoundly from the same musical note held together with other notes, in the 'total impression' which succeeds the hearing of a musical phrase, but it would obviously be better to connect this almost ineffable difference, described only through the queerest analogies, with the way in which the note 'appears' or 'is given', than with the clear-cut note itself. On the whole it seems evident, when we consider the dimensions of variability just indicated, that Moore was not talking nonsense[2] when he said in 1903 that though consciousness—or 'appearance' in our terminology—was a factor difficult to fix in introspection, and as it were 'transparent' and 'diaphanous', it was nevertheless a factor

[1] Not by any means always.

[2] As most of those who departed from his position were ultimately involved in talking. I cannot help regarding James's famous article on consciousness and its philosophical progeny, as a mistake and misfortune of the first magnitude.

that *could* be distinguished if we would only look for it with sufficient care, and in the right direction.

The term ' "appearing" ', as used in our proposed way of speaking, may also be stretched to cover all those aspects of which we prefer to speak of *feeling* something, rather than of being conscious of it. Feeling angry, determined, downcast, half-credulous, amazed, pleased, or sorry are cases in point, as well as all other experiences classed under the rubrics of 'affection' and 'conation', and some experiences, e.g. those of conviction, grouped under the rubric of 'cognition'. For here the phenomenon 'appearing' may be said to be nothing other than *ourselves* as principal agents or patients, and our own half-formed attitudes and responses. And we need not look for anything very singular in the *manner* of their appearing, beyond a certain *necessary obscurity* and lack of discriminable detail, dependent on the circumstance that the actual emotional forces, which sustain the appearances in question, are also forces readily cancelled or weakened by any attempt to devote attention to them. In these experiences we ourselves occupy the centre of the picture (even if we do not occupy its illuminated focus), and the central presence of something at once so cherished and so familiar as ourselves, imparts to the experiences in question their characteristic 'warmth' and 'intimacy'. We do not 'appear' in this picture as merely static items, but always as *ready* to embark on this or that line or style of action, whether to burst, or to smash up obstacles, or retreat inwardly, or welcome something warmly, or react with any other typical rhythm or policy. And while this readiness is sometimes richly symbolized in somaesthetic changes (which are forceful and vivid without 'appearing clearly'), it 'appears' at other times in a wholly stripped and notional form. It is strange to reflect, in this connexion, that those modern psychological developments, called 'behaviouristic', which have turned their backs so resolutely on introspection, have also enabled us to characterize our inner states more adequately than was ever possible on the previous 'analytic' assumptions. For all our ordinary talk about inner attitudes, characterizes them by analogy with rhythms or policies of outward action, of which they represent either attenuations or anticipations, and so researches which help to clarify those outward rhythms and policies will also enable us to speak more clearly of their inner analogues. The term 'implicit behaviour' applied by Watson to interpolated elements in behavioural sequences was, accordingly, more happy and more apposite than he either imagined or intended. And we find, in this connexion, no position more affronting to our sense of fitness, than Hume's strange doctrine that, 'if nature had so pleased, love might have had the same effect as hatred and hatred as love'.[1] For all our verbal instincts impel us to say that any feeling which had no tendency to expand into the acts called loving, could not have anything *in* it which deserved the name of love. Even purely inward pleasure, that most elusive of all states, is one that cannot be adequately characterized, except as the last attenuation and refinement of all those caressing, basking, lip-smacking, or exulting attitudes in which we linger and luxuriate in some present situation. We speak, therefore, as *if* outward acts were the inevitable 'expansions' of feelings, and feelings the inevitable 'condensations' of countless possible actions, and such 'condensations' may readily be said to be nothing but the highly obscure and notionally telescoped 'appearances' of the lines of action in question. As 'appearances', of course, there will be nothing peculiarly dynamic about them, but the phenomena they reveal will frequently be real forces at work in the organism, by which they, as 'appearances', are themselves nourished and sustained. The term 'appearance' is therefore quite as capable of doing good work as applied to states and changes ordinarily said to be *felt* in ourselves, as when it is applied to states and changes of which we are ordinarily said to be aware.

We may note, further, that our whole account in terms of 'appearances' agrees rather with the classic stress on 'consciousness' as fundamental in our inner life, than with the confusing modern emphasis on things emotional or 'dynamic'. And it also agrees with our deep tendency to say that if there is anything genuinely peculiar to the 'mental sphere', it is that there things are, after a manner, mirrored or *represented*. We may now say, what seems a natural 'view' of the matter, that having a mind means for an organism that it represents itself and outward objects inwardly to itself, both in their actuality and their manifold possibilities, and that it is therefore able to rehearse, as on an inward stage, programmes and policies that may afterward be translated into action. And it may also be said to mean that this

[1] *Treatise on Human Nature*, Book II, Part II, Section vi.

organism is able to enjoy, in concentrated selection and fusion, what otherwise comes up irrelevantly and dispersedly in the business of actual living.

Our aim in this article is not, however, to work out the details of our proposed way of talking, nor to suggest that it cannot be shown to have many shortcomings. We have only sought to indicate that it is possible to use analogies clearly and deliberately, so as to bring improvements and simplifications into our introspective diction. The task of building up a satisfactory introspective language is not an easy one, and has not always been forwarded by those who have mistaken their linguistic preferences for ontological rigidities, or who have yearned, in this sphere, for a quite inappropriate degree of precision. But it has been even less forwarded by those whose thwarted passion for definiteness has ended by inoculating them with that extraordinary horror of the 'private', which has for long been characteristic of transatlantic living and thinking, and now threatens to engulf the intellectual world's remaining territories. Ordinary people do something very successfully which they call communicating the quality of their inner experiences to each other: their talk moves in a region by no means wholly nebulous nor devoid of uniformities, and there is no good reason why philosophers, who have occupied themselves deeply with the ethics of speaking, should not make many profitable recommendations in this field. For though, for almost all narrowly scientific or practical purposes, the only important question before us is of what mind *does*, there remain a few guiltily leisured, reflective moments in which we still dare to ask ourselves what it *is*.

CHAPTER XVI

THE ANALOGY OF FEELING[1]

Stuart Hampshire

Grote Professor of Philosophy of Mind and Logic, University of London

1. I am concerned in this paper with only one source of one of the many puzzles associated with our knowledge of other minds. It is often said that statements about other people's feelings and sensations cannot be justified as being based upon inductive arguments of any ordinary pattern, that is, as being inferences from the observed to the unobserved of a familiar and accepted form; I shall argue that they can be so justified. I will not deny that such inferences are difficult; everyone has always known, apart altogether from philosophical theory, that they are difficult; but I will deny that they are *logically* peculiar or invalid, when considered simply as inductive arguments. I believe that modern philosophers have found something logically peculiar and problematical about our inferences to other minds, and have even denied the possibility of such inferences, at least in part because of an incomplete understanding of the functions of pronouns and of other contextual expressions in our language; in particular they have misunderstood the proper use of these expressions in combination with words like 'know', 'certain', 'verify', 'evidence'. If I am right, it becomes easier to explain why what the solipsist wants to say cannot properly be said, why solipsism is a *linguistically* absurd thesis, and at the same time to explain why it is a thesis which tempts those who confuse epistemological distinctions with logical distinctions.

2. For reasons which will become clear later, I shall introduce two quasi-technical terms. As specimens of the type of sentence, the status of which, as normally used, is in dispute, I shall take the sentences, 'I feel giddy', 'you feel giddy', 'he feels giddy', and so on through the other cases of the verb 'feel'. Any normal use of the sentence 'I feel giddy' will be, in my invented terminology, a specimen of an autobiographical statement, where this phrase is simply shorthand for 'a statement describing

[1] *Mind*, January 1952.

somebody's momentary feelings or sensations which is expressed in the first person singular'. Any normal use of the sentences 'he feels giddy', 'you feel giddy', or 'they feel giddy', will be specimens of heterobiographical statements—that is, statements describing somebody's feelings which are not expressed in the first person singular; 'we feel giddy', as normally used, would be a statement which is partly autobiographical and partly heterobiographical in my sense. It may sometimes happen that someone chooses to tell the story of his own inner life, using not the first person singular, but the third person, or some fictitious or other name; it is actually possible to write one's own obituary notice, using the third person and including within it descriptions which are intended as descriptions of one's own feelings and sensations. But on such occasions the pronouns (or verb-cases for an inflected language) are misleadingly used, and deliberately so. The ordinary function of the word 'I' (or of the corresponding verb-case in inflected languages) is to indicate explicitly that the author of the statement is also the designated subject of the statement; the exceptional, deliberately misleading uses mentioned above consciously take advantage of this fact. By 'an autobiographical statement' I shall mean a statement describing someone's feelings or sensations which explicitly shows, in the actual form of its expression, that the author of the statement is also its designated subject. A statement, e.g. in a novel, about which we can argue, by reference to evidence external to the verbal form of the statement itself, whether it is, as a matter of fact, an autobiographical statement, will not therefore be an autobiographical statement in my artificial and restricted sense.

It has often been noticed that there are certain peculiarities about these first person singular statements about feelings and sensations, particularly when the main verb is in the present tense; these peculiarities have led some philosophers to characterize them as incorrigible statements and have led others to deny them the title of 'statement' altogether; the peculiarities emerge in the use of words like 'know', 'believe', and 'certain', in combination with these sentences, or rather in their lack of use. In respect of most statements, 'I think that P is true but I may be mistaken' and 'I have established that P is true beyond all reasonable doubt' are sentences having a normal use, whatever P may be; but there are no normal circumstances in which one would say 'I think that I feel giddy but I may be mistaken' or 'I have established beyond reasonable doubt that I feel giddy', and consequently there are no normal circumstances in which it would be in place to say 'I am absolutely certain that I feel giddy'. By contrast the sentences 'you feel giddy' or 'he feels giddy' do normally occur in statements of the form 'I believe that he feels giddy but I am not certain' or 'it is known that he feels giddy', and so on; but again, 'he believes that he feels giddy' or 'he is certain that he feels giddy' have no normal use. It is the corollary of this that the questions 'how do you know?' or 'what is your evidence?' are out of place in respect of statements about momentary feelings and sensations, when addressed to the author of the statement, if he is also explicitly shown to be the designated subject of it.

One inference which might be drawn from these facts is that heterobiographical statements about feelings can never be known to be true directly, where 'known directly' means that no question arises of how the statement is known to be true and no question arises of any evidence being required to support the statement. But this, as it stands, would be a plainly false conclusion, since the person who is the designated subject of such a hetero-biographical statement does generally know directly, without need of evidence, whether the statement made about him is true or false. The proper conclusion is only that the *author* of a hetero-biographical statement of this kind can never know directly, in the sense indicated, whether the statement he has made is true or false; the author can always properly be asked how he knows, or on what grounds he believes, his heterobiographical statement to be true; he is required to produce his evidence. So the so-called asymmetry is not a matter of statements expressed in the first person singular, *as such*, being different in respect of the evidence which they require from statements expressed in the second or third person singular; both descriptions of feelings in the first person singular, and those in the second and third person, may be challenged either by reference to indirect evidence (e.g. 'I am sure you are lying; you have obvious motives for lying, and you show none of the symptoms which usually go with feeling giddy') or by a proper claim to direct knowledge (e.g. 'I can tell you quite definitely that I do feel giddy, in spite of the evidence to the contrary').

This point is obvious, but it is apt to be dangerously slurred over when philosophers talk in general of 'statements about other minds', and then go on to inquire into *the* methods appropriate to confirming or confuting such statements. They may be thought to mean by 'statements about other minds' what I have called heterobiographical statements—that is, statements describing feelings and sensations which are not expressed in the first person singular; but the so-called problems of other minds, which is sometimes presented as a problem of how a *certain kind of statement* can be tested, does not attach to *a class of statements of any one particular form*; it arises equally for first person singular statements, if in this case the position of the audience is considered instead of that of the author. The problem of other minds is properly the problem of what tests and verifications are ever possible for anyone who is not in fact the designated subject of a statement about thoughts and feelings; it arises equally for any statement about feelings, whether the statement begins with the word 'I' or with the word 'you' or 'we' or 'they'.

3. The common-sense answer to the question, so reformulated, seems obvious—indeed so obvious that simply to give it cannot possibly satisfy philosophers; something more is required to explain why it has been thought inadequate. The common-sense answer is: each one of us is sometimes the designated subject of an autobiographical statement and sometimes the subject of heterobiographical statements; each one of us sometimes makes, or is in a position to make, statements about feelings which are not inferential and do not require supporting evidence, and also makes, or is in a position to make, statements about feelings which are inferential and do require supporting evidence. All that is required for testing the validity of any method of factual inference is that each one of us should sometimes be in a position to confront the conclusions of the doubtful method of inference with what is known by him to be true independently of the method of inference in question. Each one of us is certainly in this position in respect of our common methods of inference about the feelings of persons other than ourselves, in virtue of the fact that each one of us is constantly able to compare the results of this type of inference with what he knows to be true directly and non-inferentially; each one of us is in the position to make this testing comparison, whenever he is the designated subject

of a statement about feelings and sensations. I, Hampshire, know by what sort of signs I may be misled in inferring Jones's and Smith's feelings, because I have implicitly noticed (though probably not formulated) where Jones, Smith and others generally go wrong in inferring my feelings. We all as children learn by experiment how to conceal and deceive, to pose and suppress; concurrently we are learning in this very process how to detect the poses and suppressions of others; we learn the signs and occasions of concealment at first-hand, and we are constantly revising our canons of duplicity as our own direct experience of its forms and occasions widens.

These are the common-sense considerations which seem at first glance to allow us to regard any heterobiographical statement, made by any one of us, as the conclusion of a valid inductive inference, the reliability of the method of inference used in any particular case being in principle testable by each one of us in confrontation with direct experience, that is, with non-inferential knowledge about the successes and failures of this particular method; and I think that, as is usual in these questions, the third glance will confirm the first. But before going further, it is worth noticing how the argument from analogy, as stated by philosophers, approaches what I have called the common-sense position, but also misrepresents and over-simplifies it. There is a sense of 'analogy' in which it is true that I could justify my inference that Smith is now feeling giddy by an analogy between the particular method of inference which I am now using and other uses of the same methods of inference by other people in discussing my feelings and sensations; I know by direct experience how such feelings as giddiness are concealed and revealed; both I and Smith have been in a position to test the reliability of those methods of indirect inference about giddiness and cognate sensations which we from time to time use in talking about other people. The argument from analogy, as commonly stated by philosophers, only fails because the analogy has been looked for in the wrong place. What is required is not some simple analogy between my feelings and my external symptoms on the one hand and someone else's external symptoms, and so someone else's giddiness-feeling, on the other; what is needed, and is also available, is an *analogy between different uses of the same methods of argument by different people on different occasions.* The inductive argument, the reliability of which is to be tested by each one of us, attaches both to the sentence 'I feel giddy' and to the sentences 'you feel giddy', 'he feels giddy', etc.; it attaches to my sentence of the form 'X feels giddy'; anyone hearing or using any sentence of this form, and anyone needing to test the statement conveyed on a particular occasion, can find such confirmation by looking for an analogy with occasions of its use when he was not in need of such inductive confirmation. To anyone entertaining a doubt about the justification of a particular method of inference about feelings and sensations, the reassuring analogy is between the different occasions of use of the sentence in question; for on some of these occasions the doubter, whoever he may be, was in a position to know non-inferentially that the method of inference now in question led to a correct or incorrect conclusion. Each of us is in a position to learn from his own experience that certain methods of inference to conclusions of the kind 'X feels giddy' are generally successful. Of course, if I, Hampshire, have never felt giddy myself, or had any sensation which is even remotely like this one, I would to that extent be at a loss to know whether other people are speaking the truth when they describe autobiographically this utterly unknown kind of sensation. In certain extreme cases this total failure of testability, and therefore failure of communication, does in fact happen; in such cases I am in fact content to admit that I personally have no means of knowing whether what is said by others is pure invention or not; I simply do not know what they are talking about. But over the normal range of statements about feelings and sensations of which I am either the author or audience, I can generally point to occasions on which I was the subject of the particular statement in question and other people had to use the now questionable method of inference. Suppose that Smith and I each suspect the other of deceiving and of encouraging the other to use unreliable methods of inference. This again is a testable and empirical doubt, because we each of us know how we ourselves proceed when we are trying to deceive in this particular manner. We each base our devices of deception on our observations of other people's methods of inference about us. We each know that there is something in common to our different methods of deception, since we each sometimes know that we have failed to deceive and so we each know from our own experience how such deception may be detected. But no common psychological language could be established with beings, outwardly human and sensitive, who never tried openly and in words to infer our feelings, and who never acknowledged in words our success in inferring theirs, using the one to guide them in the other in a circle of mutual correction. We would have no good inductive grounds for speculating about the feelings of utterly silent people, or of people who did not betray themselves in speculating about us. It is merely a matter of natural history, and not of logic, that total failures of communication and understanding do not occur more frequently, and that in fact we are each generally in a position to reassure ourselves about our methods of inference to the feelings of others by confrontation with the successes and failures of others in talking about us.

It has been necessary first to insist on the truism that all statements about feelings and sensations, including such statements expressed in the first person singular, are 'statements about other minds' for some people, but not 'statements about other minds' for other people; for it is precisely this feature of them which allows any one of us to test in direct experience the reliability of the numerous specific methods of inference which he uses when talking about the feelings of others. The importance of the truism can be brought out in the analogous case of 'statements about the past'; philosophers have sometimes invented perplexities by writing as if we could pick out a class of statements as 'statements about the past' and could then inquire how such statements can possibly be established as true by inductive argument; for how—it is asked—can we ever in principle confirm the validity of our inferences about the past? The mistakes which lead to this question are the same as in the 'other minds' case. We cannot pick out a class of statements as statements about the past, unless we mean merely statements expressed in the past tenses. But the tenses, like the pronouns and cases of verbs, serve (among other functions) to relate a statement to the particular context or occasion of its utterance or of its consideration; clearly the *same* statement may be a statement about past, present or future, when considered, accepted or rejected by different people in different contexts; similarly, the *same* statement may be made either heterobiographically or autobiographically. A statement in the present tense, which is in this artificial sense a statement about the present, when verified and reaffirmed, may be reaffirmed as a statement about the past, and equally a statement about the future, when finally confirmed, may be reaffirmed as a statement about the present. *The very notion of confirmation involves this possibility of comparing the different contexts of utterance of the same statement.* It does not in general lie *within* the statement itself, or in its grammatical form of expression, that it is a statement about the mind of another, or that it is a statement about the past; these are features of the circumstances of the utterance or consideration of the statement, features which are partially indicated (but not stated) by pronouns, by tenses and by other contextual expressions, whenever and by whomever the statement is asserted, reasserted or denied. Strictly speaking, there can be no class of statements about the past, standing in hopeless need of confirmation, any more than there can be a class of past events; similarly there can be no class of minds which are other minds, or class of statements about them. This confusion of contextual idioms such as 'other', 'past' with class-terms has its roots in an unnoticed double use of the idioms, which must now be explained.

3. It is often suggested that the function of pronouns and other contextual expressions ('this', 'that', 'here', 'now', etc.) is to designate or to refer uniquely to some person, thing, time, place, event, etc. Mr Strawson (*Mind*, October 1950) has suggested the appropriate label, 'uniquely referring expressions'; certainly one of the ways in which pronouns and these other contextual expressions are used is in this uniquely referring way—that is, to indicate, in a particular context of utterance, a particular person, thing, event. But it is characteristic of the contextual expressions that they are not always or solely used to refer uniquely or to designate a particular person, thing, event; they also have an important *generalized* use, in which they make no reference to a particular individual and in which they can be interpreted without any reference whatever to any particular context of utterance. Consider the slogan, 'do it *now*'; or 'never put off till *tomorrow* what you can do *today*'. In this use 'now', 'today', 'tomorrow' do not refer uniquely, but have a force in some (but not all) ways like that of a variable, and might be expanded into 'now, to whatever moment "now" may refer', or 'today, whatever day "today" may refer to'. Another example: 'the future is quite uncertain': as it stands, and without a context, this sentence is

ambiguous, and might be used to make two quite different statements, or even two different kinds of statement; 'the future'
might be used in the uniquely referring way, so that we require
to know the context of utterance in order to know what particular
stretch of history is being referred to and described as uncertain;
or 'the future' might be used in the purely generalized way—'the
future, at whatever point in history, is always uncertain'. This
familiar generalized, or quasi-variable, use is transferred to
philosophy when we talk of 'statements about *the past*', 'statements
about the *other* side of the moon', and 'statements about *other*
minds'. Confusion between the two kinds of use arises when a
transition is made within a single argument from the generalized
to the uniquely referring use, or vice versa, without this transition
being noticed; and just this is what generally happens in arguments about our knowledge of 'other minds' and in formulations
of the so-called *ego*centric predicament. The solipsistic doubter
will probably not put his question in the explicitly generalized
form, but will ask: 'How can *I* ever justify my inferences about
what is going on in *your* mind, since *I* can have no independent
means of checking *my* inferences about *your* feelings?' There may
be a muddle in this: Does the 'I' here mean 'I, Hampshire'?
Is it a lament about my, Hampshire's, peculiar isolation and the
peculiar inscrutability of you, Smith? Or does the 'I' mean
'whoever "I" refers to?' and the 'you', 'you, whoever "you" may
be?' If the latter is intended, and the pronoun is being used in
the generalized way, the question becomes: 'How can any one
of us ever justify any inference to the feelings of someone other
than himself, since no one of us, whoever he may be, has any
means of checking any inference to the feelings of anyone other
than himself?' And to this generalized form of the question the
common-sense answer again suggests itself: each and every one
of us, whoever he may be, has the means of independently
checking the reliability of the methods of inference which he
uses, although, naturally, on those occasions when he needs to
use any particular method of inference, he cannot be independently checking the inference on the same occasion. When I,
Hampshire, check in my own experience the reliability of the
various particular methods of inference which I use when talking
about the feelings of others, the statements which I make at the
conclusion of these checks are *ex-hypothesi* not themselves the

conclusions of an inference; but they are none the less efficient as checks to my methods of inference. The solipsistic problem, cleared of these confusions, can now be re-stated; whenever anyone uses the sentence 'I feel giddy', one person and one person only is in a position to know directly, and without need of inference, whether the statement conveyed is true; whenever anyone says 'you feel giddy', or 'he feels giddy', or 'Smith feels giddy', one person and one person only is in a position to know, without need of inference whether the statement is true; whenever anyone says, 'we both feel giddy', or 'they feel giddy', no one can ever know directly, and without need of inference, whether the conjoint statements conveyed are true. So the solipsist may correctly say that it is a distinguishing characteristic of statements about feelings, as opposed to statements about physical things, that at most one person can ever properly claim to know directly, and without needing to give evidence or justification, whether such statements are true. But the solipsist originally wanted to separate, within the class of statements about minds, a class of statements about *other* minds, as being dubious and problematical, from autobiographical statements, which were held to be privileged and not dubious. It is this distinction which is untenable.

Suppose that, in talking about our feelings, we each solipsistically confined ourselves to statements which we may properly claim to know to be true directly and without appeal to evidence or to methods of inference; I, Hampshire, would be allowed to say 'I feel giddy', and you, Smith, would be allowed to say 'I feel giddy'; but, since all uses of other cases of the verb require problematical inference, we would never be allowed to assent to or dissent from each other's statements, or to place ourselves in the position of an audience discussing them. Under such conditions the pronouns and cases of the verb would have no further function, and all argument and the detection of lies would be excluded: our psychological language would simply serve to convey a set of undiscussable announcements. Communication in the ordinary sense upon such topics would have ceased; for communication essentially involves the use of sentences to convey statements by an author to an actual or potential audience, in such a way that all users of the language, in denying and confirming, may change from the position of audience to author in respect of any statement made. To compare the use of personal pronouns with the uses of tenses again: because those statements which refer to events long prior or subsequent to the moment of utterance are *pro tanto* relatively uncertain at the time they are made, it might be suggested that only statements in the present tense should be accepted as completely reliable. But unless we recognize the sense of 'same statement' as something to be reaffirmed in different contexts, we remove the last possibility of correcting and denying statements, and with this we remove the possibility of all argument about them and testing of them, and also the possibility of expressing belief or disbelief; we therefore remove the essential conditions or point of statement-making; and this we would have done by failing to recognize the function of those devices which relate the same statement to the changing circumstances of its assertion. The formula often used, 'I am in a position to judge of the truth of statements about my own feeling, but not about the feeling of others', has only succeeded in misleading, because of the two ways in which the expression 'I' and 'other' may be used, and the often unnoticed shift from one use to the other; it is this shift which suggests a solipsistic conclusion—e.g. that one mind only can be known with certainty to exist and one set of feelings and sensations known with certainty to have occurred. But of course no such conclusion about *one* mind follows from the argument when correctly stated. The proper truism is, 'No one of us, whoever he may be, is in need of inference to assure himself of the truth of statements about his own feelings, but he can never assure himself directly, and without needing to appeal to evidence, of the truth of statements about the feelings of others'; stated in this form, with a quasi-variable expression as the subject term, the truism cannot serve as a premiss to any *solipsistic* conclusion.

4. The peculiarity of the word 'know' and of its cognates—that the conditions of their proper use in combination with any type of statement vary with the indicated context of utterance—is not confined to discourse about minds and feelings; it applies over the whole range of application of words like 'know', 'certain', 'verify', with whatever kind of statement they are combined. Whatever may be the topic under discussion, whether a claim to knowledge or certainty is or is not in place, must always depend upon who makes the claim, when, and under what conditions;

it can never be solely a matter of the form of the statement itself or of its topic. Any empirical statement whatever is a matter of uncertain inference under some conditions of its use or consideration. There is no mystery in the fact that a statement which may be a matter of direct and certain knowledge for one person will always be a matter of uncertain inference for another, any more than there is a mystery in the fact that the same statement which may be known with certainty to be true at one time must be a matter of uncertain inference at other times. Philosophers (Plato, Descartes, Russell) have invented the mystery by writing as if being known to be true and being uncertain were intrinsic properties of statements, properties somehow adhering to them independently of the particular circumstances in which they were made or considered. It is proper and necessary that formal logicians, who study patterns of transformations of sentence-forms, should disregard those features of statements which relate them to a context of utterance; but philosophers' questions about use and meaning hinge on the different contexts in which words like 'know' and 'certain' may occur in combination with sentences of different forms and different topics.

5. *Conclusion*. 'Past', 'Present', 'Other', are not class terms but contextual terms, and there can be no class of events which are past events, and no class of minds which are other minds, and no class of statements which are statements about either of these. 'Statements about other minds' is either an incomplete expression, requiring knowledge of the particular circumstance of its use in order that it should be intelligible—e.g. 'minds other than mine, Hampshire's'; or the contextual expression may be used in the generalized sense and mean 'statements about minds other than the author's, whoever the author may be'; if the latter is intended, then in raising the problem of other minds we are inquiring into the analogy which enables anyone to compare the situation in which he knows a statement about feelings to be true, independently of inference, with the situation in which he does not; and it is to this comparison that we refer when we talk of checking the reliability of any method of factual inference.

CHAPTER XVII

MIND AND BODY—SOME OBSERVATIONS ON MR STRAWSON'S VIEWS[1]

H. D. Lewis

*Professor of the History and Philosophy of Religion, King's College,
University of London*

The question of mind and body is a major crux in modern philosophy. It throws up very sharply the general question of the limits of empiricism, and it has ramifications that reach very far into the fields of ethics and sociology, to say nothing of religion. This seems ample justification for selecting the topic as the theme of a Presidential Address.

In my own case there is the following further reason. It is generally assumed in philosophy today, in English-speaking countries at least, that the Cartesian view of the self as a substance in some way interacting with the body is entirely mistaken. One of the assured advances in philosophy seems thus to be the rejection of Cartesian dualism. This is taken for granted so firmly that, in many quarters, argument about this issue is thought to be quite redundant, a waste of energy and a sign of philosophical naïvety which is unable to appreciate the unquestionable achievements of recent philosophy. The ghost of Descartes, a phrase we may nowadays use in more than one sense, has thus to be summoned up in and out of season for relentless chastisement. This seems essential, even for the less fashionable philosopher, if he is to prove that he is not altogether behind the times.

Let two examples suffice. The first is from the inaugural lecture[2] delivered at Edinburgh by Professor W. H. F. Barnes. Barnes is by no means a philosopher committed to prevailing fashions—did he not write *The Philosophical Predicament*? But even he cannot put in a word for 'private access' without hinting all the same that there is something radically wrong with Car-

---

[1] Presidential Address delivered to the Aristotelian Society in October 1962 and published in the *Proceedings of the Aristotelian Society*, 1962–3, Vol. LXIII.

[2] *Language, Mind and Morals.*

tesian dualism as a way of sustaining this. 'The behaviourist denial of the inner life of the mind is as much a preconceived thesis as Cartesian dualism.'[1] The 'prejudice' which lies behind the former infects the latter as well. Or so we are led to conclude.

Professor J. M. Cameron is more forthright in another inaugural lecture—at Leeds. His theme is 'Poetry and Dialectic', and he writes: 'We habitually talk of our feelings, passions, dispositions, capacities, in terms that suggest that introspection is to the mind and heart what sight and the other senses are to the world of nature. It is one of the great and, I believe, permanent advances recently made by philosophers in this country to have shown that this account, the monstrous offspring of Cartesian dualism and British empiricism, is impossible.'[2] A little later we read: 'When, at the end of *The Waste Land*, Mr Eliot depicted each man as imprisoned within his own consciousness, he gave us an image of man dwelling within the haunted palace of the Cartesians; but the palace is in ruins and the ghosts have departed.'[3]

I think this is altogether mistaken. It is not that it has gone too far, but that it is completely wrong. I do not indeed hold a brief for every feature of Descartes' dualism or for all the ways in which he presented his views. Much less would I wish to defend the views often ascribed to Descartes today and lampooned in criticisms of him. I believe all the same that he was right in essentials in his views about mind and body and that he was much more perceptive in his ways of presenting his ideas than is commonly supposed today.

I shall not attempt now to defend this view in detail. It would take more space than I have at my disposal to rehabilitate Descartes. My aim will be a more modest one. I shall make some critical comments on a view of the 'mind-body problem' (as it used to be called, and as I think it still quite proper to call it) which finds much favour among philosophers today and is an excellent instance of the way most of my contemporaries, in this country at least, believe the subject should be handled. This will enable me to indicate my own view of a central philosophical problem and to define my attitude towards some of the views and procedures of my contemporaries.

The view on which I wish to comment is that put forward by

[1] *Op. cit.*, p. 11. [2] *Poetry and Dialectic*, p. 25.
[3] *Op. cit.*, p. 26.

Mr P. F. Strawson in his much discussed book *Individuals*, and, to limit the scope of the discussion and also be as precise as I can, I shall confine myself mainly to what Strawson has to say in Chapter III of his book under the heading of 'Persons'.

I ought to add that I have chosen Strawson, not only because of his standing in philosophy today and his undoubted gifts, but also because he is widely esteemed as a philosopher with much broader sympathies than many of his contemporaries, indeed as one who is to herald a modest and perceptive return to metaphysics—not so long ago a term of contempt but one which Strawson does not disdain to use in designation of his own work.

In the chapter entitled 'Persons' in his book *Individuals*, Strawson opens his discussion with the observation that the group of questions he proposes to discuss might be denoted 'the issue of solipsism'. He realizes that this is not the customary use of those terms, but he contends that there can be no objection to his present procedure since solipsism, as normally understood, 'is not a genuine issue at all'.[1]

There can be no serious objection to the adoption of a term for a new purpose, least of all when the author is quite explicit about it at the outset. Even so the practice is not to be much commended, for it could be a source of misunderstanding. But in the present case that has less importance, for Mr Strawson hardly uses the term in the subsequent discussion, and I mention his initial move in indication of the confidence with which it is maintained throughout that solipsism is not a genuine issue. That confidence is, in my view, quite misplaced.

It is of course true that no one wishes to make a case for solipsism as a final philosophical view. No one sets out to argue that only he himself exists, or that there are no very strong reasons for believing that we can know other persons. But philosophers have to ask questions about matters which we normally do not doubt at all in order, by this 'methodological' doubt, to understand better what it is that we believe and to see what modifications in the way we normally believe it may be needed. They have thus been much concerned to discover in what way it is that we have knowledge of one another. This is the traditional problem of 'other minds', and it is the obverse of the problem

[1] *Individuals*, p. 87. All further references are to the same book.

of solipsism. The philosophers who have examined it, and very few philosophers have managed to avoid it in some form, have rarely, if ever, been seriously worried by the thought that there may be no one in the world but themselves. But they have usually thought it a difficult and fascinating question to determine how this assurance is obtained and warranted. Mr Strawson, however, thinks this enthusiasm to have been entirely misplaced and disposes as boldly of the problem of 'other minds' in a later context as he does of its counterpart, the problem of solipsism, at the outset. In both respects he seems to me unable to justify his view by satisfactory arguments and to be relying heavily on extremely dogmatic assumptions about philosophy and language.

Mr Strawson settles down to his task with a reference to some of the things we ascribe to ourselves. These include, on the one hand, states of consciousness, thoughts and sensations, and, on the other, physical characteristics like height, colouring and weight. There is no particular problem about ascribing the latter set of characteristics to 'something or other', for they can be ascribed to one's body, a 'material thing' which 'can be picked out from others, identified by ordinary physical criteria and described in ordinary physical terms'.[1] But it is thought to be very perplexing that we can ascribe states of consciousness and physical characteristics *to the very same thing*.[2]

Now here, in the very statement of the problem, there seem to me to be unwarranted assumptions which careful analysis ought to dispel. Is it strictly the case that we ascribe these different characteristics to the same thing? We certainly do so in a rough-and-ready way for ordinary purposes. We say, for example: 'I am sitting at the table', 'I am running', 'I am writing'. There are clearly two sets of characteristics involved here, as may be seen most obviously perhaps in the last example. Writing involves physical movement and it involves mental activity. We do not for normal purposes distinguish the two. It is enough to say— 'I am writing'. This is because the two activities are peculiarly closely linked and because it would be cumbersome and pointless to be always noting the distinction between them. It would be much too troublesome to say, for example—'I was intending to open the door and my body moved towards it'. It is neater and apter, for ordinary purposes, to say simply 'I went to the door'

---

[1] P. 89.   [2] P. 89.

or 'I went to open the door'. But while this is the best thing to say, as a rule, we cannot allow that to be decisive in philosophy, and I fear that that is ultimately just what Mr Strawson does.

The truth seems to be that we do not strictly ascribe corporeal characteristics and mental characteristics to the same thing. When, for example, I say 'I am tall', I am not saying anything about my mind but only about my body, which of course affects my mind in a great many ways. My mind has neither height nor length nor breadth. It would be absurd, except in a thoroughly figurative sense, to ask how big is my mind. To speak of a 'small mind' is sheer metaphor. Minds are neither big nor small. If anyone denies this let him give me the approximate length of his mind, or any other, and say how he measures it. Is it six inches, or a foot, or a mile, or what? Clearly it is none of these. The question is absurd, for tallness and so on has nothing to do with my mind, but only with my body. The much maligned Descartes was obviously right in maintaining that it was distinctive of minds not to be extended.

When this view is advanced an objection is sometimes raised in the following terms. 'You know quite well where you are now, you are not in France, not in Oxford. You are in London,[1] in this room, and you are standing at the desk in front, not sitting at the back.' This sounds plausible, but again that is only because the essential distinctions are not drawn for ordinary purposes. It would indeed be absurd and misleading for me to deny that I was not in France, or to seem to wonder whether I was in London. I know quite well where I am, when the question is put to me. But as philosophers we can also quite properly ask, 'What does this mean?' It means, in the first place, that my body is 'here in this room', and the location of that can be quite precisely specified. It is the space which my body fills. But, secondly, the experiences which I have now are conditioned in certain ways by where my body is. If my body is up at a desk where I am speaking I can only have, as visual experiences, the seeing of these particular walls, of the furniture and occupants of this room and so on, my sense of being warm and cold depends on the temperature of this particular room, the pressures on the soles

[1] The point was in fact put to me in almost these terms at Oxford in the discussion which followed one of the Wilde Lectures which I delivered there last year on a similar theme.

N

of my feet depend on the hardness of the boards, and my mental activities are affected in kindred ways. I am thinking these particular thoughts now because I am giving an address to a specific audience now. If the room were empty I should not be thinking just these thoughts, or at any rate I should not be thinking them in exactly the same way as in trying to explain my ideas to this audience. In all these regards, and in other similar ones, I am in this room. But it still does not follow that my mind is strictly in the room. Neither of course is it outside, or in France (except in a metaphorical sense if my thoughts *stray*, as we say, to a holiday in France). To deny that I was here, in any sense that implied that I was elsewhere, would be absurd. But the strict truth is that my mind is nowhere, location simply does not apply to it. My thoughts are not extended, although they are affected in many ways by extended substances, including especially my body.

To some extent Strawson takes account of this. He agrees with Descartes that 'I am not lodged in my body like a pilot in a vessel', and he goes on to refer to the ways in which my perceptual experiences are dependent on my body, on my eyes being open, on the direction of my head and so on; he toys ingeniously[1] with the possibility of one's being dependent in these ways on more than one body. That is not in fact our actual situation, and thus 'there is for each person one body which occupies a certain causal position in relation to that person's perceptual experience' and which is unique to him also 'as an *object* of perceptual experience'. These considerations seem, however, to Strawson, to leave the central question unanswered. They show why I should have a special regard for one body, 'But they do not explain why I should have the concept of *myself* at all, why I should ascribe my thoughts and feelings to *anything*. Moreover, even if we were satisfied with some other explanation of why one's states of consciousness, thoughts and feelings and perceptions, were ascribed to *something*, and satisfied that the facts in question sufficed to explain why the "possession" of a particular body should be ascribed to the *same* thing (i.e. to explain why a particular body should be spoken of as standing in some special relation—called "being possessed by"—to that thing), yet the facts in question still do not explain why we should, as we do, ascribe certain corporeal characteristics not simply to the body standing

[1] P. 91.

in this special relation to the thing to which we ascribe thoughts and feelings, etc., but to the thing itself to which we ascribe those thoughts and feelings. For we say "*I* am bald" as well as "*I* am cold", "*I* am lying on the hearthrug" as well as "*I* see a spider on the ceiling" '.[1] But it is just here that linguistic usage is made to carry far more weight than it can. We have Strawson admitting that any dependence on my body in perceptual and kindred ways does not prove his main point. It only explains why the '*possession*' of a particular body should be ascribed to the 'something', whatever it may be, to which my thoughts and feelings are ascribed, in other words it explains why I say that I *have* a body, it does not account for the fact that my thoughts and feelings are ascribed to the same thing as my physical characteristics, and to substantiate the latter claim, the crucial one for Strawson, all we have at this stage is the reference to the fact that we say '*I* am bald' and so on. But a phrase of this kind is capable of further analysis and cries out for it; it can quite properly be analysed in terms of the notion of my *having* a body, that is being peculiarly dependent on a certain body and so forth. The strict truth is not that *I* am bald, although that is a perfectly clear way of putting it for normal purposes, but that my *head* is bald. It is my *own* head, part of a body to which I stand in a very special relation, but my mind is neither bald nor covered with hair, it cannot be; and if the baldness is ascribed to me that is only to me as a complex being having a mind as well as a body or being dependent on a body; it is not ascribed to me in any further sense which requires physical and mental characteristics to belong strictly to the same entity.

I should also wish to add that my real self is my mind, and that it is only in a derivative and secondary sense that my body is said to be myself at all. In other words, in the strict sense I am not bald at all, and cannot be; it is only part of my body that can be bald, my body is not something that I *am* but something that I *have*, and here linguistic usage, if that were what we should appeal to, is on our side. The appeal to ordinary language is apt to cut disconcertingly both ways.

One wonders also why it should have been thought to be initially so plausible to suppose that my dependence on my body in perceptual experience and so on might be the explanation of

[1] P. 93.

'why I should have the concept of myself at all'.[1] Strawson is indebted in some ways to Kant, and one would have expected this to have left on him a firmer impression of at least the greater initial plausibility of an explanation of my having 'a concept of myself' in terms of some inherent feature of consciousness itself.

Strawson is not, however, unaware of the sort of objection I have brought against his main argument. He refers to two positions which might be alternatives to his own. One is the 'no ownership' view which it is thought might have been held by Wittgenstein or Schlick. On this view it is perfectly proper to refer to the dependence of my experiences on my body, and it is not very inappropriate to say further that my experiences 'belong' in this sense to my body. But, it is contended, we are apt to slide from this to the wholly inadmissible position that experiences may belong to something else not a body at all, an 'Ego, whose sole function is to provide an owner for experiences'. We fall victims in this way to 'a linguistic illusion'. This theory, however, fails, according to Strawson, because it cannot be stated without 'internal incoherence', for the exponent of it can only refer to the facts which give rise to the illusion of the ego in some such form as: 'all *my* experiences are had by (i.e. uniquely dependent on the state of) body B'. In this way ownership in some sense is implied.

It is not for me to defend the 'no ownership theory', and that theory is in fact as far removed from what seems to me to be the truth as anything can be; and yet I am not sure that it is as conclusively refuted as Strawson supposes in terms of this alleged internal incoherence. The present mode of settling arguments seems to me deceptively simple, and it does not take us very far beyond the appeal to established usage. I should not place it beyond the ingenuity of a sufficiently determined advocate of the 'no ownership theory' to find a reasonably satisfactory statement of his position. Strawson observes that the reference to experiences as mine, in the sense solely of belonging to my body, is analytic inasmuch as it adds nothing to the assertion that the experiences depend on this body. But is it quite obvious that the no ownership theory could not get along with that, does it have to bring in the word 'my' in a way that would expose it to incoherence, in other words is Strawson's present point a bar to *any*

[1] P. 93.

statement of a no ownership theory on the basis of an alleged
linguistic confusion due to ways in which we refer to the dependence of certain experiences on a certain body?

The real objection to the no ownership theory is that it is out
of accord with the facts about consciousness. There is something
left out of the account, and the incoherence arises only if the
advocate of the theory assumes this further factor in his statement
of his own position. I am not altogether convinced that he is
bound to do so, but Strawson's ascription of essential incoherence
to him does involve also stressing that the sponsor of the theory
does leave something out. But what then, in Strawson's view, is
it that the no ownership theory overlooks?

It overlooks something, we are told, which is also neglected
in the other alternative entertained by Strawson, namely the
Cartesian position. Both these mistaken positions, it seems,
overlook what Strawson rightly describes as 'a very central
thought' for him, namely, in his own words that 'it is a necessary
condition of one's ascribing states of consciousness, experiences,
to oneself, in the way one does, that one should also ascribe them,
or be prepared to ascribe them, to others who are not oneself.
This means not less than it says. It means, for example, that the
ascribing phrases are used in just the same sense when the subject
is another as when the subject is oneself.'[1]

In one sense this statement is true—at least in the main. When
I say that someone other than myself is thinking about philosophy
or planning to go for a walk I am ascribing to him the same sort
of mental state as I should ascribe to myself if I claimed to be
doing these things. In other words, for me to be thinking about
philosophy is the same thing as for you to be thinking about
philosophy. Whether this holds at all points is less certain. It has
been suggested, I think with justification, that when one person
claims to see red colour there is no absolute certainty that his experience is strictly the same as that of some other person who makes
the same claim. If red appeared consistently in my experience
when others had experience of yellow colour I should never know
of the difference and should use the word red in these situations
in the same way as other people. There are stock replies to this,
some of them taking the short way with the dissenter common
in linguistic philosophy and identifying the meaning of the word

[1] P. 99.

red with its use. But these objections seem to me to proceed on unwarranted assumptions, and I think there is a good case to be made, although I shall not make it here, for the view that there may be many radical differences between our experiences such as the one contemplated in the standard problem about seeing strictly the same colour. I have hinted at the very far-reaching character of these possibilities in my paper on 'Public and Private Space'.[1]

These are not, however, matters that I wish to press now. I have admitted that, in the main, to ascribe states of consciousness to one person is the same as to ascribe them to others in the sense noted hitherto, namely, that what is ascribed is the same. If there are exceptions to this they require to be considered carefully as a separate problem and need not worry us now.

But what about the process of ascription itself? Does not this come about in a radically different way in my own case from that of another? At this point Strawson refers to an alleged difficulty concerning the difference in the method of verification. 'How could the sense be the same', so Strawson puts the philosopher's difficulty, 'when the method of verification was so different?' Strawson himself does not think there is real cause for anxiety here. But this is not because he questions the assumption about meaning and method of verification from which the supposed difficulty arises. On the contrary it is the acceptance of that assumption that mainly underlies his own contentions, and it is an assumption for which little justification is ever offered. On what grounds, other than the dogmatic acceptance of a certain philosophical method, can it be maintained that the same sort of situation could not come to be known, in different cases, in radically different ways? We are surely not to be told at this time of day that the meaning of a statement *is* its method of verification. But what substance is there in the alleged repudiation of the original forms of logical positivism, and the supercilious contempt shown towards them, if we are to retain the present form of the principle of verification as a basic one in philosophical procedure?

Mr Strawson, as I have said, does not repudiate this principle. His position seems to be that if we ascribed states to ourselves

[1] *Proceedings of the Aristotelian Society*, 1952–3. New Series, Vol. LIII,

in a different way from ascribing them to others, there would be an insuperable difficulty arising directly from the view about 'verification' and 'sense' to which I have just alluded. It seems also somewhat partisan of him to describe this as a difficulty which gives 'trouble to the philosopher' as if it were a trouble which had generally worried philosophers in this context. It is in fact only a trouble to those who follow the prevailing linguistic and empiricist fashion in philosophy. Not that philosophers have not had troubles here. They have had indeed many well-known troubles about our knowledge of other minds, and it is these troubles which Strawson, in common with many others today, tends to thrust altogether aside, as happened in Strawson's initial reference to solipsism, as if they had no substance but were on the contrary the bogus and unilluminating problems of stupid philosophers.

Strawson believes, however, that the trouble to which he refers can be effectively eliminated. It does not really arise, not as I have observed because we must modify our views about verification, but because we are bound to ascribe states of consciousness to ourselves in precisely the same way as we ascribe them to others. We can, indeed, only identify ourselves when we also identify others. Strawson in fact puts the initial 'trouble' about ascription and verification in the alternative form of questioning 'the right to talk about ascribing in the case of oneself';[1] there can be no question of identifying oneself. We only identify other persons, and it is only in an elliptical sense that we may be said to identify ourselves when we do so *for* other persons—to tell someone else who is in pain and so on. This argument is again severely, if subtly, linguistic. It is quite true that, for normal purposes or in ordinary usage, there is no point in trying to identify ourselves or tell who we are. In practice it is always, or nearly always, a question of informing other people. But the philosopher is not concerned with ordinary aims and practices, and at the philosophical level there is a very proper problem of how it is that we know or identify ourselves. It may be that we never are in doubt, except in subsidiary senses,[2] but even so it is proper and important in philosophy to indicate the mode of awareness

---

[1] P. 100.

[2] As seem to me to be those involved in the case of loss of memory, and so on.

involved. Knowledge, notwithstanding what many have assumed to the contrary today, is not less genuine if it happens to be the sort which cannot in fact be doubted.

It is this, however, which Strawson seems to query; and it is for such reasons that he comes in due course to declare that 'one may properly be said to ascribe states of consciousness to oneself, given that one can ascribe them to others'. The point he is making is not the one that has often been made in the past by philosophers, namely that we are essentially social creatures and could not as a matter of fact have the sort of awareness of ourselves which we have as human beings, or indeed be at all the sort of persons we are, were it not for the very intimate relations we have with one another. No one would seriously dispute this point, and it is not anything so trivial that Strawson is affirming; he is concerned with a much more subtle logical difficulty about the very meaningfulness of ascribing states of consciousness to ourselves independently of ascribing them to others.

The obverse of this difficulty for Strawson is that the problem of ascribing states of consciousness to others would be insoluble if the things [sic] to which we ascribe them were 'a set of Cartesian egos to which only private experiences can, in correct logical grammar, be ascribed'.[1] For there would be no way 'of telling that a private experience is another's'. But here again there are unwarranted assumptions, in particular the assumption that if experiences are such that in themselves or directly they are private to those who have them there can be no other way in which they can also be made public or known about indirectly. To affirm that we have private access to our own experience does not preclude us from insisting also that there are ways in which these experiences may be disclosed, deliberately or in other ways, to others.[2] How that comes about is the traditional problem; in one sense we are in a world of our own and in one sense we are not. But Strawson rules this out on the ground that there can be

[1] P. 100.

[2] It is on the denial of this that Professor Ryle relies extensively in the early parts of *The Concept of Mind*. He assumes that on the 'official doctrine', about private access and so on, 'absolute solitude' must be 'the ineluctable destiny of the soul'. This has obviously never been the intention of the sponsors of the 'official doctrine', and if their position involves it, then that has to be shown, not assumed; there is little attempt to do that.

no sense in which an experience is mine unless this *expressly* involves the contrast with those of others. This seems to be the point of his saying that, on the view he opposes, 'All private experiences, all states of consciousness, will be mine, i.e. *no one's*'.[1] Here, again, we must admit that 'mine' normally implies the contrast with 'thine' and 'theirs'. This is because the words 'mine' and 'thine' usually refer to a claim, to a right or property, and this involves excluding others or limiting their rights. But, unless we are to be the slaves of ordinary usage, there is nothing here that in any way precludes my being aware of my own experiences, and thereby knowing them to be mine, in a way that does not directly involve the very different awareness I have of the experiences of others. I know that a private experience is mine in having it. I could not, admittedly, have the private experience of a human being, or reflect expressly upon it as being mine, without association with other persons. But that is quite a different matter from the curious logical point which Strawson is attempting to make.

Strawson sums up his argument up to this point as follows:

One can ascribe states of consciousness to oneself only if one can ascribe them to others. One can ascribe them to others only if one can identify other subjects of experience. And one cannot identify others if one can identify them *only* as subjects of experience, possessors of states of consciousness.

The last statement in this quotation is important as providing the link with the other main features of Strawson's central thesis. That is the insistence that we can only identify other persons and come to know about them through observing their bodies. Of human beings situated as we are in this life that is largely, if not entirely, true. We know other persons normally through the movements of their bodies, the sounds they utter, and so on; and even if there are further paranormal ways of learning about other persons, it is exceptionally hard to see how this would be possible for us if we did not have also the knowledge of other persons obtained in the ordinary way. But if we allow this, and if it is also asserted, as is done by Strawson, that we cannot identify or know ourselves except in a process which essentially and directly involves the identification of others, then it seems

---

[1] Italics mine.   [2] P. 100.

N*

impossible to ascribe experiences to ourselves at all except in ways in which our bodies have an indispensable part. The basic unit, what Strawson calls the 'logically primitive' concept, is thus, 'a type of entity such that *both* predicates ascribing states of consciousness *and* predicates ascribing corporeal characteristics, a physical situation, etc., are equally applicable to a single individual of that single type'.[1] We cannot, in other words, conceive of ourselves at all except as beings with physical characteristics.

This is much more drastic and radical than saying that in point of fact it is very hard to see how we could function independently of our bodies, that it would be difficult to identify ourselves without the sensations and experiences which are most directly related to our own bodies, that the causal dependence of mind on body is so close that it is implausible to think that the mind can function independently of the body. These are very substantial, though not to my mind insuperable, difficulties, and it is easy to see why people are daunted by them when they consider any kind of disembodied existence. But on Strawson's view discussion at this level is quite superfluous and indeed improper, since, in terms of his own very radical positions, it is out of the question to conceive of ourselves independently of our bodies, the attempt to do so stands condemned on logical grounds at the start.

To sum up the main theme in Strawson's own words: 'The point is not that we must accept this conclusion in order to avoid scepticism, but that we must accept it in order to explain the existence of the conceptual scheme in terms of which the sceptical problem is stated. But once the conclusion is accepted, the sceptical problem does not arise.'[2] As it used to be put, the traditional problem is a pseudo-problem, and when Strawson presents his own work as 'descriptive metaphysics' one wonders whether the vaunted new metaphysics is but the old anti-metaphysical philosophy in disguise.

Let me note now two supplementary arguments used by Strawson in the same context.

The first is his reply to a possible defence of Cartesianism. It might be argued, he supposes, that we do not find it difficult to identify bodies and that we could thus identify a subject as the one that stands in the same special relation to a particular

---

[1] P. 102.   [2] P. 106.

body as I stand to my own. This is wrecked, however, on the rock of the assumption implicit in it that I have already identified myself in terms of my relation to my own body—what, so it is put, 'is the word *my* doing in this explanation'? 'Uniqueness of the body does not guarantee uniqueness of the Cartesian soul.' I do not know whom Strawson believes he is tilting against here, it could hardly be Descartes himself. He certainly did not claim to know himself in terms of any relation to his own or any other body. His well-known contention is that consciousness of oneself is prior to any awareness of the external world. If he, or someone else defending substantially the same position, claimed to know his own existence, and to distinguish between himself and others, on the basis of his special relation to his own body the argument would certainly involve the absurdity[1] of assuming at the start a knowledge of the self which is also alleged to be known only through a special relation to a particular body. This is not, however, an absurdity of which Strawson's opponents are guilty— it is a Cartesian man of straw set up as a sitting target. The 'my' gets into the real argument on the basis of one's experience of oneself as a conscious being, and if Strawson wants to argue that this cannot be allowed independently of the special relation to bodies for which he holds a brief, then that has to be established on its own account and cannot be presupposed in an argument that is meant to support it.

In the second supplementary argument, Strawson again presents the alternative to his own position in another very misleading way. He declares that, whereas we should ascribe states of consciousness and corporeal entities to '*the very same things*', 'we are tempted to think of a person as a sort of compound of two kinds of subjects: a subject of experiences (a pure consciousness, an ego), on the one hand, and a subject of corporeal attributes on the other. Many questions arise when we think in this way',[2] and in seeking to cope with them we are 'apt to change from the picture of two subjects to the picture of one subject and one non-subject'.[3] I find it again hard to discover where this movement of thought is in fact found. Who are the philosophers who start in this way with the idea of two subjects? Is not the

---

[1] Ascribed also, we have seen, with more plausibility to the 'no ownership theory'.

[2] P. 102.   [3] P. 102.

reference always and from the start to one subject and one non-subject, although these are not quite the terms I should like to use? I certainly ascribe corporeal attributes to my body, but it is only in a highly elliptical sense that this may be described as ascribing them to myself. My body is not strictly myself, or some part of me. It is something to which I am very specially related, no more. One does not think of it as a subject, it is just not a starter as a candidate for the status of 'ego' or 'subject' as the terms are used in the phrase 'subject of experiences', and if the contrast of subject and non-subject is not to be understood in this way Strawson gives us no indication how then it is to be understood.[1] He simply repeats his earlier argument against the notion of a subject of experiences as such. 'For', he observes, 'there could never be any question of assigning an experience, as such, to any subject other than oneself; and therefore never any question of assigning it to oneself either, never any question of ascribing it to a subject at all. So the concept of the pure individual consciousness—the pure ego—is a concept that cannot exist; or, at least, cannot exist as a primary concept[2] in terms of which the concept of a person can be explained or analysed.'[3] But this is a reaffirmation of the original argument, and if the additional argument presupposes the earlier one, what point is there in the reference to the 'two subjects' and so on beyond saddling those who sympathize with Descartes with an impossible, and perhaps ridiculous, position very far removed from what they really maintain?

The core of Strawson's own position is well exhibited in the account which he gives, in illustration of his main thesis, of the concept of depression. I may feel depressed and I may behave in a depressed way. The behaviour, we are inclined to say, can be observed but not felt and the feeling can only be felt. There seems thus to be 'room here to drive in a logical wedge'.[4] But Strawson contends that in fact the concept of depression must cover both what is felt by me and what is observed by others. 'X's depression *is* something, one and the same thing, which is felt, but not observed, by X, and observed, but not felt, by others

---

[1] It has been put to me that he is thinking of a logical or grammatical subject. But clearly this would not serve his purpose at all, and the phrase he uses is 'subject of experiences'.
[2] There is no real concession here.   [3] P. 102.   [4] P. 108.

than X.'[1] This argument, I must confess, I find very mystifying. It is true that for rough-and-ready requirements of every day we can say that we observe the depression which X feels. But this, for a philosophical purpose, allows of further analysis and much needs it. What we strictly observe is the physical behaviour of X, his demeanour and so on, and we infer his sadness from this. His sadness does not belong to his behaviour in the sense of that which we can strictly be said to observe. We observe the physical movements and infer from these the further different process of X's feeling sad. The logical wedge is unavoidable, and it only seems hard to drive because it is obscured in the language we use for ordinary purposes which do not require special heed to the distinction in question. Unhappily, it is to language that Strawson wishes to appeal, the linguistic convention becomes the head of the corner in his argument and is made to bear the weight of all the far-reaching contentions he makes in his book. 'To refuse to accept this' (the argument I have just reproduced as he puts it) is, he adds, 'to refuse to accept the *structure* of the language in which we talk about depression. That is, in a sense, all right. One might give up talking or devise, perhaps, a different structure in terms of which to soliloquize. What is not all right is simultaneously to pretend to accept that structure and to refuse to accept it; i.e. to couch one's rejection in the language of that structure.'[2] This may not appear to be quite what was meant by the appeal to ordinary language, but is there any difference of substance here between the old linguistic veto and the new?

In the closing stage of his discussion of 'persons' Strawson turns to the 'residual perplexity of why, in view of his thesis, we ascribe to persons predicates implying states of consciousness at all. He does not claim to give an exhaustive answer but only to indicate the main clue. It is found in the nature of predicates 'which involve doing something'—going for a walk, coiling a rope. These predicates have the 'interesting characteristic' that 'one does not, in general, ascribe them to others on the strength of observation. But, in the case of these predicates, one feels minimal reluctance to concede that what is ascribed in these two different ways is the same. This is because of the marked dominance of a fairly definite pattern of bodily movement in what they ascribe, and the marked absence of any distinctive experience.'[3]

[1] P. 109. [2] P. 109. [3] P. 111.

There seems thus to be a case, our own, where we learn about 'the bodily movement' without either observation or private experiences. This releases 'us from the idea that the only things we can know about without observation or inference, or both, are private experiences; we can know, without telling by either of these means, about the present and future movements of a body'.[1] This, again, seems to me highly questionable. In the first place, do I ever strictly know that I am going for a walk without observation? I do know without observation that it is my intention to walk, but do I ever know that I am actually managing to do so without noting the position of my limbs and so forth? On the other hand, do I learn about my intention without living through the experience of intending? But what follows if we allow Strawson his point? It follows for him that, in the case of bodily movement we have something which can be known by observation and also without observation, and from this it is deduced that in observing the bodily movement of others we 'see such movements as *actions*',[2] the force of this being, apparently, that in observing the actions of others we observe what they themselves know without observation. But again we must ask what is meant by 'see' in this argument. All we strictly see or observe is the physical movement, and we then learn about the private intention by inference from what we observe. There is nothing in the situation to suggest that there is some one thing which is both visible movement and intention.

On these slender bases, and by tortuous arguments which overlook fundamental distinctions which we need to draw, Strawson sets up his final conclusion. It is that his 'remarks are not intended to suggest how the "problem of other minds" could be solved, or our beliefs about others given a general philosophical "justification". I have already argued that such a "solution" or "justification" is impossible, that the demand for it cannot be coherently stated.'[3] Implicit in this wholesale disposal of 'the familiar philosophical difficulties' is the further notion that just as we dispose of the usual distinction between mind and body, so we might also find the distinction between self and others not quite as ultimate as we are apt to assume. A 'technique' is available by which we might 'construct the idea of a special kind of social world in which the concept of an individual

[1] P. 111.   [2] P. 112.   [3] P. 112.

person is replaced by that of a group'.[1] We do already speak of groups of people engaged in corporate activities. Strawson does not develop this hint, but the mention of it is ominous indication of where we end when, in seeking to understand human life, we resort to techniques and linguistic procedures which do not take close account of what we find the facts about ourselves to be in our own experiences. Strawson says that those who find the idea of group personality absurd show none the less that they know quite well what it means. But do they show that they understand more than the *metaphorical* notion of group personality and the usefulness of this in certain legal and similar contexts?[2] The distinctness of persons seems to me ultimate, and while I cannot state the case for it here, I should like to express my conviction that few notions have done greater harm in politics or theology than that of group or corporate personality taken strictly. Recent history, in matters of thought and practice, provides abundant and appalling support for this conviction. It behoves us therefore to consider carefully how we build when we sweep aside, on flimsy and highly dogmatic grounds, the distinctions which men have usually found deep and important in their attempt to make sense of themselves and their situation.

NOTE

Mr Strawson refers also, very briefly, to the possibility of disembodied existence. He seems disposed (not, it seems to me, at all consistently with his main arguments) to allow this in an 'attenuated vicarious' form restricted to memories of present existence and 'interest in the human affairs of which he is a mute and invisible witness. . . . In proportion as the memories fade, and this vicarious living palls, to that degree his concept of himself as an individual becomes attenuated. At the limit of attenuation there is, *from the point of view of his survival as an individual*, no difference between continuance of experience and its cessation' (p. 116). This would hardly content the religious believer, or anyone else who is seriously concerned about survival. Strawson adds

[1] P. 113.

[2] In any case, to understand roughly what is meant by a theory is not tantamount to endorsing it. Or is the 'short way' with the philosophical dissenter to become now very short indeed? Thus: if I understand my opponent's view I concede it, if I do not I am not entitled to criticize it.

that 'the orthodox have wisely insisted on the resurrection of the body'. I much doubt in fact whether they have done so in senses which Strawson would intend, and the matter is certainly too complicated to be disposed of in a somewhat cryptic allusion. The believer should in any case be wary how he accepts advice from quarters very alien to his own. This I shall not pursue further. But there is one point I should like to mention.

It is that, in discussing these questions, closer heed should be paid to a distinction between partial and absolute disembodied existence. In the latter case there would be nothing even resembling bodily existence and perception. There could be many varieties of the earlier case, and there is no obvious reason why survival, if accepted, should not be one of them. But the other possibility should not be ruled out. Obvious difficulties here would be identity and communication, and of these, as I understand personality, the latter would be much the more formidable. A possible solution might be in terms of significant patterns of unexpected changes in our own thoughts which might warrant their ascription to influence exercised by some other mind. But the religious person will remember that he is dealing here with matters affected in some ways by the radical mystery of God and our dependence on Him. His faith is certainly not upset but rather strengthened by the thought that 'it has not yet been disclosed what we shall be'. If the body enters into his expectations will it not be a 'spiritual body'? That would take us very far from Strawson's M-predicates involving, as we are expressly told, a 'physical situation' (p. 102).

CHAPTER XVIII

PHILOSOPHY AND LANGUAGE[1]

A. J. Ayer

Wykeham Professor of Logic in the University of Oxford

Oxford philosophy has changed very much in the course of the present century. In so far as it has changed for the better, a large proportion of the credit must go to my predecessor in this Chair, Professor H. H. Price. Certainly the philosophers of my generation are very greatly in his debt. It is now nearly thirty years since I listened, as an undergraduate, to his lectures on *Perception*. Professor Price was, and is, an extremely good lecturer, but more than the form, it was the matter of those lectures that excited us. In the sombre philosophical climate of the Oxford of that time, here was a bold attempt to let in air and light: a theory of perception in which the principles of British empiricism were developed with a rigour and attention to detail which they had in that context never yet received. The book which grew out of the lectures remains a classic in its field. It is true that there has been a reaction against its doctrines. The theory took sense-data very seriously, and the prestige of sense-data is no longer what it was: Professor Price himself has wavered in his loyalty to them. Nevertheless the use that he then made of them enabled us to obtain a much clearer grasp of the problems which they were designed to meet. There may be better ways of solving these problems, though I am not at all sure that they have yet been found, but hardly a more effective way of bringing them to light.

In his more recent work, including his book on *Thinking and Experience*, Professor Price has addressed himself always to difficult and important questions, and he has treated them with the open-mindedness and the fertility of invention which are characteristic of him. I hope it will not be thought impertinent if I say that one of his great virtues as a philosopher is that he does not suffer from an over-dose of common sense. He is

[1] Inaugural Lecture delivered before the University of Oxford on November 3, 1960, and published by the Oxford University Press.

inclined to think that the world is a much stranger place than we ordinarily take it to be, so that even the most fanciful theories about it may be found to contain an element of truth. This results in a width of philosophical sympathy which I wish that I could emulate. But this tolerance is never lax; the theories are subjected to a very rigorous scrutiny. Neither is there anything slipshod about Professor Price's methods. He does not deal in riddles. Whatever the subject of his investigation, his treatment of it is thoroughly systematic. With his manifest enjoyment of philosophy, there goes a belief in its seriousness and importance. I can only hope that I can prove myself worthy of his example.

I

It is notorious that philosophers disagree not only about the truth of particular theories, or the answers to specific problems, but about the character and purpose of their whole activity. To some extent this is due to the vagueness with which the word 'philosophy' is used. In a bookseller's catalogue the works which are listed under this heading may legitimately range from a treatise on formal logic to an assemblage of copy-book maxims, or a romantic disquisition on the destiny of man. But there is more at issue here than a question of vagueness. It cannot always be assumed that when philosophers disagree about the nature of their subject they are merely contending for the possession of a title. For even when they are addressing themselves to the same questions, to the conflict of realism and idealism, for example, or the problem of negation, or the investigation of the nature of truth, they may still take very different views of the character of these problems, of the kind of answer that they call for, and of the standards of proof which the answers are required to meet.

In recent years, however, there has been a tendency, at least in English-speaking countries, for this range of disagreement to be narrowed. There has been talk of a revolution in philosophy: and one of its main results is thought to be that philosophers now take a more sophisticated view of their own procedures: they have become more clearly aware of what they are trying to do. The conclusion which they have reached is that philosophy is, in some special sense, an inquiry into language. How this inquiry is to be conducted, what purposes it serves, how its progress is assessed are questions which still need to be clarified. We shall in fact see that diverse answers can be given to them. But however uncertain they may be about the details, there is now a fair measure of agreement among philosophers that theirs is what is technically called a second-order subject. They do not set out to describe, or even to explain, the world, still less to change it. Their concern is only with the way in which we speak about the world. Philosophy, it has been said, is talk about talk.

This conception of philosophy is derived from various sources. In part, it is a legacy of logical positivism; it owes something to the example of G. E. Moore, still more, perhaps, to the later teachings of Wittgenstein. But these influences work in rather different ways. The logical positivists were anxious first of all to purify philosophy of metaphysics: it would then be left free to develop as a branch of logic. The language in which they were interested was the language of science, and the rôle which they assigned to the philosopher was mainly that of explicating terms which belonged to scientific methodology; he was to bring the resources of modern formal logic to bear upon such concepts as those of testability, or confirmation, or probability, or truth. He could also serve the cause of science in more specific ways, by exhibiting the structure of scientific theories, defining the expressions which occurred in them, and showing how they were formally related. If he had the technical ability to remodel scientific language, whether by redefining terms in current use or by introducing new expressions which would be scientifically fruitful, so much the better. Thus philosophy was seen as merging into science. Only the methodological problems were strictly its own perquisite: and it might be expected that they would soon be solved.

The part played by G. E. Moore is less straightforward. He himself was always careful to say that the practice of what he called analysis was only one of the functions of philosophy. Moreover, he did not conceive of it as an inquiry into language. It was concerned, in his view, not with linguistic expressions, but rather with the concepts, or propositions, or facts, for which they stood. Nevertheless, the reduction of philosophy to an inquiry into language was a reasonable consequence of the position which he held. It could be traced indirectly to his defence of common sense. For if he was right in claiming that he knew for certain that 'the common-sense view of the world' was wholly true, it followed that the propositions which comprised it were not vulnerable to philosophy: since they were known to be true no philosophical argument could show them to be false. Neither did they have to appeal to philosophy for any warrant of their truth. Admittedly, Moore did try to give a proof that there is an external world, a belief which undoubtedly figures in the common-sense view: but since his proof consisted merely in deducing that there were external objects from the fact of his knowing that he had two hands, it did no more than underline the point that the common-sense view of the world could safely be left to justify itself. But if this applies to the empirical propositions which are accepted by common sense, there seems to be no reason why it should not also apply to the empirical hypotheses of science, or to the formal propositions of mathematics and logic. They too have their appropriate standards of proof; and when they satisfy these standards they are accepted without being made to earn a philosophical certificate. Neither, on this view, can there be a philosophical foundation for any of our normative judgements; for the upshot of Moore's 'naturalistic fallacy' is that judgements of value are autonomous. But if all these domains of discourse are closed to the philosopher, in the sense that it is not his province to decide the validity of any of the propositions that occur in them, what is there left for him to do? The answer is that he can occupy himself with the analysis of these propositions. It is not his business to tell us whether they are true, but it is his business to tell us what they mean.

To conceive of philosophy as the practice of analysis is not, however, necessarily to regard it as an inquiry into language. It would seem that Moore himself was inclined to reify meanings: the concepts or propositions which philosophers sought to analyse were given the status of non-natural objects. No doubt it was not possible to apprehend them unless one understood the appropriate words, but this applied equally to many of the objects of the sciences. A philosopher who had no mastery of language would be as helpless as a mathematician who could not handle numerals: but just as the mathematician was not concerned with numerals as such but rather with the numbers which they represented, so the philosopher's command of language was merely a necessary means to the investigation of the objective properties of concepts. If this was Moore's view, it was one that he shared with philosophers of other schools. It is found among the followers of Cook Wilson, with their talk of apprehending necessary connexions between universals, and also among the phenomenologists who would make philosophy consist in what they call the intuition of essences: for these essences turn out to be meanings, regarded as objective entities.

This view of meaning is still very widely held; but it has been locally discredited through the influence of Wittgenstein. The turning-point was the shift in Wittgenstein's philosophy from the metaphor of treating words as pictures to the metaphor of treating words as tools. Linguistic signs are meaningful, but there are no such things as meanings. Instead of looking upon the meaning of a word as something which it acquires by its relation to an object, we are to content ourselves with asking how the word is used. I shall argue later on that this identification of meaning with use is neither so radical nor so fruitful a step as is commonly supposed. It is doubtful even if it does, in any interesting sense, turn questions of meaning into questions of language; but, because it is thought to do so, it completes this line of development of the notion of linguistic philosophy.

There is another important point in which Wittgenstein's idea of philosophy differed from Moore's. Though he was open-minded about questions of method, Moore clearly looked upon philosophical analysis as a source of knowledge. He believed that it issued in propositions which were true or false. To take only one example, he thought it certainly true that a proposition like 'this is a human hand' had for its subject some sense-datum, and he thought that the question what, in such a case, was being asserted of the sense-datum was one to which there was a valid answer. He did not think that anybody knew what the answer was, but he firmly believed that it was ascertainable. Once it was ascertained we should have discovered the analysis of an important class of propositions about physical objects. This would be a most valuable item in our stock of philosophical truths. For Wittgenstein, on the other hand, the idea that there could be a stock of philosophical truths was dangerously naïve. He thought that people made difficulties for themselves by failing to understand how their language worked. This led them to raise problems to which they could see no issue, to construct dilemmas which they could not resolve. In their efforts to escape from these perplexities they relapsed into talking nonsense. The remedy was to trace the muddle to its source by exposing the linguistic misconception from which it arose: and this was the rôle assigned to the enlightened philosopher. Thus the success of a philosophical inquiry would consist, not in the acquisition of a fresh piece of knowledge, but rather in the disappearance of the problem on which it was directed. We should have been made to see that our puzzlement was gratuitous.

This is an accurate account of what Wittgenstein mainly says about philosophy in his later works, but the implication that he came to look upon it merely as a form of intellectual therapy is in some degree misleading. For it must be remarked that the therapy takes the form of argument. If we fall into confusion through misunderstanding the logic of our language, it has to be shown that the assumptions which we have made about it are mistaken: and the statement that they are mistaken is itself a philosophical thesis. If it is true, it is an addition to our knowledge. In such cases, indeed, the thesis is negative in form. We are told that a view which had seemed to us plausible is false. But the theses are not always negative. It is hardly possible to say what the logic of our language is not, without making some suggestion as to what it is. Some analysis is offered of the meaning of those types of expression that are thought most likely to deceive. It is not called analysis, and it is not conducted in a systematic fashion; to a very considerable extent the reader is left to draw the moral for himself. The point is that there are morals to be drawn. What their nature is and how much they really have to do with language are among the questions which we now have to examine.

II

It should already be clear that talk of linguistic philosophy does not take us very far. The activities which the term can be made to cover are much too disparate. Not only is there a distinction to be made between the formal and the informal methods of approach, but the informal methods, in particular, comprise a number of different procedures. If I concentrate mainly upon them, it is not that I think that the use of formal methods is uninteresting or unfruitful; it is rather that the aims which it can be expected to achieve are much more easily discernible. It applies to languages of which the syntax and, if necessary, the semantics can be formalized; that is, to languages with regard to which it is possible to specify what combinations of signs count as sentences of the language; which of these sentences are derivable from one another; and, in the case where the language can be used to make empirical statements, what are the observable states of affairs which certain of these sentences designate. For a natural language, such as English, these conditions cannot be met; perhaps not even in principle, and certainly not in practice. The forms of its sentences are too multifarious and too elastic; the rules of derivation are not delimited; neither are the observable states of affairs which its most simple sentences can be used to designate. Nevertheless fragments of it can be formalized; or at any rate models can be made in which certain features of it are ideally reconstructed. By this means light can be thrown on such matters as the scaffolding of scientific theories, and the methodological conditions which they are required to satisfy.

The merits, as well as the limitations, of this way of doing philosophy can best be brought out by considering what is perhaps its most conspicuous achievement: Tarski's formal treatment of the concept of truth.[1] For various reasons, including the threat of the semantic paradoxes, Tarski makes no attempt to define the term 'truth' as it is used in any natural language. His much quoted formula, 's is true in L if and only if p', which yields such sentences as ' "snow is white" is true in English if and only if snow is white', was never meant for a general definition. It was put forward rather as a condition of adequacy which any definition of truth for a given language had to meet. The definition must be such that every sentence which was obtained from the formula by putting a sentence of the language in the place of 'p' and the name of that sentence in the place of 's' should follow from it. Tarski sought to show that definitions which satisfied this requirement could be supplied for formalized languages of a special type. The restrictions which he had to place upon them in order to maintain consistency are very significant but an account of them is not necessary for our present purpose.

[1] A. Tarski, 'The Concept of Truth in Formalized Languages': reprinted in *Logic, Semantics, Metamathematics*.

The example which Tarski chose to illustrate his thesis was that of the language of the class-calculus. His method was to specify, in a formal way, the combinations of signs belonging to the language that were to be taken as its sentential functions, and then to define, within this universe of discourse, the notion of the satisfaction of a sentential function. This was achieved by specifying the relations of class-inclusion which the values of the variables in the elementary functions had to bear to one another in order that these functions should be satisfied, and then by defining the satisfaction of more complex functions recursively. Now sentential functions are not sentences: they become sentences only when the free variables which they contain are quantified, or replaced by constants: but sentences can be treated as limiting cases of sentential functions with the peculiarity that they are satisfied by every relevant object or by none. The way was then laid open to defining a true sentence of this language as any sentence which is satisfied by every infinite sequence of classes.

On its own ground I do not think this definition can be faulted. It has been criticized for making truth a predicate of sentences instead of propositions: but the only serious objection to making truth a predicate of sentences is that token reflexive sentences, sentences which contain pronouns, or spatial or temporal demonstratives, or tensed verbs, may have different truth-values on different occasions of their use. Since none of the sentences in a formalized language, such as that of the class-calculus, are token reflexive, this objection does not here arise. But we do not ordinarily talk of sentences as being true. If anyone insists, even in this case, on speaking with the vulgar, his pedantry is easy to accommodate. All we need do is to say that a proposition of the class-calculus is true if it is expressed by a sentence which is true in Tarski's sense. The reason against doing this is not only that it is unnecessary, but that it is methodologically out of place. Truth is being defined for a language of which the sentences can be formally specified, but what it is for a sentence to express a proposition has yet to be made clear.

But even when we allow that, in cases of this type, truth can legitimately be ascribed to sentences, it is not at all evident that Tarski's achievement has much to do with any question of language. What he has primarily done is to exhibit the structure of a logical theory, with reference to its truth-conditions. This has a bearing upon language only in the trivial sense in which the description of any theory may have a bearing upon language. The account of what would make the theory true can always be represented as an account of the truth-conditions of the sentences in which the theory can be expressed. There is, however, a wider implication with regard to what is meant by truth in general. The moral which can be drawn from Tarski's definition, as well as from the schema which supplies the definition with its test of adequacy, is that to establish that a sentence is true amounts to the same as establishing the sentence itself. This means that there is, as Ramsey put it, 'no separate problem of truth',[1] but only the problem of assertion. If we understand how sentences can be used to refer to facts, and how we are justified in accepting them, we do not have to worry further about the nature of truth. The question with which philosophers have really been concerned when they have tried to develop 'theories of truth' are questions of testability and meaning. It is because it leaves these questions unanswered that they have mostly been dissatisfied with Tarski's account. But this merely shows that when they asked 'What is truth?' they were not looking for a formal definition. In that line there is nothing better than Tarski has to give.

Very much the same applies to the attempts that have been made, by Carnap and others, to develop formal theories of confirmation. It is possible and useful to work out a system for measuring the degree to which the content of one proposition is included in that of another: and it can then be stipulated that a proposition is to be said to confirm any proposition the range of which is included in its own. But if anyone is worried by Hume's problem of showing how any inductive argument can be justified, this procedure will not help him. Neither will it protect us from Goodman's paradox which purports to show that the evidence which we naturally take as confirming a given hypothesis always confirms some contrary hypothesis to an equal degree.[2] We may escape from this difficulty, as Goodman does, into a form of pragmatism; but a move of this kind is quite different in character from those that are made within a formal theory.

[1] F. P. Ramsey, 'Facts and Propositions', *The Foundations of Mathematics*, p. 142.
[2] Nelson Goodman, *Fact, Fiction and Forecast*, chapter 3.

Once more it does not appear that this group of problems has very much to do with language, except in the obvious sense that when it comes to particular instances the question whether one proposition confirms another depends upon their meaning.

A characteristic of what I have been calling the formal approach is its reliance on the symbolism of mathematical logic; but the utility of such an artificial symbolism extends beyond its application to formalized languages. It can be employed in other fields to secure a neatness and precision which is not within the resources of ordinary prose. This holds especially for attempts at what is known as reductive analysis. From the early Greeks, philosophers have been concerned with the question of what there really is: but in more recent times this mainly takes the form of trying to show that something, which there appears to be, is not. Thus it has been alleged that there are no such things as numbers but only numerals, no such things as propositions but only sentences, no such things as classes but only individuals, no abstract entities of any kind but only concrete ones, no such things as minds but only bodies, or conversely no such things as bodies but only minds. Nowadays claims of this kind are usually made in a more sophisticated way. 'Points are really classes of volumes.' 'Material things are logical constructions out of sense-data.' This brings out more clearly what issue is involved in these denials of reality. The thesis is always that some category of objects is dispensable. It can be presented as a linguistic thesis to the effect that sentences which contain expressions of one type can be replaced by sentences which contain expressions of another; that, for example, anything that we want to say about numbers can be rephrased as a statement about numerals, that talk about classes is shorthand for talk about individuals, that to speak of mental states or processes is a way of speaking about physical behaviour. The assumption is that certain types of entity are philosophically suspect, and the purpose is to show that references to such entities are nevertheless innocuous; they can be construed as disguised references to entities which are relatively less problematic.

Now clearly the best way to make a point of this kind good is actually to carry out the reduction: to supply a set of rules for transforming sentences of one type into those of another. And it is here that it may be found necessary to have recourse to an artificial symbolism. In the first place it has to be made clear what type of reduction is being attempted; whether, for example, the replacement for a given sentence has to be synonymous with it, and in that case what are the criteria for synonymity; or whether some weaker condition will suffice; such as its being possible to correlate one 'language' with another in such a way that corresponding sentences have, if not necessarily the same meaning, at least the same truth-value. Whatever condition is chosen the task of showing that it can be satisfied will not be simple. Even to sketch a method of eliminating abstract entities will be found to require more powerful tools than are available to those who insist on remaining within the confines of ordinary languages. This applies also to phenomenalism. The view that statements about physical objects must somehow be reducible to statements about sense-data has been fairly widely held; but there have been very few experiments in carrying out the transformation. One reason for this is the lack of the requisite terms at the sensory level. If the phenomenalist's claim is to have any chance of being vindicated, a 'language of appearance' must be artificially constructed.

But while the use of formal techniques may be helpful, or even essential, to the pursuit of the stated aims of reductive analysis, the interest of this type of philosophy lies elsewhere. There is no question here of supplying definitions, or elaborating concepts, which will be of scientific value; it is not claimed that talk about sense-data is more serviceable than the talk about physical objects which it is intended to replace; there is no practical advantage in making statements about individuals do the work of statements about classes. The reason why this effort is made to eliminate certain types of entity is that it is thought that they cannot be real, or at least that their reality is dubious; and the ground for this is that they are not observable. This may seem an odd reason for wishing to dispense with physical objects, but we have here to reckon with the admittedly doubtful assumption that only sense-data are directly perceived. Thus the point of reductive analysis is that it is the product of a radical empiricism. It has a linguistic aspect in so far as it seeks to show that one sort of expression can perform the office of another, but this is the outcome not of any dispassionate study of language but of an *a priori* conception of reality. It is assumed that significant discourse must in the end refer to a limited set of objects, because these are the only objects that there can really be.

III

Reductive analysis has now gone rather out of fashion. This is partly because philosophers have become unwilling to commit themselves openly to its presuppositions, or indeed to acknowledge presuppositions of any kind, partly that the proffered analyses were not convincing. Even in the cases where it seemed obvious that the reduction must be feasible, such as the transformation of statements about nations into statements about persons, or that of statements about propositions into statements about sentences, the rules for making exact translations were not forthcoming. Perhaps some weaker type of reduction was called for; but it was not made clear what form it should take, or even what purpose it would serve. As a result, the suspicion grew that this sort of analysis was a waste of time. Why should we labour to replace one type of expression by another? If we find it convenient to talk about propositions, or classes, or any other sort of abstract entity, why should we struggle to eliminate them? It is not as if we had any difficulty in understanding what was said about them. But are we not then overcrowding our picture of the universe? Can we really believe in the existence of such Platonic entities? Rightly or wrongly this bogey has lost its power to scarify. If the objection is not simply ignored, it is met cavalierly with a plea of metaphysical innocence.

The trouble with the reductionists, it is now maintained, is that they had too little respect for language. Though they did their best to torture it on their Procrustean bed, it proved too strong for them: they were unable to obtain the avowals that they wanted. What we must do instead is to approach language without preconceptions, to see how it actually does work.

But why should this be of any philosophical interest? One answer, which we have already noted, is that it will free us from certain deep perplexities for which our misinterpretations of language are responsible. Another more positive answer is that a careful examination of the workings of our language will give us an insight into the structure of the world which it describes. Let us now try to see how far these claims are justified.

The principal method of catching language at work is to study examples of the ways in which certain expressions are actually used. There are, however, significantly different manners of putting this into practice. One is to take a group of kindred terms and try, by giving examples, to show exactly how they differ in meaning. Thus one may inquire how being disingenuous differs from being uncandid, and how both of them differ from being insincere. Is it really true, as the dictionary says, that 'disingenuous' is the opposite of 'ingenuous'? Surely to deny that a remark is ingenuous and to assert that it is disingenuous is not to say the same thing. But then what is the opposite of 'ingenuous'? 'Sophisticated'? 'Uncandid'? Perhaps there is no single word. With skill and patience we may be able to construct examples which will make these nuances clear.

But what shall we have gained? If it is said that knowledge of this kind is to be valued for its own sake, well and good. Certainly the work of the lexicographer is neither trivial nor easy. But how far does this sort of inquiry take us towards the solution of anything that has ever been regarded as a philosophical problem? No doubt my actual example was not especially favourable. Moral philosophers might indeed be interested in the question of sincerity, but hardly in determining the different types or shades of insincerity that might be denoted by different English words. But are there much better examples to be found? It has indeed been claimed that examining the use of words like 'inadvertently', 'deliberately', 'mistakenly', 'intentionally' would help us to deal more effectively with the problem of free-will, perhaps even to dispose of the problem altogether. The idea is that we can learn in this way what are the circumstances in which we credit people with responsibility for their acts and on what grounds we are ready to absolve them; and it is agreed that the extent to which they are responsible is the measure of the extent to which they are free. But while this is, no doubt, a useful way of making clear how we do in fact proceed with the ascription of responsibility, it touches only lightly on the problem of free-will. For those who are troubled by this problem are perfectly well aware that we are in fact trained to distinguish between the cases in which an agent can 'help himself', and those in which he cannot. Their trouble is that they do not see how this distinction can be justified. If all human actions are causally explicable, is there not a very good sense in which no one can ever help doing what he does? Now it may well be that this reasoning is muddled; and if so that the muddle can be shown up. But then some other method must be chosen; it is no answer to the denier of free-will merely to pin-point ways of using language in which the falsity of his position is already presupposed.

But is it not an answer? Surely the mere fact that we are able to employ a certain type of expression in ordinary speech is a proof that it has application. If it is ever correct to say that anyone acts freely, then he does act freely. For what can it be to act freely if not to behave in a way which satisfies the conditions under which the expression 'acting freely' is properly applied? If an expression X is correctly used to apply to just those things that have the property Y, then for anything to have the property Y it must be sufficient that X can be correctly applied to it.

This argument is plausible, but I believe that it is unsound. It overlooks the fact that there is no sharp dividing line between the description of facts and their interpretation; even at the level of common sense our ordinary language will be found to carry a considerable load of theory. One may allow that an expression is being used correctly if it is applied to a situation which has certain characteristic features, but one is not therefore bound to accept the interpretation of those features which the use of the expression tacitly implies. Thus in a society which believes in witchcraft it is perfectly correct in certain circumstances to say that a person is bewitched: the symptoms which are commonly regarded as the sign of demonic possession may be quite clearly marked: it does not follow, however, that demons really are at work. In the same way, when there is evidence that a man has deliberately done whatever he did, that he was in full possession of his faculties, that he was not under constraint, it may be correct to say that he acted freely and it may be in accordance with common practice to hold him responsible for what he has done. But if the implication is that his action was not causally determined, one may consistently reject it; and the way in which one expresses this rejection may be to say that the man was not really free at all. I do not say that this is the implication, or even that if it were, it would not be true. My point is only that this is the question on which the dispute about free-will has mainly turned; and that it cannot be settled merely by giving a careful and accurate account of customary usage.

The argument which we have been discussing has come to be known as the argument from paradigm cases. It is used as a weapon against philosophical scepticism in the interests of common sense. Thus when a philosopher says, as many have, that it is not certain that there are physical objects, he is asked how he thinks that words like 'chair' and 'table' came into common use. Did he not himself learn the use of these words by being shown specimens of what they stood for? Surely then the undoubted fact that we constantly came upon situations to which such words apply is an incontestable proof that physical objects exist? This is, indeed, as favourable an example as one could hope to find, but even so the argument is not conclusive. The question is how much our use of these words is taken to involve. If, for example, it commits us to the theory that there are things which exist independently of being perceived, then a philosopher may consistently doubt or reject this proposition, even though he admits that there are situations to which the words that are commonly taken to stand for physical objects are properly applied. People have been trained to use these words, and do correctly use them, when they have certain perceptions; but this is no guarantee that the interpretation of these perceptions, which is involved in the claim that there are physical objects, is itself correct. Again, I am not saying that such a philosopher would be right. The arguments which lead him to doubt or deny that anything can exist without being perceived may be demonstrably fallacious. All I am saying is that he is not refuted merely by the fact that words like 'chair' and 'table' have a customary use.

The reason why he is not refuted is that his doubts bear upon what Moore would call a question of analysis, rather than a question of fact. It is a matter of fact that the criteria by which we actually determine that there are such things as chairs and tables are very frequently satisfied; and if the statement that there are physical objects is construed simply as a consequence of this fact, it is not open to question on philosophical grounds. On the other hand, it may be construed not just as claiming that these criteria are often satisfied but as affirming the common-sense view of what this satisfaction comes to; and in that case it is entirely open to philosophical argument. When it is a matter of interpretation, there is nothing sacrosanct about common sense.

The difficulty here is that the distinction between questions of fact and questions of analysis is not so easily drawn as most philosophers now seem to think. If one takes the view that ordinary language is perfectly in order, one will assign to the statements, which it is used to make, only such interpretations as will allow them in many cases to be true. Thus a sophisticated behaviourist need not deny that there are what are ordinarily classified as mental facts: he does not have to claim that we are wrong in supposing that we think and feel. We are not wrong, he may say, because all that we really mean by this, though we may not know it, is that we are disposed to behave in certain ways. If our ordinary language were thoroughly animistic, then, even assuming behaviourism to be false, we should not be wrong in personifying all the works of nature, or at any rate not wrong on any question of fact; for what we should really mean by this talk would be exactly what we now really mean by talking about physical objects. If primitive people who do speak in this way make any mistake at all it is a mistake in analysis: they do not understand the logic of their language.

I think that this view is tenable, but it rests on a theory of meaning which its advocates commonly fail to make explicit. The theory is not new; it is summed up in the verification principle on which the logical positivists relied for their elimination of metaphysics. In very rough terms, the assumption is that the meaning of a sentence is yielded by a description of the observations which would make it true. Thus the animists' language is translatable into our own, inasmuch as the statements which it is used to express are verified by the same observations as serve to verify the statements which we make about physical objects. The fact that they believe themselves to be talking about spirits merely shows that they are poor philosophers. Their language is burdened with metaphysical trappings from which ours is taken to be free. If we are more tolerant, we may just say that they have a different conceptual system: but the difference is then a difference in form and not in factual content.

For my part I have no wish to disown the verification principle, though it suffers from a vagueness which it has not yet been found possible to eradicate. I doubt, however, if it is a wholly effective means of distinguishing questions of analysis of interpretation from questions of fact. The trouble lies with the assumption that it is possible to supply a neutral record of facts, which is free from any taint of theory; a common bedrock for divergent interpretations. But this is highly dubious. It is claimed, for example, that a naïve realist and a follower of Berkeley do not differ with regard to any matter of fact. Whatever they may respectively think that they mean by their perceptual judgements, they accept the same observable states of affairs as showing them to be true. But what are these observable states of affairs? The Berkeleian describes them in a way that the naïve realist finds unintelligible: the naïve realist describes them in a way that the Berkeleian might regard as begging the question against him. It is common ground, at least for those who accept the verification principle, that in the normal way, when a man sets out to describe what he perceives, he manages to assert something which is true; but what this is may be a matter for dispute. It has been thought that it could first be stated and then analysed; but it would seem that in the very attempt to state it one already commits oneself to some form of analysis.

If this is right, it appears that philosophy does after all intrude upon questions of empirical fact. Once it is established what is to count as a fact, that is, once the criteria are settled, it is an empirical and not a philosophical question whether they are satisfied. But adoption of these criteria implies the acceptance of a given conceptual system, and the appraisal of conceptual systems does fall within the province of philosophy. To maintain that ordinary language is perfectly in order is to declare oneself satisfied with the conceptual system that we actually have, or at least with that part of it which is contained in the terminology of common sense. But however well the system works on the whole, it is not immune from criticism. Even among its categorical features there may be some which prove on investigation to be ill adapted to their purpose. The concept of 'cause' is a possible example. No doubt such concepts can be reinterpreted so as to escape the objections to which they were exposed. But it does not seem plausible to maintain with respect to every such redefinition that it merely records what was intended all along.

o

IV

Not only does the verification principle play an essential part in the vindication of ordinary language; it also sustains the doctrine that the meaning of an expression is to be identified with its use. At first sight, it is by no means clear what this doctrine comes to: for a given set of words can be employed for many different purposes, to inform, to persuade, to amuse, to deceive, to threaten, to distract, sometimes simply to show off; and yet on all these occasions they may have the same meaning, The fulfilment of the purpose depends on the meaning, but it does not constitute it. Sometimes again, there may be no connexion at all between the meaning of a word and the use to which it is put, as when it is employed purely for decoration, for example as part of a *collage*. So if one is to maintain that the meaning of words consists in their use one will have to specify what sort of use this is; and the only plausible answer is that it is a matter of what they are used to signify, of what it is that they are used to name, or designate, or state, or question, or command, as the case may be. For the sake of simplicity, let us confine ourselves to the example of declarative discourse, as expressed in indicative sentences. The thesis is then that the meaning of such an indicative sentence is identical with what it is used to state.

This seems innocent enough, indeed rather too innocent: for on the face of it to say that the meaning of an indicative sentence is identical with what it is used to state is to say no more than that its meaning is what it means. The point of talking about 'use' emerges only when we go on to consider how we are supposed to determine what a given sentence states; and it is here that the principle of verification once more comes in. For the answer is that to specify the use of a sentence, in this sense, is to describe the situations to which it is applied; in other words, to describe the situations, the states of affairs, by which the statement it expresses would be verified.

The employment of this principle, in some manner or other, is characteristic of all types of informal analysis, but it can be made to operate in various ways. Thus in the work of philosophers like Wittgenstein or Ryle, no special attention is paid to niceties of language. I do not mean by this that they are not careful in their choice of words, but only that they are not concerned with discriminating shades of meaning. They approach language not in the spirit of a collector, in search of rare or interesting specimens, but rather in that of a diagnostician. They are concerned with those concepts, or families of concepts, which, for one reason or another, have given trouble to philosophers, and their aim is to dispel the confusions which have grown around them. As I said before, this aim is not merely negative: the removal of our philosophical perplexities should leave us with a better understanding of the rôles that these concepts really do fulfil; in certain cases it may even put us in a position to amend them.

The method is simply to take a new look at the facts. Thus when Ryle sets out to destroy what he regards as the myth of the ghost in the machine,[1] he tries to make us fix our attention on the actual phenomena of what is supposed to be our mental life. He asks us to consider what actually happens in typical cases when someone is acting intelligently, or working out a problem, or yielding to a motive, or doing what he wants, or in the grip of some feeling or emotion. Do we invariably find that some inner process is at work, that there is some private object or occurrence with which the intelligence, or the emotion, or the motive, or the act of will can be identified? If we do not, this is a proof that the existence of such ghostly entities is not an essential feature of these 'mental' facts. The official thesis that everything that ranks as a mental phenomenon unfolds itself upon a private stage is refuted by the production of counter-examples. Of course this is not enough to lay the ghost: it still remains possible that there are performances which do take place upon the private stage, however little part they play in what are ordinarily regarded as the principal operations of the mind. The physicalist position may also be exposed to counter-examples. But my object here is not to criticize Ryle's conclusions, but to consider the method by which they are reached.

The questions which he raises may also be put in a form which makes their character appear more linguistic. Instead of asking what actually happens when someone does, for example, act intelligently, one may ask what makes it correct to say that someone is acting intelligently: what are the typical circumstances in which we should ordinarily say that someone was yielding to such and such a motive; how do we in fact use such sentences

[1] G. Ryle, *The Concept of Mind*.

as 'he is very angry' or 'I intend to go to London tomorrow'? In this way the emphasis is apparently made to fall upon our verbal habits. But this appearance is delusive. The question is not: when do we say this rather than that; when, for example, do we say that someone intended to do something, rather than that he meant to do it, or that he designed to do it? Neither is any interest taken in the philological or social reasons that there may be for our employing a particular form of words. The question is, given that we do make statements of such and such a sort, what are the circumstances that would make them true? In short, the emphasis is not on our verbal habits themselves, but on the situations to which they are adapted. It is true that an account of the facts which verify a given statement will also be an account of the way in which the words that describe these facts are used; but it still makes a difference where the emphasis falls. The difference is between starting with the words and then looking for the facts to which to fit them, and starting with an identification of the facts and then seeing how they can best be described.

In Wittgenstein's later work there is on the face of it a much greater emphasis on language; so much so indeed that at one point he speaks of his own investigations as grammatical: philosophical problems are to be solved 'by looking into the workings of our language, and that in such a way as to make us recognize those workings in despite of an urge to misunderstand them'.[1] But when we examine how this process of looking into the workings of our language is actually conducted, we find once again that it is chiefly a matter of the meticulous inspection of a certain range of facts. When Wittgenstein, for example, asks us to consider the English word 'reading', or the German word *lesen*, he does not in fact direct our attention to the multiplicity of uses to which these words are put. We hear nothing about lip-reading, or reading fortunes, or reading the expression on a person's face. We are asked rather to consider what actually happens when, for example, someone reads a newspaper. Since reading words is more than merely looking at a series of shapes, we are inclined to say that reading consists in 'a special conscious activity of mind'.[2] But is this hypothesis really borne out by the

[1] L. Wittgenstein, *Philosophical Investigations*, i. 109.
[2] *Op. cit.*, i. 156.

facts? In reply, we are given a series of examples, some of them very subtle, the moral of which is that 'in different circumstances we apply different criteria for a person's reading'.[1] Again, this can be taken as showing that what a dictionary might represent as one particular use of the verb 'to read' is in fact a family of uses; but again this would put the emphasis in the wrong place. What is being brought to our attention is the variety of the phenomena in which reading of this sort may consist.

The effort which we are urged to make, both by Wittgenstein and Ryle, is to see the phenomena as they really are, to divest ourselves of any preconception which may lead us to distort the facts. But, as I have already tried to show, no record of the facts can be free from all interpretation. One's account of what actually happens is governed by one's idea of what is possible. To put it in linguistic terms, the way in which one construes a given type of statement depends upon one's general view of meaning. Thus when Wittgenstein declares that an inner process stands in need of outward criteria, when he denies the possibility of a private language on the ground that there can be no language without rules of which the observance can be publicly checked, he is fashioning a mould into which the facts must be made to fit. These principles are not derived from an open-minded study of the way in which the English, or the German, or any other language happens to work: they set limits to what any use of language can achieve, and so help to decree what facts are possible; for if anything is a fact it can be stated. Since they lay down what we are capable of meaning, any account of what we do mean will be expected to conform to them.

This is not in itself an objection to Wittgenstein's procedure. There must always be some method of approach. The value of the method can be tested only by its results. Here, however, there is the difficulty that the results themselves must be evaluated. If they are tested by the same criteria as are used in obtaining them, they are bound to be favourable so long as the method is consistent. But then this whole proceeding lies open to the charge of begging the question. On the other hand, it is not to be expected that one should employ any other criteria than those which from the outset have been assumed to be correct. Thus, so long as it is free from inner contradiction, it is hard to

[1] L. Wittgenstein, *op. cit.*, i. 164.

see how any philosophical thesis can be refuted: and equally hard to see how it can ever be proved. Let us take for example the thesis of physicalism; that all statements which ostensibly refer to mental states or processes are translatable into statements about physical occurrences. The obvious way to refute it is to produce a counter-example, which in this case seems quite easy. There are any number of statements about people's thoughts and sensations and feelings which appear to be logically independent of any statement about their bodily condition or behaviour. But the adherent to physicalism may not recognize these examples: he may insist that they be interpreted in accordance with his principles. He will do so not because this is the meaning that they manifestly have, but because he has convinced himself on *a priori* grounds that no other way of interpreting them is possible. Our only hope then is to make the interpretation appear so strained that the assumptions on which they rest become discredited. As for the proof of any such thesis, it rests on the absence of any refutation of this sort. So long as we cannot find any convincing counter-example, the thesis is allowed to stand. In this respect the procedure followed in philosophy is like that of the natural sciences.

I have argued that what passes for linguistic philosophy, at least as it is represented in the work of such authors as Wittgenstein and Ryle, is concerned with language only to the extent that a study of language is inseparable from a study of the facts which it is used to describe. To use a somewhat imperfect analogy, the interest lies in the photographs, and not in the mechanism of the camera by which they happen to be taken. In Wittgenstein's case, indeed, there is a predominant concern with the general problem of the way in which language is related to the things of which it speaks; but, while they are illustrated by examples, his answers to this question are not based upon the special features of any given language. They do not so much elucidate our actual uses of words as determine what uses are possible.

The aim, then, is to see the facts for what they are. Sometimes it is enough to have them simply pointed out to us, but often reasons must be supplied for thinking that a given description of them is correct. And here we may come upon a form of argument which is straightforwardly linguistic. It consists in appealing to the fact that certain combinations of words do or do not make sense. Thus when Ryle is concerned to distinguish between knowledge and belief, he points out that whereas the English word 'belief' can be qualified by adjectives like 'obstinate', 'wavering', or 'unswerving', which are also appropriate to nouns like 'loyalty' or 'addiction', this is not true of the word 'knowledge'. We say of a belief, but not of knowledge, that it is slipped into or given up: we can say of someone that he is trying to stop believing something, but not that he is trying to stop knowing something: we can ask why people believe things but not why they know them; we say 'How do you know?' but not 'How do you believe?'[1] The point of all this is to show that knowing, unlike believing, is not a disposition which is actualized in events: the possession of knowledge is an achievement; it marks a capacity for getting something right. If we recognize this we shall avoid the mistake of looking for the essence of knowledge in some special state of mind; we shall not be taken in by the philosopher's myth of there being 'acts of knowing' which mysteriously guarantee the truth or reality of the 'objects' which are known.

This appeal to what it makes sense to say is not a new device in philosophy. It goes back to the ancient Greeks. When Socrates in the *Theaetetus* is attacking the suggestion that perception is identical with knowledge, one of the arguments which Plato makes him use is that what can be said of the one cannot be said of the other. We talk of things being perceived distinctly or indistinctly, clearly or faintly, from a distance or near at hand, but these are not ways in which anything can be said to be known. The conclusion is that perception and knowledge cannot be identical.[2] It should, however, be added that while Plato is sure of this conclusion he mainly relies on other arguments to establish it. The weight which he attaches to this verbal argument seems to be relatively slight. Thus when Socrates, a little later in the dialogue, is made to deliver a speech against himself in Protagoras' name, he raises the objection that he has not dealt with Protagoras honestly. He ought to have examined more carefully the reasons which induced Protagoras to identify perception with knowledge 'instead of taking as a basis the ordinary meaning of nouns and

[1] G. Ryle, *The Concept of Mind*, p. 134.
[2] Plato, *Theaetetus* 165 d.

words, which most people pervert in haphazard ways and thereby cause all sorts of perplexity in one another'.[1]

No doubt this overstates the danger of relying on inferences from ordinary usage. Even so the most that can be established by the fact that words which it is permissible to couple with one expression cannot significantly be coupled with another is that the two expressions are not strictly synonymous. If it is a necessary condition of the identity of A with B that everything that can be said of A can equally be said of B, then it follows that the references of the two expressions are not identical. It does not follow, however, that one cannot be defined in terms of the other. The facts which Ryle adduces concerning the different ways in which we talk of belief and knowledge do not entail that knowledge cannot be defined in terms of belief. They entail only that the definition cannot take the form of simply equating them. They do not prove even that it is a mistake to talk about 'acts of knowing'. For if a philosopher is convinced that there are such things as he intends this expression to designate, he will not mind admitting that he is using the word 'knowing' in an unusual sense: he may even maintain that it is legitimate to extend its use so that it comes to refer to the processes of which it commonly signifies the successful completion. Nevertheless, if it can be shown, as it surely can, that such a view would be mistaken on other grounds, then the verbal argument does have its point. Not only does it reinforce the other arguments, but it supplies an explanation of the mistake. It shows how philosophers may in fact have come to grief through misunderstanding the grammar of their language.

V

What I have been calling a verbal argument is one in which the premisses consist of facts which relate to the special features of some natural language; such facts as that a certain group of English words is not ordinarily found in combination, or that various English words, which perform roughly the same function, are actually used in subtly different ways. It would be a good thing, perhaps, if the appellation of linguistic philosophy were restricted to arguments of this type. In a more extended sense,

[1] Plato, *Theaetetus* 168 c.

however, it may be said that most philosophical arguments are linguistic; for they mainly consist in stating that one proposition does, or does not, follow from another; and whether or not one proposition follows from another depends entirely on the meaning of the sentences by which they are expressed. The trouble is that very often when these alleged entailments are of philosophical interest, their validity is in dispute. The meaning of the crucial terms is just what needs to be settled. In such a case, there is little profit in researching into the niceties of English, or French, or German idiom; again the procedure is rather to try to look freshly at the facts. If one proposition does not entail the other, it should be possible to find, or at any rate to imagine, some state of affairs in which one proposition would be true and the other false. In short, it is once more a question of searching for a counter-example. Of course there is still the danger that what one takes to be a counter-example will be interpreted in a different fashion by those whom one is trying to refute. It is, indeed, partly for this reason that philosophical problems so long remain unsolved.

Among the most obstinate of these problems are those that relate to the theory of knowledge. As I have tried to show elsewhere,[1] these problems are best presented in the form of the need to find an answer to a certain type of scepticism. By raising the question how we know that propositions of some familiar sort are true, the sceptic tries to demonstrate that our claim to knowledge is unwarranted; that not only do we not know such propositions to be true, but we do not even have any good reason to believe them. Now it might well be thought that, here if anywhere, the solution would lie in some form of linguistic analysis. How do we actually use the sentences in question? What are the typical circumstances in which we unhesitatingly accept the propositions which they express? Suppose, for example, that the sceptic is maintaining that one has no good reason to believe in the existence of other people who have thoughts and feelings like one's own. Need we do more than simply draw his attention to the familiar situations in which we do ascribe these properties to other people? Is it not just an empirical fact that propositions of this sort are very often verified?

Once more this is the argument from the paradigm case; and

---

[1] See *The Problem of Knowledge.*

o*

it suffers from the weakness which we have already exposed. The situations to which we draw the sceptic's attention have to be interpreted. Are we to say that the mental life which one ascribes to others is somehow to be identified with their observable behaviour? Are we to say that this behaviour which we point to is the basis for an inductive inference? Or can we find another, more subtle form of answer? In the first case, the sceptic may claim that his point has been conceded: in the second, he will want to know how the inference can be justified: in the third, he will demand to be shown what other form of answer is possible, and exactly how it meets his arguments. Neither will it help us to point out that when we talk of someone's knowing what another person thinks or feels we are using the word 'know' in a way that accords with ordinary practice. For the contention which we have to meet is that ordinary practice is here at fault; not that the word 'know' is being used incorrectly, but rather that the claim, which it is rightly understood to make, turns out on investigation to be incapable of being justified.

It is not my purpose here to consider how in such an instance the sceptic can best be answered. The point which I wish to make is just that when it comes to problems of this kind it is not sufficient merely to reinspect the facts. If the sceptic's arguments are to be effectively challenged his presuppositions must be brought to light: if we think that he misrepresents the evidence, we must furnish some other principles of interpretation; if it is his idea of proof that is erroneous, we must devise a better theory of our own.

In general, I think that the current philosophical emphasis on fact, as opposed to theory, has been overdone. Too often, the claim to dispense with theory is a way of masking assumptions which, whatever their merit, had better be brought into the open. But, apart from this, the distrust which is rightly felt for speculative metaphysics is not a sufficient ground for limiting the scale of philosophical analysis: there is no reason to suppose that the only concepts which are worth investigating are those that have a comparatively narrow range, or that all that we can usefully do is to describe how concepts of this kind are actually employed. It is equally possible, and perhaps of more importance, to examine the architectonic features of our conceptual system; to apply analytical techniques to the investigation of categories.

There are, indeed, very welcome signs, for example in the recent work of Mr Strawson[1] and Professor Hampshire,[2] of a movement in this direction. To some extent the movement marks a return to Kant; a revival not exactly of Kant's doctrines but of his method of approach.

There is, however, a danger in following Kant too closely. It consists in succumbing to a kind of *a priori* anthropology, in assuming that certain fundamental features of our own conceptual system are necessities of language, which is the modern equivalent for necessities of thought. Thus it may be maintained that it is impossible for there to be a language which does not recognize the distinction between particulars and universals, or that physical objects must of necessity be the primary particulars in any universe of discourse which is comparable to our own. Such theses do indeed become more plausible when they are restricted to language whose capacities are required to match those of ordinary English, but this qualification also runs the risk of making them trivial. For it may then be argued that the work which a language does depends upon its categorical structure; so that no language which differs radically from our own in this respect can be capable of doing exactly the same work. But the answer to this is that, even if they are not strictly inter-translatable, languages of different structure may still be equipped to give substantially the same information; to every fact which can be stated in the one there will be a correlate which can be stated in the other. For example, a language without tenses, or other token-reflexive signs, cannot be an exact model of a language which possesses them. It will have no precise equivalent for a sentence like 'I met him yesterday'. Nevertheless, if the language affords the means of describing the persons to whom the pronouns refer, if it enables us to name the date which is indicated by 'yesterday' and also perhaps, in order to get the full effect of the past tense, the date at which the sentence is formulated, then substantially the same result will be obtained. There will be a loss of economy, but no loss of information.

This being so, I see no *a priori* reason why even such an important concept as that of a physical object should be regarded as indispensable. Might not substantially the same facts be

[1] See P. F. Strawson, *Individuals*.
[2] See S. N. Hampshire, *Thought and Action*.

expressed in a language reflecting a universe of discourse in which the basic particulars were momentary events? And there are other possibilities. One which is worthy of consideration is that regions of space-time be treated as the only individuals. Neither is it certain that there need be any reference to individuals at all. The main tendency of Russell's theory of descriptions, as developed especially by Professor Quine,[1] is towards the elimination of singular terms. It may indeed be contended that the attempts so far made to achieve this have not been wholly satisfactory, but I can see no ground for simply assuming that it is not feasible.

But why should one concern oneself with questions of this kind except as an exercise in ingenuity? There may be various reasons. For example, the elimination of singular terms may be seen as the only way out of the difficulties which are attached to the notion of substance. But the most convincing answer is that there can hardly be a better way of gaining an understanding of the work that these concepts actually do than by seeing how it would be possible to replace them.

Finally, whatever view one may take of the more specialized interests of linguistic philosophy, there still remains the problem of elucidating the concept of language itself. One of the debts that we owe to Wittgenstein, and before him to the pragmatists, is a realization of the active part that language plays in the constitution of facts. If 'the world is everything that is the case',[2] then what can be the case depends upon our conceptual system. But exactly what this comes to, and how it is to be reconciled with the objectivity of fact, are problems that still need to be resolved. They also bring into consideration the possibility of devising a general theory of meaning. At the present time such questions tend to be suspect just because of their extreme generality. My own view is that this is rather a reason for pursuing them. I believe it to be the best way of preserving analytical philosophy from the scholasticism which has been threatening to overtake it.

[1] See W. V. Quine, *Word and Object.*
[2] L. Wittgenstein, *Tractatus Logico Philosophicus*, i.

CHAPTER XIX

USE, USAGE AND MEANING[1]

J. N. Findlay

Professor of Philosophy, King's College, University of London

I am in great agreement with what I regard as the substantial points in Professor Ryle's paper.[2] His definition of language I think rather arbitrarily narrow; for him it is a 'stock, fund or deposit of words, constructions, *cliché* phrases and so on'. I should have thought it would be wrong not to include in a language the various syntactical and other *rules* which restrict our employment of the capital of expressions mentioned by Professor Ryle, though perhaps I am wrong in thinking he meant to exclude them. That adjectives must agree with the gender of their substantives in certain cases would certainly be held to be part of the French language, as it is not part of the English. There is also, I think, a further arbitrariness in excluding sentences from *language*, and in making them the units of *speech* which are produced when we say things. I think we can and should distinguish between the sentence *Je ne sais quoi* as a mere possibility permitted by the French language, and the same sentence as used or produced by someone to say something. I can in fact see no good reason why one should not have a narrower and a wider conception of a language. On the narrower conception, a language includes a vocabulary and rules, whereas on the wider conception it includes also *all* the possible sentences that could be framed out of the vocabulary in accordance with the rules. In this sense French or English would include all the permissible sentences that could be framed in it, whether anyone ever uttered or wrote or thought them or not. If this conception of a language makes it absurdly wide, the conception of it as a vocabulary plus rules makes it unduly narrow. Certainly, however, I think we want to distinguish between a sentence as a grammatically permissible word-combina-

---

[1] This paper was originally published as the second contribution to a symposium in *Proceedings of the Aristotelian Society* 1961 Supplementary Vol. XXXV.

[2] Published as the first contribution to the same symposium but not here presupposed in detail.

tion, and the utterance or writing down or silent thinking of that sentence by someone on some occasion to make an allegation, raise a query, express a doubt, etc. etc., and in the latter case I find a language of *use* or *employment* more natural than Professor Ryle's language of *production*. I think therefore that Professor Ryle is legislating rather vexatiously in forbidding us to speak of sentences as parts of language, or to say that such sentences can be *used* by speakers. I do not, however, think that this vexatious piece of legislation is in the forefront of Professor Ryle's intentions.

What Professor Ryle is mainly concerned to do seems to me to be to distinguish between grammatical faults in the use of words in constructing sentences, and faults in what may be called 'logical syntax' or 'logical grammar', which involve the use of words to construct perfectly grammatical sentences, but which none the less violate a deeper set of rules, the rules of sense, the rules of logic, the rules regulating the mutual relations of categories, etc. etc. With all this I am deeply in agreement, because it involves precisely the recognition that different sorts of words, as it were, make different sorts of abstract *cuts* in their subject-matter, or help to execute different sorts of abstract *cuts*—some, as Aristotle might say, tell us *what* things are, others *how* they are, others *how many* they are, others *conjoin*, others *emphasize*, others *bracket*, etc. etc.—and that in making such quite different types of cross-section they become subject to the relations necessarily obtaining among such cross-sections, so that some verbal combinations which are smooth and pretty grammatically none the less make hideous nonsense. Professor Ryle, it seems to me, is here suggesting that it is the relations of different sorts of *meanings* to one another which determine the depth-grammar of words, and that these meanings and their relations are matters that must be *independently* considered if we are to study logical as well as grammatical syntax. If this suggestion is not implicit in his words, perhaps he will explain what sort of abuse of words it is that is logical or depth-grammatical as opposed to merely surface-grammatical abuse. Incidentally, I feel in the contexts invoked by Ryle that it is doubly tempting to talk of the *use* and *abuse* of grammatical sentences. The sentence is there, a fully-fashioned grammatical entity, and it is its use to express a categorically possible combination of meanings which is at times possible and legitimate, whereas at other times there is really only an abuse.

Having expressed my agreement and disagreement with Ryle, I may perhaps allow myself to dwell a little on the famous dictum which he quotes and which has dominated philosophical discussion for the past twenty years: 'Don't ask for the meaning: ask for the use.' I wish to make against it the not often raised objection that the use for which it bids us ask, is of all things the most obscure, the most veiled in philosophical mists, the most remote from detailed determination or application, in the wide range of philosophical concepts. There is, I think, a use of 'use' which is humdrum and ordinary, but in which a study of the use of expressions is of only limited philosophical importance and interest. There is also a use of 'use' characteristic of the later writings of Wittgenstein which is utterly remote from the humdrum and ordinary, and which has won its way into the acceptance of philosophers largely because it has *seemed* to have the clearness and the straightforwardness of the ordinary use. We are all proof against the glozing deceits of words like 'substance', 'being', 'nothingness', 'consciousness', etc., etc.: we at once see that some occasions of their employment are really only abuses—but we are not yet proof against the fascinations exerted by the singular abuses of so ordinary a term as 'use'. When these abuses are exposed, the whole attitude represented by the slogan quoted by Ryle reveals itself as completely without significant basis, which unfortunately puts an end to all but a limited emphasis on 'use' and 'usage' by philosophers. Since the suggestion that use and usage—in some acceptable sense—*are* philosophically very important, certainly underlies Ryle's paper, I need not apologize for irrelevance in proceeding to demolish this suggestion.

The reason why it is absurd to tell us *not* to attend to the meaning of expressions but to concentrate on their use, is perfectly simple: it is that the notion of use, as it ordinarily exists and is used, presupposes the notion of meaning (in its central and paradigmatic sense), and that it cannot therefore be used to elucidate the latter, and much less to replace or to do duty for it. The notion of use is a *wider* notion than the paradigmatic notion of meaning: it covers many *other* things beside the meaning of an expression, but the meaning-function in its paradigmatic sense is certainly *one* of the things it covers, and it is not possible to give a clear account of use without presupposing this function. What I am saying is simply that we cannot fully say, in a great many cases, how an expression is used, without saying what sort of things it is intended to refer to, or to bring to mind, and just how, or in what angle or light, it purports to refer to them, or to bring them to mind. And in cases where it would be wrong and absurd to say that an expression *independently* brought something to mind, or presented it in a certain light, it would none the less be incontestably right to say that it *helped* to do such things in some definite matter, so that what was brought to mind would be *different*, or *differently presented*, if the expression were not part of our total utterance. Thus if I make use of the word 'dragon' in a large number of contexts, I use it to refer to a human being or beings, generally mature and female, and I use it also to represent such a human being or beings as being restrictive, uncompromising and somewhat terrifying. And if I *apply* the term in a certain context I see that to which I apply it in the light connoted by my words. And if I use the words 'such a' before uttering the word 'dragon', these words certainly help to suggest that what I am describing is *very* restrictive, *very* uncompromising and *very* terrifying, i.e. they contribute to the force of my description without playing an independent part of it. In saying what the use of my expression is, I therefore have to say what, in the ordinary diction of logicians, they denote and connote, what their precise reference is or what their general scope, or how they contribute to connotation or denotation, and it is not thought possible to say how many expressions are *used*, without bringing in such connotative and denotative particulars.

The notion of use of course goes far *beyond* that of connotation and denotation, and it is one of the extremely important discoveries of modern semantics that there are *some* expressions whose use, in certain contexts, is *not* to connote or denote anything, nor even to help to do either, but to do such things as give voice to feelings and wishes, evoke certain attitudes in others, or *perform* certain formal social acts, e.g. promises, which have certain definite social consequences, etc. etc. That *not* all expressions, on all occasions of their *use*, perform the functions of reference or characterization, or assist in such performance, is certainly a discovery not to be underestimated, which has cleared the deck of much tangled tackle and many stumbling-blocks. But this kind of *non*-referential, *non*-connotative use is parasitic upon a connotative, referential one, and could hardly exist without it.

It is one of Wittgenstein's more irresponsible fancies that there could be a language composed *only* of commands, or *only* of curses, or *only* of greetings. The concept of use also certainly covers all the hidden *implications* and *suggestions* which attach to the writing or utterance of a word or a sentence, but which are not strictly part of what it means or says: thus when I say 'He did not commit this murder' I may use this sentence to imply that he committed certain other murders, that I absolutely believe him to be no murderer, that we live under laws forbidding the taking of life, etc. etc. But all such implications and suggestions are likewise dependent upon the function of directly connoting or denoting something, and are in fact an extension of the same. Use also obviously covers the mere requirements of accidence and syntax, though these, as Ryle has shown, are mere instrumentalities in the task of significant diction.

What is implicit, however, in the slogan 'Don't ask for the meaning: ask for the use' is not that use covers much *more* than the connotative and denotative functions of language, but that it somehow resumes and completely explains the latter, that we can completely see around and see through talk about the reference and connotation of expressions by taking note of the way people operate with such expressions, how they combine them with other expressions to form sentences, and the varying *circumstances* in which producing such sentences is reckoned appropriate or fully justifiable. This study of verbal manœuvres, and of appropriate and justifying circumstances, must not, however, be confined to the single instant of utterance: it must point *backwards* to the all-important situations in which use was *learnt* or *taught*, and it must point *forwards* to the innumerable situations in which the utterance in question will again be found *appropriate*, or will be found to be more and more abundantly *justified*. The study of use therefore includes a genealogy and a prognosis of the most indefinite and complex kind, much more extensive than any that occurs in a merely grammatical or philological study. In another respect, however, the slogan gives 'use' an extraordinarily restricted interpretation. The operations involved in use are not to be operations conducted privately in anyone's head, or at least such operations can only be brought into consideration in so far as they can be narrowly tied up with other non-private operations, and the *circumstances* in which such operations are conducted must all be circumstances belonging to what may be called the common public environment, circumstances in which bricks are being assembled into buildings, apples taken from drawers and handed over to customers, railway-signals altered, or hunting expeditions conducted. The sort of change which is a mere change in perspective or in conscious 'light' is *not* among the circumstances mentionable in describing use.

And there is yet another most extraordinary restriction placed upon our account of the *circumstances* in which a word is correctly used: we must not employ the word or its equivalent to explain those circumstances. We must not, e.g., say that when a man is confronted by three apples in a drawer, or by an apple and another apple and yet another apple, he is then justified in employing the word 'three' in connexion with such apples. The word 'three' may be employed in describing the circumstances justifying countless *other* sorts of utterance, but not the circumstances justifying its *own* employment. In the same way we must never say that it is when a man is confronted by a red object, or has learnt to discriminate its colour, that he is justified in calling it 'red'. Such accounts are held to be wholly trivial and unilluminating, and are moreover held to suggest various deep philosophical fallacies: the belief that meanings exist 'out there' in the things we deal with *before* we find the appropriate words to 'pick them out', or that they exist 'in the mind' or the understanding before we find words to express them. Whatever we suggest by our accounts of use, we must never suggest that there are *pre-existent meanings*. Words enjoy meaning and reference in and by our use of them, and our use cannot be explained in terms of any meaning that antedates the use of words. And since understanding and thinking are defined in terms of the operation with signs, we must never speak as if we could understand or think anything before we dispose of appropriate verbal expressions and have been taught to employ them. The programme of this extreme 'utilitarianism'—as one may perhaps call the use-doctrine—is impressive: it resembles nothing so much as the brave empiricist programme of Locke and Hume, in which no idea was to be admitted into the charmed circle of thought and knowledge without producing a genealogy purer than any required by the Nuremberg laws, exhibiting a proper origin in sensation and reflexion, and a derivation from these by approved processes.

But, like that brave programme, it faces the crucial objection that it cannot be carried out completely, and that no comprehensive account of use and usage can be given which does not contain some members of impure origin. That the brave programme was hopeless Wittgenstein himself perhaps obscurely realized, when he wrongly said of the *Brown Book*, the most profound and wonderful of his writings, that it was *nichte wert*. But if success, rather than stimulus and provocation, is the criterion of philosophical value, his judgement was entirely justified.

I need not range far nor cite many instances to make plain the totally unilluminating, indeed deeply obfuscating character of attempts to give a complete account of the use of expressions in terms of merely public operations and circumstances. The very conception of a *rule*, central to the 'utilitarianism' in question, abounds in difficulty. For we are expressly told that to follow a rule is not necessarily to be guided by a spoken or written formula, since each such formula admits of interpretation in terms of another formula, and this in terms of another, and so on indefinitely. Nor is the following of a rule to be identified with any sort of inner personal understanding of that rule which can guide one's subsequent performance, since to hold this would be to accept pre-existent meanings resident in the queer medium of the mind. Nor can the following of a rule be identified with one's actual performance up to a point, since this is always compatible with an infinity of rules. In the end it would seem that following a rule must be an ineffable sort of affair: it must be something that can be accomplished in one's *doing* (in this case, speaking), but not effectively spoken *about*. It is something that one can know how *to do* without being able to know how what one does is done. The conception of a linguistic rule has, in fact, all the irretrievable obscurity of the structural resemblance constitutive of meaning in the *Tractatus*, which cannot be expressed but only *shown*. If it is at least *possible* that a rule should at times be understood or grasped in thought, we can understand what it is like to follow it without thought, but if grasping is a function of following, the whole activity of following dissolves in mystery. I do not myself know how it differs from the most arbitrary irregularity except that it mysteriously *feels* right at every stage, and that others, standing at my side, mysteriously agree in such feelings. And if it is hard to throw light

on the following of rules in terms of outward circumstances and
performances, how much harder it is to say in what lies conformity
to an *open* rule, one which is to be applied over and over *indefinitely*.
While the *thought* expressed by the phrase 'and so on indefinitely'
is most absolutely simple and easy to entertain, it is a thought
logically impossible to evince adequately in one's performance.
Much has been written, from the standpoint of the use-doctrine,
about the difference between closed and open games, but the
discussion ends up with very much what it started from, that is a
difference in the *spirit* with which the respective games are played.
A man, e.g., using an open arithmetic simply has a system or
general rule for constructing numerals *indefinitely*. That a spirit
is operative in this case I should not care to deny, but that it
consorts well with the use-doctrine, or establishes its superiority,
I cannot conceive.

Similar difficulties confront us if we consider the use-account
of the use of descriptive adjectives like those of colour. We are
forbidden to talk of prior colour-differences in objects, or prior
colour-discriminations in persons, as this would involve the grave
error of positing pre-existent meanings. We are introduced to
imaginary tribal activities which involve the picturesque carrying
about of charts of colour samples and their comparisons with,
or imposition on objects, but these it would seem explain little
or nothing, since the charts are dispensable and admit moreover
of a wrong use. From the use of charts the tribe progresses to the
use of colour samples carried somehow in the mind's eye, and
ultimately to the mere unhesitant pronouncement, after sufficient
training, of certain colour-words in the presence of certain
objects. With this pronouncement others as unhesitatingly agree.
From the Scylla of holding that 'blue' stands for a discriminable
blueness in objects, or expresses an awareness of blueness in one's
mind, one proceeds to the Charybdis of saying that those things
are blue which we and others agree, and have been trained, to call
so. It is plain, of course, that one must have ultimates somewhere, and it is plain also that there are different possibilities of
colour-discrimination corresponding to different possibilities of
usage: what is *not* plain is why one should prefer such a strange,
secondary ultimate as a *use* to the more obvious, understandable
ultimates of discriminating thoughts in the mind, or discriminable
features in things.

The most superb example of the problem-increasing character of the use-semantics is, however, to be found in its treatment of cases where men use expressions without obvious reference to any palpable feature of the public environment, when they give voice, e.g., to recollections or anticipations, or describe their personal feelings or impressions, or report their fantasies or their dreams. Here the course is followed of attempting to account for such uses by supposing men to be such as *spontaneously* to want to use expressions taught in certain contexts in contexts where their normal justification is absent, and that these non-normal needs, so strangely universal among us, constitute the basis for a new *secondary* set of linguistic usages, while the sole fact that we agree in feeling certain linguistic urges is the sole criterion of their correctness. Thus children perhaps spontaneously run over the names of objects recently presented to them, or can be encouraged to do so without difficulty: meaning can then be given to the *past tense*, and they can learn to say that they *had* a ball, a stick, a rattle, etc. To 'refer to the past' is merely to learn to employ the past tense in such circumstances, an account as amusingly free in presupposing pastness and temporal passage in the *circumstances* of the learning, as it is firm in denying any non-verbal *understanding* of them. Men then spontaneously begin to use the past tense where there is no such recent provocation: we then give a use to talk about 'remembering', particularly if others agree in such spontaneous inclinations. The reference to the past in memory is therefore not the ultimate, mysterious thing that Husserl, Broad and others have supposed it to be: it merely reflects the strange tendency of men to talk preteritively beyond the limits of recency, and the further linkage of this fact with the readings of instruments, the report of others, and many other observed matters. It may now happen that men waking from sleep spontaneously talk in the past tense *as if* recalling happenings which no one remembers, and which do not fit in with the observable contemporary state, or with the memory-inclinations of others. The concept of 'dreaming' now makes its *début* to take care of these extraordinary performances. Malcolm, the admirable exponent of a preposterous analysis, admits that on it dream-language is very odd: it is *as if* one is faithfully recalling something, but one cannot explain this fact by saying that one *did* experience what one is disposed to report, since this would involve an unintelligible hypothesis, one excluded by the guiding assumptions of the doctrine of use. What these queernesses surely show is the profound mistakenness somewhere of these guiding assumptions. To make use of a gnostic principle used by Moore in other contexts: we *know* certain facts about meaning much more absolutely than we can be sure of the premises, or the inferential rules, of semantic arguments designed either to establish them or to explain them away. Obviously we cannot make straight sense of many linguistic usages without postulating just those pre-existent understandings (not confined to matters in the public forefront) and the possibility of communicating such understandings to others, which it is the whole aim of the use-doctrine to exclude.

The use-doctrine may further be objected to for its profoundly circular, question-begging character. This is a point ably made by Mr Gellner in a book where some of the most profound criticisms of the use-doctrine and its consequences lie hidden under a somewhat popular exterior. To have seen an unacceptable, unargued naturalism behind Wittgenstein's brilliant façade of exposition, is no mean insight. By describing the functioning of linguistic expressions exclusively in public and social terms, we at once go *too far* in assuming such approaches to be wholly justified and clear, and we also *do not go far enough* in refusing to recognize aspects of language not fitting an approach of this sort, or in 'proving' them to be misguided or senseless. These two lines of objection really coincide, since it is by turning away from aspects of language it cannot readily accommodate that the use-doctrine is unable to see its own difficulties and obscurities. The use-theorists have dwelt much on the profound subtlety of ordinary language, but they have been far from recognizing *how* subtle it actually is. For it not only uses expressions to point to, or to throw light on, ordinary objects, but it also uses them *reflexly*, in the manner studied in Husserl's *Logische Untersuchungen*, to point to or throw light on its own *meanings*, thereby setting up an order of objects as clear-edged and partial as its normal objects are fuzzy and full, and as delicate in their abstraction as they are indispensable for the higher flights of thought. That a phrase like 'the third door on the right' can be used both straightforwardly to refer to a door, and reflexly to refer to its own meaning, is a truth plain to babes, but occasioning headaches to the semantically over-wise and prudent. Ordinary speech, further, provides us with an instrument for communicating with others about matters public and common, which is also an instrument for purely personal use, in which different observations, different views, different judgements provide much the same complementary parallax, and the same corrective or confirmatory testing as in the interpersonal case. But not only is it thus double in its use, it also manages to incorporate the personal in the public use, and the public in the personal, in a regress pursuable as far as ever we choose. Thus we all understand other people's first-person talk by analogy with our own, and its imperfect public intelligibility is also perfectly and publicly intelligible, since everyone makes just such first-person statements in his own case. The manner in which we smoothly swing over from another man's perfectly understood use of the first-person pronoun 'I', and replace it with 'he' in reporting the content of his statement, and expect the other man to do the same in regard to us, as well as the children's games in which these proprieties are amusingly violated: all these show an understanding of the antithesis of contrasted privacies, and of their overcoming in a wider publicity, of which the use-semantics betrays no inkling. In the same manner, ordinary speech has in it the germs of what may be called the Cartesian or the Lockean inversion, the reversal of the ordinary approach from outward things to the mind, into an approach to outer things from the facts of our subjective life. Though the language in which we talk of and to ourselves—the best subject-matter and audience—may have had its *source* in contexts of public ostensibility, it can, by a profitable ingratitude, use the personal language thus painfully acquired to cast doubt upon, or to throw light on, its own origin. We may illuminate our understanding and knowledge of public matters in terms of just those personal experiences and pre-existent understandings which talk about public matters first renders possible. And this personal Cartesian or Lockean story can then achieve the widest publicity, since to have back rooms continuous with those opening on the public square is the most universal, most inescapable of predicaments. It is no doubt by a creative transformation that the rumour of the square penetrates backwards, and is re-echoed in the small back rooms, and it is likewise by a creative transformation that these transformed echoes rejoin the rumour of the square. All this, however, unquestionably happens, and it is the task of a philosophical semantics to make sense of it, and not to declare it unintelligible.

Nothing that has been said in the foregoing is meant to reflect on the painstaking, detailed study of linguistic usage, or the actual manner of its teaching, if used to show how we actually come to mean what we undoubtedly do mean, or to throw light on the complexity and subtlety of our meanings, or to show how we come to be misled into supposing we mean what really conflicts with the 'depth-grammar' of our meanings. Our criticisms are only of a radical use-theory carried to extremes, which constructs fables as to how we might have been taught the meanings of words in order to buttress *a priori* doctrines as to what we *must* or *cannot* mean. If anyone thinks such doctrines archaic and superseded, and so not requiring rebuttal, he is wide of the truth. Wittgenstein's accounts of language-games are so arresting, so novel, so subtle in their detailed development, so daring in their frank embrace of the unplausible, so imbued with intellectual seriousness and earnestness, and so great, finally, in their aesthetic appeal, that it is hard to see through them or around them. They fascinate the philosopher in the same way that Wittgenstein claimed that philosophers were fascinated by the forms of ordinary language, and against such fascination determined steps are necessary. The steps I have taken in this paper may not have been sufficiently subtle, and may have involved certain misunderstandings of detail: I shall hope, at least, to have incited others to do better.

All this should not, of course, be taken as reflecting on the philosophical greatness of Wittgenstein. Wittgenstein is the author of three wholly differing accounts of meaning, all of which merit entire rejection: meaning is *not* reduplication of structure, it is *not* verification or verifiability, it is plainly *not* what he meant by 'use'. It is not these things, though it is of course intimately connected with them all, but it will be best illuminated by construing further the old humdrum notions of connotation and denotation, and by seeking painfully to throw light on the 'thought behind our words', for which, on account of the peculiar categories it involves, it would seem that no adequate surrogate has been, or can be, offered. It is, I surmise, in the 'intentional nature of thought' that the true solution of the problems of meaning is to be found. But by formulating these three inadequate accounts, Wittgenstein has given the semantic problem the central place it deserves in philosophy, and has contributed vastly to its solution. Through his inability to account satisfactorily for certain linguistic performances, he has indicated the precise nodes where language makes its various creative leaps and has thereby given philosophical semantics its opportunity and its task. Moreover, each of Wittgenstein's frequent rhetorical questions is such that, if answered in the sense *not* intended by the question, it will lead to an illuminating result: they are practically all arrows which, if read in the reverse direction, point unerringly to some truth. A philosophy of meaning so valuably wrong does not differ profoundly from one that is systematically right.

Subject Index

Index of Proper Names